Live&Work in
The USA

Eleanor Turner

Fifth edition

crimson

Published by Crimson Publishing, 2009
www.crimsonpublishing.com

4501 Forbes Blvd., Suite 200, Lanham MD 20706
Westminster House, Kew Road, Richmond, Surrey TW9 2ND

Distributed in North America by National Book Network
www.nbnbooks.com

Distributed in the UK by Portfolio Books
www.portfoliobooks.com

A catalogue record for this book is available from the British Library.

ISBN 978 1 85458 428 1

Printed and bound in China by Everbest Printing Co. Ltd

The United States of America was founded on the belief that individuals can take control of their destiny and create their own favourable environment. American history is full of examples of people making that journey, from the arrival of the Pilgrim Fathers escaping religious persecution, to the shiploads of new immigrants arriving in New York Harbor. The USA is a nation that still believes opportunities should be taken and hard work rewarded. If this mythology is too rose-tinted, at least we should acknowledge that it is a reputation which remains highly attractive, particularly to those who are willing to take a gamble to improve their quality of life. In this seductive scenario the successful (the alternative is not often considered), are showered with rewards

In almost every suburb in America, newly-arrived families from around the world are seeking the good life: a home with a yard, decent education and healthcare, a prosperous retirement, and opportunities for their children. Today's immigrants are less likely to be escaping persecution and dire poverty than to be seeking a new life or change of pace. Many are educated professionals who are transferred from one office of a multinational company to another, while some are hand-picked by companies for their special skills.

The devastating impact on the USA of terrorism on September 11 undoubtedly had an effect on the nation's psyche. In the 2004 re-election, the two biggest vote winners turned out to be moral issues and the war on terror, while the 2008 Presidential campaign – where history was made with the Democrat Barak Obama becoming America's first black president – focused more heavily on universal healthcare, the declining economy and inflated oil prices. It seems that the issue of war has taken a backseat to concerns regarding the economy and weakened dollar, with fear mounting that America may not be the world's sole superpower for much longer.

Not since the Japanese assault on Pearl Harbor have Americans felt so beleaguered. While many parts of the world, including Europe, have long coped with terrorism and violent conflict, American citizens have usually felt safe at home. The rest of the world has, until recently, seemed very far away. To protect themselves, Americans have introduced effective counter-terrorist measures, stricter visa controls, and intensive checks at entry ports. Travelling by plane now entails far greater patience and reserves of time.

America's recent economic downturn, reminiscent of the 2001 recession, has prompted both an increase in tourism to the USA and a decrease in domestic spending. However, it is expected that the most recent slowdown will not last, and indeed, it has not affected immigration rates at all so far. Business investment, exports and government spending have all remained steady, and America continues to welcome investment from foreign nationals. Despite periodic and inevitable economic downturns, the USA continues to exude an almost mystical appeal. American influence on world culture remains enormous and its economic power stretches to every area of global activity. Many people around the world harbour dreams of emigrating to the USA, or at least wish to spend a substantial amount of time living and working in this seemingly blessed country.

This revised edition of *Live & Work in the USA* explains how to navigate your way through the complex immigration requirements, and includes information on how to find a job, home or school. You'll also learn how to adapt to American life, what to expect when you're out there, and how to find help, should you need it. Whether you are an employee or entrepreneur, a student or a retiree, this book should provide a useful and informative introduction to life in the USA.

Live & Work in the USA is one of a series of books which guide individuals through the opportunities for work, business, or retirement in North America, Australasia, Asia and Europe. The purpose of the *Live & Work* series is to build up a comprehensive database of information concerning the many and various regulations and practicalities involved in moving from one country to another.

The USA immigration system is far more complicated than those which allow free movement of Europeans around the European Union, or inter-movement between New Zealand and Australia. Furthermore, the immigration system is unequivocally biased towards those whose qualifications, skills and experience are deemed to be of benefit to the USA. When it comes to eligibility, the system is extremely selective. *Live & Work in the USA* explains the entire system, how best to go about maximising your chances of being accepted as an immigrant and where to get professional help with your application. The book also helps to prepare for – and lessen the potential shock of – the difference in culture and daily life by giving guidance on socialising USA style.

If you do not wish to live permanently in the USA, you can spend six months of the year there as a property investor/holiday-home owner. Many retirees (as well as younger people) do this already. This book can help you find relevant property agents and also indicates the most likely places for retirement or holiday homes.

North America is not a continent easily left once you have established yourself; its respect for the individual, its big-heartedness, its pace and extraordinary diversity, are all part of the attraction. I hope that *Live & Work in the USA* will help you make the move successfully.

Eleanor Turner
November 2008

T he author and the publishers of this book would like to thank all those people who have contributed to the content over the years. In this revised edition special thanks go to:

Fiona Bootes, Sue Ward, Jane Hunt, Tony and Mandy Kirk, Kate Whelan, and Leo Dillard for kindly contributing their lives as case studies; Hannah Stern for her enormous help with information on New York City and Kristen Cruze for her help with California; all the photographers who allowed their work to be reprinted in this edition, particularly Brian Ching and Melanie Hagen; Lucy McLoughlin and Beth Bishop for editing and guiding me from start to finish; my family and my husband's family for helping us achieve our own immigration dream and finally my wonderful husband, Mike, who helped and encouraged me to complete this book.

The publishers would like to thank Pam Lomax, Richard Geer, Julia Calderwood, Jennifer Smith and Anna Rice for the kind use of their photos in the book.

How to use this book

Telephone numbers

Please note that the telephone numbers in this book are written as if you are calling that number from inside the same country. To call these numbers from outside the country you will need to know the relevant international access code; in the UK, this is currently 00.

To call the USA: dial the international access code + 1 + the complete number as given in this book.

To call the UK from America: dial the international access code + 44 + the complete number as given in this book – but omitting the first 0 in the British number.

Currency conversion chart						
Currency	**US $**	**GBR £**	**Euro Đ**	**AU $**	**NZ $**	**¥en**
1 US$	1	0.50	0.62	1.03	1.32	106.5
1 GBR €	1.98	1	1.25	2.05	2.61	211.4
1 Euro Đ	1.59	0.80	1	1.64	2.09	169.4
1 AU $	0.96	0.48	0.61	1	1.27	103.1
1 NZ $	0.76	0.38	0.48	0.79	1	80.9
1 ¥en	0.009	0.005	0.006	0.009	0.012	1

Contents

Why Live & Work in the USA?

■ ABOUT THE USA

Official Name:	United States of America
Capital City:	Washington, D.C.
Currency:	US Dollar ($)
Time Zones:	Mainland USA has four zones: Eastern Standard Time (GMT-5), Central Standard Time (GMT-6), Mountain Standard Time (GMT-7) and Pacific Standard Time (GMT-8). Offshore USA has a further two: Alaskan Standard Time (GMT-9) and Hawaii-Aleutian Standard Time (GMT-10).
Wealth:	$13.8 trillion GDP (2007)
Population Size:	303,755,274
Largest City:	New York (population 8,143,197)
Ethnic Make-Up:	73.9% White, 12.2% African-American, 4.4% Asian, 7.24% Other, 2.0% Two or More Races. The USA's 14.8% Hispanic or Latino population is derived from within these racial groups.

The world is fascinated by the USA. While Americans may see Europe as a wonderful land of history, castles, and misbehaving aristocrats, and Australia as the laid-back capital of the world, we often look to America as the embodiment of all that is modern, glamorous and sophisticated. This perception is now changing, as a heightened speed of communication means that products that were previously unattainable are now in our hands as soon as we hear tale of their creation.

Nevertheless, there is still something exciting about America – it is certainly true that no other country is as visible and as talked about. We grow up on a rich diet of films and television from the States and find that we know rather a lot about the country and its inhabitants: what they eat, how they dress, how they talk. Many children in Europe have seen the Rocky Mountains or Monument Valley a hundred times before they have even heard of the Matterhorn or Tokatoka Peak. Even so, what usually takes the visitor by surprise is the sheer foreignness of it all. Sure, the people speak English, but that is often the only point of contact. Attitudes and ways of life are so different from what we are used to that some Europeans and Australasians are lost. Nothing could seem more foreign than New York late at night, when your head runs with horror stories (as the author Norman Mailer said, visitors to New York 'just want to be reassured that they are not going to be mugged within the next few hours'); or a redneck nightclub in Phoenix where the customers wear Stetsons and the temperature outside is in the high nineties.

For hundreds of years people have been flocking to America – millions of them escaping hardship and repression in their home countries. In recent

TIP

■ America is a complicated and diverse country. To truly know it you would have to travel for 20 years. Every state is a country in itself, with Utah as different from Louisiana as London is to Prague. Every state is as American as anywhere else and there is no such thing as a place that is more typical of the USA than any other.

years, however, America has been closing its doors to immigrants and making it more and more difficult to plead economic hardship as a reason to get into the country. Despite such difficulties and the risk of poverty that may face such immigrants, many still come over the desert from Mexico and across the sea from Cuba. For those who are successful, of course, the dream comes true, and this is how the myth lives on: it is the millionaires who shout loudest about the American Dream. When the novelist G. K. Chesterton said that 'there is nothing the matter with Americans except their ideals', he wanted them to keep a firmer grip on reality. America does sometimes seem full of contradictions. The land of opportunity has some of the strictest immigration laws in the world and has, to date, executed 1099 people since 1977 – all of these despite a strict allegiance to the notion of human rights.

Skyscraper advertising in Times Square, New York

Despite all of this, America is a stunningly beautiful country. Americans often talk with wonder and respect of the beauty of the land, and you know that they feel privileged to live there. The Grand Canyon or the autumn colours of New England are famous sights, but the real beauty of America is in the size of it. In Europe there are few open spaces on the scale of some of the great national parks in America. In Yosemite it is possible to wander for days without seeing another soul and there are roads that never seem to end, vanishing into the horizon. It is a country in which you can disappear with ease, which is one of the reasons why hitch-hiking is forbidden in most states.

The American people are famously friendly. It is true that to the typically reserved British they might seem overly so, but if you are newly arrived you will be delighted by the attention and the interest you receive. If you are naturally outgoing you will fall easily into any community, while if you have a more solitary personality you will be able to find an isolated spot, somewhere in the Rockies perhaps – or Arizona or upstate New York – where you will be bothered by nobody. This is the greatest attraction of America: it has something for everyone. You cannot say it is too cold, too hot, too mountainous, or too populated – America is the land of opportunity, and you simply have to decide where to go to find your ideal environment.

■ REASONS TO LIVE IN THE USA

The economy

Those who decide to move to the USA will be assured of a standard of living as high as anywhere in Europe or Australasia. At the same time, they will find that the cost of living is a good deal lower than many other countries, despite the much-feared 2008 recession. America is an exceedingly attractive country to live in, which is one of the reasons that it is so difficult to get permission to do so.

For much of the 1990s the USA enjoyed a period of enormous economic growth and prosperity. A combination of deficit reduction by the Clinton administration in 1993 and significant innovation in computing and technology drove the economy to new levels of prosperity. Investment in internet stock and even the war in the Middle East helped boost the economy through much of the late 1990s and early 2000s, but the bubble has begun to burst in recent years. The subprime mortgage crisis of 2007 and the historic weakness of the US dollar have led to an unprecedented recession, with a predicted slowdown in annual growth rate to just 2.2%. The inflated price of oil can be seen on American streets, as car owners search for smaller, more fuel-efficient vehicles instead of gas-guzzling SUVs. Petrol tanks, too, cost three times more to fill up than they did in 2002. Having said this, while Americans may complain that their cost of living has gone up, petrol prices are still well below those in the UK and beyond.

Investment opportunities

While UK and Australasian entrepreneurs and would-be exporters have the advantage of a shared language, the US government is anxious to attract as much inward investment as possible. States are given federal grants with which to start up business advisory centres and to offer investment initiatives. There is no control over the nationality of those benefiting from these grants, and many states actively encourage foreign investment. The UK government has fostered links between UK businesses and the USA, and US chambers of commerce have opened in the UK in order to encourage business enterprise between the two countries.

Taxation of businesses in most states is lenient, payroll regulations are straightforward and the bureaucratic burden is generally lighter than in most of Europe. The downside of this is, of course, the competition that you will be up against. It may be easy to register your business, but it is another matter entirely to make it work. Experts advise that unless you identify a niche that has not been exploited, you will quickly be overcome by aggressive home-grown competition. The federal and state governments will help you set up, but will not hold your hand while you are encircled by sharks.

Hard work ethos

Britons who are employed by a US company may find a few differences in the way things are done. The US work ethic is famous: 'Rise early, work late, strike oil' was John Paul Getty's formula for success. Even

■ Setting up a business need not be difficult, and can be accomplished in some states in a matter of days. If you run a business that employs people and invests in the US economy, you are eligible for a visa that will allow you to stay as long as the business is surviving.

if you can't manage the third, you will be expected to do the first and second.

In America, more than any other country, success is measured in two concrete terms: money and position. The drive to do well is enormous; the nation was built by people who for one reason or another were driven out of their homelands. Many arrived in the USA with no money and no belongings. The boss who 'built himself up from nothing' is a stock character, but one who has left his mark on the American company.

The rewards of hard work are substantial: wages in the USA, especially at senior management levels, are high. The housing and rental sector is cheaper than in Europe: a typical middle manager lives in a three-bedroomed detached house on its own plot of land. Out of the office, great demands will be made on your free time in the form of recreational activities. Americans work hard and, as a result, they set out to enjoy the little leisure time that they have. You will be invited to sports clubs, theatrical evenings, debating clubs, fishing weekends and mountain walks, and are unlikely to ever be lonely.

There are many advantages to living in America, but of course there are also a few disadvantages. The exceptional popularity of the country is the reason for one of these major drawbacks: immigration laws. It is very difficult to get permission to stay more than three or six months at any one time, and even more difficult to work legally as a non-immigrant unless you can prove that no American can do your job. Unless you are married to a US citizen, the chances of getting a green card (and permanent resident's status) are somewhat easier for victims of repressive regimes or for individuals of certain nationalities. Each year there is a green card lottery but only certain nationals are eligible each time because the process is designed to increase the diversity of the population and encourage nationals from countries with low rates of emigration to the US. See *Before You Go* for more information on the Diversity Visa Lottery.

Beliefs and customs

Once you do get permission to work (or if you decide to work illegally, as thousands do, at the risk of deportation), you may find that many prejudices about the US are confirmed. Inner-city areas sometimes suffer high rates of crime, particularly involving guns. This can be shocking to people more used to living in Europe or New Zealand, where gunfire on the streets merits headline news. Racial tension also remains a distinct problem in American society, though there has been improvement since the 1960s with the creation of many federal programmes to limit discrimination and improve economic assistance for minorities.

America is a foreign country, with many customs and attitudes that outsiders find difficult to understand. What is seen as a joke in the office in London may land you in trouble in New York. America's greater sensitivity

Lake Michigan Pier at sunset

toward the constituent parts of its society involves some adjustment, but it is simply reflecting its truly diverse character. The national ideal of a melting pot is taken seriously.

To a foreigner, Americans have strange habits. They play an incomprehensible version of rugby (which they call football though it is nothing like football), they are the inventors of the Big Mac, and they eat strawberry jelly and peanut butter. They have strange names, their beer is weak and dress sense poor, they are too friendly, and they are too loud. But all criticism says more about the critic than the criticised.

Trying to compile a comprehensive list of the pros and cons of living in America would be never ending, but the summary of the main reasons either to move to the USA or not, is a reasonable enough exercise for a prospective immigrant to carry out. At the end of the day, the fact remains that if you are willing and eager to adopt the culture and customs of your new country, their strange habits suddenly won't seem half as strange any more.

Standard of living

The US offers a distinctly better standard of living than most of Europe and obviously better than the developing world. In many parts of the country,

FACT

■ The rewards
of hard work
are substantial:
wages in the USA,
especially at senior
management levels,
are high.

especially on the coast, the climate is temperate and appealing. Life, as a rule, is generally easier than in the congested cities of Europe, and commercial choices are endless: shopping malls offer abundance at good value and services are delivered with a smile around the clock. America continues to have an enduring appeal, largely because self-improvement is so central to the culture. That hackneyed phrase, 'the American Dream' has staying power because it reflects the nation's cultural support of individual self-improvement.

Pros and Cons of Living in the USA

Pros
- High standard of living
- Comparatively healthy economy with good prospects
- The Special Relationship: European\US business relationships are friendly
- Incentives for new businesses and investment
- Few bureaucratic burdens on business
- Low taxation
- Common language
- Locals are very friendly and open
- High wages with high disposable income
- Beautiful and diverse country
- Housing and rental sector remains reasonably priced

Cons
- Visa and immigration controls
- Unstable economy with housing market downturn
- Distance from Europe
- Bureaucracy on domestic level can be a problem
- Executive job prospects are not as good as they once were
- Punishing work ethic – few holidays and poor maternity leave benefits
- Weak regulation of guns
- Unfamiliar customs, such as restaurant etiquette and national sports

■ PERSONAL CASE HISTORIES

Fiona Boote

Now living in Sacramento, California, Fiona was born and raised in Stoke-on-Trent and London in the UK. Originally an IT trainer in the City of London, unforeseen circumstances led her to travel extensively as a Commercial Yacht Captain for several years, before meeting her husband, Darin, and settling in the USA in 2007.

What was your life like pre-moving to the USA?

When I lived in the UK, my life went through lots of changes. I was married in 2001 and worked as an IT trainer in London, but a few days after the ceremony the events of 9-11 happened. The ripples of that cascaded all the way into my life and had a profound effect on me. I lost my job and couldn't find another, and the stress of that meant my husband and I separated. I then worked in child protection for a while, before deciding to focus on the things that made me really happy. I decided to sell my house, obtain my Yachtsman's Licence and start sailing for a living. I went to the Pacific Islands, Australia and Europe and lived on a boat for a number of years.

How is it that you came to move to the USA?

As part of my interests I got involved in an eco group called Tribe Wanted.com, which works on sustainable solutions for an island in Fiji. They hold parties all over the world for members to meet up, and I ended up staying with friends in Sacramento, CA and Kalamazoo, MI while I attended a party in Chicago. It was during this trip I met my husband for the first time. I spent some more time sailing around Australia, and came back to the USA for another visit with friends later on. I was re-introduced to my now husband and we were marred within two or three months!

What were your first impressions on arriving in the USA?

Well, I had visited the States a number of times before for work or to see friends, so I knew a little about it already. When my husband and I got married it was my first extended stay. I'd say Americans look similar and sound similar, but there's something so very different about them too. I think people expect America to be just like it is on TV, but it isn't! On TV there's almost an entire population or demographic missing: Mexicans and Hispanics. Certainly in the area where we live the number of legitimate or heritage Hispanics is vastly different from how it's portrayed on the screen. Another thing I found interesting was the amount of driving people do over here and the extreme religious nature of the country. A much higher proportion of people attend church in the USA than in the UK, even though similar proportions call themselves Christian.

Has it taken long to acclimatise?

Well, I don't have very deep roots. I left home when I was eighteen and I've been very independent ever since. I think it's led to me feeling settled wherever I go: I'm happy living in the 'right now'. It's also meant I don't get homesick, which is great because I think it's very easy to become homesick over here.

What is the social life like?

It's *really* different. I live in suburbia, and one thing that's really apparent is the lack of pubs at the end of every street. Bars here aren't the same, which I think is left over from the Prohibition Era. You can't go into a bar here for a typical pub lunch, and you don't see many 'ladies' in them either! I don't have the same social life as I used to – people don't go out for a quick drink after work, for example – so I've had to work harder to make friends as an adult, especially as I don't have young children. Social lives seem to rotate around families and church, not the pub.

How did you go about looking for work?

By the start of '08 I hadn't worked for over two years in the conventional sense, and I was going brain dead! Once my permanent resident status came through in January I started looking for something local (we only had one car at that point) and a job at a chiropractor's office down the street came up. By the end of January I was working there and although I call it my 'little job', I still really enjoy it.

What comments do you have about the American working environment?

Oh, there are loads! California is an 'at will' employer state, which means employers and employees don't have to give any notice when they leave. It means I don't have any real job security, which I find really shocking. As a courtesy I'm asked to give two weeks' notice, but I'm not under obligation to do so. I'm also paid every two weeks, which I find very strange on a salary! I'm used to working with people thanks to my previous jobs, and I love my current work because I'm with patients all day.

What is your visa status? Is it easy to change once you're in the country?

Well, my husband and I were fortunate in that our application went very smoothly. I actually came to America on the VWP to visit friends, so we had to apply for all the paperwork after we were married and adjust my status. I wouldn't advise any one else to go by that route as we cut it very fine, but it made more logical sense to us to do it the way we did, rather than for me to return to the UK and apply for a fiancée K visa. It's also important to remember that I had absolutely no intention of staying in the country longer than my plane ticket allowed for! I didn't lie at the port of entry and we consulted a solicitor to help us adjust my status. In fact, it was only after we were married and had applied for my permanent residency that we even realised we could have done things differently.

What is American bureaucracy like? How does it compare with the UK?

When we went for our interview to grant me PR status, we were asked to prove our marriage was real. The immigration officer told us a marriage certificate didn't count, as anyone could produce one, and she wanted to see evidence of a marriage, not a wedding. Luckily we had some receipts from the formal ceremony we held for our friends and family after our legal one, and the office said that that was a very good indicator we were real! Other bureaucracies are very strange. Banking is a killer! I find having to endorse cheques on the back weird, and not being able to transfer money easily and for free. Cell phones too! I've owned pay-as-you-go phones in the UK, Spain, Australia and here, and this is the only country that charges you for incoming calls. I think it's a product of Americans not travelling abroad as much as other nationalities, and not experiencing how other countries do things.

What do you like about the Sacramento area?

Well, if it wasn't for my husband I probably wouldn't choose to live here. The weather is so hot sometimes that it's like living on the face of the sun. In fact, I haven't seen any rain here since April. I do like the history and culture of the area, though. It's Gold Rush country and there are lots of places to visit and nature paths to walk on. It's also got lots of entertainment facilities such as theatres, opera houses and other shows. There's easy access to San Francisco and as it's the state capital it's fairly cosmopolitan. You can even walk into Arnie's state office and pick up his business card, as my Dad once did!

How does the standard of living compare to the UK?

With one trip to Wal-Mart, you can see this is the land of plenty. Actually, the excess of living here is a bugbear of mine. There's lots of stuff to buy. You also see tons of yard sales every weekend with people getting rid of their stuff, so everything's very disposable over here. There are a number of foreclosures in my local area, and in fact, we bought our house recently for only 50% of what the previous owners bought it for two years ago. I haven't encountered abject poverty in this city yet though, but it's probably because I live in the suburbs. I'm sure if I looked hard enough for it, I'd find it.

How did you find the process of finding a place to live? How did you go about it when you first arrived?

Well, when I first arrived I didn't have a credit score to speak of, so we bought the house on my husband's salary. We went to a mortgage broker to get pre-approved for a loan, and then we started looking for a house online. I wanted to be closer to my friends, but also needed somewhere fairly diverse for my husband's family.

What are your favourite places to visit in your new country?

I really love San Francisco – it's probably my favourite place I've been to in America. It feels very British, and has a strong European flavour to it. It's also nice and diverse, which I like, and it gets cooler than Sacramento as it's closer to the ocean. I didn't really like New York as it's too 'in your face', and LA was full of posers and very obvious poverty. Chicago was great but I didn't see much of it.

What do you like most about the USA?

Transitioning to living here was very smooth, and I've liked all the countries I've been to.

What do you like the least?

The excess and the fact my social life is so different from what it used to be.

Do you think you will stay in the USA?

Well, I felt confident and settled enough to buy a house, so we'll definitely stay for the foreseeable future. My husband and I have talked about maybe moving to somewhere like Australia at some point, but it won't be soon. Realistically we might move to Portland in Oregon, but for at least the next 5–7 years we'll stay here. For me, that's a very long time to stay in one place!

Did you have any regrets about leaving the UK?

No regrets, absolutely none! I don't believe that someone has an ultimate plan for us, so it's important to make life as enjoyable as you can. Seize opportunities and be happy and content.

What advice would you give someone thinking of going to live and work in the USA?

My strongest advice would be to go via a regular visa route if you're planning on getting married to a US citizen. If you have to do it the way I did it, make sure you get the advice of a solicitor and that you have enough time to submit paperwork. Most importantly, don't lie at the port of entry.

Sue Ward

Sue lives and works in Florida with two of her three sons. She planned to move from Essex, England, to Florida in 1998 on an L visa, after falling in love in America during a holiday to Orlando in 1989. She then made the permanent move in 2003 and now owns and operates two internet-based companies from her home: www.floridavillas.com, and Flamingo Properties Inc. Sue also runs the website www.expatsvoice. org. Her husband's death in March 2006 and application to have her third son join her in Florida have been the cause of extreme turmoil in her family's life and Sue has self-taught herself immigration law to try and overcome the varied obstacles in her path.

What was your life like prior to your move to the USA?

We had a good lifestyle and lived in Chingford in Essex in our own home. My husband worked for the Ministry of Defence and we owned our own business selling Florida properties to Brits. We were also both Special Constables for the Metropolitan Police.

How is it that you came to move to the USA?

We took a holiday to Florida in 1989 with our three sons and fell in love with the place. During the same holiday we impulsively bought a house through a broker that our insurance agent owned! My husband then applied for an L-1 visa through our own company and set up an office in the USA. He and one of my sons were able to move in 1998 and I spent part of my time in the UK and the rest in the USA on a spouse's L-2 visa until 2003, when I moved permanently. My youngest son was able to move with me and attend school, but my middle child turned 21 before the application was approved, so he had to apply separately at a later date. Unfortunately an administrative error with American bureaucracy meant that he was initially denied and, although this matter was cleared up, we have had to file several applications to have his case judged as of before his 21st birthday, rather than after. We are in the process of filing a lawsuit to achieve this using the Child Status Protection Act (CSPA) and are expecting a decision later this year.

At the time of the interview, Sue's son had yet to be approved for a visa based on his pre-21st birthday application and has yet to join his family abroad.

What were your first impressions on arriving in the USA?

Well, we made the move in stages so I had a long time to gain a first impression. I love the lifestyle, the weather, and how clean it is, and Florida is very friendly. In terms of living and working here, the tax is less than at home and everything is cheaper. Our first impression in 1989 when we came for a tourist holiday was so good we decided to stay.

Has it taken long to acclimatise?

No, not long. There are good and bad things about living in America, just like there are in Britain. I'd say there are more opportunities in Florida but it's all relative. If you work hard in America you reap the rewards – probably more so than in the UK – but, generally, because I made the move in stages, it didn't take me very long at all to acclimatise.

What is the social life like?

In the UK we didn't socialise much, just sat at home and watched the telly in the evenings. Now we're in the USA, we tend to have friends round more often and often use our swimming pool for parties. I think it's better. There are some British-style pubs around here but they're more like bars so we don't visit them much and we weren't really pub drinkers in the UK anyway. Everything is further away here than at home but because everyone travels to socialise, it's fine. It's perfectly normal to travel a long way to see friends now.

How did you go about looking for work?

I work from home for my own companies so I didn't really look for work out here. My husband was able to move by using an L visa, so we had to keep our companies operating in order to stay here. I use the phone and the internet, and receive visitors in my office at home. I employ a few people, including two of my sons. My customers are mainly from the UK and Europe, but I'm slowly gaining more US clients the longer I'm here.

What comments do you have about the American working environment?

It's no different really. I employ eight people but because it's a family business my way of working hasn't really changed much. The people I employ service the holiday villas we sell by cleaning the pools and buildings and performing maintenance on them. They tend to be American citizens so perhaps my style of working has changed by simply working with non-Brits, but generally not a lot has changed.

What is your visa status? Did you find it easy to change your status once you were in the country?

I arrived on an L-2 visa and am now a green card holder, but since my husband died things have been a little difficult. The fact my middle son is still unable to join me means my feelings on changing status and the immigration procedure in general are very bitter. I am able to live and work here permanently but I hate the fact my son's not here with me and I can't visit the UK very often because of my job. I have studied immigration law as a hobby for the past 10 years in order to resolve the situation.

What is American bureaucracy like? How does it compare with the UK?

Prior to September 11, it was really easy to obtain a social security number and driving licence and all the other identification you need to live and work here. Since then, however, immigration law has really tightened up and it's much harder to gain entry than before, which is why my son's case has been so difficult. My concern is about people who gained entry before September 11 and who are still living here, even if they're here illegally. I don't think they're really being checked up on as much as the newcomers.

What do you like about Florida?

I love the weather and the friendly people you meet. The lifestyle is also a lot less stressful! I do find, though, that people can be blinkered about the outside world and aren't as aware of international situations as they are in the UK. People don't tend to think 'outside the box' as much, although it's a trade off, because everyone in the UK is far more negative than they are here.

How does the standard of living compare with England?

In 1990 it cost us £1,000 to set up our business in the UK and we've been able to successfully expand it overseas in the USA. We have no cash flow problems so our standard of living remains pretty high. I think immigration is often a case of the grass is greener but people should remember that it's a privilege, not a right, to live in America if you're a foreigner. For me, my quality of life is impaired by not having my other son with me so it's not an option for me to do nothing. I'm fighting to have his case brought to court but if it fails I don't know whether or not I will return to live in the UK.

How did you find the process of finding a place to live? How did you go about it when you first arrived?

Our insurance agent in the UK owned a house in Florida and we purchased it from him via a broker on the spur of the moment. It wasn't our wisest decision and we've had a lot of problems with it since. I'd recommend going through a broker to other people.

What are your favourite places to visit in your new country?

To be honest, I don't take many holidays. Since my husband died I've had to manage our companies by myself so I don't have the time. If I did go anywhere it would be back to the UK to see my son.

What do you like most about the USA?

The same things that I like about Florida – the prices, the people and the weather.

What do you like the least?

My least favourite thing is definitely the low wages Americans are paid. We try to pay our staff quite well but I'm constantly shocked by the minimum wage out here. People who are paid $10 an hour can't afford to buy a house and are living almost on the poverty line. A friend of mine is paid $12 an hour by a large superstore and seems really pleased about it, but she hasn't been given a raise in years and I don't think it's good enough. Medical coverage is bad too and very expensive. I don't like the fact it's not equal for all.

Do you have any regrets about leaving the UK?

My only regret is that my family and I didn't all leave at the same time. It would have saved a lot of heartache.

What advice would you give someone thinking of coming to live and work in the USA?

I would recommend they join my website (www.expatsvoice.org) for some really good advice because we have lawyers and community leaders as members and a discussion forum where people can ask and answer questions. I'd also recommend doing lots of research and homework before you do anything else and don't use a one-stop-shop with ulterior motives. A lot of members of my website have been ripped off that way. I'd check the credibility of anyone you employ to help you make the move, but don't do it yourself unless you really know what you're doing. If you do it wrong you're stuffed!

Jane Hunt

Jane is a professional violinist with the Irish Sopranos and moved to New York City, New York, in 2005. She was able to use an O-1 visa as a person of extraordinary ability after graduating from the Royal Northern College of Music in Manchester and has been living and working in the USA ever since.

What was your life like prior to your move to the USA?

Before I moved over here my life was dedicated to the violin. I studied at the Royal Northern College of Music for four years and dreamt of being able to earn a living doing what I loved. My family also lived in Manchester so I saw them more often than I do now and, although I was a student, I studied a lot so didn't really live as a student in the traditional way, with lots of parties and drinking.

How is it that you came to move to the USA?

I studied a lot at summer courses in America and with schools in New York City like the Juliard School, so I became very familiar with the New York music scene and made lots of contacts here. When I was close to graduating, I saw an advert for a guest soloist for the Irish Sopranos and auditioned. Once I'd got the job my agent organised my O-1 visa for me and my employers took care of the cost, so it was pretty easy to do. Now that I've been here a while I have to reapply for my visa and take care of the cost myself, which I'm about to start doing.

What were your first impressions on arriving in the USA?

I loved it! It was just like the movies and a complete dream come true. I was pretty fresh faced and naïve so everything was really vivid. I really liked the seasons in Central Park and seeing everything in reality for the first time. I had seen some stuff before when I'd been on summer courses but it was really different actually living here.

Has it taken long to acclimatise?

No, not long at all. I haven't been back to Manchester since I moved two and a half years ago, and although it still doesn't really feel like my permanent home, I don't think I'll ever move back to the UK. I might move to Italy for a while at some point but I'm starting to put down roots in New York so I now call this city home instead. I probably wouldn't go back to the UK because of the weather!

What is the social life like?

I work a lot, and, because I'm a musician, my work tends to be during the evenings and at weekends. When I socialise I go to cafes and restaurants with my fiancé and friends, which is wonderful, and I also take my puppy for a lot of walks. The great thing about New York is that it seems to be the centre of the world and everything's available any time of day. If I do want to go to a club at 5am, I can.

How did you go about looking for work?

All my work has come through the Irish Sopranos and nothing has really changed since I first came over here apart from the fact that I am now a permanent (instead of a guest) violinist. I had the job before I moved abroad so I never really 'looked' for work. Also, because I'm a musician I'm not really judged on qualifications, but on my playing experience and the concert halls I've played. I don't think my experience can therefore compare to other people's.

What comments do you have about the American working environment?

The New York music scene is crazy. I was lucky in that I was employed by an established company so my social security number and driving licence were taken care of for me, but I've generally found that the working environment here is similar to the UK's. Sometimes it's like you're still in Britain. I think it might be a bit less relaxed than in the UK because I'm under more pressure to be a success over here, but it's pretty similar. One drawback is that because I'm self-employed I don't get any healthcare but I've joined a musicians' agency that does provide some for me. I think it takes a lot more money to live well in New York than in Manchester and New York is definitely not a good place to be poor.

What is your visa status? Is it easy to change your status once you're in the country?

My first O-1 visa was taken care of for me but I have to renew or reapply now, and then again every three years or so. I can eventually apply for a green card, I think, but there's a really long waiting list and I'm not sure about doing it just yet.

What is American bureaucracy like? How does it compare with the UK?

I think it's pretty easy here but I have had a lot of help organising everything, including setting up my bank account, getting a social security number and my driving licence.

What do you like about the New York area?

I love the Upper Westside and Central Park. It's such a massive city, it's easy to lose yourself in it and sometimes when you're in the middle of Central Park it's like you're in a meadow.

How does the standard of living compare with England?

Because I'm self-employed it's harder to make ends meet, particularly if I need medical care. Luckily I haven't needed much because I haven't been ill very often. If you're wealthy then New York is a great place to live, but it seems that everyone who lives in the city is massively rich. If you're poor, it must be very hard.

How did you find the process of finding a place to live? How did you go about it when you first arrived?

When I first arrived I slept on a friend's couch while I was looking for a place to live. I didn't want to pay a broker so I looked on the website www.craigslist.org for places that needed a roommate. You have to be really careful and not end up living with someone crazy, but as long as you take your time until you're happy then living with a roommate is perfectly safe. I have a long-term boyfriend and we've just got engaged so I now live with him. I think the process of finding a place to live can really be affected by your financial situation.

What are your favourite places to visit in your new country?

Because I'm part of a touring musicians' group, I'm lucky in that I've seen a lot of different places in America. It's great because I get to experience the diversity and different people that make up the USA. In New York my favourite place is Central Park, but there are a lot of really nice cafes and European coffee shops. I spent a lot of time in Spain as a child so I'm really comfortable in those types of places. I love the fact you can walk everywhere in New York, too. I have a 24-hour deli underneath my apartment which I use a lot as well.

What do you like most about the USA?

I like the fact that everything in New York is so tall! It's an island, so the city is unable to expand outwards and has to expand upwards. I also like the seasons.

What do you like the least?

I don't like the scenes of massive wealth in New York City or the focus on money. The whole city is money orientated, even the children are! It can be lonely sometimes, but generally I really like the city. The good outweighs the bad.

Do you think you will stay in the USA?

I might live in Italy for a little while as part of my job as a musician, but I wouldn't return to the UK. I think I'll stay in New York for a long time because I'm putting down roots here.

Do you have any regrets about leaving the UK?

None, really. I think I'd be a different person if I'd stayed in the UK but the music industry is tough in any country. I'm happy with the choice I made.

What advice would you give someone thinking of coming to live and work in the USA?

I would advise people to make as many contacts as they can because unless you know people, you shouldn't do it. I had to have a petitioner apply for my O-1 visa for me, which involved a 20-page document full of press clippings and recommendations. I wouldn't have been able to do it without my agent and record label to sort everything out for me and I needed my contacts to get that document filled. You can Google anything you need these days and join networking sites so I think it's probably easier than it used to be to make the move and I wouldn't discourage anyone from trying to do it. It's different for every individual. For someone in a similar situation to me, I'd recommend looking at the option of going through a school such as Juliard or the Manhattan School, joining a musicians' website, and making good use of existing contacts.

Tony and Mandy Kirk

Originally from Mansfield, England, Tony Kirk, a British citizen and American resident, has been married to Mandy, an American citizen, since 2001. After spending two seasons in Columbus, Ohio, as an intern, Tony accepted a job in New Hampshire where he met and married Mandy. Now living in St Joseph, Michigan, Tony works for the appliance firm Whirlpool as an industrial designer.

What was your life like prior to your move to the USA?

I was living in Letchworth in Hertfordshire in a comfortable one-bedroom flat and working at a design consultants. Letchworth is a quaint English village and quite small. The approach to the technology I was developing at the design firm seemed very different from the experience I had as an intern in the USA. In America it's very business orientated, whereas in the UK it's more about developing the technology, then working out how to use it in the real world. I grew up on a farm near Nottingham; my dad was a farm worker and my mum worked for the local electricity board. My world has gotten a lot bigger since then!

How is it that you came to move to the USA?

I went on an intern programme in 1996, and again in 1997, in Columbus. During those trips I made some friends and kept in contact with them, so when a friend mentioned an opportunity at a sister company in New England, I was very interested. The company was expanding their team to be more culturally diverse, recruiting from the entire USA and abroad, so coming from the UK and sharing a language gave me an advantage. The friend who mentioned the opportunity was also from the UK and was getting married in Boston, so he invited me to the wedding to see the area and possibly meet with the company. At the wedding I met the bride's sister, started dating her, and Mandy and I were married in 2001. I got the job in New England and was on an H1-B visa for three years initially, so that when it came time to renew the visa I suggested we apply for a green card instead, as I was now married to a US citizen. It was cheaper than applying for the H1-B again so the corporate lawyer agreed and helped us out.

What were your first impressions on arriving in the USA?

When I went to Ohio for my internship in 1996 it was my first time visiting the USA and I loved it. The USA was very alluring to me as I'd grown up with *The A Team* and *Knightrider* shows, and life seemed very easy over there. There's a focus on convenience which doesn't exist in the UK. When I first landed in America it was in Atlanta during their Olympics and I remember thinking of the U2 lyrics from *Bullet The Blue Sky*: 'Outside is America...'! Also, the very first shop I saw at the airport was a WHSmith, but it was also the last familiar brand name I saw during my trip.

I was intrigued at being in a foreign country and Americans were intrigued about me being there. I was treated as special and different, and most people were genuinely interested in my background and culture. I got the usual questions about having tea at 4pm and driving rules, but I found that the differences were subtle. It's certainly not as different as, say, going to Japan, because at least in America the common language enables a rich conversation and dialogue.

Has it taken long to acclimatise?

Not really. I decided, before I got married, to make a three-year plan. The plan was to have no plan! I decided to see a lot, soak up a lot and wait for the end of the three years before making a decision about whether or not to stay in the USA. The marriage has obviously made my living here permanent, but giving ourselves that freedom to just enjoy the country before making any major decisions meant that I eased into American life easily.

What is the social life like?

America is a country obsessed with the pursuit of leisure, so I find it odd that workers only get two weeks of annual paid leave. Mandy and I live in St Joseph in Michigan, which is right on Lake Michigan and is a small, quaint town of around 10,000. It reminds me of New England – except there's better parking and wider roads! In town there are loads of restaurants, bars and places to eat out, and because we're on the lake there are also plenty of beaches, so people tend to use them a lot.

How did you go about looking for work?

Well, I used the contacts I already had from my internships in Ohio to find out more about jobs in New Hampshire. My previous experiences working with American companies helped me to land the job, and they also really helped me out with my permanent residency. Mandy and I wanted to move back to Ohio to be closer to her parents, and I ended up getting a job with Whirlpool in Michigan, which was a lot closer than New England.

What comments do you have about the American working environment?

It's the subtle differences which make it amusing. There is still a language barrier, even now! Expressions like 'the cheque's in the post' are not used here and can often bring meetings to a complete standstill as everyone looks at me. I watch my spelling and pay attention to my own language to make life easier. In my line of work I'm sometimes caught out by the words 'aluminium' vs. 'aluminum', so it's important for my career that I get it right.

What is your visa status? Is it easy to change your status once you're in the country?

I came over on an H1-B visa but am now a green card holder because I married an American citizen. It was a lengthy process but fairly simple, and we had the help of the corporate lawyer.

What is American bureaucracy like? How does it compare with the UK?

The immigration process so far hasn't been too bad. I'm considering becoming a US citizen at some point, and all the forms seem to be easy to file as they're all pdf-based and online. I think the US government is dedicated to making it more straightforward. I had to visit the Boston city hall to get my green card and although it was really long and laborious, I was actually disappointed that they didn't ask us to play the expected version of The Newlyweds Game! I was all prepared to answer questions about where Mandy kept her toothbrush and stuff, and they only asked us really simple, boring questions instead. In terms of other bureaucracies, I think American post offices are great – I'm really happy with them.

What do you like about the St Joseph and Michigan areas?

I think the area where we live is really beautiful, with the waves crashing on the lake shore. Lake Michigan is so big it looks like an ocean. The Michigan economy is suffering from having the car industry shaken out, and St Joseph is actually built on an old brownfield site where Tier 2 and 3 industries used to be. It's now all redeveloped and Whirlpool is the largest employer, along with the local hospital. In 2009 they're opening a Jack Nicholas golf course and although I'm not a golfer I'm pleased it'll also have a hotel, water sports and mariner development alongside it. It's partly sponsored by Whirlpool and their local interest scheme so that if Whirlpool ever changed locations the area wouldn't be derelict. Detroit isn't great but its surrounding cities are, though I really don't like Flint. I think a lot of Detroit's surrounding cities are a blueprint for success, and there's a sense of optimism in Michigan. Attitude is important at the moment, as is being flexible.

How does the standard of living compare with the UK?

I think it's ridiculous how nice a house can be in the USA for the money you pay for it. My parents' home in the UK is much smaller than its cost equivalent here. I like the high disposable income here, but Americans spend it on very strange things! I was considering buying a new lawnmower and asked my neighbour if he thought John Deere would be a good brand to buy. He told me that they were, but that they had no power for going uphill backwards and probably wouldn't tow a boat! Everything in America is bigger, better, faster, stronger.

How did you find the process of finding a place to live? How did you go about it when you first arrived?

We had our house built for us according to our plan, and even then the cost was half of what it would have been in the UK. I think we pay about 30% of our salary into accommodation costs for a very nice home. I was paying around £400 a month in the UK about twelve years ago for a small, one-bedroom apartment which wasn't in London, and I don't even know how much that would be these days. The process of buying in the USA is very easy because real estate agents work purely on commission. You're therefore more of a partner in the whole process. Our agent helped us to find the land, plan our new house and sell our old one all in one. Construction techniques are very different over here and my mum and dad back home were surprised to see everything being built of wood, and shingles used instead of clay tiles. We also chose to go with a certified green builder so everything in our house is made from sustainable resources, and we still managed to stay within budget.

What are your favourite places to visit in your new country?

My favourite place is Chicago because it's a Midwestern city that happens to be big. New York and Seattle are character cities, whereas Chicago has nice people, good food, excellent shopping and is a convenient hour and a half for us to get to. We'll often go and stay overnight, and Chicago has some very nice but cheap hotels. Even hotels belonging to the same chain of hotels that they have in New York are cheaper there. I also really like New Hampshire – I think it's my favourite state. I like the scenery and it's a great location.

What do you like most about the USA?

I like the size of the USA – it's ridiculous. We once drove across pretty much the entire country and saw the diversity and amazing landscapes here. The cultures and scenery are fantastic. You can take a short plane ride anywhere in the USA and find yourself somewhere completely different.

What do you like the least?

I always moan about the lack of vacation time. I also think the political system has a lot of flaws and is a bit of a disappointment. It's an odd system, but I suppose the spirit of the country is still intact.

Do you think you will stay in the USA?

We will probably stay forever, but then nothing's forever, is it? We're flexible enough that we could make changes to our plans. I like the lifestyle out here, but I think there's an over-reliance on cars which cannot be sustained.

Do you have any regrets about leaving the UK?

No, not really, but there's stuff I miss. Life can be difficult when your parents live in another country, particularly if they don't travel much, like my dad. The relationship you have with your family will always be different when you move, unless they move with you.

What advice would you give to someone thinking of coming to live and work in the USA?

They need to be flexible and malleable. Everyone's experience will be different, so be respectful and adventurous. After all, why would you come over here if you didn't want it to be different? I don't understand why British people go to Spain year after year and complain that they couldn't find a decent cup of tea or bag of chips. If you want it to be the same you should stay put. You can learn a lot from the residents around you, and although you might need UK things around you sometimes, you shouldn't rely on them to get you through. Learn to be an American!

Kate Whelan

Born and bred in Adelaide, Australia, Kate was a keen traveller in her youth. While backpacking in Europe, she met her American husband, Brent, in London and they settled in Madison, Wisconsin, in 1998. Having trained as an interior designer, Kate is now a stay-at-home mum, looking after her two small children full time.

What was your life like prior to moving to the USA?

I was kind of in a transition phase. At the time Australia , and particularly Adelaide, was experiencing a bad economy and jobs were becoming scarce, so I was looking for a way out. I also think, as an Australian, there is a tendency to feel a bit isolated from the world and I wanted to see it, so after I graduated from university I spent about eight or nine months backpacking around Europe alone. I eventually ran out of money, so I returned to London to get a job. I met my husband by chance in a unisex room in a youth hostel and we only really settled in the USA after travelling some more together in Australia and America.

How is it that you came to move to the USA?

After we met, my husband and I corresponded for a while, then I took a holiday to the USA to visit him. After that I took a job as summer camp counsellor in Lake Geneva, near where he was working, and we followed that by travelling in Oz for four months. While we travelled we decided to get married, so I came over to the USA on a fiancée visa. We then got married and I became an American resident.

What were your first impressions on arriving in the USA?

My first impressions were formed on holidays and as a camp counsellor. On my first visit, I landed in Florida and we drove the entire way to Wisconsin through the Deep South. It was January when we arrived in the Midwest and it was the first time, at the age of 24, that I'd ever seen snow like that before! It was a real shock to the system, but didn't seem to faze me when I eventually agreed to move here. My husband got a job offer in Janesville but my impressions of that town weren't great. We'd visited Madison before, so we decided – on a whim – to live here instead!

Has it taken long to acclimatise?

To be honest, it's an on-going process — I'm not completely acclimatised. I'm really homesick for Australia in the winter and, although there's an attractive anonymity in being a foreigner here, I miss my family a lot. It's taken me several years to get used to living here – longer than I thought. Living in a large city like London was actually easier to acclimatise to than Madison. It's also been hard to live here as a liberal: my husband's family is very conservative, so I want to fit in but it's really hard not to rebel!

What is the social life like?

It's definitely different. I grew up in a small town in South Australia called Renmark, which had a population of about 8,000 people, and later lived in Adelaide, a city of a million people. The USA, in general, is more reserved and I have to watch my mouth more. I find myself saying 'hell' sometimes and getting really strange looks from people! We recently moved to McFarland, where there are lots of young families, and it's really nice. I've made some more friends here, but it seems that you have to go to the same church as most of the families to really make friends. I'm not really into that but I've tried to meet new people in other ways. I think people here are open to chatting with you but aren't necessarily prepared to invite you over for social events.

How did you go about looking for work?

When I first came over I looked for an administrative assistant role for about two months but I guess I was over-qualified. I worked for twelve months in a communications department because I wanted to get into writing, but I was hired as a union worker and the job I really wanted was non-union. It meant that I eventually changed jobs and company and worked for EDS, which was the fiscal agent for the Medicaid programme in Wisconsin. I was writing Medicaid provider publications and doing a bit of desktop publishing but although I was writing, it was a bit dull and boring, and I wanted to do something creative. When we bought our first house, we decided to renovate it. I enjoyed it so much that after we had our first child, I resigned from my job and enrolled in an interior design course at a local technical college, which led to a job at a commercial interiors' firm involving space-planning and using AutoCAD. Unfortunately my position was made redundant in November 2007 and I now stay at home full time to look after my two children.

What comments do you have on the American working environment?

My job at EDS was exactly like the movie *Office Space*! I worked with a guy who was just like the one with the red stapler (and also a bit like Dwight in *The Office*).

What is your visa status? Is it easy to change your status once you're in the country?

I came over on a K-1 fiancée visa in December 1998 and technically we got married the following January. However, we wanted a celebration with friends and family, not just a photo by the court commissioner's photocopier, so we staged a second wedding in June 1999. We even pretended to sign the official papers again for the benefit of those who hadn't joined us the first time! After we were married,

I obtained permanent residency, which I think is easier to get if you enter the country on a K-1 visa. I'm now considering becoming an American citizen but until recently Australia didn't offer dual citizenship, so I was involved in the movement to make that a possibility. One of my children is a dual citizen but the other isn't yet. I also don't think it's been a good time (until recently) to become a US citizen, but the longer I leave it the more expensive it becomes.

What is American bureaucracy like?
How does it compare with Australia?

Visiting the Immigration and Naturalization Service (INS), now the United States Citizenship and Immigration Services (USCIS), was really hard. There were really long lines everywhere and everyone was shouting. It helped if you were an English speaker, but even the most intelligent non-English speakers were treated badly. Some weren't even allowed to use interpreters and a few even approached me to ask for help! The signage was bad there too: I had no idea which of the really long queues I was supposed to join and got shouted at for even asking about it. I think it's now moved venues and it's a lot better. They have bullet-proof glass there, which I guess is important if you treat people as badly as they did... One aspect of the bureaucracy which went wrong for me was the nationality they had written on my green card. Instead of being Australian, they had me down as French Polynesian! I was told it would cost me $100 to change it, even though it was their mistake, so I ended up having to get a letter from my local congressional office which enabled me to have it changed free of charge. The staff at USCIS were really unhelpful and rude about it, which didn't help.

What do you like about the Madison area?

I like McFarland, which is just south of Madison, but I have problems with the people sometimes. I find I connect more with people who aren't from Wisconsin in general, because they're more likely to know what's going on in the rest of the world and have travelled a bit. I don't know if my life seems threatening to locals here but, unlike in Australia, there isn't an expectation that they'll ever travel anywhere. Maybe that's why I struggle to relate to them sometimes.

How does the standard of living compare with Australia?

The cost of living here is higher than it used to be but it's still nothing compared to living in Australia. Our house in McFarland cost around $400,000 when we bought it, but it would have probably cost around $1,000,000 in Australia. Everything is getting a little bit more expensive now, with the recession, so I used to spend about $250 a week on groceries, but now I'm spending more like $300 instead. I'm more careful about using up everything in the fridge before I buy new stuff and I plan my errands out so I don't have to make unnecessary trips.

How did you find the process of finding a place to live? How did you go about it when you first arrived?

We rented a place when I first came over and during our second year we kept a 'get out' clause in our contract so we could leave early, buy a house and not have to worry about sub-letting. My husband works in banking so we knew how to get a loan easily, and we were in our first home in Madison for seven years. When we knew we wanted to move again we purchased a 'spec home' in McFarland that was in the process of being built. That was great because we got to choose some of the finishing touches as it got completed. The housing market was dead in November 2006, which meant we didn't actually move until February 2007. It did mean that several of the buyers we saw were actually serious about buying, particularly at that time of year in the Midwest. My background in interior design also helped us sell our old house, which seemed to appeal to more of an East Coast sensibility, and it was an East Coast couple who eventually bought the place for its asking price.

What are your favourite places to visit in your new country?

We took our honeymoon in Santa Barbara, CA, which was amazing but a bit like la-la-land! The city was beautiful, the climate was wonderful and there were lots of famous people around. I also like Boulder, CO, which is where my husband went to university. There are a lot of places I'd like to visit – New York, Boston, Washington, D.C., San Francisco, etc. It's a bit hard to travel when you have young children and we tend to use up our vacation time with trips home to Australia every couple of years.

What do you like most about the USA?

I like the standard of living and the quality of life. The school district where we live is also great.

What do you like the least?

I hate not having much support with my children because my family lives so far away. My parents visit nearly every year, so I'm very lucky, but it's hard to bring up two children in an area where you don't have much of a support system. One of my children has special needs too, which I find exhausting a lot of the time.

Do you think you will stay in the USA?

I hate thinking that I will stay for ever! My husband isn't good with constant change, but he loves Australia and knows more about Australian sports teams than I do! He fits in really well there with the Aussies so maybe we'll go back there at some point, but the career opportunities for him are far better over here. It's just hard thinking that I will be away from my family permanently.

Do you have any regrets about leaving Australia?

I regret leaving my family, particularly my brothers. I also regret leaving when I did! The economy wasn't good back then, but now Australia's economy is better than America's. I think I was also a bit naïve and followed my husband for love instead of thinking the whole thing through!

What advice would you give to someone thinking of coming to live and work in the USA?

I would say to investigate it thoroughly. I would think about where you'd be living and what job you'd have, but also think about if you end up having kids. Can you afford to go home or for friends and family to visit? There's more isolation than you'd expect, but mass communication can improve things. Also, check if there are any expat organisations in the area you're moving to. It's nice to have a few friends who understand where you're coming from in terms of culture. Generally though, I'd tell people to treat it as an adventure!

Leo Dillard

Originally from Hereford, England, Leo spent six months in Phoenix, Arizona, as part of an American Studies university exchange programme. Now back at home, Leo recalls the different learning styles and climate he had to adapt to when studying abroad, and how life as a student can have a very different focus in America compared to the UK.

What was your life like prior to moving to the USA?

I was studying at university in the UK and was in the middle of my second year. My university offered a six-month spell abroad as part of my degree, which was great as it meant my course would still finish in three years and I didn't have to take an extra year to get everything done. I was living in halls of residence, which was fine, except everyone else around me was in their first year and wanted to have fun all night. I had got all that out of my system the previous year and was settling down to do some real work, so I was kind of glad to leave for the second part of the year.

How is it that you came to move to the USA?

As I said, my university offered this six-month exchange programme to the USA as part of the American Studies course. It was such a fantastic opportunity that I jumped on board as soon as I heard about it. It meant that I could sample an American college without having to change degree schemes or take an extra year out, and I'd always wanted to travel there anyway. My uni had been offering the exchange for a few years so were able to organise everything for me. All I had to pick was which college I wanted to go to, and which classes I wanted to take when I got there.

What were your first impressions on arriving in the USA?

That it was really warm for January! The airport was air conditioned, which I thought was odd for that time of year, until I stepped outside and it was about 75°F! I also thought that Phoenix was the most planned city I'd ever seen – it was even more grid-like than Milton Keynes, but without the roundabouts. It was extremely easy to get around, which was great for a newcomer like me.

Did it take long to acclimatise?

As the winter turned into spring and the weather got hotter, I found it actually got harder to acclimatise over time. I really hated the weather by the time I left in mid-June. In terms of learning styles, I thought the pace and style of teaching was faster, but easier, at Arizona State. Also, it was hard at the start to get used to missing my family and friends because I was the only one from my group to exchange with Arizona, so I was completely alone and didn't know a soul when I first stepped off the plane.

What was the social life like?

I'm an August baby, so I wasn't even 20 when I went out there, which meant I couldn't buy or drink alcohol. That made the social life very different from the UK for a start! Of course I drank in private with friends, but it meant I couldn't get served in bars. If I'd tried using a false ID and been caught I could have been thrown out of the country and had my visa revoked, so it wasn't worth the hassle in public. Students over there who are too young to drink tend to watch DVDs together and cook more meals as a group to socialise, especially as it starts to get too hot to even go outdoors after a while and you can't be bothered to leave the house.

How did you go about looking for work?

I wasn't allowed to work on my visa unless it was on campus, and because I'd arrived in the middle of the year all the campus jobs had already gone, so I didn't bother to get work. I did have a friend who did some babysitting in the area, so sometimes I'd go with her to help out and she'd give me half the profits. Generally though, I was there to study so I took it quite seriously.

What comments do you have about the American working environment?

Well, because I was over there to learn I didn't see much of the working environment, but I did think the lecturers and professors were stricter. They tended to set 'homework' every class instead of one or two large essays a few times during the semester, like in the UK, and they expected it to be in on time. Sometimes it felt more like my A-Levels than university, but the quality of teaching was extraordinarily good.

What was your visa status? Is it easy to change once you're in the country?

I went out there on a J-1 visa, so I couldn't change it very easily. I didn't want to though, as I fully intended to go back to the UK once I was done and finish getting my degree. I think I could have stayed out there longer if I'd arranged it in advance; I think the limit is something like eighteen months on a J-1.

What is American bureaucracy like? How does it compare with the UK?

The American Embassy in London was insane! There were so many queues and people and guards and I wasn't prepared for how long it would take me to get done what I needed to. I think I was there for about four hours in total, and I was almost the first through the door when they opened. I think the US government is really paranoid. Also, my family came out to visit in April for Easter and we flew down to

Mexico for a few days, so I had to tell the International Students Office on campus that I was planning on leaving the country. They gave me some paperwork to fill in that I had to present to the border patrol guards when I flew back into Phoenix. That struck me as both odd and really unnecessary.

What do you like about the Phoenix area?

It's very easy to get around and I like Scottsdale a lot. The houses up there are all worth well over a million dollars, so it was a favourite pastime of ours to drive around up there and pick out which house we'd like to own! Also, they have these strange brass boxes covering up their utility boxes to make everything look prettier. I have no idea why, but it looked nice! Scottsdale also had the best bars and shopping.

How does the standard of living compare to the UK?

I didn't see much of the city outside of the campus as I wasn't really there long enough, but there seemed to be a real divide between the rich and the poor in Phoenix. It was quite stark. Most of the students had cars with them, which is really different from the UK, and books were a lot more expensive than at home. Other supplies were cheaper though, and the standard of accommodation was really good.

How did you find the process of finding a place to live? How did you go about it when you first arrived?

My university had a reciprocal agreement with Arizona State, so I continued to pay tuition and halls of residence fees while I was abroad, which covered my costs. For that reason I had to stay in a residence hall in Phoenix on campus, which was fine, but I didn't have any choice in the matter. It also meant I moved into a suite of rooms with three other men who already knew each other. They were great and we got on very well, but it was hard being a stranger at first. I missed home quite a bit at first because of it.

What were your favourite places to visit in your new country?

To be honest, I didn't travel very much because the scheduling of classes was so tight. I was in class for about twenty hours a week, and had homework and test preparation on top of that. I saw Mexico when my family came over, which was amazing, but that doesn't really count, does it?!

What did you like most about the USA?

I loved the weather at first, although that swiftly changed when it got warmer! I liked the large shopping malls because they have these weird water mister things spraying all the time to keep you cool, and everywhere is air-conditioned. I loved the ease of everything over there: if I wanted fast food at 3am, I could find it! I did miss fish and chips though...

Do you think you would have stayed in the USA?

Probably not. Or at least, I wouldn't have stayed any longer in Phoenix. I'd like to visit other areas of the country as a tourist and maybe use some of my American friends as tour guides, but a desert climate is so inhospitable sometimes. I also couldn't stay any longer as a student because my visa ran out. I might consider working there on a different visa one day, but I have plenty of time to make decisions like that.

Did you have any regrets about leaving the UK?

When I came back and visited some friends at home, I felt completely out of the loop. It was really hard at first to settle in out there, but once I had it was hard to leave again. I made some extraordinary friends, many of whom I keep in touch with online, but I'll probably not see them ever again. Now I have to change my focus again and start getting back into the learning groove in the UK. I also wish I'd been able to see more of my family while I was out there, as it was the first time I'd been out of the country without them.

What advice would you give someone thinking of going to live and work in the USA?

As a student, I'd advise other students heading out there to thoroughly research which subjects they want to study while abroad and make their college choice according to that. I'd also take into account climate and distance, and suggest they call their home and friends in the UK once a week, but no more and no less. I made sure I took lots of money and opened a US bank account while I was out there, which was really worthwhile as it meant I had electronic funds in addition to cash. I think my best advice would be to bite the bullet and do it! You're only young once!

Before You Go

■ VISAS, WORK PERMITS AND CITIZENSHIP

Although over a million people a year emigrate to the United States (7.9 million between 2000 and 2007), it still has some of the strictest and most daunting immigration laws in the world. There are more than 65 types of visas and derivatives, and a number of different ways to obtain a green card. Consular bureaucracy, which often requires the production of many personal documents such as birth certificates or property details, can make visa applications an ordeal. Despite the complexity of the process, however, more than 90% of British are successful in their application for a visa.

British emigration to the US currently accounts for 2% of the USA's total immigration figures. This amounts to around 14,500 people British citizens granted resident status. Such a high figure explains why the British (except those residents from Northern Ireland) are not eligible for the green card lottery (known officially as the 'diversity visa lottery') – because they already fill the quota set aside for each nationality. The lottery is designed to give greater access to nationals who might not have such a high degree of skills and to ensure that emigration to the US is culturally and ethnically balanced. Most European countries are eligible each year, with the exception of the UK, Poland and Russia, and all Oceanic countries were eligible in 2008.

The UK leads the world in the number of citizens living in the US after being granted working visas (temporary workers, intra-company transferees and exchange visitors). There are over 100,000 British citizens and approximately half as many German or Italian citizens working or studying in the US in the above capacities, which illustrates that with sufficient help, resources and determination, it is highly feasible to consider the option of living and working in the US. Despite the bureaucratic hurdles, thousands of individuals pull off the ambition of spending part of their lives across the Atlantic.

For those set on going one step further and permanently emigrating, you will require even more persistence and dedication. The most recently published figures for persons acquiring permanent resident status during 2007 suggest that increasing numbers of immigrants are arriving from Australia and Western Europe, which is perhaps a reflection of a strengthening of international relationships and a weakened US dollar. Nevertheless, regardless of an individual's reason for leaving their home country, the numbers demonstrate that while the option of becoming a permanent resident is certainly viable, it remains one that requires tremendous commitment.

At present there are two ways of living and working legally in the USA. The first is to have the appropriate non-immigrant visa, and the second is to have an immigrant visa. An immigrant visa holder is processed

FACT

■ British emigration to the US currently accounts for 2% of the USA's total immigration figures.

FACT

■ The UK leads the world in the number of citizens living in the US after being granted working visas.

for a Permanent Resident Card (PRC), known as the 'green card'. Both are covered in detail later in this chapter, but the essential differences between them are that the green card, granted to those in possession of an immigrant visa, is a permit to live and work permanently in America with most of the rights of a citizen, while a non-immigrant visa is always temporary. It is quite possible, however, to spend many years living and working legally with the right kind of non-immigrant visa, without ever having to, or being able to, apply for a green card.

Up until 1990, one of the prime qualifications for successful immigration was to be a relative of a US citizen. Green card quotas were designed to favour those with family connections above most others. Getting a green card through employment had also been a successful route for many people.

The 1990 Immigration Act brought about substantial changes in immigration policy. Although it is still extremely helpful to be related to a US citizen or permanent resident when petitioning for a green card, the Act created several new immigrant and non-immigrant categories which are based on the personal qualifications of the applicant. There is now more priority given to the employment categories and if you are a person of 'extraordinary ability' in the arts or sciences, or an outstanding academic, it is slightly easier to get a green card than before. The Act created the

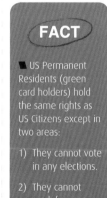

FACT

■ US Permanent Residents (green card holders) hold the same rights as US Citizens except in two areas:

1) They cannot vote in any elections.

2) They cannot work for many government agencies, including the Post Office.

H-1B category of working visa to allow qualified people to fill shortages in hospitals, universities, computer programming companies and among other occupations, with the possibility of applying for residency at a later date. There are 65,000 H-1B visas available annually and Congress passed a law in 2000 allowing an additional 20,000 H-1B visas a year under an 'advanced degree' section for those who hold Master's degrees or higher. If you wish to pursue permanent residency through the H-1B category, however, there are no guarantees. An employer must sponsor you to apply through the H1-B visas to get a green card, and they are under no obligation to do so. You may, therefore, end up being tied to one employer for a number of years and then sent back home.

In addition to working visas, a special programme called the EB-5 investment visa has been introduced. This is particularly desirable as, like family-based visas, it provides a route to a green card, although it does also require a minimum 'at risk' investment of $500,000. Most non-family based visas are linked to a specific job or investment which can prove restrictive, and since the 21st Century Department of Justice Appropriations Authorization Act in 2002, the EB-5 has been no different. Previously, the investor didn't need to have active day-to-day involvement in the investment other than retaining a net asset value of at least $1,000,000, which enabled the holder (and his or her immediate family) to take any job, own any business, and even retire. Now, however, an active day-to-day involvement is crucial in maintaining visa status and the Immigration and Nationality Act requires the holder to 'actively engage' in a new commercial enterprise.

Further changes to the law came in with the Illegal Immigration Reform and Immigrant Responsibility Act of 1996 as well as through various acts of legislation brought in at the end of 2005. Most of the changes relate to enforcement of the law, and include such things as an automated entry-exit control system matching your next entry with your last exit, the setting up of inspection stations at foreign airports, and the provision of 10 full-time immigration enforcement agents in each state. Penalties for illegal immigration have become more draconian – an illegal alien forced to leave is barred for five years, and any subsequent removal will result in a 20-year bar. Even harbouring illegal aliens can now land you a three-year minimum prison sentence.

Anyone working for a multi-national company with offices in the USA, is uniquely privileged and intra-company transfers (L category visa) cover this category. Many foreign nationals seem to slip into New York's financial world with ease. However, for the majority of foreign nationals it is difficult, but certainly not impossible, to get permission to work in the USA. Experts advise that if you do not fit into any of the visa categories, you should change your circumstances until you do. The visa system has many quirks; for example, a category may require a 'degree or degree equivalent'. This might make it seem as though those without degrees have little chance of getting through, but there are also a number of qualifications that will satisfy the USCIS, including, in some cases, the right sort of experience. If you have done City and Guilds exams in the UK, an AQF Certificate IV or Diploma in Australia, or if you have 20 years experience as a senior engineer, this could, for example, qualifty as a 'degree equivalent'. There are several companies who will transcribe qualifications, and it may be worth investigating them to see if your qualifications meet the standard required for a specific visa.

For an individual hoping to find work in the USA, the process of obtaining permission to do so is uncertain and requires a degree of determination and commitment. Naturally, it's hard to apply non-vocational qualifications to the common working visa, the H1-B, particularly an arts degree like History or English. However, these degrees often offer an advantage in that they can apply to a range of jobs. Describing yourself as a 'researcher' with specialist knowledge in an area corresponding with your degree is one solution. With the assistance of an experienced immigration lawyer, it is possible to obtain one of the working visas, but you will need to have the support of an employer in America first, patience second, and sufficient funds to support the often lengthy legal process third.

The system is complicated and the USCIS (United States Citizenship and Immigration Services) is strict in its interpretation of the requirements. To many people it may seem unfair, but it is worthwhile to keep in mind that although the system cannot be deceived, it can be worked to your advantage. The essential thing is to know the categories and to take the greatest care in ensuring that you fit into one of them.

Immigration is a contentious issue within the USA because it remains such a popular destination. Anyone other than Native Americans is, by definition, descended from immigrants. Historically, it is a nation that has welcomed immigration, and the huge ethnic and cultural diversity of urban neighborhoods remains extraordinary as new waves of immigrants continue to arrive at the melting pot. Occasionally, however – and especially during times of growing unemployment – certain pressure groups will campaign to restrict the numbers of new immigrants. Critics argue that Americans are being squeezed out of employment opportunities and that the country is facing problems of population density.

Virtually anybody wishing to enter the USA as an alien (i.e. anyone who is not a US citizen or holder of a green card) must hold a valid passport and an appropriate non-immigrant visa, even if they are only there for a tourist holiday. The good news is that in 2000 President Clinton signed the Visa Waiver Permanent Program Act. The Visa Waiver Program (VWP) allows visitors from 27 countries (including the UK, most of Western Europe, Australia and New Zealand) to stay as a temporary visitor for up to 90 days without a visa. You must travel with an airline that has agreed to take part in the scheme (this includes the main transatlantic carriers) and during the flight or at check-in they will hand out visa waiver forms which need to be completed and given to immigration control on arrival. It is, of course, worth checking with the airline before you fly as to whether they subscribe to the Program or not. Since 2006, all VWP travellers have had to be in possession of individual machine-readable (biometric) passports. When you arrive at your port of entry you may be subjected to rigorous questioning as to the reason for your journey. You may need to prove that you have sufficient funds to finance your stay and that you have somewhere to stay. You may also need to make a convincing case that you are intending to return to your own country of residence within the 90-day time limit. One simple yet crucial element of this is to purchase a return ticket for your flight as you cannot enter on the VWP without it, though you may also have to produce proof of continuing employment at home or enrolment in higher education. American immigration can be tough even to the point of putting you on a return flight home, so bring enough material to persuade the officials that you are truly just visiting for business or pleasure.

If you are ineligible for the VWP, or simply want to apply for a straightforward B visa (for tourists B-2 and temporary business visitors B-1), the process is simple and should not require assistance from a lawyer. It becomes more complicated when you want to stay for more than six months at a time, or when you want to work, so it is essential to be quite sure which visa category you are applying for. If you are in any doubt about your status or what kind of visa you want, seek professional advice. There is a list of US immigration lawyers operating in the UK at the end of this chapter, and a list of useful websites at the back of the book.

US consular officials base their decisions on the applicant's documentation and, in most cases, a short interview. The US Embassy in London currently has a wait time of up to 25 days before an appointment is scheduled for non-immigrant visas. The wait time for embassies in other countries may be shorter. In the eyes of the consular officer every visa applicant is deemed to be an 'intending immigrant', and the burden of proof rests on you to convince the officer that you have a 'compelling commitment' to return to your own country. In most cases this is straightforward; if you are applying for a B visa and have a job or a college place to return to, this would count.

There are two common reasons for refusal to grant a B-1 or B-2 visa. The first is when you want to extend your trip over the six-month limit, and have no definite commitment to a job or a place at university when you return. The second is that you may have left your job in the UK in order to look into the possibilities of starting or investing in a business in the USA, so that you can qualify for an E-2 (treaty investor) visa. In both cases it is up to you to convince the consulate that you are not an intending immigrant.

After you have been issued a visa there is a further hurdle in the form of the US Customs and Border Protection officer at the port of entry. These officers are unpredictable. They might search your luggage and demand to know why you have brought an ironing board and a full set of cutlery if you only intend to stay three months. They will certainly want to know how much money you have on you, and what access you have to more funds. They will ask questions that might seem difficult to answer if your reason for visiting the country differs even slightly from your visa category.

Once you are in the USA it is no longer possible to get your visa changed to another non-immigrant visa without leaving the USA, unless you are a student. All other revalidation of visas must now take place in the person's home country or place of usual residence or abode. Another caveat: while changing your mind is one thing, 'willful misrepresentation of a material fact' is another. If you apply for one visa with the intention of changing your

FACT

■ If you need to stay longer than 90 days, you should apply for a visa in the US consulate of your home country as only in the rarest cases or in the context of a status adjustment are they issued in the USA itself. If you are temporarily abroad you can apply in the US consulate of the country that you are staying in.

TIP

■ In **all** immigration cases, honesty really is the best policy.

status when you arrive, you may get into serious trouble and find yourself ineligible for future visas. For example, if you have changed from B-1 to E-2 status once, and then return to the USA on another B-1, hoping to change status again, your application would almost certainly be turned down, and the USCIS would regard with extreme suspicion any future application.

The most important thing is to apply for the right visa in the first place. If you are thinking of staying for a long time, looking for work, or are going out as a student but want to stay on, you will eventually have to apply for a green card (see below). This is a long and difficult process, especially for a Western European.

The US Embassy can supply a full list of all the visas available, but the following is a summary of the main categories.

> The most important thing is to apply for the right visa in the first place. If you are thinking of staying for a long time, looking for work, or are going out as a student but want to stay on, you will eventually have to apply for a green card.

Visa categories

A Visa – Diplomatic Visa

To qualify you must be travelling to the US on behalf of your national government to engage solely in official activities for that government. Issued through diplomatic channels with separate A visas for ambassadors, employees and family.

B Visa – Temporary Visitors for Business or Pleasure

If you are visiting the USA solely for business or pleasure, and are not eligible for the visa waiver programme, then you should apply for a B-1 (business) or B-2 (pleasure) visa or a combination of both (B-1/B-2). Business in this case means coming for the purpose of conferences, conventions or seminars, negotiation of contracts, consultation with business associates, and/or litigation whilst under the employment of a non-US company. You are allowed to purchase or incorporate but not to be employed by a US company, or to manage a US business, while visiting on this visa. However, you may acquire property and sign contracts. A B-2 visa means that you may not take part in any business-related activities at all. B-1 visas normally provide admission for up to one year, B-2 visas for a maximum of six months. It is possible to use the B-2 as often as you like. If you have a holiday home in the USA and can prove that you have another, permanent, residence in your own country it is perfectly possible to spend six months of the year in the USA, using your visa each time you come back in. B visas are valid for a maximum of ten years.

C Visa – Transit Visa

Most European and Oceanic visitors can simply transfer flights under the Visa Waiver Program. Aliens who are ineligible for the VWP will need a C visa under one of its three classifications, including United Nations employees and government officials. Check with the local US embassy or consulate for information.

Example of Treaty Traders visas

A UK-owned business begins trading heavily with an American company. They apply for an E-1 Treaty Trader visa for at least one employee by proving that the volume of trade is high enough to warrant a permanent base in the USA and that the UK company has sufficient experience dealing with American businesses. It is approved. The new base in the USA must now trade at a level of at least 50% in America and it is favourable that it employs many US nationals. The E-1 visa holder has to be, and remain, a UK national.

D Visa – Crew Member

D visas are issued to crew members of international airlines and to aliens required for the normal operation and service of a vessel. They are similar to C visas, but specific to airline employees.

E Visa – Treaty Traders and Investors

E visas are for business or investment use. They are valid for up to five years at a time, are renewable, and not subject to quota restrictions. E-1 visas are for citizens of countries which have the appropriate treaties with the USA (this includes the UK, Australia and Canada, but not New Zealand or South Africa). The US company that you work for can be owned by you or by another person, but they must be of the same nationality as you. At least 50% of its business activities must consist of trade between the USA and your own country and it must employ high numbers of US nationals in the company as well as those who are of the same nationality as the visa holder.

You are restricted, with E-2 visas, to working only for the employer or self-owned business which acted as your visa sponsor. E-2 visas are available to those who have made a qualifying 50% investment in a US company (of any size), or who are working for a UK company which has made an investment of at least 50% in a US company. E-2 visa holders can apply for a green card through the EB-5 special programme once they show they have made the minimum investment in the company ($500,000) and have hired 10 new workers.

F and M Visa – Students

F visas are issued to full-time academic or language students and M visas are for vocational, technical or other non-academic students. Both are renewable and the privileges and restrictions that apply are also more or less the same, except that with an M visa you can work legally on or off the campus if the work is considered practical training for your field

E-2 VISA

Privileges

- You can work legally in the USA for a US business in which a substantial *cash* investment (at least $100,000) has been made by you or other citizens of your home country.
- You may travel in and out of the USA or remain there continuously until your E-2 visa expires.
- There is no legal limitation on the number of extensions that may be granted.
- E-2 Visas can allow you to live in the US on a prolonged basis, provided you continue to maintain E-2 qualification.
- Visas are available for your spouse and all unmarried children under 21 though while they may study in the USA, they cannot work.

Limitations

- Visas are available only to nationals of countries that have trade treaties with the USA.
- You are restricted to working only for the specific employer or self-owned business which acted as your E-2 visa sponsor.
- Accompanying relatives may stay in the USA with you, but they may not work.
- When children reach the age of 21 and wish to continue living in the USA they must apply for their own visa.
- You must renew your white I-94 (Arrival-Departure Record, completed on flight) every year.

of study. Restrictions are that you must first be accepted by a school or college in the USA before you can apply, and you can only attend the school for which you were issued that visa. A spouse and minor children (those under 21) may qualify for a non-immigrant visa.

G Visa – International Organisations

The G visa is for UN, IMF and similar organisations. Dependants may qualify for a derivative visa and may be permitted to work.

H Visa – Temporary Workers

Most non-resident foreigners given permission to work are admitted on an H visa. There are four different types of this visa and subdivisions within them. Remember that you will need to have obtained a firm offer of employment first before making an application to the US Citizenship and Immigration Service (USCIS).

- **H1-B visas** are issued to temporary workers in 'specialty occupations' – those that require a degree or certificate of higher education. Architecture, engineering, mathematics, physical sciences, social sciences, medicine and health, education, business specialities, accounting, law, theology, and the arts are all considered speciality occupations. H1-B visas are limited by a quota, which currently stands at a base limit of 65,000 each year, plus an additional 20,000 for those in possession of an 'advanced degree'. This makes the chances of getting one slimmer at the end of the financial year, and frequently the quota is filled on the first day it opens in April each year. The application process has been sped up with a 'fast stream' system that allows employers to obtain visas for prospective employees within seven days. The employer is required to submit a petition (a form of sponsorship) to the USCIS; and a 'labor condition application' must also be submitted to the Department of Labor. When these have been approved the employee applies to the consul in his or her own country.
- **H1-C visas** are for registered nurses working temporarily in the USA and are valid for up to three years.
- **H-2A and H-2B visas** are for those skilled and unskilled workers going to the US to perform a job which is temporary or seasonal in nature and for which there is a shortage of US workers. Technicians and skilled tradespeople can apply in this category. There is an annual quota of 66,000 in this category.
- **H-3 visas** are for trainees. The training cannot be available in your home country and must be for future employment outside the USA.
- **H-4 visas** are available for spouses and dependants. Employment is not permitted on this type of visa.
- An H visa is valid only while you work for the employer who sponsored your application. If you change jobs you must apply for another visa, with a new employer's petition. You can only possess an H visa, whether with the original employer or a number of employers, for a maximum of six years. On expiration you must reside abroad for a total of one year before applying for another visa.

I Visa – Representatives of Foreign Media

I visas are available to people who are working in press, radio, film, television, print or other forms of media in their own country. They are issued for multiple admissions and are valid for an extended period. Holders are obliged to work only in the occupation for which the visa was issued. Freelancers must prove that they have a contract for work produced in the US. Spouses and dependants may accompany an I visa holder, but they cannot work.

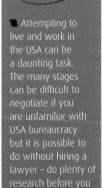

TIP

Attempting to live and work in the USA can be a daunting task. The many stages can be difficult to negotiate if you are unfamiliar with USA bureaucracy but it is possible to do without hiring a lawyer – do plenty of research before you take even the first step and keep all paperwork for future reference.

J Visa – Exchange Visitors

J-1 visas allow you to come to the USA to participate in a specific exchange visitor programme approved by the United States Information Agency (USIA). These include summer employment programmes, intern programmes for university students, teachers, or scholars, and au-pair programmes (for further information, visit www.travel.state.gov). Dependants receive J-2 visas and may study, but not work. The USIA sponsors organisations such as BUNAC (see *Employment*), which provides those qualifying for its programme with the J-1. They are valid for 12 to 18 months, and allow multiple entries, as long as permission is sought from the sponsor organisation and arranged in advance. You can work in a wide variety of occupations but you are restricted to those which are specified in the organisation's programme. There is also a two-year foreign residency requirement for J visa holders. This means the visa holder is obliged to remain in their home country for at least two years after the expiration of their J visa before they can apply for permanent residency or an H, L or K visa.

K Visa – Fiancé(e)

The K visa is for the fiancé(e) of a US citizen only; they have to travel to America to marry and will take up indefinite residence after marriage. The K visa can only be issued when the fiancé(e) is outside the USA and the couple must be married within 90 days of a K visa holder being admitted entry to the USA. A K-3 (spouse) and K-4 (child) visa has been created to reunite families that have been separated for a long period of time while their visa immigrant applications are being processed.

L Visa – Intra-company Transfers

L visas are available for certain executives, managers, or employees with specialised knowledge who are transferred to the USA to work for their employer, its parent, its branch subsidiary or affiliates. This visa category can be valid for a total of seven years for executives or managers and for up to five years for workers with specialised knowledge, and it allows multiple entries. Any legal form of doing business is acceptable, including but not restricted to, corporations, limited companies, partnerships, joint ventures and sole proprietorships. The USCIS is becoming increasingly more restrictive in allowing L-1 visa holders to convert to the green card by filing an I-140 Permanent Employment petition, although L visa holders are eligible to apply after just one year of working in the USA. The USCIS reserves the right to re-evaluate all L-1 visas when you apply for the green card through the I-140 route.

N Visa (NATO Visa) – Visas issued to NATO aliens, spouses and children

International organisation special immigrants may be eligible for a NATO visa if their organisation has instructed them to visit a military headquarters in the USA.

L VISA

Privileges

- You can be transferred to the USA and work legally for a US company that is a branch, subsidiary, affiliate or joint venture partner of a company which already employs you outside the USA.
- Visas can be issued quickly.
- You may travel in and out of the USA or remain there continuously until your L-1 status expires.
- Visas are available for your spouse and all unmarried children under 21.
- If you have an L-1 visa for an executive or managerial level position in the US company and want to apply for a green card through employment you can do so after one year (the USCIS is becoming more restrictive in allowing this form of conversion).
- When you enter the USA your I-94 (Arrival-Departure Record) will be issued for the length of your L-1 approval.

Limitations

- You are restricted to working only for the US employer who acted as your L-1 visa sponsor and the US company must be a branch, subsidiary, affiliate or joint venture partner of the company that currently employs you outside the USA.
- Visas can initially be approved for one year (new US company) or three years if your US company has been trading for more than one year. Extensions of two years at a time may be allowed until you have been in the USA for a total of seven years if you are a manager or an executive.
- When children reach the age of 21 and wish to continue living in the USA they must apply for their own visa.

O, P, and R Visa – Temporary work visas for selected occupations

The Immigration Act of 1990 created a number of highly-specialised working visa categories. O and P visas are available for people with outstanding ability or achievement in business, the sciences, arts, education, entertainment, and athletics. R visas are for religious workers who have been a member of a religious denomination which has a bona fide non-profit religious organisation in the US. The application requires written evidence from an appropriate individual or organisation to back it up. These visas are often issued for a particular event or occasion (such as a festival) and are valid for the duration of that event, up to a maximum of three years. They are also renewable.

Q Visa – Exchange visitors coming to the USA to participate in international cultural exchange programmes

Nicknamed the 'Disney Visa' because it was lobbying by that organisation that helped create it, the Q visa is granted to those who will be working in a job where they will be sharing a practical training with Americans, or the history, traditions or culture of their country. Nannies and au pairs (although they normally qualify for a J-1), or teachers of unusual arts would qualify. The visa is valid for up to 15 months, and has to be applied for by the prospective employer. It is also only renewable if the visa holder returns to their home country for at least one year before the visa is re-issued. It differs from the J visa in that it does not relate to specific exchange programmes.

S Visa – Suppliers of information in criminal or espionage cases

Usually only issued and expedited by federal and local government agencies, holders of an S visa are witnesses or informants in matters of political law, legal cases or criminal investigations.

T and U Visa – Victims of trafficking or abuse

Victims of severe human rights crimes may enter the USA on these visas, accompanied by spouses and dependants, to assist federal authorities in their investigations.

V Visa – Dependants of Lawful Permanent Residents

Spouses and children of permanent residents who have been waiting three or more years for immigrant visas may use temporary V visas to enter the USA under the LIFE Act. V visa holders may wait in the USA for an immigrant visa and are eligible to apply for a work permit.

The green card

The green card, or the Alien Registration Receipt Card – the I-551 which includes a photograph, biometric indicators, and a fingerprint in the chip – is the best-known and most coveted of immigration documents.

Significantly, the green card entitles you to live and work in the country, though you must physically live there as a permanent resident. If the USCIS suspects you of having another home abroad, and if you spend more than a certain amount of time out of the country (usually a year), you may lose your green card. You have to satisfy the authorities that you are, and mean to remain, a permanent resident.

This can cause problems if you want to apply for a visa and then for a green card, because a requirement of most visas is the absolute intention not to remain permanently. A certain amount of ingenuity is often needed to explain a sudden change in circumstances, so be prepared to do some homework and possibly answer some tricky questions.

A green card holder is a tax resident of the USA, and has the right to apply for US citizenship after a certain time, depending on which route you took to become a permanent resident. One of the only differences between citizenship and green card status is that the latter does not give you the right to vote.

Everyone has an equal chance of getting a green card. Although some people consider that it is more difficult for a Western European to make a successful application, everybody applying through one of the normal channels (for example through employment, as a family member of a US citizen, or through a minimum investment of $500,000) has the same status whatever their nationality. The fact that many Western Europeans in the USA do not have green cards may be because they do not see themselves as permanent residents. It is more common for them to stay for the duration of a non-immigrant visa and to return periodically to their own country, whereas many people from the developing world and from Eastern Europe tend to come to America to stay for good.

TIP

■ If you have previously been admitted entry to the USA on a specific visa and now wish to apply for permanent residency, it is worth checking online at www.travel.state.gov to see if there are any foreign residency requirements. You may have to remain in your home country for an extended period of time before applying for a green card.

 Although most Britons are not eligible for the Green Card Lottery, an exception is made for individuals born in Northern Ireland. A complete list of eligible countries is available at www.travel.state.gov.

Another reason for the lack of Britons with green cards is that for several years they have not been eligible for the Green Card Lottery (see below), which is only open to nationals of countries which have not sent more than 50,000 immigrants to the US in the past five years.

There are a number of websites dedicated to facilitating entry to the lottery, but be wary of those who wish to take money from you, as entry to the lottery is free for the first stage.

 Application submissions and paperwork can be reviewed at www.dvlottery.state.gov.

The only case in which certain nationalities are favoured above others is in the Diversity Immigrant Visa program – popularly known as the Green Card Lottery – by which 50,000 green cards are reserved each year for

TIP

■ Another reason for the lack of Britons with green cards is that for several years they have not been eligible for the Green Card Lottery

> **Many Europeans in the USA complain about the system, its expenses and difficulties. As one past applicant says;**
>
> British people and Europeans have a very hard time staying here, and have to move through the immigration system from one visa to another and finally to a green card. This is a very difficult process which I can testify to first hand. Many circumvent the system by marrying, although even then the immigration department checks up on them to see if the marriage is valid.

countries which traditionally have not seen many emigrants cross over to the USA. An additional 5,000 are available through the Nicaraguan and Central American Relief Act (NACARA) to applicants from certain countires in Central America who meet certain criteria. The Immigration Act of 1990 introduced this category as a way of encouraging ethnic diversity in the US population. The odds of being selected are about one in 20 for progressing to the second stage of applications and less than one in 100 for getting a final permanent residency visa, according to USCIS.

Certain categories are favoured above others: the vital distinction is whether you come from a country with a repressive regime. Political refugees are given priority above many other categories. Other ways of getting a green card include investment in the USA – although as a minimum of $500,000 must be invested, it is not an option open to many.

Applying for a green card

Applying for a green card is usually a two-step process consisting of the filing of a petition (by your relative, spouse or employer) with USCIS, and the application, which can be made at the US embassy or consulate in your home country. You can file with USCIS if you are in the USA on a non-immigrant visa at the time, although you may have to reapply for a work permit while you wait for an Immigrant Visa Number to become available. As applications differ depending on the category, you should ask the advice of the consulate.

The following summary lists the categories of those who are eligible for green cards:

- **Immediate Relatives:** Including spouses of US citizens; unmarried people under the age of 21 who have at least one US citizen parent; or parents of US citizens if the son or daughter is over 21.
- **Preference categories:** These are usually people with family members who are US citizens (under these categories certain family members will be given precedence over others: children of US citizens have priority over brothers and sisters, for example). The second preference category is those with job skills that are wanted by US employers

and are in short supply in the USA, such as medical professions, manufacturing jobs and even teaching positions. Skill shortages often depend on the state and city.

- **Diversity Immigration Lottery (also known as the Green Card Lottery):** 55,000 green cards are given to those countries that in the past have sent the fewest immigrants to the USA. If you are a national of one of these countrues, you must register by a certain date each year, and if the registration is accepted you file an application, along with documents such as birth and marriage certificates, at a consulate. You must provide proof of a high school education or its equivalent, or two years' work experience within the last five years in a job which requires at least two years' training or experience. Although an astonishing six or seven million people from six geographic regions apply to enter the Lottery, there are only 90,000 places available. Of those who successfully enter, only half of those will then go on to win a green card. There have been instances of fraudulent websites posing as official US government sites and 'scam' emails soliciting funds so if you plan on applying for the Lottery, always do so through the official website at www.dvlottery.state.gov. Notification of success will come from the Kentucky Consular Center in the form of written notification and will never solicit payment.

- **Investors:** As a result of the Immigration Act in 1990, 10,000 green cards are now available through an EB-5 visa for those who invest $1million in either new US businesses that will hire at least 10 full-time workers, or in an existing business that will hire an additional 10 full-time workers. The minimum is reduced to $500,000 if the investment is made in a Targeted Employment Area, which is either rural or where unemployment is 150% of the national average. The requirement to employ 10 citizens is also waived if the investment is made in specific areas designated as Regional Centers and a competent professional, such as an economist, quantifies that it will stimulate employment. Many Regional Centers have immigrant investor programmes which offer investments designed to meet the immigration requirements. Some extremely useful information on the EB-5 route to residency is available at the law office website of attorneys Chang and Boos; see www.americanlaw.com/investor.html.

- **Special Immigrant:** Over the years, various laws have been passed covering certain 'special categories' of immigrant. These include religious workers, foreign medical graduates, former employees in the Panama Canal Zone, foreign workers who were formerly long-time employees of the US government, and several others. Check with the US consulate for details or go online at www.uscis.gov.

- **Refugees and those seeking political asylum:** To qualify for residency through this route you must be fleeing political or religious persecution in your own country and have held refugee or asylum status in the USA for at least one year. Economic refugees (those escaping poverty) do not qualify.

■ **Amnesty:** The Immigration Control and Reform Act (ICRA) in 1986 gave amnesty to aliens who had been living illegally in the USA since 1 January 1982, by giving them green cards. Under the ICRA those who had worked in agriculture for 90 days between 1 May 1985 and 1 May 1986 were given green cards under two categories: Special Agricultural Workers (SAWs) and Replenishment Agricultural Workers (RAWs). The second category (RAWs) is specifically for those who worked for 20 days within a calendar year and registered before 31 December 1989, and who were entered into a lottery. This system will be revived whenever there is a shortage of agricultural workers.

■ **Temporary Protected Status:** This is not a green card category: Temporary Protected Status is given to those fleeing persecution who need a temporary safe haven. It will not lead to a green card and once a country has been removed from the TPS list, the protected person reverts back to their original visa status.

Immigration documents

If you fall into one of the categories listed above and are eligible to apply for permanent residency, you may wish to start accumulating some or all of the following documents **for each person immigrating** before taking any other steps. Please note that not all of these documents will be necessary for each applicant, and some applicants may require other proof or documentation not listed opposite.

Documents required

Valid passport for applicant	Ensure your passport is valid for at least another 5–10 years after you first apply. The application process may take considerably longer than you think, and switching passport numbers in the middle may delay it further.
Valid passport or ID for sponsor	Your sponsor (spouse, parents, child, employer, etc.) will need to prove their citizenship and right to sponsor you.
Birth or adoption certificate	This will need to be a full, original copy. If you do not have one, visit the UK General Register Office (www.gro.gov.uk), the Australian state or territory Registrar of Births, Deaths and Marriages (www.passports.gov.au/Requirements/BirthRegistrars) or the New Zealand Department of Internal Affairs (www.bdm.govt.nz) to obtain a new copy for a small fee. European applicants must visit their relevant country's registrar, which can be located at www.europa.eu.
Marriage certificate or licence	If applicable, this will also need to be a full, original copy. Visit your home country's registrar listed above to obtain a copy if you do not have one.
Divorce certificate or decree	Full, original document(s).
Death certificate	Although not always necessary, it may be worth obtaining any death certificates for deceased spouses, parents or children, particularly if your application is dependent on them.
Police certificate	At a later stage of the application process, you will need to prove a clean criminal history. A copy of your history can be obtained by visiting your local police force and applying in person. Although it may take a few months to receive a copy. They are valid for only six months and incur a fee, so don't apply for one too early.
Vaccinations or medical history	During one of the very last stages of the process, you will need to schedule a medical check-up and x-ray with an embassy-approved medical practitioner. Take with you proof of all vaccinations received, as you may be required to receive them again for a large fee if you cannot prove them. Your doctor will usually provide your medical history for you.
Sponsor's tax returns	Your sponsor will need to submit evidence of tax returns for the past three years. Copies can be obtained from the IRS (www.irs.gov) and they currently need to show an income 125% above the current poverty line for each year.
Passport photos	You will send off numerous passport-sized photos, so it's worth starting to collect them before you apply. Make sure they are sized for USA regulations, which are different from almost everywhere else in the world (2" x 2", with at least 1" of face and $\frac{1}{2}$" of space between head and top of frame).
Money	Every form you submit usually has a fee attached of between $85–$250, so ensure you have plenty of funds available before you start your application. Money will need to be sent by either a cashier's cheque or postal order in US.

It is also wise to start accumulating any address changes you and your parents have had since you were 18 (particularly for the police certificate) and a complete employment history. While you may not need this for the application stage, it will make job hunting a lot easier once you're living in the USA. School transcripts for any children making the move will also be of use to you once you are abroad.

Finally, it is worth remembering that the application process may well take a lot longer than you think, and, as a general rule, you may need to apply 1–2 years before you want to make your physical move. For this reason, don't book any flights or removal firms until you have the permanent residency visa in your hand.

US citizenship

To be a US citizen you have to renounce citizenship of all other countries, although your country may not accept the renunciation, and may enable you to keep dual citizenship. It is worth checking on your own country's immigration service website for clarification of dual citizenship laws (www. ukba.homeoffice.gov.uk for the UK, www.europa.eu for members of the European Union and www.immi.gov.au for Australia). US immigration laws are complicated, and there are many ways in which people qualify for citizenship without realising it. The rules governing whether or not a child born out of the country is a citizen or not have changed several times over the last 50 years. The basic law is that in order to qualify, one or both of your parents must be US citizens, and have to have spent a certain amount of time in the USA.

If you think that you may qualify as a US citizen, contact the consulate for details of the law as it stood when you were born.

■ If you were born between 1952 and 1986, and only one parent was a US citizen, he or she would have had to have spent at least 10 years (at least five of them after the age of 14) in the USA.

■ Since 15 November 1986, the 10-year residence rule changed to five years, with two years of compulsory residence after the age of 14.

■ When parents become naturalised US citizens, their children automatically have the same right, provided that they hold green cards and are under the age of 18 at the time of their parents' naturalisation.

■ The Child Citizenship Act of 2000 ruled that a child under 18 who has been adopted and emigrated to the USA immediately acquires US citizenship, providing their adoptive parents are also US citizens.

■ Proof of US citizenship can be given using a birth certificate from a state government, a US passport, certificates of citizenship, or certificates of consular registration of birth.

■ A child born on US soil is automatically a citizen of the USA no matter what the laws of the parents' country. Children born in the USA to foreign diplomats are an exception to this rule: they are deemed to have been born on foreign soil.

Naturalisation

To become a naturalised citizen of the US you must be at least 18, and you must have held a green card for at least five years. You should also be a person of good moral character, have knowledge of the English language, and be familiar with American government and history.

At least half of the five-year waiting limit must have been spent in the USA. If you leave the country for more than six months and less than a year it is deducted from your total, and if you leave for one year or more this wipes out any time added up to the five years, and you must start the waiting period again.

If you are married to a US citizen the waiting period is reduced to three years, while if your spouse works for the US government abroad there is no waiting period.

The process for naturalisation is surprisingly simple. The application is made with the USCIS on form N-400, which can be obtained from www.uscis.gov. After this form has been processed (which may take anything from a few months to over a year) you will be called to an interview in which you will have to demonstrate the required knowledge of history and government, and spoken English. You may be asked the date of US independence, the meaning of the stars and stripes, what happens if both the president and the vice president die in office, who the governor of your state is, or what the name of the national anthem is and who wrote it. These questions are designed to imbue in anyone who wants to become a citizen a sense of the importance of what they are doing, and sample questions are available on the USCIS website. It is not an exercise in nationalism, more a matter of taking your new country seriously by taking the trouble to know something about it. Many city councils in the USA run free citizenship classes to prepare residents for the process of naturalisation.

The final part of the process is the swearing-in ceremony, when you will take the Oath of Allegiance to swear allegiance to the USA, and renounce citizenship of all other countries.

Illegal papers

Many of the estimated eight million illegal immigrants in the USA hold counterfeit green cards – but that is getting more difficult to do. In 1998, the then INS spent $38 million developing a green card they believe is impossible to counterfeit. Embedded with microscopic portraits of all 42 presidents, a hologram of the Statue of Liberty and other hi-tech wizardry, it tries the skills of even the cleverest forger. You can still buy a fake for

FACT

■ 'Bad' moral character can cover anything from committing a crime, being 'a habitual drunkard' or non-payment of taxes.

FACT

■ All you used to need to fake a green card was a typewriter, a pot of glue, a cheap laminating machine and a Polaroid camera. Not any more!

anything from $5,000–$15,000, but be warned that the government is notoriously strict in dealing with illegal immigrants, and if you are discovered with fake papers you will certainly be deported, and may never be allowed back into the country. Beware also of phoney 'immigration consultants' who claim to increase your chances of success in the green card lottery. They will tell you they have never had an application rejected, or that they are affiliated with the government. The process for entering the lottery is free and simple, and there is nothing anyone can do to increase your chances of success.

Summary and resources

Once you have succeeded in getting the visa that you want, make sure that you work and live within its limits. It would be pointless to blacken your name by trying to cheat the system. Once you are on the files of the USCIS you will be amazed by how familiar they are with your circumstances and how soon they get in touch if you outstay your welcome.

Bear in mind also that many people spend years in the USA without getting permanent residence status, or applying for the 'ultimate goal' – citizenship. The latter may, of course, not be an option for many Europeans who do not wish to renounce their nationality for the sake of it.

If you have had an application turned down it would be best to get a lawyer. There are two schools of thought on this subject. Some say that it will do you no good, that the system is quite easy to work without resorting to expensive advice; but, on the other hand, for between $1,000–$3,000 you can get enough help to open doors that you were not aware of, and it could save months of frustration.

Useful websites

The most useful websites come from law firms and other licensed organisations specialising in visa applications; a small selection of the best are listed here. There are also hundreds of personal homepages made by people who feel the need to share their visa application sagas – some of them make interesting reading!

www.uscis.gov: the official site of the US Citizenship and Immigration Service providing information about fees, applications, regulations and offices.

www.travel.state.gov: the official site of the US Department of State, including advice and guidelines on travel and immigration.

www.dvlottery.state.gov: the official site of the Diversity Visa Lottery. Entry and information can be obtained here.

www.americanlaw.com/investor.html: the law office website for Chang and Boos, hosting a wealth of information and helpful legal advice.

www.visanow.com: site providing online immigration law services that also offers guidance and hosts online applications.

> **TIP**
>
> ■ Treat lawyers with caution, and make sure that they are fully qualified to deal with your situation: avoid using 'visa specialists' as they are not regulated or qualified and may attempt to scam you. Your local US Embassy will supply a list of qualified, experienced and authentic lawyers upon request.

www.lawcom.com/immigration: the immigration homepage from the law office of Richard Madison. An excellent and informative site.

www.us-immigration.com/imm.htm: straightforward immigration information from the American Immigration Center.

www.imwong.com: from the law office of Margaret W. Wong and Associates.

Useful addresses

US embassies:

US Embassy: 24 Grosvenor Square, London W1A 1AE; 020 7499 9000 (main switchboard); 09042 450100 (operator assisted visa information line); www.usembassy.org.uk

US Consulate General Scotland: 3 Regent Terrace, Edinburgh EH7 5BW; 0131 556 8315; www.usembassy.org.uk/scotland

US Consulate General Northern Ireland: Danesfort House, 223 Stranmillis Road, Belfast BT9 5GR; 028 9038 6100; www.usembassy.org.uk/nireland

US Citizenship and Immigration Services: US Embassy, 5 Upper Grosvenor Street, London W1A 2JB; 020 7495 0551; www.uscis.gov

Foreign embassies in the USA

British Embassy: 3100 Massachusetts Avenue, Washington, D.C. 20008; 202 588 7800; www.britainusa.com/embassy

Irish Embassy: 2234 Massachusetts Avenue NW, Washington, D.C. 20008; 202 4623939; www.embassyofireland.org

Australian Embassy: 1601 Massachusetts Avenue NW, Washington D.C., 20036; 202 797 3000; www.austemb.org

New Zealand Embassy: 37 Observatory Circle NW, Washington D.C., 20008; 202 328 4800; www.nzembassy.com

Visa services and immigration lawyers

Brownstein, Brownstein & Associates: Immigration Department, 6000 Cote de Neiges, Suite 590, Montréal, Quebec, Canada H3S 1Z8; 416 601 1800; contact@brownsteinlaw.com; www.brownsteinlaw.com. Canadian immigration lawyers with associates worldwide, including in the USA.

Ferman Law: 27 Bruton Street, London W1J 6QN; 020 7499 5702; info@ fermanlaw.com; www.fermanlaw.com. An American attorney specialising in US and Canadian immigration, setting up businesses, and taxation.

Four Corners Emigration: Strathblane House, Ashfield Road, Cheadle, Cheshire SK8 1BB; 0845 841 9453; info@fourcorners.net; www.fourcorners. net. Specialists in assisting with immigration and visas to the USA. Full support with relocation and resettlement is also given.

Global Visas: 28 Great Tower Street, London EC3R 5AT; 020 7190 3903; www.globalvisas.com

Laura Devine Solicitors: 11 Old Jewry, London EC2R 8DU; 020 7710 0700; enquiries@lauradevine.com; www.lauradevine.com

New Horizons Group: 2555 Porter Lake Drive, Suite 102, Sarasota, FL; 34240; 941 387 3829. Also Devlin House: 36 St George Street, Mayfair, London,

W1S 2FW; 01252 761419; info@usafl.com; www.newhorizonsgroup.com. One-stop relocation service to the USA.

Richard S. Goldstein: 96A Mount Street, 1st Floor, Mayfair, London W1K 2TB; 020 7499 8200; lawoffices@goldsteinvisa.com; www.goldsteinvisa. com. Also at 145 West 57th Street, 16th Floor, New York, NY 10019; 212 957 0500; lawoffices@lorsg.com.

Travel Document Systems: 925 15th Street NW, Suite 300, Washington, D.C. 20005; 202 638 3800; support@traveldocs.com; www.traveldocs.com

USA Immigration Law Center: 1717 K Street NW, Suite 600, Washington D.C. 20036; 202 973 0168; info@usailc.com;; www.usailc.com

Walter F Rudeloff: 4 King's Bench Walk, Temple, London EC4Y 7DL; 020 7267 1297;. American attorney at law providing professional immigration services to obtain any type of US visa or green card.

Workpermit.com: 11 Bolt Court, Fleet Street, London EC4A 3DQ; 020 7842 0800; london@workpermit.com; www.workpermit.com. Global corporate immigration service affiliated with the UK's Computing and Software Services Association.

Employment and investment specialists

Ambler Collins Visa Specialists: Eden House, 59 Fulham High Street, London SW6 3JJ; 020 7371 0213; info@amblercollins.com; www.amblercollins. com. A firm specialising in providing advice on all categories of US visas. Also assists with applications to appropriate government offices.

RWH International Inc: 3223 3rd Avenue South, Suite 200, Seattle, WA 98134; 416 636 3933; info@usjoboffer.com; www.usjoboffer.com. A firm which assists with the job-hunting process in the US.

Robinson O'Connell: 10 Greycoat Place, London SW1P 1SB; 020 7960 6057; visas@robinsonoconnell.com; www.robinsonoconnell.com. Specialists in the EB-5 investment visa, particularly those linked to Regional Centers for retirees.

Other interesting websites

www.britishexpats.com: a site dedicated to assisting new and old expats from all over the world, particularly – but not exclusively – British. Hosts a wealth of articles and a fun, social discussion forum.

www.expatsvoice.org: similar in theme to British Expats, with a focus on assisting those who have had a troublesome time obtaining visas.

www.matesupover.com: expats forum for Aussies and Kiwis living far from home.

www.en.wikipedia.org: online encyclopedia with definitions to assist even the most inexperienced immigrant.

◼ LANGUAGE

English is the principal language of the USA by virtue of the fact that it is the first language of the majority of the population. It does, however, have no constitutional status as the official language. For the rest of the population, English is a second language, and many people hardly speak it at all. There are some states where more than 23% of the population speak a language other than English at home, a list that includes those bordering Mexico, New York State and New Jersey. There are 21 million people who speak Spanish as a first language, although half of them were reported to speak English 'very well' during the last census. Surprisingly, French is spoken by 1.6 million people at home, and is the largest foreign language after Spanish and Chinese. French has official standing in Louisiana (which was a French possession until 1803), and has evolved into two main branches: Cajun Acadian, spoken by the descendants of Canadian refugees, and Creole French, spoken by the descendants of slaves from Southern Louisiana. Significant minorities speak Italian, German, Korean, Greek, and Japanese. Spanish is an official language in New Mexico, and California, Texas and New York State have the greatest concentration of Hispanic immigrants.

There are very few languages that are not spoken somewhere in the USA, and there are a few that are not spoken anywhere else in the world. In eastern Pennsylvania, around 150,000–250,000 people speak Pennsylvania Dutch (or Pennsylvania German); a mixture of German and Dutch dialects. There are no records showing how many of them speak it as a first language, although the Amish people are the most famous and continuous speakers. On the coast of Georgia and South Carolina some people still speak a language called Gullah, a dialect of the original African language brought to the US by slaves. There are also speakers of Yiddish, Hungarian, Russian, Polish, Serbo-Croat, Ukrainian, Czech, Arabic, Eskimo, Aleut, and Tagalog, the official language of the Philippines.

FACT

◼ Of the 304 million inhabitants of the country, about 254 million speak English at home.

Native languages

Of the 2.2 million Native Americans (American Indians or Alaska Natives) 350,000 speak an Amerindian language at home. The biggest group is Navajo, with 150,000 speakers living in Arizona, Utah and New Mexico, though there are also around 15,000 Apache, Cherokee, Choctaw, Dakota and Ojibwa speakers. The many other Indian languages are spoken by a diminishing number: 8,000 speak Blackfoot, Creek, Keres or Passamaquoddy; around the same number speak Arapaho, Cheyenne, Chickasaw, Comanche and Crow; 300 speak Flathead and less than two hundred speak Mohave, Seminole and Pawnee. It is likely that many of these ancient languages will be extinct within the next two generations as

FACT

◼ There are 550,000 Gypsies in the USA who use Romany as their first language.

English continues its relentless advance, although dedicated work is being carried out to preserve endangered languages through the internet.

■ BANKS AND FINANCE

Bank accounts

American banks tend to operate on a regional or state basis. They offer the same sorts of facilities as UK banks with a few, sometimes quite frustrating, differences. The standard retail bank or building society is called a Savings and Loan, or 'thrift' bank. Individuals may open current ('checking') or deposit ('savings') accounts, money may be transferred, and banker's drafts can be ordered. American banks do not usually have foreign exchange facilities, although with an international credit card such as Visa or American Express, dollars can be withdrawn and charged to your account in your own currency. This is of course an expensive way to get cash, as the commission is usually high.

How to open a bank account

You should have no difficulty opening a bank account, providing your visa has either generated a temporary Social Security Number (SSN) or you are able to prove you have foreign national status to the bank's auditors. You will also need a proof of address in the USA, in which case use a rental agreement or paystub from your employer until utility bills start coming through. Most banks will require a minimum opening balance of $25–

$200, and, in some banks, it is necessary to keep a minimum balance in your account. Falling below this may result in harsh charges being levied. Some banks may charge between $300–$10,000 a year, depending on the account, to waive minimum balance requirements, or else they may charge monthly maintenance fees or even charge you to open and close your account. As with all banking systems, read the small print carefully before opening an account and choose the one that suits your needs best.

It is advisable to check what identification is required to open an account. You may wish to take two or more of the following documents with you when you go to the bank, as most accounts cannot be opened online or from another country:

- Passport
- Visa (with temporary SSN if appropriate)
- Social security number (apply to the Social Security Agency if you do not already have this)
- Driving licence (apply to your local DMV or use the original from your home country)
- Proof of residency for the USA or your home country (green card or passport)
- Proof of your address in the USA (utility bill, tenancy agreement, wage slip, etc.)
- Proof of your address in home country

Social security numbers are usually generated automatically for new permanent residents and are sent to your new address within a month of your arrival. If you do not receive a card with your number on within this time, go to your local Social Security Administration office with your I-551 (visa or green card) and find out more information using your Alien Registration Number. If you are on a non-immigrant visa a temporary SSN will have been printed on the visa in your passport.

If you need a credit rating, you could try opening an account with a major department store such as Sears. This will automatically give you a credit rating which will be accepted by the bank, although the route to a high credit rating in the USA is difficult and can often take years. The best way to start improving your credit score is by taking out one or two small credit cards and paying them off each month, making sure you receive an income, pay bills on time and maintain a bank account.

FACT

■ The route to a high credit rating in the USA is difficult and can often take years.

Internet banking

American banks offer both savings and deposit accounts, and will usually offer you free internet or telephone banking as standard with either one. Internet banking is a fantastic resource, particularly for expats who may wish to view their account while in another country, so take advantage of the flexibility they offer. You can also help save paper by signing up for online statements instead of paper ones, and can arrange direct debits, transfer money and pay bills through your online account. Having your balance at your fingertips is a great way to manage your money when abroad.

ATMs, cards and banking procedures

There is a network of Automatic Telling Machines (ATMs) across the country. Most accounts include cash cards and debit cards, and networks such as Cirrus and Plus are interstate and countrywide. There are also local networks in the major cities, such as the New York Cash Exchange. It would be worth opening an account with a bank that is a member of one of these networks. Banks usually charge non account-holders commission for withdrawing cash from their ATM, which is another good reason for banking with one of the larger banks. Link cash cards, issued by many UK banks and building societies, can be used in Plus machines to withdraw cash from the holder's UK current account. Cards issued by Natwest (Royal Bank of Scotland), HSBC and the Nationwide, Halifax, and Woolwich building societies will be accepted. If you intend to return to the UK after a period in the USA and don't have an account already, it would be worth opening one at one of the banks or building societies that participate in the Link\Plus network, as your current account will continue to accumulate interest while you are abroad. HSBC and the Royal Bank of Scotland (known as HBOS in the USA) now own and operate branches in America, as well as online.

Cheque guarantee cards are not issued in the USA, although debit cards are confusingly called check cards. Cheque fraud is rife, and many places, such as restaurants and service stations, will not accept them as a matter of course. If you do pay by cheque, you may be asked for one or two pieces of identification such as student ID or passport, and driving licence or credit card. It is worthwhile getting a state ID if you do not have a driving licence: both of these are available from the Department of Motor Vehicles Licensing Office (www.dmv.org) in your state.

It is essential not to go overdrawn on a current account. Fees for bounced cheques can be punitive: $10–$35 per cheque. As well as this, the cheque is sent back to the payee, which, if it is a shop or organization, is likely to charge another $10–$35 fee. Individuals who knowingly write bad cheques may be charged with fraud.

Chequebooks are not free, and have to be ordered in bulk from the bank, usually in sets of 20. This will cost around $25, although you can pay more to a private company and have cheques printed in any number of designs, including a favourite sports team, cartoon character or even a home photo. It is common to have your full name, address and telephone number on your chequebook.

Finally, before opening an account, you should check to see that the institution is federally insured so that your deposits are guaranteed up to $100,000 in case of corporate bankruptcy, fraud or theft. Banks which are

TIP

Most banks offer overdraft protection for a small one-time fee, which can be a helpful feature, especially for students.

included in this scheme advertise with special federal deposit insurance stickers in the window.

US banks can also arrange mortgages and other low-interest loans. If a bank provides this service it will be called a savings bank. High-interest accounts are available at most US banks, although their rates tend to be higher for online-only accounts. These are of between two- and five-year deposit terms, and, at the time of writing, were seen to be offering interest rates of between 3.5% and 4%.

Savings Banks in the USA do not generally deal with any but the very smallest business customers: they are almost exclusively for private bank accounts. Businesses are catered for by the commercial banks, such as US Bank, Chase Bank or the Bank of America.

Transferring money

The most common form of international transfer is instantaneous and electronic. Because of the five to eight-hour time difference, UK and European banks are able to transfer funds at same day value, meaning that when you order funds from your UK or European branch the money will be changed into dollars at the exchange rate that is in effect at that moment, and not at the next day's rate. Likewise for Asia and Australasia – a money transfer will be exchanged at the rate it held on the day it was ordered, although it will obviously be arriving one day later due to the time difference.

An express transfer costs around $40, and a standard transfer, which takes about five days, $20. Other companies do offer money transfers, such as MoneyGram (www.moneygram.com) and Western Union (www.westernunion.com), but they may charge you more than a bank and are only able to send money to other branches. Both MoneyGram and Western Union are commonplace in Europe, Australasia and the USA, and can be easily found at local shops or post offices. Other forms of international transfers are banker's drafts and international money orders. These are sent by post and are relatively uncommon.

FACT

■ Most banks are able to send money transfers or drafts to any foreign bank providing they have the IBAN (International Bank Account Number), bank name and sort code of the receiving account.

■ Internal money transfers

These can be arranged by electronic transfer (the SWIFT system or the CHIPS system) between banks across the country. The cost would be between $10 and $25, depending on the distance, although if both accounts are owned by the same bank it can be done for free online.

Currency

The US monetary unit is the dollar ($), which is divided into 100 cents. Dollar notes (referred to as 'bills') come in the following denominations: $1, $2, $5, $10, $20, $50, and $100. Naturally, the dollar and British pound exchange rate fluctuates and is determined by the money markets. In the past few years sterling's strength against the euro has slightly declined,

The dollar has grown increasingly weak, due to the current economic downturn

though it has still outstripped the US dollar as the American currency becomes increasingly fragile internationally. Recently, the dollar has drifted downwards against the pound and the euro with a direct effect on tourism, international trading and oil prices. The current exchange rate on the dollar is around $1 = £0.50 and $1 = €0.62. Exchange rates can be checked before departure at www.xe.com or through any major search engine.

US bank websites

The following is a list of several major national banks. It is not exhaustive as most banks in America have branches in more than one state, but are not necessarily nationwide.

Bank of America	www.bankofamerica.com
Chase Bank	www.chase.com
Citi Bank	www.citi.com
Key Bank	www.key.com (online only)
US Bank	www.usbank.com
Wells Fargo	www.wellsfargo.com

◼ COST OF LIVING

Upon initial arrival in the States, many foreigners find they have more money than at home. Wages are often double what they are in the UK, but accommodation costs are around half. New immigrants may therefore find that they have a far higher disposable income than in their home country. An administrative assistant from anywhere in Western Europe for example, may have earned around £16,000 (€20,000) per annum at home and now finds themselves earning $30,000 for the same work in the USA. Their rent has halved though, from £750 (€930) per month to only $650, leaving a balance of $1,850 every month before taxes. In Europe, they would have only £583 or €740 ($1,160) left. Even taking exchange rates into consideration, it's still around half of the USA earner's monthly disposable income.

TIP

◼ Once you get over the initial 'wow, it's all so cheap!' factor, remember that you're now earning in dollars and spending in dollars.

The cost of living in the USA is on the rise, particularly with its current economic slowdown, and newcomers should be aware that all finances are relative once you start earning. The price of food, petrol and entertainment have all seen increases in 2008, so while you may have more disposable income at first, once you start paying taxes, insurance and monthly bills, it may seem less than when you first emigrated. Accommodation in the UK generally accounts for between 60% and 70% of a monthly income; in the USA it's around 35%, although if you're living in a large and expensive city, costs will naturally be greater. It is all comparative though; the administrator from the first example now earns $2,500 a month in America but pays $9 for a ticket to see a movie. In the UK they earned £1,330 (€1,660) a month but only paid £5 (€7.50) to go to the cinema.

One important element of calculating disposable income figures is what will happen to the money once it reaches your wallet. If you have more money each month to play with than before you moved, your expenses may soon catch up. If you have enough to purchase an additional car for example, the payments on it will absorb some of your funds and you'll have less left over each month. America is a very easy place to spend your hard-earned dollars, so just remember: it's all relative.

Below is a table with averaged estimated costs of basic items and services you may encounter while living and working in America. Prices for individual items will obviously fluctuate widely depending on where you purchase them, what type of goods you're buying and if you're insured! More information can be found in the *Setting Up Home* section of this book.

Costs of basics		
Service		**Average Cost ($)**
Monthly rent	(2-bedroom house)	1,050
	(1-bedroom apartment)	650
Dinner for two		50
Lunch for two		15
Cinema ticket		9
Single journey on NY Subway		2.50
Visit to doctor	(GP, co-pay)	10
	(GP, uninsured)	175
Cup of coffee	(coffee house)	
	(gas station)	
Glass of beer		2
Haircut	(women)	40
	(men)	15

■ GETTING THERE

It is often relatively cheap to fly to the USA from Europe and Oceania, depending on when you wish to fly and with whom you want to fly, but fuel price increases are gradually increasing ticket prices. There are dozens of scheduled airlines and countless charter carriers who fly to destinations all over the USA. In many cases flying from the UK means you have a choice of UK airports for your departure and searching around for the best combination of price, dates and distance from home can be a bit of a daunting task but worthwhile. Finding the best-priced ticket takes some searching around on the web or in the advert pages of newspaper travel supplements and backpackers' magazines like *TNT* or *Southern Cross*. The most useful websites are not those that promise the lowest prices, but those that offer flexible booking options and up-front figures, including taxes. Some of the most useful and reputable are listed below.

In the UK, the London *Evening Standard*, London listings magazine *Time Out* and the colour supplements of the Saturday and Sunday newspapers are also useful sources, as well as Teletext. Cheap, direct fares normally have an advance booking requirement of just two days online, though with charters you cannot change the date or time of the booking once it has been made. Most operators can cater for those who wish to fly to one US city and return from another; these are known as 'open jaw returns'. For details of travel insurance and health insurance within the US see 'Daily Life'.

The peak (most expensive) periods are usually between June and September and over Christmas/New Year. At other times it is generally easy to get cheap tickets for the date you want, particularly if you book far enough in advance. In the low season, flights from London to Miami are priced around £450 ($900) return and London to New York about £300 ($600).

When making a booking online, be sure to check various sites and multiple combinations of dates, destinations and departure cities. Most websites now have a flexi-date option, allowing you to see up to three or four days before and after your selected date and the differences in prices charged for these days, and this can be extremely helpful. Also bear in mind that it is often cheaper to fly mid-week and to larger cities and then to hire a car and drive to your final destination. Some helpful websites for making flight bookings include the following:

FACT

■ Most websites now have a flexi-date option, allowing you to see up to three or four days before and after your selected date and the differences in prices charged for these days, and this can be extremely helpful.

Expedia	www.expedia.com	Good, all-purpose site
Lastminute.com	www.lastminute.com	Handy for late planners
Opodo	www.opodo.com	Great for general travel
STA Travel	www.statravel.com	Excellent for those under 26 or students
Travelocity	www.travelocity.com	Great for multi purpose bookings
Travel Supermarket	www.travelsupermarket.co.uk	Good site for making comparisons

A reliable, independent booking service for low-cost flights on scheduled and charter services to the USA is available from Flightclub (0845 880 1808; www.flightclub.co.uk), who are members of ABTA.

Other agents specialising in the USA include First American Travel (020 8673 8888; www.1111trip.com), Unijet (0870 600 8009; www.unijet.aero), and Trailfinders (020 7938 3939; www.trailfinders.com). Airline numbers and websites for US flights include:

Air Canada	0871 220 1111	www.aircanada.com
American Airlines	020 7365 0777	www.americanairlines.co.uk
Continental	0845 607 6760	www.continental.com
United Airlines	0845 844 4777	www.unitedairlines.co.uk
US Airways	0845 600 3300	www.usairways.com
British Airways	0844 493 0787	www.britishairways.com
Delta	0845 600 0950	www.delta.com
Virgin Atlantic	0870 380 2007	www.virgin-atlantic.com
Northwest/KLM	0870 507 4074	www.nwa.com or www.klm.com
Qantas	0845 774 7767	www.qantas.com
Air New Zealand	0800 028 4149	www.airnewzealand.com

Insurance

Working travellers and those on speculative job-finding trips to the USA are strongly advised to take out comprehensive travel insurance. Insurers offering reasonable and flexible premiums include Expatriate Insurance Services Ltd (dial 0870 330 0016 from the UK or 1 800 436 6267 from within the USA; info@expatriate-insurance.com; www.expatriate-insurance. com). They specialise in arranging international travel, health, and life insurance. Insurance can often also be purchased through the same website through which you booked your flight, or through your existing insurance provider.

■ PLANNING AN INTERNATIONAL MOVE

Removals firms should be affiliated either to the Association of International Removers, or a national organisation such as the British Association of Removers (see below for a list of websites and addresses). Removal companies are not regulated by law in any case, and this is the best guarantee of protection. Affiliated companies are inspected for their business practices and for their financial security, and they are also covered by shipping guarantees and bonds in case they go out of business while your goods are in the mid-Atlantic.

Most companies will offer a certain number of weeks' free storage and will undertake to move absolutely anything door to door, including motorbikes, cars and pets. Most international removal firms require that you do not pack up your home yourself, and that their team packs everything for you. While this often sounds too good to be true, it also ensures the removal firm has packed goods to their specification and it should generally

> **James Dasey, International Manager at Doree Bonner International, gives the following advice:**
>
> For any international removal, the costs involved are based specifically upon the volume of goods an individual is looking to ship. Generally speaking, the larger the volume, the more cost effective the shipment becomes. It is not advisable to ship electrical items into the USA as problems will be encountered because of the voltage differences. Problems will also be encountered with the shipment of vehicles but other than this, if an item has a useful and usable life span upon arrival, it is generally worth sending.

prevent goods being damaged en route. Costs vary widely depending on the destination: shipping to a port in the USA is generally reasonable, but as soon as the goods have to be transported any distance inland, the price escalates. It is therefore a good deal cheaper to ship to Los Angeles or New York than to Las Vegas or Chicago.

Moving the average family home consisting of three or four bedrooms from the UK to the US will cost, on average, £5,000. Air freight is usually not considered an option because of the expense: household goods are priced by bulk rather than by weight. Shipping, then, is the common method. Items can take anywhere from 4 to 12 weeks to arrive. The contents of an an average family home will fit into a 20-foot (6m) container, but it is possible to use a 40-foot (12m) alternative.

Employers are not required to report to the Internal Revenue Service any moving expenses paid directly to a third party (the removal firm) on behalf of an employee. Therefore for US tax purposes your employer should pay your moving expenses directly to the removal firm rather than reimburse you for the cost of moving.

Useful addresses
The British Association of Removers: 01923 699 480; info@bar.co.uk; www.removers.org.uk
Avalon Overseas Movers: 020 8955 1079; www.avalon-overseas.com
Bishop's Move Group: 020 8391 8222; international@bishopsmove.com; www.bishopsmove.com.
Britannia Movers International: 020 8256 1700; sales@britannia-movers.co.uk; www.britannia-movers.co.uk
Davies Turner Worldwide Movers: 020 7622 4393; T.Hutchison@daviesturner.co.uk; www.daviesturner.co.uk/movers
Doree Bonner International: 020 8303 6261; moving@dbonner.co.uk; www.doreebonner.co.uk
International Federation of International Removers (Belgium): 32 2 426 5160; fidi@fidi.com; www.fidi.com
John Mason International: 020 8667 1133; www.johnmason.com
Oceanair: 020 8805 1221; sales@oceanair-int.co.uk; www.oceanairinternational.com.
PSS International Removals: 020 8686 7733; sales@p-s-s.co.uk; www.pss.uk.com.

Customs regulations

US customs regulations are pretty liberal when it comes to those moving house. Almost all household and personal effects that are more than one year old can be taken in, except for certain spices, meat products, seeds and plants, fruits, ivory, crocodile and alligator skin products, switchblades (flick knives) and the obvious things, such as drugs and firearms. If you are on prescriptive drugs you will need a doctor's letter. A duty will be levied on goods that have not been used, or were bought less than one year before. If you have anything that looks very new, take proof that it is more than a year old. Unaccompanied baggage can be sent, but it should arrive within five days of the passenger to avoid storage charges, and it must be declared when you arrive to be eligible for customs exemptions.

Returning US residents are allowed to import duty free up to $400 worth of goods bought abroad, as well as 200 cigarettes, one litre of spirits, and reasonable quantities of perfume. Non-residents are allowed to import duty free gifts of up to $100 in value, plus alcohol and cigarettes as above. If you need more information on import procedures, contact the Department of Homeland Security Customs and Border Protection at the US Embassy (020 7894 0771) or visit their website at www.usembassy. org.uk/ukcustom.

Importing procedures

Imported goods must be entered on US Customs form 3299, and submitted to the customs office at the port of entry. You will be handed this blue form either when you check in at an airport, or during the flight by flight attendants. All goods must be listed on the form, with particular detail given to goods that are less than a year old, as duty will be charged on these at a rate of 4%–10% of their value. On arrival in the USA you must provide an address to the customs office, which will then contact you when your shipment arrives. All shipping firms are fully aware of import procedures, and you will find that everything is taken care of, unless you are shipping independently. In the USA, contact the local customs office for your port of entry, listed in the telephone directory under US Customs.

Importing vs buying a car

FACT

■ If you are bringing in a car for less than a year you will be exempt from US emission control and safety standards but you will need to take the registration document with you.

There is no import duty for non-residents, visitors or first-time immigrants importing foreign-made cars. For returning residents, the duty is 2.5% of the price for cars, and 1.5%–2.9% (depending on cylinder capacity) for motorcycles. But there is little point in importing your car to the USA unless it is particularly valuable or sentimental to you, as the cost of buying a new one and selling it when you leave would certainly work out cheaper.

As long as you hold a valid driving licence you are allowed to buy a car in America; you don't have to have a US licence. Buying a new car can be a good deal cheaper in the States than in Europe or Australasia. Many dealers will offer to take care of insurance in the form of a loan, but it would be advisable to arrange this for yourself – the dealer will be going to the same sort of bank or insurance company as you, and will be taking a commission himself.

Buying a used car comes with many attendant problems. Try to find a dealership outside the city limits to avoid city sales taxes. If you are buying privately, try to buy in a wealthy area: the car may cost more, but it will be in better condition. There is a publication called the *Kelley Blue Book* (available at most bookstores, or online at www.kbb.com), which gives information on standard values for new and used cars.

◼ IMPORTING PETS

In order to bring in a dog or cat to the USA you will need to present a health certificate from a vet. If coming from the UK, there will be no quarantine requirement (unless required by state or local authorities) when you arrive in the USA, as the UK is free of rabies,. However, all other animals and birds are subject to strict customs regulations and quarantine. The exceptions are the states of Hawaii and Alaska, which have additional regulations. To take a dog, cat, or bird into these states you have to have an Interstate Health Certificate from a vet, issued no more than 10 days prior to shipping. Hawaii is rabies-free, and all dogs and cats (except those coming from continental USA or Australia, New Zealand or Britain) must be quarantined for 120 days.

The UK has now introduced the Passports for Pets scheme (to avoid the six-month quarantine process for bringing a pet back into the country) but the USA does not yet qualify to participate because it is not classified as rabies free. Information on exporting pets from the UK to outside the EU is available from local Animal Health Divisional Offices. A list of these offices can be found at www.defra.gov.uk. The only exception is the state of Hawaii because, as mentioned previously, it is free of rabies.

TIP

◼ The US Embassy will supply current regulations concerning the import of pets. Alternatively, you can visit the *US Public Health Service* and *Centers for Disease Control and Prevention* website at www.cdc.gov. The *American Society for the Prevention of Cruelty to Animals* (www.aspca.org) also has useful information about the keeping of pets in the USA.

Setting Up Home

America continues to be a favourite choice for emigrants. According to the UK Office of Population Censuses and Surveys, around 32,000 people a year leave the UK and 7,200 leave Australia in order to spend a year or more in the USA. Wherever you go, you will meet Europeans, and, if you spend time in areas with the greatest concentration of foreigners, such as Arizona, California, Colorado, Florida, Illinois and New York, you will find ready-made communities to welcome you. Of course, buying a house in the USA can be as traumatic as it is in your own country, but generally the US property industry is well-regulated, efficient and fair. The recent sub-prime mortgage crisis has slowed down the rate of sales in America but an average consumer will still find a wide variety and choice of homes to purchase. There are so many foreigners buying property (especially in certain states), that extensive networks exist to ensure the buying process runs smoothly. There are large numbers of UK property companies that deal with the USA and relocation agents will steer you through the entire process, from identifying properties to organising visits. The more a company is doing for you, the more important it is to brief them thoroughly: you do not want to make a series of abortive visits across the Atlantic to look at unsuitable houses.

Venice Beach, California, famous for its circus-like Ocean Front Walk, which is full of entertainers and vendors

In the UK, another way of getting in touch with US property professionals is to go to one of the major international exhibitions aimed at domestic homebuyers. The main event for information about buying property in the US is the Homebuyer Show held annually in March at the ExCel centre in London's Docklands. There is an extensive section there that is dedicated to buying property abroad and exhibitors include developers, agents, attorneys, removal companies, overseas lenders and property magazine publishers, all displaying their services. The show is an excellent opportunity to familiarise yourself with prices, locations, and so on, and to collect addresses of companies which might be useful in the future.

> For more information about the Homebuyer Show, visit the website www. homebuyer.co.uk or contact the organiser (020 7069 5000; enquiries@ homebuyer.co.uk). The Home Buyer Show held at the Brisbane Convention and Exhibition Centre in Brisbane, Australia, during July is a similar event and details for that can be found at www.bcec.com.au.

House prices vary enormously from state to state. It is more expensive to buy in a city than in the country, and generally cheaper inland than on the coast. You will also find the south cheaper than the north and Midwest. Of the 10 most expensive places to live according to the American Chamber of Commerce Researchers Association (ACCRA) however, a surprising number are outside of this general rule. Three are in Alaska (Fairbanks, Anchorage and Juneau) and only two are in California (Los Angeles and San Diego). The rest are spread throughout the USA (in Seattle, Ann Arbor, Philadelphia, Boston and New York). Of course, New York tops the bill. Other expensive metropolitan areas include Jersey City (New Jersey), Stamford (Connecticut) and Honolulu (Hawaii). The cheapest housing is in Wyoming, Nebraska, Idaho, Wisconsin and Alabama. The most affordable urban areas are Tampa Bay in Florida, Houston in Texas, St Louis in Missouri, and Minneapolis in Minnesota.

Much of the hassle of long-distance planning can be eased by using the internet. Here, you can search property listings, check prices, and make contact with attorneys, real estate agents, schools, and local authorities. One useful starting point is the *Life in the USA* website (www.lifeintheusa. com), which provides new arrivals with a guide to American society and culture. Joining an online forum group will also provide you with tips, advice and friendly chatter.

■ CHOOSING WHERE TO LIVE

The standard of living in the USA is considerably higher than in many European countries. In a country of over 300 million inhabitants this can only be an average: there is also terrible poverty and deprivation, and not only in the inner cities. Some rural areas, such as the Appalachians and the Mississippi

TIP

■ Be warned that if an exhibiting company wants to take any money upfront, you'd be well advised to steer clear. Take their details and check out their credentials online before paying any fees. Upsetting as it may seem, not all exhibitors have scruples.

TIP

■ Although this is an excellent time to buy, in some cases the decision whether to buy or not will not arise: if you are on a short-term job placement and are not in a position to buy, or if you are intending to live in a major city where prices are high even for the seriously wealthy, you may wish to rent instead.

Delta, suffer crushing poverty. But the national standard of living is high. The median household income is $44,334 and 89% of households own a motor vehicle, while more than 99% have a refrigerator, 76% a clothes washer, and nearly 44% central air conditioning. More than 98% own a television, 34% a freezer, 28% an outdoor grill, and 12% a waterbed heater.

By 2008, 68% of Americans owned their homes, which translates as nearly seven out of 10. The US Department of Housing and Urban Development specified a national homeownership goal of 70% by 2006, but the slump in the housing market in recent years has slowed ownership to the point where it is now declining everywhere except the Midwest (72%). For those who do own a property, it is likely to be an apartment or condominium in a town, or a house (or bungalow) in the suburbs, with its own garden, called a yard. Land is not the scarce commodity it is in most of Europe, and although 80% of Americans live in urban areas, high-density housing is rare.

FACT

■ 89% of American households own a motor vehicle, while more than 99% have a refrigerator, 76% a clothes washer, and nearly 44% central air conditioning. More than 98% own a television, 34% a freezer, 28% an outdoor grill, and 12% a waterbed heater.

The vast majority of the population live in big city suburbs which spread for miles, with few limits on growth. Suburban living is encouraged by car ownership, and by the opening of out-of-town shopping complexes, which, in turn, cause city-centre businesses to close down. As shops and communities collapse in the inner cities, those who can afford to move out do so, leaving fewer and fewer reasons for anyone to remain there – except those who are trapped by poverty.

There are more than 50 metropolitan areas with populations in excess of three quarters of a million. Some of these are huge – in terms of area, rather than density of population. On the west coast, Los Angeles County is a vast urban sprawl stretching over 4,060 sq miles; and on the east coast there is a chain of large cities, from Boston to Washington, D.C.. A quintessentially American phenomenon is the Edge City. This is a suburb that has become a town, with shopping malls, cinemas, offices and streets of houses. It often has no name, and belongs to no particular place. There are more than 200 of these in the USA, commonly found near automobile routes.

A third of all Americans live within 20 miles (32km) of the old Route 1, the first federal highway, which starts on the Canadian border and runs all the way along the East Coast to the tip of the country at the Florida Keys. The majority of people who emigrate to the USA live on either the east or west coast: Florida is a favourite of retirees, both European and American.

With such a vast and diverse country, any generalisations are aure to be misleading. However, it is possible to make some observations about how

Hollywood, a district in Los Angeles that now personifies the American film industry

the average American family lives. Every country has its stereotypes, and Americans seem to be lampooned by Europeans with more than average frequency. Just as Americans are delighted when they meet someone who conforms to their picture of the stuffy, polite, tweed-suited, red-faced Englishman, many Europeans expect Americans to be as brash and loud as the popular conception has it.

In America, things often are on a larger scale than any European is used to. Even portions of food can seem immense. The average family lives in a bigger house and on a bigger plot of land. It is important to be aware of the great differences between states, as a family in Los Angeles will lead a very different life from one in New England. On much of the west coast, three time zones away from the east, life is as 'American', and sometimes as foreign, as it comes.

In Illinois, between Chicago and Springfield, there is a town called Normal. The population of Normal is around 50,500. It is not quite in the geographical centre of the USA, but in terms of history, racial mix, lifestyle, and attitudes it is probably as near to a 'normal' American town as you could find. It has a high school, a city hall, a police department headquarters, a flagstaff, a cinema and a shopping mall. It has average problems. The police are worried about the number of guns there are in the town and it has a minor drug problem. It also has a more serious problem with racism, possibly stemming from the fact that Illinois has one of the largest

FACT

■ In America, things often are on a larger scale than any European is used to. Even portions of food can seem immense. The average family lives in a bigger house and on a bigger plot of land.

Hispanic populations in America. To describe how an American family lives you could do worse than imagine the average family in the average town, and in Normal, Illinois, that is as near as you are going to get.

A middle-class family in Normal will live in a three-bedroom house on the outskirts of town. It may be a bungalow, and no more than 20 years old. It would not appear very sturdy to a European or Australasian, but the family may not expect to stay there forever. They certainly will not think that their children will remain in the same house when they are grown up, though there is probably an expectation that their children will at least remain in the same town. The house will have a garage and a garden. Everybody in the area will have one or two cars – public transport is highly unlikely to come near to the house, even if it exists in the town. There will be a well-cared-for front lawn, in accordance with neighbourhood agreements. The inside of the house will be clean and roomy, and all the furniture will look new. There will be few old-fashioned decorations or knick-knacks, unless the inhabitants are elderly, and there will be three landline telephones. The kitchen will be packed with electric gadgets, as will the rest of the house. In a power cut, the refrigerator, freezer, microwave, toaster, electric coffeepot, popcorn-popper, can opener, electric carving knife, television, cable box, DVD and DVR players, computer, stereo, alarm clock, answerphone, garage door opener, clothes washer, dishwasher, magi-mix, and electric toothbrush would all be rendered inoperable. Europeans travelling in the States 20 or 30 years ago were always amazed by the gadgets; the sheer variety of *things* that Americans had in their homes. This has changed now, and our jaws no longer drop at the electric boot-wipers and heated pet blankets, but what still probably has the capacity to astonish is the size of the refrigerator in an American home. It will invariably be of industrial size: at least six feet tall with doors which open like a wardrobe, and covered in magnets, photos and children's scribbles. This is to contain enough food for a family of four. The family shopping will be done once a fortnight, or once a week for 'soda' and fresh vegetables, and the fridge and freezer will be stocked full.

The high standard of living is reflected in more than the size of the refrigerator. The children will have bedrooms groaning with toys, all more expensive, more automated, and generally able to *do* more than other kids' toys from other places. A European or Australian 10-year-old visiting his American counterpart is usually delighted and envious at the magical kingdom in the bedroom.

With all this in mind, it does not need pointing out that millions of Americans live in vastly different circumstances. The cities hide families that sleep three to a bed, and do not have hot water, let alone electric toothbrushes. The USA has some of the worst inner-city poverty in the developed world. For every affluent household in Normal, Illinois, there is a family living in a trailer park in a jobless community in a former industrial

heartland, victims of recessions and the relentless closure of factories. Even parts of the same town can hide extreme poverty and neglect, or ghost towns – the presence of which are often unfairly blamed on cultural differences or immigration. Travelling by train will probably take you through burnt-out and decaying urban neighbourhoods which have been left behind after failing industries have closed down. America has more millionaires than any other country, but its cities and rural areas can be poverty-stricken and squalid. Neither the country's wealth nor its poverty represents a true picture: they are aspects, rather, of the same reality.

◼ REGIONAL GUIDE

Pacific Alaska region

Includes States: Hawaii, Alaska, Washington, Oregon and Idaho
Major Cities: Seattle, WA; Portland, OR; Honolulu, HI; Anchorage, AL
Average House Price: $256,000

Lifestyle: The Pacific Alaska Region encompasses three different climates, with Alaska experiencing three months of the year in complete darkness, Hawaii playing host to sun, sea and sand seekers all year round and Washington and Oregon having a not-dissimilar climate to the UK. It is

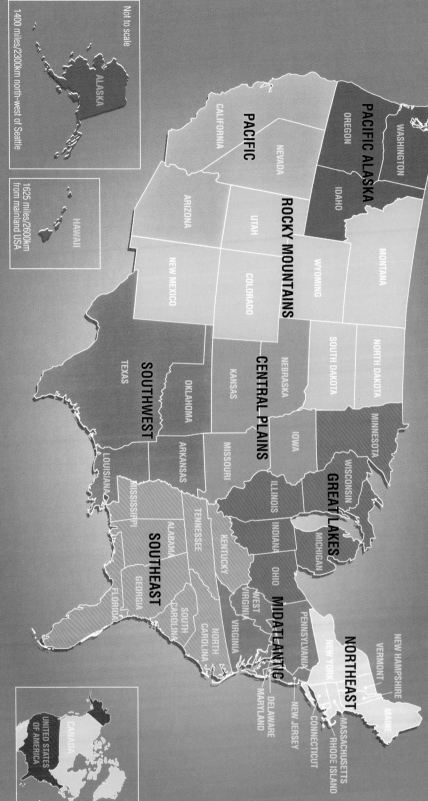

REGIONS **OF** THE **USA**

NORTH →

Not to scale

1400 miles/2300km north-west of Seattle

ALASKA

1625 miles/2600km from mainland USA

HAWAII

UNITED STATES OF AMERICA

CANADA

UNITED STATES OF AMERICA

PACIFIC

PACIFIC ALASKA

ROCKY MOUNTAINS

CENTRAL PLAINS

SOUTHWEST

GREAT LAKES

SOUTHEAST

MIDATLANTIC

NORTHEAST

WASHINGTON
OREGON
CALIFORNIA
NEVADA
IDAHO
MONTANA
ARIZONA
UTAH
WYOMING
NEW MEXICO
COLORADO
NORTH DAKOTA
SOUTH DAKOTA
NEBRASKA
KANSAS
TEXAS
OKLAHOMA
ARKANSAS
MISSOURI
IOWA
MINNESOTA
WISCONSIN
ILLINOIS
INDIANA
MICHIGAN
LOUISIANA
MISSISSIPPI
TENNESSEE
ALABAMA
KENTUCKY
OHIO
WEST VIRGINIA
GEORGIA
FLORIDA
SOUTH CAROLINA
NORTH CAROLINA
VIRGINIA
PENNSYLVANIA
NEW YORK
MARYLAND
DELAWARE
NEW JERSEY
CONNECTICUT
RHODE ISLAND
MASSACHUSETTS
NEW HAMPSHIRE
VERMONT
MAINE

A stretch of road in Santa Monica, California, along the beach

hard, therefore, to select one specific lifestyle which describes all its areas. Generally, the pace of life in this region is gentler and quieter than in the Pacific Region, houses cost less, incomes are lower and there is less tourism. Of all the states, the anomaly in this group is Alaska, whose sheer distance away from the mainland means imports are pricey and both the cost of living and, consequently, typical incomes, are among the highest in the country. The largest city in the group, Seattle (www.seattle.gov), has all the usual draws of a major town, such as the Seattle Space Needle tower, parks, zoos and fine dining, but also has the unusual benefit of reasonably-priced housing and a climate almost identical to the UK. One unusual fact about the Pacific Alaska region is that drivers are warned that there is a very real danger of hitting a moose while out on the highway.

Pacific region

Includes States: California, Nevada and Arizona
Major Cities: Tucson, AZ; Phoenix, AZ; San Francisco, CA; San Diego, CA; Sacramento, CA; Los Angeles, CA; Las Vegas, NV
Average House Price: $342,300

Lifestyle: California is one of the USA's wealthiest states, which isn't surprising when you consider the type of industry and tourism generated in the area. California, Nevada and Arizona are well known for their tourism:

The terrain of Montana, in the Rocky Mountains

deserts, gambling and the movies are as much a part of America as cattle ranches and fast food are. Living in the Pacific Region usually reflects this too, with house prices the most expensive in the country and industry booming. States in this region are famous for their cheese, wine and technology products, as well as high Native American populations on their many reserves. The area's migratory Hispanic population helps provide a seasonal workforce for agricultural areas of the region and while it is common to want to live in one of the large Californian cities (www.ca.gov), it's also very easy and comfortable to live in a rural district. A word of caution though: the wealthy parts of the Pacific Region are likely to stay wealthy while the poorer, more rural areas are likely to get poorer.

Rocky Mountain region

Includes States: Montana, North Dakota, South Dakota, Wyoming, Utah, Colorado, New Mexico
Major Cities: Albuquerque, NM; Denver, CO; Colorado Springs, CO; Sioux Falls, SD; Fargo, ND; Helena, MT, Cheyenne, WY
Average House Price: $158,300

Lifestyle: If you like to play winter sports, the Rocky Mountain region is the place to live. Its climate is extremely seasonal and changes from extreme heat and humidity in the summer to snow, ice and freezing temperatures in the winter. House prices are reasonable too as these huge states are sparsely populated and contain great swathes of untouched, unowned land. The beauty and size of the Rocky Mountains are a major tourist attraction for millions of visitors to the USA and owning a home close to them is a dream come true for many. In fact, one of the area's largest cities, Denver, can put part of its size and popularity down to the fact it's a convenient hop-off point for the ski resort to the wealthy, Aspen. It's a quiet, gentle pace of life in the Rocky Mountain region and the average person is likely to list their occupation as either farmer, rancher or service provider. Famous sites include the Black Hills in South Dakota and Mount Rushmore in North Dakota.

Enjoying the great outdoors, at Barton Springs, Austin Texas

Southwest region

Includes States: Oklahoma, Texas, Arkansas and Louisiana
Major Cities: Tulsa, OK; Oklahoma City, OK; New Orleans, LA; Austin, TX; Houston, TX; Dallas, TX; San Antonio, TX; Little Rock, AR
Average House Price: $178,900

Lifestyle: One of the largest regions on the list, the Southwest is known for its stereotypes. From the Texan cowboy to the Louisianan jazz musician, a large percentage of tourism in these states is as a direct response to the Southwest's Americana. These states are also known for their fierce beliefs, right-wing religions and extremes of weather, with tornadoes, thunderstorms and hurricanes a common sight in the Tornado Alley area. Amusingly, there are still many Texans who openly choose to fly the state flag instead of the Stars and Stripes, refusing to acknowledge Texas' admission to the Union. Nevertheless, Texas is one of the most popular destinations for expats and the entire Southwest region is booming with business development. The Southwest's location along the Gulf of Mexico means it draws a summer crowd and the entire area is famous for its 'Southern hospitality'.

Downtown St Louis, Missouri

Central plains region

Includes States: Nebraska, Kansas, Iowa and Missouri
Major Cities: Wichita, KA; St Louis, MO; Omaha, NA; Kansas City, MO; Des Moines, IA
Average House Price: $161,400

Lifestyle: The Great Plains region is known for its vast expanses of flat land and, thanks to irrigation, subsequent fields of crops. There are several thousand miles of land with fewer than six people per sq mile, a statistic backed up by the fact this part of America has actually seen a drop in its proportionate population since the 1920s. However, farming and ranching remain the main sources of employment and export for this region and despite the rural flight, gross state product continues to rise for each of its member states. It's not for nothing this region is known as 'the Breadbasket of America'. The route of the original trans-America railroad runs through the Great Plains region, and Nebraska hosts the headquarters of the Union Pacific Railroad company. In company with the Southwest and Great Lakes regions, the Central Plains states tend to experience extremes of weather: they're hot and humid in the summer, with colossal thunderstorms and tornadoes, but get buried under several feet of snow as soon as winter comes along.

Great Lakes region

Includes States: Minnesota, Wisconsin, Illinois, Indiana, Michigan and Ohio
Major Cities: Minneapolis, MN; Milwaukee, WI; Indianapolis, IN; Chicago, IL; Detroit, MI; Columbus, OH; Cleveland, OH
Average House Price: $181,700

Lifestyle: If for nothing else, the Great Lakes region is famous for the friendliness and generosity of its people. However, in addition to this, the Twin Cities in Minnesota boast one of the highest standards of living in the USA, and the influence of Chicago, Milwaukee and Detroit on the international music scene cannot be denied. Minneapolis is also one of the world's most popular international locations for corporate headquarters, a fact completely disproportionate to its size. Along with the Great Plains, the Great Lakes region is mainly agricultural, and it's entirely possible to drive for hours without seeing a single township or vehicle other than a tractor. Although a highly religious group of people, the population of this cluster of states doesn't tend to be as conservative or rigid as those in the South; rather they welcome newcomers to church functions as friends and are famous for their hospitality. The weather in the Great Lakes region is, along with the Great Plains, record-breaking. If you like your winters cold and your summers hot, The Great Lakes are a very good choice.

Southeast region

Includes States: Kentucky, Tennessee, North Carolina, South Carolina, Mississippi, Alabama, Georgia and Florida
Major Cities: Nashville-Davidson, TN; Louisville-Jefferson County, KY; Memphis, TN; Atlanta, GA; Jacksonville, FL; Miami, FL; Charlotte, NC; Charleston, SC
Average House Price: $168,900

Lifestyle: Perhaps one of the broadest groups of states in terms of culture, the Southeast region of the USA stretches up from Florida to almost the centre of the country in Tennessee. The Southeast is famous for its 'Deep South' cooking, angry heatwaves, and country and western music. It's also known for its cash-crop agriculture as the heat lends itself well to the production of tobacco, cotton and citrus fruits. The area boasts some of the nation's top tourist attractions: Walt Disney World in Florida and the music city of Nashville, Tennessee, to name but two. The Southeast is also home to a great deal of Civil War history, artefacts dating back to the slave trade, and battlegrounds which showcase frequent re-enactments with authentic uniforms and weapons. Interestingly, this region also hosts many of America's top college cheerleading teams, whose professional displays are always worth a watch for the sheer grace and athleticism of its competitors. Many Americans consider the Carolinas to have the nicest climate, biggest houses and most beautiful scenery, although prices are often higher there than in the rest of the region.

Mid-Atlantic region

Includes States: Pennsylvania, New Jersey, Delaware, Maryland, District of Colombia, West Virginia and Virginia
Major Cities: Washington, D.C.; Virginia Beach, VA; Philadelphia, PA; Baltimore, MD; Charleston, WV; Trenton, NJ
Average House Price: $276,400

Lifestyle: Many of the states in the Mid-Atlantic region were members of the original 13 states and colonies to make up the Union in 1776. There is therefore plenty of British and European influence to be found, ranging from place names and architecture to food and drink. Mammoth plantation-style houses line wide, tree-lined roads in the Virginias, bringing with them Civil War history and 'old money' sentiments. This region is also home to the Amish people, whose very existence harks back to a simpler, pre-Union time, with strict religious rules and their own language. The District of Columbia stands alone within this group of states as it is actually a city and district combined into one: Washington, D.C. because the Union didn't want one single state to lay claim to the nation's capital. The states

New York can be overwhelmingly busy, but it's one of the most popular places to move to

to the north in New England are famous for their colours as the season changes into autumn; tourists say the New England Fall colours are truly a sight to behold.

Northeast region

Includes States: Massachusetts, Maine, New Hampshire, Connecticut, Vermont, New York and Rhode Island
Major Cities: New York, NY; Boston, MA; Augusta, ME; Concord, NH; Montpelier, VT; Providence, RI
Average House Price: $287,700

Lifestyle: The Northeast region can lay claim to having much in common with the Mid-Atlantic region, as its member states were also some of the original 13 to make up the Union in 1776. There are, therefore, one again plenty of British and European influences and the same New England Fall colours every year. However, this region can boast the largest and most cosmopolitan city in the USA: New York. This alone makes it stand apart from the crowd as it's one of the biggest tourist attractions in the country and a business and shopping centre like no other. (For more information, see the 'City Neighbourhoods Guide', below). The Northeast is famous for its seafood, and Boston crab and Maine lobsters are considered

Boston town houses in the city centre

quite the delicacies here. Vermont is known for its snow and skiing, and Buffalo, in the state of New York, has one of the strangest and heaviest lake-effect snowfalls in the country. This region is also home to the smallest state in the USA: Rhode Island is only 1,545 sq miles (4,002 km) in area, smaller even than many of the nation's metropolitan areas.

◾ CITY NEIGHBOURHOODS GUIDE
New York, New York

New York is commonly considered to be one of America's cultural capitals and most important cities. Since its founding in 1625 by Dutch settlers it has grown to be not only the largest city in the state of New York, but also the largest in the USA, now housing over 10 million people. It has always been a popular destination for immigrants and much of its trade and industry has been built there as a result. In fact, the very idea of America being a 'melting pot' was born in New York City.

New York comprises five boroughs: The Bronx, Brooklyn, Manhattan, Queens and Staten Island – the most famous being Manhattan (see map opposite). Manhattan continues to be the epicentre of New York life, due in part to its plentiful shopping, museums, art galleries, restaurants, public transport and expensive housing. The rich and famous live a fabulous life there, tourists enjoy the sights and sounds, and beggars line the streets at night searching for scraps in dustbins. Like America as a whole, New York is melting pot of different nationalities, races and social statuses. It's also a tremendous amount of fun.

DISTRICTS**OF**NEW**YORK**CITY

NORTH ↑

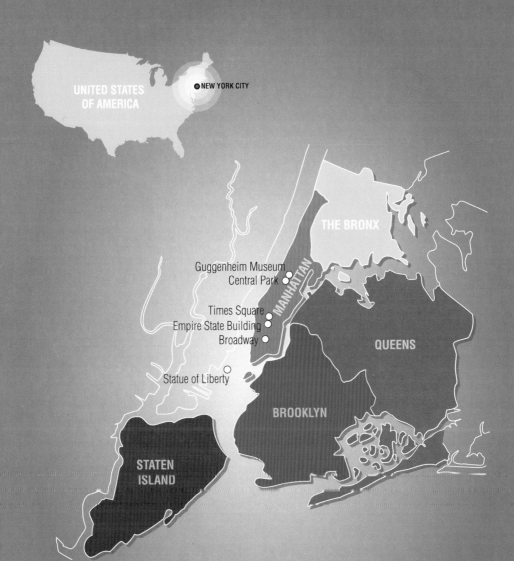

UNITED STATES
OF AMERICA

● NEW YORK CITY

THE BRONX

MANHATTAN

Guggenheim Museum
Central Park ○

Times Square ○
Empire State Building ○
Broadway ○

○
Statue of Liberty

QUEENS

BROOKLYN

STATEN
ISLAND

When choosing a location for your house or apartment in New York, consider carefully the differences between boroughs. Chances are you won't be a multi-millionaire and thus able to purchase a property on Park Avenue in Manhattan, so instead consider setting up home in either Brooklyn or Queens.

Brooklyn is located on the southern tip of Long Island and has become a popular place to call home for families, artists, or those simply seeking respite from the sky-high property prices of Manhattan. Before the early 1990s, Brooklyn was plagued by high crime rates and poor infrastructure, leaving land values low and property very cheap. When Mayor Rudy Giuliani came to office in 1994, however, he made cleaning up New York City a priority, and reversed the slow decline of Brooklyn into a ghetto. By the time Giuliani left office in 2001, Brooklyn and other New York suburbs were wealthier, safer and a viable alternative to Manhattan. Bohemian apartments and ex-factory spaces became a cheap, safe and fashionable alternative to living in the centre of the city, and improved public transport also assisted this process. Housing is now commonly a 'Brownstone' (a tall,

Trendy Brownstone town houses in Brooklyn

Winter in Central Park

slender house commonly built in terraced blocks using brown bricks) or a modern apartment block converted from old factories and warehouses. Schools are of a good to excellent standard, and independent shops nestle between the larger, faceless department stores and fast food restaurants. In short, it seems that if Manhattan is where the tourists go, Brooklyn is where the New Yorkers go.

Home to the world-famous Yankee Stadium, The Bronx borough of New York has seen several metamorphoses over its lifetime. Once a haven for bootleggers and drug dealers, the borough has undergone a transformation over the past 20 years to become a leading centre for rejuvenation and urban development. Between one fifth and one quarter of The Bronx is given over to parks and wildlife reserves, including Van Cortlandt Park and Pelham Bay Park (which also includes a large man-made beach). As with most New York districts, The Bronx can also boast a fairly substantial mass-transit system. Unfortunately The Bronx is one of the poorest areas in the USA although it does have an extremely diverse ethnic make-up. It's also the most popular destination for immigrant Ghanaians and other West Africans in the USA.

The New York borough of Queens has a population of about 2.2 million, a figure larger than most other US metropolitan areas and even some of the states. Known as a very Democratic borough, residents of Queens have not voted for a Republican en masse since 1972, a trend which seems set to continue for some time. It's also considered to be one of the more mature boroughs of New York, despite only having a median age of 35 at

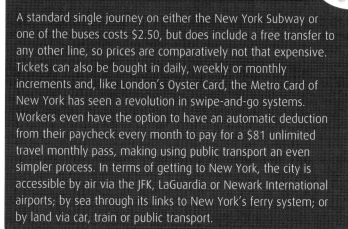

Getting around New York

A standard single journey on either the New York Subway or one of the buses costs $2.50, but does include a free transfer to any other line, so prices are comparatively not that expensive. Tickets can also be bought in daily, weekly or monthly increments and, like London's Oyster Card, the Metro Card of New York has seen a revolution in swipe-and-go systems. Workers even have the option to have an automatic deduction from their paycheck every month to pay for a $81 unlimited travel monthly pass, making using public transport an even simpler process. In terms of getting to New York, the city is accessible by air via the JFK, LaGuardia or Newark International airports; by sea through its links to New York's ferry system; or by land via car, train or public transport.

the last census, with just 12.7% of its population aged 65 or older. Queens is home to the John F Kennedy (JFK) International Airport, which is one of the busiest in the world, and the New York Mets baseball team.

Staten Island is the least populous of the New York boroughs. Reached mainly by ferry and bridge, Staten Island is literally that: an island. Statistically speaking, there are more Italian-Americans living in Staten Island by percentage than any other single county in the USA, a fact which is supported by the many Italian-themed restaurants and grocery stores in the area. The island also boasts the oldest school in the country, The Staten Island Academy, which remains an independent private grade school and a leader in a very strong educational borough. The economy of the borough is also strong, exceeding the average per capita income of both New York City and New York State.

Good for:	Less good for:
Young professionals	Less economically stable
Families	Elderly
Living	Working
Parks and activities	Businesses and socialising
Average rental property prices:	
One-bedroom apartment	$1,800 p/m
Three-bedroom house	$3,550 p/m

A view of Los Angeles, nicknamed the City of Angels

Los Angeles, California

Los Angeles, CA, was founded in 1781 and incorporated into the Union when California became a state in 1850. It has a warm sunny climate year round, but due to its location – nestled between two large hills – residents and tourists often complain about smog and pollution. With a population of around 3.8 million, LA is the second largest city in the USA, comprising 10 general districts: Downtown Los Angeles, San Fernando, Northeast, Eastside, Wilshire, South Los Angeles (South Central), Westside, Harbor Area, Hollywood and Crescenta.

Downtown Los Angeles is the city's epicentre, with its financial, historical, recreational and political centres all located here. Of the 10 districts, Downtown is the smallest, although it does manage to pack in Chinatown, Little Tokyo, Historic Core, Skid Row and even Toy District, to name but a few of its famous neighbourhoods. Not known for its fantastic living quarters, Downtown is LA's financial, cultural and entertainment district, rather than a place to bring up families. The majority of the city's public transportation is focused on Downtown.

The Northeast and Eastside districts are heavily populated by Latino communities, ranging from impoverished to affluent, and the area is surrounded by hills. Both the Northeast and Eastside boast a variety of neighbourhoods with titles to reflect this, such as the upscale Montecito Heights and University Hills, populated by young professionals. Lincoln Heights, another neighbourhood with uneven terrain, has poorer, working-class families, as does Boyle Heights, which is a traditional destination for LA newcomers.

South Los Angeles, still known to locals as South Central, is most remembered for its history of violent crime and urban decay. Certainly it remains an area popular with dangerous gangs and clashes between ethnic groups are common. It is frequently immortalised in rap music as a result of this. These days, parts of South Los Angeles, such as Watts, are still considered to be ghettos, but there are more prosperous districts developing too, such as West Adams and Baldwin Hills. Efforts to improve the situation in South Los Angeles have included A Place Called Home (APCH), which aims to guide the district's youth towards family values, trust and respect.

Harbor Area provides Los Angeles with a direct route to the Port of Los Angeles. Its main neighbourhood is San Pedro, a beach-based community with mainly working-class residents, and because of its ocean connections, much of the interest of Harbor Area is water-focused. It has a large Maritime Museum, several moored navy ships and the Cabrillo Marine Aquarium. It is also a popular location for film and television shoots and has clocked hundreds of scenes in various movies and serials.

Hollywood, perhaps the most famous district of Los Angeles, actually comprises an extremely affluent Hollywood Hills at its highest point, leading down to poorer neighbourhoods at its lowest. Known as the cultural centre of the movie-making industry, much of Hollywood is now occupied by props, effects and post-production companies, as many sound stages, movie lots and television studios have moved into surrounding neighbourhoods instead. The average household income

San Fernando Valley, part of the city of Los Angeles, with the Santa Monica Mountains in the distance

in Hollywood is around $33,500, which stands in stark contrast to the legendary paychecks of the hill-dwelling celebrities, and there is much in the way of redevelopment and rejuvenation in the area to help it keep up with its reputation.

Famous landmarks in Los Angeles include the Walt Disney Concert Hall, the Getty Center, Grauman's Chinese Theatre, the Hollywood Bowl, the Kodak Theatre and Capitol Records. Los Angeles is very much a tourist town, if only to gawp at minor celebrities and 'beautiful people', but as its population of 3.8 million Angelenos can testify, it's also a beautiful, sunny place to live with very good schools, fantastic places to eat and shopping and business centres galore. The official website of Los Angeles city can be found at www.lacity.org.

Good for:	Less good for:
Car-owners	Users of public transport
Big businesses	Small businesses
Young professionals	Retired people; families
Sunshine	Pollution control
Average rental property pices:	
One-bedroom apartment	$735 p/m
Three-bedroom house	$2,100 p/m

Miami, Florida

Miami has a reputation for being both a place for quiet retirement and for loud partying. It's this dichotomy which manages to ensure Miami is never far from the news. A centre for drug-dealers and violent crime, Miami also plays host to millions of families and holiday-makers every year from both the USA and abroad, all coming to soak up the sun, sunbathe on the endless golden beaches and watch the beautiful people pass by. Miami has some fairly unique wildlife, beautiful year-round weather and a variety of both expensive and reasonably-priced homes, making it a favourite destination for foreign expats and American snowbirds (a term for travellers who live in warm weather states for the winter and cooler, northern states for the summer). Miami is broken up into a fairly substantial central city with a number of suburbs surrounding it, although its boroughs aren't as distinct as some other American cities as it lies on the coast. In fact, it has the smallest land area of any major US city and a metro area of only 2.5million people.

Miami's climate is wet and warm, with tropical storms a frequent occurrence. Many homeowners take out flood and hurricane insurance to protect their properties from the damage such severe weather can do. Houses and apartments really vary here, with cool, Mexican-style

Spacious bungalows are popular purchases in Florida. Most come with a good sized garden, and many with pools

whitewashed bungalows and tall, luxury condo buildings. Nearly all of them have parking availability, as Miami, like Los Angeles, doesn't have a particularly impressive public transport system. Unlike many other cities, however, a lot of people walk to where they need to go in Miami – the weather and casual pace of life doesn't make it seem such a chore! Miami also boasts several colleges and universities, including the University of Miami. The public school system usually emerges with average scores academically, but students and parents often rate it much more highly.

Landmarks of Miami include the Miami Freedom Tower, the Merrick House and Gardens, a Spanish monastery and the Port of Miami. As a major tourist destination, it is also home to hundreds of hotels and places to stay, and many tourist attractions. This has led to a booming service industry in the city, which continues to thrive despite recent cutbacks on flights in and out of Miami due to increases in fuel costs. Shopping is excellent in the city, with a number of good-quality boutiques and fashion-forward stores, and you can also find a fantastic array of Mexican and Cuban food stores to browse through on any street corner.

Good for:	Less good for:
Holiday homes	Permanent homes
Extroverts	Introverts
Small businesses	Large business
Wildlife	Urban development
Average rental property prices:	
One-bedroom apartment	$1,100 p/m
Three-bedroom house	$2,100 p/m

Chicago, Illinois

Chicago is possibly the most famous city in the USA outside of New York. The background for hundreds of movies and television dramas (including *Blues Brothers, Batman: The Dark Knight* and the medical series *ER*), Chicago is also one of the birthplaces of jazz and deep-pan pizza. It is frequently referred to as a Midwestern town that just happens to be

big, so friendly and welcoming is its atmosphere. Chicago is divided into four main districts: Downtown (and the Loop), North Side, South Side and West Side. The east side of the city is actually the shore of Lake Michigan.

Originally founded in 1683 by a Catholic priest, Chicago is now a bustling centre of finance and business, and is one of the hub cities of the Midwest. The Chicago O'Hare International Airport is amongst the busiest in the country for internal flights, aided by its location as a stopping point in the middle of the country. The smaller Midway International Airport also follows close behind. Chicago boasts an impressive amount of culture and entertainment opportunities, with groups such as the *Blue Man Group* establishing permanent bases there. Most of the activities take place Downtown, where the old cable-car system known as the Loop (now an elevated train track) provides a convenient circuit around many of Chicago's commercial, industrial and business ventures. There are ample shopping and restaurants in the middle of the city and along the Magnificent Mile, and there are even opportunities to fish for your own dinner on the shores of Lake Michigan, although it's not highly recommended in the middle of a highway.

Dusk looking out at Lake Michigan, Illinois

Chicago's public school district is fairly impressive, but it's the higher education facilities that get people excited: the University of Chicago is a world leader in many fields, including sociology and economics, and enrolment is highly competitive. Housing is also competitive, particularly on the North Side, where the most densely populated areas of Chicago lie. The South Side tends to be more spread out, with larger houses for single families and space for greenery and garages. It is the largest and most sought-after district. The West Side is less affluent, with social and economic problems and high rates of poverty, although Chicago is generally a fairly comfortable place to live for most of its inhabitants.

As with all Midwestern cities, Chicago suffers from extremes of temperatures. Record snowfall over the 2007–2008 winter pushed its resources to the limits, and the city ran out of salt for its snowplows and gritters more than once. Seasonal change into a hot summer then left many of the roads in and around Chicago broken up and full of potholes, which led to an increase in vehicle collisions. For a city born and bred in hard, seasonal weather, it seems Chicago still hasn't worked out to cope with its weather system.

Good for:	Less good for:
Families	Young people
Mass-transit users	Car owners
Employment	Self-employment
Travel within the USA	Travel abroad
Average rental property prices:	
One-bedroom apartment	$900 p/m
Three-bedroom house	$1,500 p/m

RENTING PROPERTY

Most apartments in the USA are rented unfurnished, although a refrigerator, oven and dishwasher are normally included. Post-war apartment blocks in cities like New York and San Francisco have public basements which have laundry rooms with coin-operated washing and drying machines – an in-house launderette, in short. The more modern and luxurious apartment blocks will have a swimming pool, gym and sauna. Rented furnished accommodation will have all mod cons, including air conditioning (in the older buildings the units will be window mounted) and central heating. The cheapest apartments go by a variety of euphemistic names: bachelor apartments, studios, or efficiency apartments. These will be very small with just a bedroom, bathroom, and a curtained-off cooking area.

Useful rental terms	
Apartment:	flat
Dormitory:	student hall of residence, often with single or two-person rooms
Duplex:	apartment on two floors (sometimes called a split-level)
Half-bath:	room with toilet and sink but no bath
Walk-up:	studio or flat in a block without a lift
Cold-water apartment:	flat without hot water (relatively rare except in the oldest buildings)
Efficiency, bachelor:	bedsit or studio flat
First floor:	ground floor (therefore the second floor is the same as the British first floor, and so on)
Roomer:	lodger
Roommate:	flatmate
Rooming house:	a house in which rooms are let
Closet:	wardrobe or cupboard
Flatware:	cutlery
Washer:	washing machine (clothes)

How to find a rental property

Local newspapers and magazines have 'Apartments for Rent' sections, and free monthly rental guides are published in most areas. These are available from chambers of commerce (see *Regional Guide* for addresses), and can also be picked up from visitor centres, supermarkets, and street racks. Most of the larger real estate agents have rental sections, and major apartment blocks and condominiums have their own rental offices. Other places to look are noticeboards in colleges, company offices, shopping malls, supermarkets, and visitor centres. One of the most fruitful sources of information will of course be friends and colleagues, and websites such as www.craigslist.org.

Tenancy agreements

Renting an apartment requires all the usual documentation and guarantees of income, such as a passport, driving licence, social security number (SSN) and three recent paystubs. Consult the *Moving to the USA* section for a brief how-to guide to obtaining these documents if you do not yet have them. You will have to complete an application form (most states have standard lease forms, available from real estate offices and stationers) and usually not only agree to, but actually pay for, a background check using your SSN. Agents will not be happy finding you an apartment that is going to take up more than 25%-30% of your monthly income. The

TIP

■ Beware of referral services and 'apartment finders', who will try to charge a commission, or demand a deposit in advance for a variety of services such as property listings, viewing fees and so on. This is illegal: you should pay nothing except to either an established real estate agent, or the owner of the property.

application form will include references from your employer or business, your bank, and credit and personal references. If you have recently moved to the USA and your credit rating is still low, you may be able to pay several months up front as collateral instead. Similarly, if do not yet have a job, you may have to pay more up front to start a lease agreement. If you are living with an American resident or US Citizen, you could use just their name on the lease at first, and have yours added once you have secured a job and have a stronger credit rating. Each landlord will have a different practice, so it may be wise to check their regulations before you pick an apartment.

If you pay a deposit it should be put into an escrow account. Tenants in the USA do not have the same sort of security that they do in the UK and much of Europe. The law is generally weighted in the landlord's favour, so it is essential to read everything carefully before signing. Look out for leases with automatic renewal clauses, which will penalise you if you do not inform the landlord that you are leaving before the first term expires and the second term automatically begins. Landlords are able to evict tenants with just one written notice and force tenants to pay for normal wear and tear, so be sure to read and re-read a contract before you sign it. It is advisable to take out renters' insurance if you have any qualms about your contract as you can be insured against damage to your property which was not caused by you, such as fires in adjoining apartments, which otherwise the landlord may force you to pay for.

FACT

It is fairly uncommon for landlords and banks to look at overseas credit histories, so you may need to pay a little more initially and wait for your American credit score to get raised.

> The website www.rentlaw.com has details of rental laws pertaining to each state, should you have any concerns.

Rental periods, lease regulations, amounts of deposit, and agency (brokerage) fees vary from state to state. In Florida, two months' rent in advance is the normal rate while in Illinois, standard leases contain a transfer clause: one month's notice and a fee of $50–$100 is required to break the lease. Leases are normally for one year, with an option to renew. In some states rental periods are seasonal: most leases in towns or cities with universities, for example, expire in May or September, so it is extremely difficult to rent at any other time of year.

Some states have 'rental control' schemes, based on the Consumer Price Index, which keep rent increases within a certain limit. The idea behind this is to keep a regular supply of affordable housing in the market and ensure a balance of population demographics is maintained. In Los Angeles, for example, most rented accommodation is covered by the scheme which guarantees that every 12 months rental increases of not more than 8% and not less than 3% will be allowed. This is put into effect as soon as an apartment is occupied; when it is vacated, the landlord can increase the rent as he likes. Contact local chambers of commerce or real estate agents for details of schemes.

Rental costs

Like tenancy agreements, once again these vary enormously from state to state and city to city. New York City is possibly the most expensive city in the USA to live in. Rents per month can range from $850 for a studio in The Bronx to $24,000 for a three-bedroom apartment with a doorman in the Upper East Side of Manhattan. Other areas of the country will be much cheaper. Los Angeles, a city of comparable size, offers much better value. A studio, for example, will cost approximately $925 per month while you can rent a three-bedroom house for $4,000 and a four-bedroom for $6,000. Elsewhere, a two-bedroom apartment in Houston will, on average, cost $1,300 a month while the same apartment would cost $1,650 in Boston, $2,200 in Atlanta and Washington, and $3,000 in Miami. As any estate agent will tell you, the three most important rules of property pricing are location, location, location.

In blocks of apartments there may well be a doorman who guards access to the building and provides general security. They may also provide other services, such as taking delivery of the mail, letting in repairmen, and keeping an eye on the apartment while you're away. Doorman guarded buildings are more expensive to occupy but they provide an added sense of safety in urban areas. There may well also be a building 'super' who maintains the upkeep of the building. Remember that these building employees may expect generous tips, usually around the end of the year in the Christmas season. It's not unusual for tenants to give tips ranging from $50 to more than $200 in either cash or gift vouchers for the help and service they receive during the entire year.

TIP

■ Finding rented housing in some cities can be as difficult as in Europe simply because demand is high. Properties go quickly and prices can be steep. Often you'll be asked to put down one month's rent as deposit and one month's rent in advance.

 Tipping etiquette is often something foreigners find confusing or uncomfortable in the USA, so for a simple guide to seasonal and everyday tipping, try www.tipguide.org.

Relocating agencies can advise on average prices within an area or you could contact a real estate agency directly. Students attending universities and colleges should approach the student advisor or housing office for assistance in finding rented accommodation.

Useful contacts

The World of Florida: 01432 845645; homes@worldofflorida.co.uk; www.worldofflorida.co.uk. Specialists in villas to rent and buy in Florida.
Property Abroad: 0845 2000 467; sales@property-abroad.com; www.property-abroad.com
Rightmove: 01908 308 500; talk-to-us@rightmove.co.uk; www.rightmove.co.uk.

◼ BUYING A HOME

Buying a home can be a stressful experience at the best of times, but if you have never bought property abroad before and don't know where to start it can make the experience even more daunting and stressful. The following guide sets out key regulations in the US property market, as well as some useful tips and websites to use when considering the purchase of a new home in America.

Purchasing and conveyancing procedures

Useful terms

Amortize: To make regular payments covering both the principal balance and the interest and thereby to write off the cost of the asset over time.

Binder: Written document binding both parties to sign a sales contract. Sometimes supported by a small deposit ($100–$1,000) known as 'earnest money' or 'good faith' deposit.

Certificate of Title, or Title Insurance Document: A document, signed by a title examiner, stating that a seller has an insurable title to the property.

Closing: Completing the deal.

Comparable Market Analysis (CMA): A survey of comparable houses either on the market or recently sold.

Earnest money: In some states this is referred to as a binder (see above). It can also be the deposit paid on signing of the contract.

Escrow: A fund or account that is held by a third party (often a bank, or a closing agent) until all conditions of the contract are met.

Lien: A security claim, usually against a debt. If a property has a lien on it, the holder of the lien has a legal claim on the property until the debt is discharged.

Title search: A detailed examination of the document history of a property.

Finding a property

The American system of property purchase is efficient and well organised. Most qualified real estate agents are members of Multiple Listing Services (www.mls.com), which allow them access to local and nationwide databases of all the properties for sale. This means that you do not necessarily have to contact an agent in the particular area in which you intend to buy: a member agent in New York will be able to key in your criteria and produce a list of properties in California, for example.

The internet, with its capacity to cross-reference and link to literally millions of pages of information, is the ideal vehicle for seeing what sort of property is around. You'll still want the services of an estate agent, but you could do worse than browse a few sites to see what is available,

perhaps starting with www.realtor.com. The US Home Exchange (www.ushx.com) is also a free listings site with thousands of houses listed state by state. The sites listed in the 'Mortgages on the web' section below have links to real estate services.

Auctions are also a popular means of purchasing property in the USA. At an auction you'll receive the particulars and conditions of sale outlining the property and the terms of the auction. Once you've made the highest bid and it is accepted then you are legally obliged to buy the property. Usually, 10% of the purchase price must be paid as a deposit one to three months after signing the agreement. The US Treasury runs regular auctions in conjunction with the IRS for seized assets such as houses and cars, and listings can be found at www.ustreas.gov/auctions. The best preparation for an auction is to organise your finances in advance with approval to bid up to a pre-arranged amount.

> **Philip Jones found accommodation difficult to find:**
>
> New York real estate is impossible. Like London it is prohibitively expensive and hard to find. We were fortunate enough to buy an apartment in TriBeCa, a region near to the financial district, eight years ago. Property has gone up substantially in price since and we certainly would be unable to buy it now! We were very lucky.

Estate agents

Real estate agents act both as agents and as lawyers in property transactions. In order to become a member of the National Association of Realtors (NAR), or be licensed by their state regulator, they are required to take examinations in estate law, finance, surveying and other subjects. After a certain amount of time spent practising, and further exams, they can then qualify as a broker. There will usually be two realtors in any transaction, although the commission is charged only to the seller.

Estate agents do not normally have street premises with photographs of properties for sale in the window, although they will provide detailed reports with photographs for properties you express interest in. Look in the *Yellow Pages* at www.yellow.com (under Residential Real Estate Agents), contact the relevant state Chamber of Commerce (see the *Employment* chapter for contact details), or get in touch with the National Association of Realtors(www.realtor.org). for the address of the Real Estate Commission local to you These are set up by the state government and can also be found through the state Justice Department. The Sunday newspapers are also fruitful sources of advertisements for agents, mortgage brokers and private sellers and buyers.

Dealing with estate agents

When dealing with estate agents the usual rules of caution apply. Remember that they are usually acting for the seller, not for you, and the bigger the sale price, the bigger their commission. Some agencies will advertise themselves as operating under 'buyer's brokerage' or 'buyer's agency' principles, which means that they are supposed to act solely in the buyer's interests. It is strongly recommended to buy any property through a qualified broker in order to be sure that they are fully conversant with the market and the regulations. This is doubly important if you are new to the country and are unsure of the mechanics of house buying.

When looking at a property it is perfectly acceptable to go over it thoroughly, particularly as it is extremely uncommon for the homeowner to be present while you are looking around. Turn on all the taps (faucets) to check the water pressure, check under the sink for drips, run the garbage disposal, the dishwasher, the Jacuzzi, and any of the other electrical gadgets that may be part of the sale. Ask the seller for copies of the latest water bills and check with the water company that usage for that size of house is normal. You can also ask for gas and electricity bills so that you can get an idea of how much it costs to maintain the house. A full structural inspection by a qualified house inspector will usually be a condition of the mortgage and an appraisal (valuation) may also be necessary – you are entitled to a copy of this.

If you aren't disturbed by the thought of benefiting from another's misfortune, it is possible to pick up foreclosed homes (repossessions) from the US Department of Housing and Urban Development. These houses are often in very poor condition, but they are extremely cheap, only a small deposit is required, and the HUD will often take on the closing costs as well. In the USA's current economic climate this is becoming an increasingly popular method of buying a home. More information, including contact details for the HUD, is given below.

Condominiums and cooperatives

An alternative to a detached house or an apartment is a condo or a co-op. Condominiums are effectively apartment blocks (or sometimes housing estates) that are owned and run by a management company. Units can be bought directly, with the company that owns the building sharing a

TIP

In the UK, one starting point is to visit a trade fair dedicated to buying property or one dedicated to emigration. At the annual Homebuyers Show at the ExCel Centre in London (www.homebuyer. co.uk) you can find estate agencies and services specialising in American property.

FACT

The National Association of Realtors and state authorities guarantee the credentials of their members. The term 'realtor' is actually patented by the NAR, and anybody calling themselves a realtor must be a member and abide by a strict code of ethics.

common interest with you in the grounds and facilities. You are in charge of what happens inside the unit, while the owner is responsible for the communal fabric of the building and the grounds.

Cooperative apartments don't belong directly to the buyer; you buy shares in a corporation that owns the entire building. While you are still responsible for the inside of your unit, a residents' committee, or management company, deals with the day-to-day running of the common areas.

Purchases are normally financed by a conventional mortgage (although buying shares in a co-op tends to be more complicated). There are also monthly payments, called maintenance fees, association fees or homeowners' dues, which pay for the operating costs of the building.

It is important to look at the structural state of the building and grounds. If the paintwork looks tired and the common areas are a mess, you should leave the property well alone. Contracts normally specify a percentage that unit owners have to pay for major structural repairs, so you could be faced with a $50,000 bill for curing the building of dry rot.

It is equally important to check the state of the management company and the owner. This should be part of the estate agent's job: he will need to supply you with information about the cash reserves of the company, its operating budget and its legal status. If it is inefficient, or simply crooked, it will hopefully come to light.

You could also go to an owners' or shareholders' meeting, which will give you an idea of the way the operation is run. Get hold of a copy of the condo or co-op rules from the building's Board of Directors to make sure that there are no exclusion clauses that don't allow you to keep pets or throw parties.

Professional assistance

Buying a house in your own country can be a stressful experience, but the traumas are magnified when buying abroad. Although American property law is based on English common law, with emphasis on proof of title, a contract, and a closing (what in the UK is called 'completion'), customs and practices are very different. It is absolutely essential to get the advice of a lawyer before signing anything at all. Contracts are exchanged much earlier in the deal than in Europe, and you might find yourself signed into something that you cannot back out of. If you are being pushed into something and you are afraid that you might lose the house of your dreams, put in a clause saying that the contract is subject to approval by your lawyer.

If you are intending to buy an American property from the UK it will be difficult to handle the legal aspect with a British-based legal practice as there are so few solicitors working in the US property market. However, if you do need help contact the Law Society of England and Wales (020 7242

1222; info.services@lawsociety.org.uk; www.lawsociety.org.uk). It is best to hire a relocation agency to find an American property attorney or find one yourself by contacting the American Bar Association (1 800 285 2221; www.abanet.org) for a referral.

Title insurance is an area that can be confusing. The title of a house ('title deeds' in the UK and Australasia) shows that it belongs to the person or people it is supposed to belong to. Title insurance does not guarantee the title, but it compensates the holder if the title is found to be defective. With this insurance Americans sometimes decide that they do not need a lawyer to do a search on the property. However, it does not insure such things as right of way, use conditions or zoning restrictions. In other words, you are covered if your house is found to belong to someone other than the person you have bought it from, but not if you discover that it cannot be used for business purposes as you thought, or if it has a right of way going through the back yard.

The mortgage lender will carry out a physical inspection of the property to confirm that it is safe to lend on. You should also get an inspection done yourself. Be careful of asking friends or relatives to do it, however expert they are: it is difficult, or impossible, to sue them if they fail to notice a major fault that might have stopped you from buying the house. Advice on inspections and inspectors can be had from the National Association of Home Inspectors (contact details below) who are a non-profit organisation comparable to British surveyors. Alternatively, contact the appraisal section of the NAR.

In many real-estate transactions a third party, called an escrow firm or title company, will conduct the closing (completion) of the contract. It will hold the down payment, oversee all the paperwork and distribute the money when all the terms of the contract have been met.

If you are buying US property from the UK it's best to use an agency that is a member of the *Federation of Overseas Property Developers, Agents, and Consultants (FOPDAC)*, now commonly known as part of the *National Association of Estate Agents* (01926 417 790; info@naea.co.uk;www.naea.co.uk). They are a trade association which regulates the overseas property market. FOPDAC can provide a list of accredited agencies and can also supply fact sheets on buying or selling property abroad. Most British agents working in the US tend to specialise in Florida because the state is the largest market for expats. For property purchases in other states it might be best to contact a relocation agency or a property company in the US directly.

Running costs

Remember that in addition to mortgage costs and taxes, any financial calculation needs to include annual running costs. Taxation is, as one can imagine, a complicated subject, and rates can vary from state to state and county to county. Websites such as www.taxnetusa.com can provide some

TIP
■ US lawyers charge anything between $100 and $500 per hour. You are likely to pay around $1,500–$2,000 for contract checking, looking at the abstract (the title deeds) and coordinating the closing. Administrative expenses will be added on as extras to the basic legal fee.

TIP
■ A full house inspection will start at $200– $300 and rise according to the extent of the inspection and size of the property.

TIP

■ Management costs for a home might be $150 per month and utilities such as water, electricity and gas may cost $200 each per month. On top of these you might want to pay someone to clean the house and maintain a pool and a garden, particularly in warmer states.

assistance. If you're thinking of buying a property it's best to conduct some research about your preferred location first. Property taxes in Florida, for example, cost about 1% of the value of the property and are re-evaluated every three years.

A home in Florida costing $175,000 to purchase may well cost $1,700 per month in expenses, which includes mortgage payments, taxes and maintenance costs. This is a substantial figure, but to be expected. It only begins to look steep if the house functions as a second, holiday home. If this is the case, however, it is likely you will offset costs by renting the house out while you are occupying your primary residence.

As a rough idea, someone who owns a house in Florida that is valued at $175,000, of which 20% ($34,948) was paid as a deposit, would have a monthly mortgage payment of around $750. Therefore, if they rented out the home for nine months (40 weeks) of the year and had the tenant pay all running costs for a total payment of $1,700 a month, they would make an annual profit for those nine months of $2,250.

Useful mortgage terms

Adjustable Rate Mortgage (ARM): variable rate mortgage

Annual Percentage Rate (APR): the finance rate on a loan

Assumption of mortgage: means that the buyer assumes responsibility for an existing mortgage note held by the seller. Subject to approval by the lender

Balloon payment: large accelerated payments due at the end, or during the life, of some loans

Caps: national limits on interest rates within an ARM

Federal National Mortgage Association (FNMA, Fannie Mae): private corporation created by Congress that buys mortgage notes from local lenders. It can also set guidelines used by lenders to assess borrowers

Origination fee: application fees for processing a mortgage

PITI principal, interest, tax, and insurance: the basis of monthly mortgage repayments

RESPA statement: the Real Estate Settlement Procedures Act (RESPA) sets out a good faith statement which gives a breakdown of closing costs

Mortgages overview

American lenders will demand an astonishing amount of information before they will consider lending to you. As well as the standard information – such as current and previous names, addresses, education and social security numbers – you will be required to supply at least three years of pay slips, rental cheques, tax returns, credit reports, credit card accounts and any liabilities. Interestingly, they like to see evidence of small sums of money owed, and are suspicious of a regularly-cleared credit account, which may indicate you're not to be trusted with long-term credit.

Mortgage lenders come in many forms, but the most commonly used is a bank. The first and most important step you should take is to approach the bank where you would like to take out a mortgage and, if you haven't already done so, open a checking or savings account with them. This process will begin a relationship with the bank; a crucial step in acquiring a decently rated loan from them. Once you have an account with them, ask to speak to their loan officer and discuss with them the qualifications you would need to meet in order to obtain a mortgage.

Once a bank has agreed to finance a loan for you, they will provide you with a pre-approval for a fixed sum. This figure will give you a good idea of how expensive a house you can afford on your current salary and economic situation, helping you when you visit a real estate agent. After you have chosen the house you wish to purchase, and agreed on a price with both the seller and the real estate agent, you can take the final figure back to the bank and begin the mortgage purchasing process.

With the current housing market in the USA, house prices are falling and a low rate on a mortgage loan is becoming more common. A borrower with a large down payment (5% or over) will therefore be able to command a much better interest rate than in previous years, particularly if they have high-earning power as well. Walking into a bank or lending institution with 5% savings in cash sets you apart from the majority of American borrowers in the current climate, so if you don't yet have any savings it may be time to start.

Local lenders (banks and other financial institutions) will take on loans from brokers and real estate agents, tie around 100 together, and sell them onto large loan institutions, like the Federal National Mortgage Association, Countrywide or Northwest Mortgage. This buying and selling of unhealthy or unsupported loans contributed dramatically in 2008 to the failure and subsequent bail-out of the Fannie Mae and Freddie Mac institutions.

The company *Conti Financial Services* (01273 772811; enquiries@ mortgageoverseas.com; www.mortgageoverseas.com) can offer specialist advice on obtaining a mortgage in 45 countries, including the USA.

Mortgages on the web

Until recently, the prospect of getting a mortgage online was too daunting for most people to contemplate. Issues such as security were uppermost in borrowers' minds, and the amount of variables involved – such as matching the best type of loan to the borrower – seemed to need human input. But computers are the ideal tool for matching infinite numbers of variables. There are now web-based search engines built specifically for mortgage packages from companies such as Microsoft, Intuit, E-Loan, Amex, Finance Tree and the intriguingly-named HomeShark, all of which allow you to compare and contrast current loan rates, and also give a complete picture of loan costs and terms, and information on how mortgages will affect individual borrowers. Some packages will ask how long you intend to stay in your

TIP

■ Some American financial advisors recommend that to build up your credit over a long period of time you should open several credit cards and use them regularly, paying off the balance each month. Keep them open even if you don't use them, as their sheer existence will improve your credit score.

FACT

■ Most American banks and mortgage brokers operate on a 5-15-80 system, where 5% of a purchase price is needed as a down payment, 15% can be obtained through a bridging loan and 80% forms a 30-year mortgage loan. Prior to the sub-prime housing crisis, the system was more like 20-80, but a recent slump in the housing market has forced banks and lenders to find ways of encouraging people to buy again – hence the 15% bridging loan.

TIP

■ Walking into a bank or lending institution with 5% savings in cash sets you apart from the majority of American borrowers in the current climate.

home and will guide you to a shorter or longer-term mortgage accordingly. It is also possible to purchase CD packages for your home computer which calculate mortgage rates based on certain variables. California-based E-Loan has a facility called E-Track which tracks the progress of your loan and posts regular updates on your application. Be warned however, that it is easy to set up online mortgage websites without proper regulation, so don't hand over any money unless you've done plenty of research on the company and you're certain it's not a scam.

 One of the most useful government sites for property matters is the US Department of Housing and Urban Development's (HUD), found at www. hud.gov. It offers straightforward and easily accessible information.

The US Department of Housing and Urban Development (HUD) is a federal agency responsible for national policy and programmes that address America's housing needs. Its website has information on all aspects of home buying, from finding an agent to arranging a mortgage. The National Association of Realtors (estate agents) also runs a helpful site at www.realtor.com, which acts as a central reference source for finding information about realtors, properties for sale and moving services. It also offers advice on finance and insurance.

Online borrowing has a long way to go before the majority of borrowers are getting their mortgages straight off the screen – the reams of paperwork still make a human facilitator essential – but some of these sites are worth a look, if only to give yourself an idea of what to expect from a visit to the mortgage-lender.

Many of the websites listed below offer enormous quantities of relevant information ranging from the latest borrowing rates to special tools which help you calculate the costs of buying a property:

www.bankrate.com: a comprehensive site for financial reference, giving current mortgage rates and banking products.

www.realtor.com: the official site of American realtors (estate agents), it includes advice on financing and moving services.

www.eloan.com: a site providing well set-out information on all aspects of borrowing.

www.homeshark.com: provides information for buyers, sellers and renters. Another excellent site for the financially uninitiated.

www.quickenloans.com: a comprehensive site offering information on home loans, refinancing and financial services.

www.mortgages-expo.com: details financing options.

Types of mortgage

The recent sub-prime mortgage crisis in the USA has led the Federal Reserve to drop interest rates to encourage borrowing, allowing banks to set fairly low rates for their own mortgages. For all of 2007, 30-year fixed-rate mortgages stood at around 6.34%, but the housing freefall forced a drop to just 5.92% in 2008. Mortgage rates are predicted to fall further if the housing market doesn't begin recovery by 2009.

The US mortgage system is essentially similar to that in other countries such as the UK, but there are differences in procedure that need to be noted. The Federal National Mortgage Association (sometimes referred to as. 'Fannie Mae') is a privately-owned corporation set up by Congress that is responsible for mortgage guidelines used by the majority of lenders. Details can be found at wwwfanniemae.com.

The main types of mortgage are:

Fixed rate: the most popular type of mortgage, usually carried over 30 years.

Adjustable Rate Mortgage (ARM): similar to a variable rate mortgage. Initial payments can be 2%–3% lower than the current rate, although rates can 'balloon' with changes in the interest rate. ARMs take account of national interest rates, and repayment is controlled by a cap on the mortgage. Lifetime Caps set the limits over the lifetime of the mortgage, Annual Caps regulate your interest rate over the year, and Payment Caps allow for one adjustment a year.

Convertible mortgage: can be converted from a fixed to an adjusted rate at certain times during the course of the loan. There is also the option to spread payments over 40 years or increase individual payment amounts to pay off the loan earlier.

Graduated payment mortgage: this has a low initial rate that increases over a period of time. The lender assumes that the borrower's income will increase in order to be able to service the higher rates and is often an option for those who would not normally qualify for a fixed-rate mortgage.

Two-step loans: fixed or adjustable rate mortgages with a built-in rate increase after five or seven years. Initial rates are usually low, but in the latter stages of the mortgage you will pay more than the going rate.

Fifteen-year mortgage: must be paid off within 15 years.

Registration and mortgage costs

Some states require documentary stamps on mortgage and transfer deeds, although often at a low rate. In Florida, for instance, if you are buying a property you will be charged 35 cents per $100 of mortgage amount. If you are selling a property, you are obliged to pay 70 cents per $100 of the full selling price. In states where you are required to record title documents there will be further charges for this. Some states also levy 'intangible taxes' on the loan amount ($2 per $1,000 of loan in Florida). And other states impose various transfer taxes and other duties. New York, for example, has a transfer tax of $2 per $500 of price, and a mortgage recording tax of 1% of the loan. There are many permutations.

Added to these are the closing costs, which, depending on the state, will include mortgage recording fees, state and local closing taxes (as above), legal fees, inspection fees and other general costs. These can total between 2% and 6% of the purchase price. Mortgage lenders also usually charge one or two 'points' (a point is 1% of the total loan). The other main monthly costs associated with a mortgage are what are commonly known as 'PITI': the Principal mortgage payment, Interest, Taxes and Insurance. PITI costs can be calculated online at www.realestateabc.com and state-by-state guides to fees, taxes and hidden costs are available at www.hud.gov. Annual property taxes can be between 1% and 3% of the purchase price.

The lowest down-payment that can be given is usually 5% (though it is possible to negotiate less). Normally, the buyer will put down 20% of the purchase price, although the 5-15-20 scheme is more popular now the housing market has slowed down. Financial planners advise against paying more than 28% of your gross monthly income in mortgage repayments, although the lending environment makes it easy to shop around: look under 'Real Estate Loans' in the Yellow Pages, at www.yellow.com, or on any internet search engine if you don't wish to use your own bank. Overall, the typical monthly house payment, including insurance and taxes, is around $75 per $10,000 of the house cost per month. So, if you purchased a house for $200,000, your monthly payment would be roughly $1,750.

Title insurance is sometimes purchased to protect the buyer from an invalid or unenforceable title deed to their new property. For example, if their new house did not actually belong to the seller and the real owners demanded the house back, a full refund would have to be granted to the purchaser because the title was unenforceable. Title insurance can be a requirement of the mortgage and the lender will not close the deal without proof that a policy has been arranged, although not every buyer takes it out.

You will also be required to take out hazard, or homeowners, insurance. It is advisable to get an all-risk policy, which includes liability cover; there are frequent claims against homeowners by people who have been injured on their property. The average premium on a $120,000 house would be $700–$800. For more information on insurance contact a real estate agent or the National Consumer Insurance Helpline on 1 800 942 4242. The Insurance Information Institute (www.iii.org) can also answer all your questions concerning the nature of home insurance and the options available to house buyers.

Closing costs often take people by surprise as they are demanded upfront, and can be sizable. With mortgage points (percentage to the lender), house inspection survey, appraisal and lawyers' fees you should expect to pay $3,000–$4,000. In some states, closing costs are much higher: in Florida the average is between $6,000 and $8,000. Some lenders will offer free closing costs to attract new borrowers but they may make up the difference in other ways, so once again, do your research before signing up.

Non-resident and UK mortgages

If you hope to buy a property with a US mortgage without being a resident, you face certain restrictions on the amount of money you can borrow. US banks will not usually lend more than 80% of the market value of the desired property, or a maximum of 70% for an investment property. If you want to pay less than a 20% deposit you will be asked to take out a private mortgage insurance policy (PMI) which will pay off the outstanding balance on the mortgage should you be unable to continue payments. Many banks will require overseas purchasers to put down a deposit of six months' mortgage payments, insurance fees and due taxes.

It is generally not a good idea to take out a mortgage in your home country for a foreign property. Arranging a mortgage within the US may be easier because foreign banks need to know that if they repossess the property, they are guaranteed to recoup the loan. If you do choose this option, you may have to put your house in your home country up as security. This is unwise. It's best to arrange your US mortgage so that it poses as little threat as possible to your home lifestyle. As well as this, US rates are usually cheaper than, say, UK rates (though the gap is closing), so there may be no saving to be gained. There can also be tax problems.

Mortgages from UK offshore banks (or from onshore banks with offshore branches) should present no problems, depending on the particular policy of the bank. Contact any major UK bank for details of their offshore accounts. The base rate in America is just 2% compared with 5% in the UK.

UK and USA Useful addresses

National Association of Home Inspectors: 800 448 3942 or 952 928 4641; info@nahi.org; www.nahi.org

American Society of Home Inspectors: 60016; 800 743 2744; www.ashi.com. North America's largest organisation for home inspectors.

US Department of Housing and Urban Development: 800 333 4636; www.hud.gov

Insurance Information Institute: 212 346 5500; www.iii.org. A primary source of insurance information for consumers.

LaVigne, Coton & Associates: 407 316 9988; attylavign@aol.com; www.lavignelaw.us. A law firm handling both real estate and immigration.

National Association of Realtors: 30700 Russell Ranch Road, Westlake Village, CA 91362; 805 557 2300; www.realtor.com

Prudential Florida WCI Realty: 954 449 2700 or 020 8257 9988 (UK office); www.prudentialfloridawcirealty.com

The World of Florida: 08080 252 626; homes@worldofflorida.co.uk; www.worldofflorida.co.uk. Specialists in villas to buy and rent in Florida.

TIP

■ If you hope to buy a property with a US mortgage without being a resident, you face certain restrictions on the amount of money you can borrow.

Useful publications

A Place In The Sun (2002 Fanny Blake, Channel 4 Books,). A companion book to a television series explaining how to buy a holiday or retirement home in a warm climate. The series included Florida.

Emigrate America A monthly newspaper which includes news and information for people who want to live, work or emigrate to the United States, including information on immigration law and any developments that might affect prospective emigrants. The paper also has many relevant advertisements for legal and relocation services. Available on subscription by telephoning 01323 726040 or visiting www.emigrate2.co.uk.

World of Property Magazine Available at www.worldofproperty.co.uk, the magazine regularly features Florida property and buying tips.

Contracts

One of the major differences between the US, English, and Welsh (though not Scottish or Australian) conveyancing procedure is in the contract. In England and Wales nothing is settled until the contract is signed, and then the buyer must complete the deal on pain of severe financial penalties. At any stage before that, the seller can take a better offer and the buyer can be gazumped. Gazumping does happen in the USA because nothing is binding until the seller accepts the offer, but it is far less common, primarily because of the greater involvement of the agents and brokers, and because the contractual process begins when an offer is made. It is, in many ways, a much fairer system; the contract is signed much earlier, and it is equally binding to buyer and seller, although with let-out clauses for any major problems.

Once your offer is accepted by the seller you immediately sign a contract, usually in the realtor's office. You then pay a deposit (sometimes called 'earnest money') of around 5%–10% of the purchase price into an escrow account that is held by a bank or another regulated body. This ensures that if you have to pull out of the deal you will see the money again. Under federal law you have a right, when buying a residential property, to have the deposit put in an escrow account, unless you agree otherwise. Many builders' contracts (if you are buying a new home) contain a clause that you *do* agree otherwise – this should be negotiated out if possible.

Standard contracts contain let-out clauses for the buyer if the mortgage does not come through or if the inspection uncovers major structural problems. You may also be able to persuade the seller to allow a clause which makes the contract conditional on sale of your current house. A closing date will be specified and this should be realistic – it can take five or six weeks for the mortgage to come through.

Another essential clause specifies that the house conforms to all local, state and federal real-estate regulations. Title insurance should also be taken out by the buyer (see the 'Professional assistance' section above). When you sign the contract you give the seller a deposit (a percentage of

FACT

■ Gazumping does happen in the USA, but it is far less common than overseas.

the purchase price) which goes towards the down-payment, which in turn is handed over on completion of the purchase.

House prices	
Median single-family house values in selected metropolitan areas, 2007 **(*Source: National Association of Realtors*)**	
North-east	
Hartford, Connecticut	$263,200
Boston, Massachusetts	$395,600
Pittsburgh, Pennsylvania	$120,700
New York, New York	$469,700
Mid-west	
Cincinnati, Ohio	$140,800
Lansing, Michigan	$126,800
St Louis, Missouri	$145,400
Minneapolis, Minnesota	$225,200
Chicago, Illinois	$276,600
South	
Atlanta, Georgia	$172,000
Houston, Texas	$152,500
Miami, Florida	$365,500
Memphis, Tennessee	$137,200
West	
Denver, Colorado	$245,400
Las Vegas, Nevada	$297,700
San Francisco, California	$805,400
Phoenix, Arizona	$257,400

Relocators

Relocation companies specialise in moving people to live and work in foreign countries. Many work principally with the human resource departments of large companies but can accommodate individuals if required.

The process of adjustment will vary depending on an individual's experience of international life and to what extent a company is proactive in helping employees settle into a new life in the USA. On a practical level, a relocation company will organise all the visa arrangements and smooth out any other legal and financial issues such as pension planning and taxation. Similarly, they will arrange the actual shipping of households.

Relocation packages may also assist with searches for housing, schools and specialist services such as asthma clinics, along with offering cross-cultural training to cover issues such as the culture of the country, its politics,

> **Weichert Relocation Resources Inc points out that a particular issue for individuals moving to the United States from the UK is that they can sometimes underestimate the degree of adjustment needed:**
>
> There's an assumption that, because there is a shared language and a degree of cultural exchange, the move there will be simpler than, for example, one to India. But bear in mind that the United States is a continent encompassing wide regional differences. Moving to New York will be quite a different experience from living in Houston.

TIP

■ Sometimes an assignment may actually fail if an employee is not properly prepared for the move.

FACT

■ Because the US is so large and relocation a common fact of career progression, American employers expect to carry many of the costs.

religion, history and attitudes. Orientation days are sometimes provided which teach an individual or family how to use the local supermarket or post office, or how to hire a television. There's even support for what is indelicately referred to as the 'trailing spouse'. Often spouses are not allowed to work and are in the most need of support.

After an initial interview, during which they will find out as much as possible about you and your family, the relocator will bring in an American firm (most of the large European relocators have sister companies or associates in the USA) which will take over the business of finding a property, schools (if necessary), and other essentials. Your belongings will be transported door to door and all customs formalities will be taken care of: in short, your hand will be held until you feel you can cope on your own.

Relocation is not cheap. Often, though, if an employee is being moved by their present employer then most – if not all – of the costs will be carried by the employer. If you have been offered a job through an application process, relocation costs are also likely to be part of the employment package. Alternatively, it's something that can be negotiated before acceptance of the job offer. As a rough guide, a home search will cost £1,800 with a school search an extra £300.

To move the possessions of an average British household would cost approximately £5,500, but insurance will need to be added and that figure depends entirely on the value of the goods being moved. An insurance assessor will need to make a valuation of the items being moved before giving a quote.

For individuals and small companies wanting to relocate, it is an expensive business, and the best option would be to contact a US real-estate agent who deals with relocations. Most agents have access to Multiple Listing Services – local and nationwide databases of properties for sale – and they are equipped to offer a more complete service than most European agents. You can also look up relocators in the *Yellow Pages*, though keep in mind that there are a number of things to look out for.

Some of the smaller operators will not abide by any code of practice and will be taking a commission from real-estate agents: they will take you round properties but will not be bargaining entirely on your behalf. In the USA, the Employee Relocation Council has 1,200 members from corporations that relocate their employees, as well as 10,000 members from the relocation, real-estate and associated professions. In the UK, the Association of Relocation Agents, although dealing mainly with the UK, has US contacts and can give advice on relocating to the USA.

The company Four Corners Emigration (listed below) differs slightly from other relocation firms in that it concentrates on assisting with immigration and visas, although its clients do receive full support with their relocation and resettlement.

Useful relocation contacts and resources

Worldwide ERC: 703 842 3400; webmaster@worldwideerc.org; www.erc.org

Association of Relocation Agents: 08700 737475; arp.relocation@gmail.com; www.arp-relocation.com. This UK-based trade association lists many companies specialising in international relocation on its website.

Anglo Domus: 01865 514458; relocation@anglo-domus.com; www.anglodomus.com

Avalon Overseas Movers: 020 8955 1079; www.avalon-overseas.com

Community Connections: 650 327 0577; cci@communityconn.com; www.communityconn.com.

www.directmoving.com. An international relocation web portal. Contents include information about jobs, health and insurance, immigration and expatriate contacts.

Four Corners Emigration: 0845 841 9453; info@fourcorners.net; www.4-corners.net

Moves International Relocations: 020 8267 6000; enquiries@moves.co.uk; www.moves.co.uk

Pricoa Relocations UK: 020 8966 1200; www.pricoarelocation.com

Weichert Relocation Resources Inc: 877 882 1290; marketing@wrri.com; www.wrri.com

Runzheimer International: 262 971 2200; marketing@runzheimer.com; www.runzheimer.com. International relocation specialists.

www.homestore.com. (805) This site, move, [name of site wanted by editor] is principally concerned with real estate but has sections dedicated to moving, home improvement, and decorating.

Holiday-home income

Florida – and to a lesser extent Arizona and Colorado – are the most popular states for Europeans buying holiday homes, and real estate agents there are experienced in buying, selling and managing homes for expatriates and summer visitors.

Holiday homes can be less of an expense if you rent them out for the months that you are not there. Income derived from this should normally be taxed at the standard 30% rate of federal income tax as income not effectively connected with a US business. However, because this would deter foreigners from investing in US real estate, you can choose to have the income taxed as if it were effectively connected with a US business. It is then taxed on a net basis (after deducting all expenses), and at a graduated rate.

Renting out your property can be a headache. Many management companies guarantee a certain rental income, but once you've paid the purchase price and the various commissions, such a guarantee will almost certainly fail to live up to its promise. Remember that management of your home will make a decent profit for builders and management companies, so don't feel you are doing them a favour by letting them handle it. If you are dependent on rental income to support the property, make sure that there are no zoning (local property regulation) or other restrictions on short-term rentals, and that you will be able to recoup enough money to cover the mortgage at a 75% occupancy rate, which is probably the most you can hope for. You must also take into account maintenance costs. Depending on the state, the income will also be subject to state taxation (state income tax or sales tax), and licence fees of some sort. Most importantly, your income will agian be taxable in your country of residence, subject to any available double taxation relief.

Contact a real estate agent, a solicitor, or an accountant for advice. Alternatively, you can download the relevant forms (non-resident alien) from the Internal Revenue Service at www.irs.gov or call 1 800 829 1040 within the USA.

Insurance and wills

Home insurance

Americans like to insure themselves against all eventualities, which is arguably sensible in such a highly litigious society. As a consequence the insurance industry is huge. Last year nearly $2.87 trillion was invested in life and health insurance in the USA and $9,400 per head is spent on the many types of insurance every year. One of the reasons for this is that there is far less mandatory insurance, in the form of social security deductions and payments, than in most European countries. Health insurance is essential and the importance of obtaining it cannot be stressed enough. Most people in employment will be covered by a company policy but the self-employed must take out their own policies.

A homeowner's insurance policy usually consists of casualty insurance and liability insurance. The first covers the fabric of the house and your possessions, and the second insures against an injury sustained by a third party while on your property. It is not unknown for friends to sue friends, and for families to meet in court over an ankle sprained on the porch steps, although it is not an everyday occurrence. It is recommended that your liability insurance covers you for at least $300,000: check the policy for this, as the basic sum is usually $100,000.

Policies come in basic and more comprehensive packages. The basic (HO-1) policy insures your home and possessions against 'common perils' such as fire, lightning and other natural disasters; personal and medical liability; theft, and vandalism. Broad policies and all-risk policies cover many more eventualities, and it is wise to pay the extra on the premium to be covered for damage from smoke, sprinkler systems, or leaking air conditioners. Earthquake insurance is (obviously) expensive in high-risk areas like California, and only a small percentage of people take it out.

Condominium and co-operative buyers need to take out different types of insurance. A master policy, held by the owners, will cover the basic building, but will not cover things such as refrigerators and kitchen units, and any decorating or improvements. You must also be insured in case the master policy is inadequate after a loss, in which case individual owners will have to make up the difference. Tenants of rented accommodation will also need renters' insurance to cover personal belongings, theft and damage to the property.

In the UK, advice is available from the Association of British Insurers (020 7600 3333; info@abi.org.uk; www.abi.org.uk); and in the USA from the National Consumer Insurance Helpline (1 800 942 4242) or from the Insurance Information Institute (212 346 5500; www.iii.org).

Wills

All adults should make a will, no matter how large or small their assets. In the USA, the process is more or less the same as in most of Europe although the specifics vary from state to state. If you are a non-resident you can specify that your estate be subject to non-US inheritance laws. If this is not specified in the will, US law automatically applies. It is possible to make tax-free bequests to charities: if you have assets of more than $2 million (an exemption that will increase to $3.5 million in 2009) you will be liable to estate tax and you should consult an attorney about your will. Otherwise, most states have standard will forms that allow you to leave your possessions and money to your spouse and children, or a charity if you wish. A will must still be drawn up and witnessed using the proper legal process.

You may also want to look into the possibility of creating a trust, which is a way of bequeathing your money before death. This has valuable taxation implications: a trust can be used to shift income to a beneficiary (usually a close relative or child) who is in a lower taxation bracket. An attorney or accountant should be consulted about the various options open to foreigners in this situation. See also *Understanding Living Trusts* (Vickie and Jim Schumacher, Schumacher Publishing, 2003) and check the wills and probate section of FindLaw at www.findlaw.com for lawyers countrywide specialising in wills.

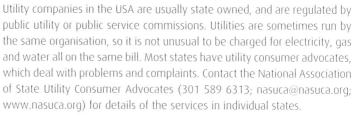

■ SERVICES AND UTILITIES

Utility companies in the USA are usually state owned, and are regulated by public utility or public service commissions. Utilities are sometimes run by the same organisation, so it is not unusual to be charged for electricity, gas and water all on the same bill. Most states have utility consumer advocates, which deal with problems and complaints. Contact the National Association of State Utility Consumer Advocates (301 589 6313; nasuca@nasuca.org; www.nasuca.org) for details of the services in individual states.

If you're renting a property the leasing office will provide you with a sheet of useful phone numbers when you move in so that you can change the names on the bills. Real estate agents may provide the same service for homeowners, but you might also have to be prepared to ask neighbours for provider names and numbers. Costs for changing names over will vary, and you could have to not pay anything at all, or, alternatively, have to pay a deposit (which is returnable) of between $50 and $300. If you are in any doubt, contact NASUCA and they will point you in the right direction to get started.

Electricity

The electricity supply is generally 110–120 volts, AC 60 cycles, single phase and flat two-point fittings are normal for most appliances. European appliances rated at 240 volts AC can be used with an adaptor, although this is not always the case: check that your favourite curling tongs are usable on the US current before you go as appliances have been known to melt or blow components if used incorrectly abroad. Electrical goods are considerably cheaper in the USA than in Europe, and most people decide to buy new radios, razors and so on when they arrive. Check your electrical devices to see if they have a 110\240 volt switch, in which case they will work in the USA. Alternatively, purchase an adaptor with a built-in converter.

Gas

Gas is available in all cities and in most apartments. In rural areas it may not be piped, but will be delivered in bottles and stored outside. In some rented apartments the gas supply may be included in the rent. There is no need to shop around for the cheapest supplier of bottled gas: in most areas there will only be one company.

Water

The water supply is entirely safe to drink. In the west and the south there are often restrictions on the use of water, particularly after snow-free or dry winters. In many areas the cost of the water is included in the local property taxes: in others, you'll find each apartment or building has its own water meter, and that you are billed by the municipality. Water rates are generally low.

Refuse, recycling & snow clearing

Most districts have weekly or fortnightly refuse collection, and more and more states are implementing recycling schemes. Some states will give you between 1¢–5¢ for each plastic bottle, plastic bag or aluminium can you recycle, while others will pick up your recycling straight from your driveway but do not give you any cash back. In areas where there is regular and heavy snowfall it is possible to arrange for snow to be cleared from your entrance and driveway.

FACT

■ It is possible to have your mail picked up from your own mailbox so you don't have to make that late afternoon dash to the nearest post box before it gets picked up.

Mail

The United States Postal Service tends to operate differently from mailing corporations in other countries. In the USA for example, it is possible to have your mail picked up from your own mailbox so you don't have to make that late afternoon dash to the nearest post box before it gets picked up. Public post boxes also exist though, and can be found on street corners and near shops in an easy to spot shade of bright blue. Houses and apartments do not usually have letterboxes in their front doors, as mailboxes are the usual practice and are placed either at the end of driveways (for houses) or built into the foyer wall (in apartment buildings). You will probably need a key to open either. Mail tends to be delivered later than in the UK (around 12pm) and it is far more common to ship goods using a private mailing company such as FedEx or UPS than it is abroad.

Telephones

The American telephone system is entirely deregulated into regional companies and consumers have a number of different choices

of line and apparatus. You can buy your own phone from a retailer – regional telephone companies are not allowed to manufacture or sell telephone equipment. Connection costs are between $50 and $100, depending on the area, and it normally takes only a few days to be connected. All telephones should be approved by the Federal Communications Commission. You will be billed monthly and different companies have varying charges for local, long distance and on and off peak calls so it's wise to shop around if you can. The average charge for a local call is 10 cents, but in some states all local calls are free, particularly if you pay a minimum sum to your provider each month. In some areas there is a local free call allocation (between 20 and 75 calls a month), after which you will be charged a basic rate. Monthly line charges are between $10 and $15. More than 500 companies now compete in the long-distance call market, so it is a good idea to contact a number of companies, and ask colleagues and friends, before deciding which one to choose.

The major long-distance carriers are AT&T, MCI/Verizon, Time Warner Cable and Sprint:

- AT&T   www.att.com
- MCI/Verizon   www.consumer.mci.com
- Sprint   www.sprint.com
- Time Warner Cable   www.timewarnercable.com

Mobile phones

When thinking about purchasing a mobile phone (or cell phone, as they are commonly referred to) for yourself, bear in mind that you may need a social security number and good credit history to sign up for a contract, so it may be wise to invest in a pay-as-you-go phone until such necessities are established. Contracts tend to run for either two years or 18 months so look out for flexible plans with benefits. Plans could include free roaming charges so you won't be charged for making calls outside of your home state, cheap long-distance and national calling, and free calls to numbers of your choosing. Text messaging is not as popular in the USA as it is abroad, so you may wish to avoid signing up for additional texts in your plan until you can be sure you're going to make good use of them. The largest mobile phone companies are AT&T (www.att.com), Sprint (www.sprint.com), T-Mobile (www.t-mobile.com), US Cellular (www.uscellular.com) and Verizon Wireless (www.verizonwireless.com).

The internet and pay TV

If you have a home computer you will almost certainly want and need the internet. Most internet companies are also home phone or cable companies and will offer broadband and wireless internet as part of a package. Signing up for all three with the same company will save you money, but you may end up with services you don't want. Time Warner Cable for example, will currently provide you with a free high-definition DVR box to record any show on television without the use of a VCR, but in order to qualify you must purchase one of their more expensive and extensive channel packages, which may include channels you'll never watch. It's important to shop around, but once you've decided on a company and package to suit you signing-up is easy. A technician will be round to your property to get everything working as soon as it is convenient for you and will even demonstrate how to work your new technology.

TIP

■ The mobile phone industry in the USA is finally catching up with Western Europe and Australasia, and nearly everybody over the age of 13 has a cell phone now.

Daily Life

◣ CULTURE SHOCK

There is often so much expectation put upon a new country that immigrants can be disappointed when they finally arrive and settle in. One major reason for this is culture shock. There are several things any new immigrant should look out for in this vein, including homesickness, frustrations with bureaucracy, and the realisation that you area not able to take things for granted in the same way you're used to doing.

Homesickness should not be dismissed lightly. If you are used to having family and friends close by, the reality of living thousands of miles away and only being able to contact them by phone or email can be traumatic. Even if you are moving with your immediate family, the loss of friends and extended family can affect you more than you think. A couple of ways to prepare yourself for the change are to create photo albums of loved ones and update address books with current contact details so that when you need a little pick-me-up you have pictures to look at and phone numbers at hand. Letter writing may seem old-fashioned these days but for many people it's therapeutic to write a letter and exciting to receive one, so keeping in contact this way may ease the transition to a new country. Sending photos and videos via the internet or using a webcam is another fantastic and convenient way to stay in touch. However, while it's important to maintain contact with 'home', it should not replace integrating into your new community. Make sure you're not so homesick and pining for loved ones that you forget all the wonderful reasons you moved countries in the first place.

You may only be accompanying the main visa holder and, as such, are not allowed to enter into employment. Or you might have arrived in the country without an immediate job and have to begin your search once you've settled in. The repercussions of these situations can include loneliness, boredom and alienation from the community. In extreme cases it can lead to resentment and even depression, so should not be underestimated. The best way to avoid situations like this is to keep yourself busy. You could join a gym, take up a new hobby or work online for a company based in your home country.

 Websites such as www.volunteermatch.org and www.dosomething.org offer thousands of opportunities to volunteers in many fields, providing interesting ways to keep yourself occupied, meet new people and give back to your new community. It can also be an interesting item to add to your résumé.

For some, the journey to their new life has been accompanied by endless paperwork and form-filling, and there's a belief that all that bureaucracy ends once you arrive. Unfortunately it's often only just begun and in America you'll need new forms of identification for absolutely everything, and the paperwork involved can be daunting and frustrating. You may find yourself running around in circles trying to get one government agency to talk to another or waiting for months for a single document to come through the mail. If the bureaucracy does seem endless and too difficult you could try talking to your local congressional office, which is there to fix problems such as this.

i Try www.house.gov for a list of representatives and local offices.

Culture shock can be a response to unfamiliar customs which bring you out of your comfort zone. If you are used to driving on the left, for example, driving on the right and making right-hand turns on a red light will seem strange at first and may make you doubt your driving skills. America has different national sports, different foods, different approaches to raising children and different religious beliefs from many other English-speaking countries. Day-to-day living can be completely removed from what you're used to, although the non-existence of a language barrier does help.

While culture shock isn't something to dismiss lightly, it also isn't something to be afraid of. Accept that it will happen, that it will probably be a delayed reaction rather than immediate and learn how to deal with its impact before you set off for the airport. Having a healthy outlook such as this will really ease the journey.

FACT

■ It's important to assimilate and adopt as many aspects of the American culture as you can, but don't lose yourself too much. Part of the fun of being an immigrant is having 'an accent' and a different approach to tasks; it makes you popular and actually helps you assimilate faster.

■ SHOPS AND SHOPPING

America, the land of shopping malls and supermarkets, can still surprise visitors with its small, independent shops. True, these are mostly in the big cities, and the cosy street of shops in the small town has long gone, but shopping need not be the air-conditioned nightmare that we are led to believe. Wherever you shop, you will find that prices compare very well with Europe.

One of the great charms of some cities, particularly New York and San Francisco, is how old-fashioned they are. Visitors are surprised by how small and interesting the streets are at ground level. It is worth walking around New York's Greenwich Village, SoHo, or Haight-Ashbury in San Francisco, to see that America is not a land of soulless malls. It is easy to find excellent little shops, selling everything from T-shirts to walking sticks, if you only look for them.

FACT

■ Food, clothes, books, CDs and electrical goods are all cheaper in the USA than in Europe and Australasia.

Mall of America is the USA's largest retail and entertainment complex, and a visit can be overwhelming

As out-of-town shopping centres and high street arcades spring up all over the UK and Europe, the awesome power of the American shopping culture becomes less of a novelty, although it is, still, an experience. It is no exaggeration to say that America is a shopper's paradise (although paradise can mean many things according to different tastes). Since the first 'Shopping and Entertainment Complex' opened in Bloomington, Minnesota in the 1950s, the shopping mall has become the American shopping experience personified. We are now used to malls all around the globe, and so to describe one would be pointless. What you must be ready for, however, is that the biggest American malls are bigger, shinier, more air-conditioned, with more pervasive 'muzak' and longer and quieter escalators, than anywhere in the world.

The best shopping is to be found on a handful of famous streets: Rodeo Drive in Beverly Hills, Lake Shore Drive in Chicago, Worth Avenue in Palm Beach, and 5th and Madison Avenues in Manhattan. It is an experience to walk down one of these streets and to feel, for once in your life, that you are sharing the same space with the truly rich. Of course, the dream is rudely shattered when you step into one of the shops and are treated with a certain coolness by the assistants, who can often place you in an income bracket before the door has sighed shut behind you.

FACT

■ The first shopping mall ever opened was in Bloomington, Minnesota during the 1950s.

Away from the large cities, shopping in small-town America has nearly disappeared, as huge out-of-town shopping centres have sucked all the custom away from downtown (the town centre), to leave a grey expanse of vacant lots and boarded-up shops. The well-heeled residents have fled to the suburbs, leaving the poorest families to make what they can of it. This is a bleak picture, but it is happening all over the country.

Dedicated shoppers should not despair, however. The mall has its peculiar attractions – essentially that you can find anything you could possibly want under one (very big) roof. Shopaholics should head for the great department stores like Macy's or Bloomingdales in Manhattan, or Saks Fifth Avenue for big-name men's tailoring. In San Francisco, Ghirardelli Square or the San Francisco Shopping Center combine shops, restaurants and 'entertainment'. For the biggest of them all, in the unlikely setting of South Dakota and attracting 20,000 tourists a day, Wall Drug combines drugstore, mall and museum of American eccentricity in one.

Factory shops ('outlets') are also popular, selling goods direct from the manufacturer at discounts of up to 70%. They are usually located outside city centres and may contain hundreds of different outlets under one roof. There is a comprehensive list of outlets at www.outletbound.com, which also publishes a paper guide listing 11,000 factory outlet stores in the USA and Canada.

i For information on the big department stores, you should look on their (generally very good) websites: www.sears.com, www.bloomingdales. com and www.walmart.com are just three.

Food is usually purchased from large grocery stores, which are local to individual states and sell fresh, frozen and grocery products. Larger stores will also carry imported food from abroad – look for Heinz Baked Beans, Cadbury's chocolate and Mars Bars without almonds in the Ethnic Food aisle. Food stores are one of the quickest and quirkiest introductions to American life, and spending a few hours browsing through American versions of your favourite dinners can provide you with a literal slice of American pie. Another option is to attend local farmers' markets, held during the spring and summer months. Stay for a few hours to pick up fresh, locally-grown produce and breads, then eat lunch cooked from the best ingredients found in your town. They are also a wonderful way to meet and support the local community.

WalMart is the largest grocery retailer in the United States

■ MEDIA AND COMMUNICATIONS

Newspapers

There are more than 3,000 daily, weekly and monthly newspapers published in the USA. Some of them are among the oldest newspapers in the world: the *Philadelphia Inquirer* was established in 1771, for example. All the larger cities support several newspapers, and even small towns have their own free journal. Only a handful of titles like *USA Today, The Wall Street Journal* and the *New York Times* are distributed nationally, though even these do not compare to European titles, which have a genuine national readership and wide demographic appeal. Americans tend to rely on the news broadcasters for national and international news. The American newspaper market is much more regional in nature because of the country's vast size. Even in a city the size of New York or Los Angeles the political and cultural establishment are usually obtaining comment and analysis from a single broadsheet. Other papers with a national readership are the *Los Angeles Times*, and the *Washington Post*, although these are obviously aimed at their local markets.

Foreign newspapers such as *The Financial Times*, which prints an American edition, are of course available in all big cities. Another widely available international edition is *The International Express* and *The Guardian Weekly*, which produce editions summarising British news, politics and sport over the previous week and are aimed specifically at expats. They are available from newsagents and on subscription. In the USA, contact Speedimpex (www.speedimpex.com) for information about local distributors.

 Almost all newspapers of any size now have their own websites which publish most of that day's edition online with other supplementary information like entertainment guides and classified advertising. Many large cities publish local interest magazines like *Time Out New York* or the *Los Angeles Magazine*. Citysearch (www.citysearch.com) runs a network of 105 national city guides which allow users to interact with the local community – whether it's concerning buying tickets online, searching for a movie or finding a house to rent. Digitalcity (www.digitalcity.com) runs a similar network of local information. For lists of all American newspapers and publications consult www.newslink.org, which lists more than 4,000 with an online presence, or, alternatively, the media section of www.yahoo.com.

Contact details for two major publications with national distribution are as follows:

USA Today: 703 276 3400; www.usatoday.com
The Wall Street Journal: 1 800 369 2834 (US); 020 7842 9609 (UK); www.wsj.com

The following is a list of newspapers published in selected states

Arizona
Arizona Republic — www.azcentral.com

California
San Francisco Chronicle — www.sfgate.com
Los Angeles Times — www.latimes.com

Colorado
Denver Post — www.denverpost.com

Connecticut
Hartford Courant — www.courant.com

District of Columbia
Washington Post — www.washingtonpost.com

Florida
Miami Herald — www.miamiherald.com

Georgia
Atlanta Journal-Constitution — www.ajc.com

Illinois
Chicago Tribune — www.chicagotribune.com

Indiana
Indianapolis Star — www.indystar.com

Louisiana
Times-Picayune — www.timespicayune.com

Massachusetts
Boston Globe — www.boston.com

Michigan
Detroit Free Press — www.freep.com

Nevada
Las Vegas Review-Journal — www.lvrj.com

New Jersey
Star-Ledger — www.nj.com/starledger

New York
Financial Times — www.financialnews-us.com
New York Post — www.newyorkpost.com
New York Times — www.nytimes.com
Village Voice — www.villagevoice.com
Wall Street Journal Eastern Edition — www.wsj.com
Irish Echo — www.irishecho.com

Pennsylvania
Philadelphia Inquirer — www.philly.com

Texas
Dallas Morning News — www.dallasnews.com

Washington
Seattle Post-Intelligencer — www.seattlep-i.nwsource.com

Magazines and periodicals

Of the 10,000 magazines published in the USA, the most popular achieve circulations that newspaper editors can only dream of. *Reader's Digest*, for example, has a US circulation of 11 million, a figure quite alien to most European magazine publishers and even domestic newspapers. A study of the most popular magazines would show that Americans are most concerned with how to fill their free time (the *TV Guide* is one of the top 10, as well as other hobby magazines like *Better Homes* and *Gardens*), and that the massed ranks of the retired are poised to take over the country. The two best sellers for retired

people are the *American Association of Retired Persons (AARP) Bulletin* (circulation 21 million) and *Modern Maturity* (a close second at 20 million). Other top national sellers are the aforementioned *Reader's Digest* and *TV Guide*, along with *USA Weekend*, *National Geographic*, *Time Magazine*, *Family Circle*, *Good Housekeeping*, and the *Ladies' Home Journal*. Among the most entertaining periodicals are the 'schlock' magazines such as the *National Enquirer* and the *National Examiner* (also available in many UK newsagents). Headlines such as 'Woman Gives Birth to 200lb Baby', and stories about children that are half-bat and half-boy, can enliven a dull day.

As with most American goods, the cost of magazines and newspapers is very reasonable, and most monthly publications cost less than $5. Subscriptions tend to offer 12 or 14 copies a year for the price of 10 or 12, and will often come with a free gift as an incentive.

Television

The US has the greatest number of TV sets per head of any country in the world – 219 million according to the CIA World Factbook, which is nearly one set for every two people. There are several main TV networks, of which the best known are CBS, NBC, ABC, and Fox. Unlike in Europe, these networks operate much like a franchise, whereby locally-owned stations act as affiliates and broadcast the network's content. In addition to these network stations are literally hundreds of cable networks broadcasting specialised content like sports or movies. The USA is now in the process of switching its entire network from analogue to digital reception, so those families who do not have cable television or a digital receiver must switch by 2009 or they will not be able to watch TV any more.

Anyone remotely conversant with TV just about anywhere in the world will be no stranger to the best – and worst – of American television. Shows

> **TIP**
>
> ■ Magazines and newspapers are most commonly bought from grocery stores and large multi-purpose shops such as Wal-Mart or Target. The humble newsagent is a far less familiar sight in America unless you're in a large city, and you're far more likely to use a small newsstand for your latest copy of a favourite magazine even then.

FACT

■ The average US family has 2.1 televisions, and watches around seven hours of TV a day.

such as the various strands of the *CSI* and *Law & Order* crime series, the hospital drama *ER* and *24* are massively popular critical hits in the UK and abroad. *Friends, Seinfeld, Frasier, Will and Grace, Scrubs* and *House* have achieved cult status, and many of them are still repeated internationally, long after they ceased production in the US. Add to that cartoons like *The Simpsons, Futurama, King of the Hill* and *South Park,* and it's easy to see why European TV bosses are constantly looking across the Atlantic for top-grossing American shows to buy. Much of the success of comic writing in the US is attributed to the fact that they are made by teams of writers numbering as high as 15. These writers sit around large tables each week bouncing comic ideas off each other in contrast to the traditional image of a writer struggling alone to come up with the gags.

Naturally, with such a huge market and proliferation of channels, the best is hedged around with the worst. American TV can be very bad indeed – channels have to appeal to as wide an audience as possible and often serials and sitcoms become an indistinguishable blur. There is also a craze for distasteful real-life TV, with 'confessional' hosts such as Jerry Springer inviting misfits and inadequates to work out their domestic quarrels on screen, sometimes with extreme – and often choreographed – violence. Broadcasting standards tend to only censor expletives and nudity in these shows, and any violence is often left to air in full.

The Public Broadcasting Service (PBS) is a non-commercial station that does not carry advertising and shows a mixture of documentaries, discussion programmes and quality foreign drama. It is non-profit-making, state-focused, and is financed by public subscriptions and federal government funds.

Reality TV

One interesting phenomenon of recent years is the reversal of shows being sold across the ocean. The huge success of New Zealand's *Popstars* led to an explosion of similarly themed reality shows such as the UK's *Pop Idol* and the USA's *American Idol*. Other concept shows to have been sold include *Strictly Come Dancing*, which became *Dancing with the Stars* in the USA and *Changing Rooms*, which morphed into America's *Trading Spaces*. The phenomenon of *Big Brother* was also not an American original, despite an attempted lawsuit to the contrary: the very first version of the show was broadcast in the Netherlands in 1999 and has since been sold to over 70 other countries, including the USA. It seems that although the USA may be king of the serial drama and comedy series, it looks to the rest of the world for its reality show inspiration.

One distinctly bizarre, but characteristically democratic feature of American television is the presence of local cable stations which allow individuals and groups to broadcast 'home-made' shows. These can range from an amateur musician performing cabaret in their own home to mediums taking calls from anxious viewers hoping to find reassurance about their love lives. Schools and colleges also broadcast sports matches, dance and cheerleading competitions and even spelling bees on these channels, thus bringing community events directly into your home.

Radio

There are around 10,000 commercial radio stations in the US: 5,000 AM, 5,000 FM, and any number of tiny local stations that you will find by twiddling the dial. Depending on where you are you will find an abundance of rock and roll or country and western (the late Tammy Wynette is bigger than Bruce Springsteen in the USA) on the music stations, as well as the usual assortment of talk shows and religious broadcasts.

The radio is a much more satisfying medium than the TV for many people for all sorts of reasons: it requires more concentration for a start, but more importantly it is not dominated by powerful networks, and so it is more intimate and idiosyncratic. If you are driving, there is no better way of getting the feel of the locality you are entering than to start picking up the local stations.

 The BBC World Service is also available in the USA on many stations, or can be listened to on the internet. For full details of names, frequencies and times, log on to the World Service at www.bbc.co.uk or telephone the BBC on 08700 100 222.

Books and bookshops

Books are reasonably cheap in the USA, although they are becoming more expensive, with the recent surge in nationwide prices. Books are more or less all discounted if you know where to shop, and the usual, undiscounted, price of $9.99 for a paperback is less than we are used to in Europe and Australasia. Bookshops are huge and well-stocked, although for more academic or literary works it is best to look for smaller specialist bookshops. These are common in university towns. The biggest chains are Doubleday, B. Dalton, and Walden books, and the massive stores include Barnes and Noble, and Borders.

During the 1990s, the larger urban stores began adding cafes to create a place where book lovers could 'hang-out' over a coffee, a trend that has now also crossed over to the UK. Bookstores have now begun to resemble libraries and clubs where you can spend a snug afternoon in an armchair or as a place to meet friends. Bookstores also now sell far more than just books, including CDs and DVDs, audio books, newspapers and magazines, board games, jigsaw puzzles and stationery.

FACT

■ The advancement of satellite radio has made tuning in even easier and more interesting in the USA, enabling listeners to locate stations that play only their favourite songs.

Post

The USPS Federal Mail has a mixed reputation. Letters can go missing, but – like earthquakes and tornadoes – it is a risk that you have to take. Next-day delivery can seldom be guaranteed: at standard rates letters can take up to seven days to arrive. For some reason, New York delivery times are always longer.

All long-distance internal mail is sent by air without a surcharge, and overnight express for guaranteed delivery the next day is available at an extra cost. Air mail between northern Europe and the USA usually takes five to six days but varies according to destination and can take a week or more to reach the West Coast, Alaska or Hawaii. Surface mail takes approximately six weeks. Post Offices are usually open Monday to Friday from 7am to 6pm, and until midday on Saturday; main post offices in larger cities are open 24 hours. Mail boxes in the street are dark blue and stamped 'US Mail'. They can also be found in the sides of major buildings and in hotel lobbies, in which case there will be a flap, also marked US Mail.

Addresses consist of the name of the person, the street number and street (or PO Box number), the city, state and zip code. Zip codes (similar to post codes) refer to a specific district in the country. They are always five digits long, with the lower numbers in the north-east and the higher ones in the west. For example, a Boston zip code might be 02116, and a

FACT

■ In the major cities bookstores are open late, often until midnight, and most are open on Sundays.

Hawaii one might be 96815. Some zip codes are followed by a second sequence of four digits: this is not essential but might speed up delivery. The table below lists the two-character abbreviations of state names that precede the zip code.

An alternative to the federal postal service is to use one of the many express delivery services which promise overnight delivery at a price. The most extensive networks belong to FedEx and UPS which own a fleet of aircrafts, on the scale of a passenger airline, to take parcels and mail rapidly across the country. Most towns and cities have offices belonging to these services and they also offer home collection. Setting up an account will produce discounted rates and is an ever-more popular method of delivery in the USA.

State postal abbreviations

Alabama AL	Montana MT
Alaska AK	Nebraska NB
Arizona AZ	Nevada NV
Arkansas AR	New Hampshire NH
California CA	New Jersey NJ
Colorado CO	New Mexico NM
Connecticut CT	New York NY
Delaware DE	North Carolina NC
Florida FL	North Dakota ND
Georgia GA	Ohio OH
Hawaii HI	Oklahoma OK
Idaho ID	Oregon OR
Illinois IL	Pennsylvania PA
Indiana IN	Rhode Island RI
Iowa IA	South Carolina SC
Kansas KS	South Dakota SD
Kentucky KY	Tennessee TN
Louisiana LA	Texas TX
Maine ME	Utah UT
Maryland MD	Vermont VT
Massachusetts MA	Virginia VA
Michigan MI	Washington WA
Minnesota MN	West Virginia WV
Mississippi MS	Wisconsin WI
Missouri MO	Wyoming WY

TIP

 Stamps can be bought in drugstores, hotels, bus and train stations and many other places, although oddly they are 25% more expensive anywhere other than in a post office.

Telephones

Telephone numbers consist of a three-digit area code and the seven-digit main number, and are usually written thus: 000 000 0000. If you are calling from outside the area, use the area code (most cities are also divided into different areas, so if you were calling Manhattan from Brooklyn, for example, you would have to use the area code). Many large public companies and offices will also have a toll-free number which is denoted by 1 800 instead of the area code. These numbers can be called from outside the US, but aren't free if you do so; 900 numbers will get you the latest sports results or your horoscope but will charge premium rates.

The operator, reached by dialing 0, will help you in a variety of ways which vary from telling you the weather forecast to giving you information on dental and health services. Other telephone information is available on 411, and directory enquiries for toll-free numbers is on 800 874 4000. Directory enquiries can be reached in any area by dialling the three-digit area code plus 555 1212: if you are outside Manhattan and need a number there, for example, dial 212-555 1212. Some numbers are expressed as letters, such as 1-800-CALL-ATT. The letters on the dialling buttons correspond to numbers on the telephone and many companies advertise their numbers in this way as a marketing gimmick and as a way of helping you remember a number. For a tongue-in-cheek guide to all things American, including using letters for telephone numbers, read Bill Bryson's *The Lost Continent* (1990 Harper Perennial), available at www.amazon.com.

For information on domestic telephones, mobile phones and the internet see the 'Utilities and services' section in 'Setting Up Home'. For emergencies, see the appropriate paragraph later in this chapter.

TIP

■ Payphones take nickels, dimes and quarters, and also credit cards and phone cards. You can charge any call to your credit card by ringing the operator and giving them the credit card number, or by punching in the number if the phone will allow you to.

■ CARS AND MOTORING

America is a land of rootless dreamers, forever shifting back and forth, north and south, east and west. Kerouac wrote his great road novel in 1957, but in films, in books and in everyday life, the vision is still the same. From *Bonnie and Clyde* in 1967, through to *Easy Rider* (1969), *Thelma and Louise* (1991), and the appropriately named *Road Trip* in 2000, the road movie is as much a part of the American dream as Thanksgiving Day. It's usually an illusion – frustrated by dull lives, its heroes (or anti-heroes) take to the road and usually head west in search of adventure and the unknown. The films often end in disaster – Peter Fonda and Dennis Hopper blown off their choppers by savage rednecks in *Easy Rider*, Thelma and Louise driving off a cliff – but still, for most Americans the car and the open road represent the ultimate freedom. For a country founded on emigration, the idea that finding the end of the rainbow involves one more journey remains irresistible. The pioneering movement of people to settle in the 'wild west'

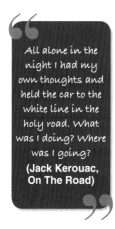

All alone in the night I had my own thoughts and held the car to the white line in the holy road. What was I doing? Where was I going?

(Jack Kerouac, On The Road)

is still an important aspect of the American mythology. Remember that today Americans will frequently leave their home towns to relocate for new jobs or to improve their career prospects. In a country the size of a continent, movement and travel are an ingrained aspect of life.

In the USA, cars and petrol are cheap compared to other countries, and only the poorest do not own a car, which partly explains why public bus services can be so rudimentary. Americans own 145 million cars, one for every two people, and they use a billion gallons of petrol each year. As Britain invented the railway, so in the following century the USA created the first automobile society. America today has 42,500 miles of freeway, and four million miles of secondary roads. In some cities, the vast majority of people – even those on low incomes – own a car: in Los Angeles, for example, a city without extensive public transport, it would quite simply be difficult to travel anywhere without one.

The government is aware of the environmental problems caused by the volume of traffic in cities (in LA, pollution makes the sunset a brilliant toxic pink), and it is introducing legislation to try to restrict car use. In most states there is a special freeway lane, called the carpool or HOV lane (for High Occupancy Vehicles) which is reserved for buses and cars with more than three occupants. These are heavily policed and using one without the requisite number of passengers (or blow-up dolls) as passengers in your car will incur a heavy fine.

The highway system consists of a bewildering variety of differently named roads, ranging from 'super-highways' with six lanes each way, to single-lane country roads. The freeway system is linked by the national arterial Interstates, which connect cities and states, and are designated by the prefix I-, and a red, white and blue shield. Many of the old and famous roads, such as Route 101 from Los Angeles through San Francisco and northern California, have been supplanted by the fast but characterless Interstates, but are well worth taking if you have the time. National and local maps (as well as the more modern satellite navigation systems) will show 'scenic routes', which can also be worth the trouble to investigate. Freeways can be controlled-access, and may be known as turnpikes, expressways or toll-roads: they have all the characteristics of motorways – a central barrier and no cross traffic. As with motorways, plan your journey on the freeways and interstates: you cannot stop or turn around, but you do have the convenience of restrooms in every petrol station, fast food restaurants built just off exit ramps, and even the latest introduction of UK-style service stations called Oasis. America is definitely more driver-friendly than the majority of the world.

Driving regulations

These vary from state to state, so it is best to check with the local branch of the American Automobile Association at www.aaa.com (known as 'Triple A')

TIP

The automobile market is slowing down as a result of gas prices and an economic slowdown and Americans are more likely to shun their SUVs in favour of smaller, more economical cars these days. It is a far-off day when Americans stop buying cars altogether though.

TIP

Tolls in the USA are usually two to three cents a mile, and some states such as Illinois have them on every single major road, so take plenty of change with you on your next road trip.

if you want to be sure of speed limits, seat belt rules and so on, in the state that you are driving in. If you are staying for any length of time in the USA and are planning on driving a lot it would be worth joining the AAA, which provides breakdown service, and also maps and travel information. Basic membership costs $53 a year for breakdown service, tyre change and travel to the nearest repair facility, regardless of distance. There's also assistance if you find yourself locked out of your car, and AAA Club guarantees for a personal cheque of up to $250 worth of repairs. The *BP Motor Club* is another, less widespread motoring organisation (details below).

Speed limits in congested city areas are usually 20–25 mph (32–40 km/h), and on highways 55–65mph (88–104 km/h). Highway police have all the usual tricks for detecting speeds over the limit, from radar to automatic cameras that are triggered when your car passes the limit. Speed limits are often rigorously enforced and tickets can be very expensive, so if you do insist on speeding keep an eye out for police cars and hidden cameras.

In most states you are allowed to turn right at red traffic lights, provided it is not explicitly forbidden at a particular junction. Motoring laws, much like other areas of daily life, do vary from state to state so it's best to check when you move to California from Florida, for example.

Parking rules are also enforced with varying strictness in different states and towns. Never park in front of a fire hydrant or on a bus stop but

always park facing the same direction as traffic. Look out for signs warning you of street cleaning between certain times on certain days of the week and move your car the night before; learn what different coloured kerbs mean: generally, red is no parking at any time, yellow denotes a limited truck loading zone, green a limited waiting period, blue is for handicapped drivers, and white means set down only. These colours will vary from state to state. In some states there will be designated snow streets, which have to be left free for snow ploughs in winter. Parking on highways in rural areas is generally forbidden, and camping, apart from in designated areas, is often prohibited. Parking in cities and towns is often controlled by private companies as well as the city police, who will tow away or clamp illegally parked cars. To get your car back you will have to pay a fine, show proof of ownership, ID, insurance, registration and your licence. Private and municipal parking lots charge $10–$30 a day; you will also find private outdoor parking lots, where you pay by stuffing notes into a slot corresponding to your parking space.

Driving while under the influence of alcohol is taken very seriously in the USA. In some states (such as Utah) you are not allowed to carry alcohol anywhere in the car, and in other states it must be carried, unopened, in the trunk (the boot). For all states the legal blood alcohol level at which you are permitted to drive is less than 0.8%, which for a person weighing 140lbs (10st or 63.5kg) equates to about one and a half drinks.

Useful contacts
AAA Foundation for Traffic Safety: 202 638 5944; info@aaafoundation.org; www.aaafoundation.org. Also produces the useful publications *How To Help An Older Driver* and *Road Rage: How To Avoid Aggressive Driving* as well as other safety leaflets.
Department of Transportation: 202 366 4000; www.dot.gov
American Automobile Association: 407 444 7000; www.aaa.com. The AAA is organised by clubs at a state level. You can use the website which will direct you to your nearest AAA club. Alternatively, if you don't have access to the internet, call directory enquiries within each state for contact information.
BP Motor Club: 1 800 732 9600; www.bpmotorclub.com

Breakdowns and accidents

All accidents should be reported to the nearest police station immediately, especially if personal injury or property damage is involved. If you are driving a hired car you should follow the accident procedure laid out in the rental agreement. Almost all car rental companies are full members of the AAA, which means that when you do break down you will be taken to your destination free of charge. If you break down on a freeway, raise your hood (bonnet) and wait for a state trooper. You may be advised to hang a white

TIP

Pack your car with a torch, tools to change a tyre, a first aid kit, a couple of blankets and some food, especially when driving during the winter months.

cloth on the driver's side, but this can look like too much of a distress signal and imply vulnerability. Interstates have emergency roadside telephones – you should note your location by the small green mileage markers on the side of the road or use your SatNav system to be even more accurate. On a long journey, especially across the remote mountainous and desert areas of the west, it's advisable to take a mobile phone with you, otherwise you might be stranded after a breakdown.

Insurance

Just as with your driving licence, every time you drive a car in the USA you must have with you proof of insurance and ownership title, so it's best to keep copies in your glove compartment. If you are in an accident or are stopped for speeding, you will need to show these documents to the police. Your insurance company will provide you with a handy credit card sized slip for this express purpose.

Insurance varies between states, but it is usually necessary to be resident in the state in which you take out a policy. It is possible to buy a short-term tourist policy, but these can be double the price of the basic policy. It is essential to check that the policy comes with a collision damage waiver (CDW) and a theft waiver (TW). Similarly to the mandatory UK third-party insurance, car insurance in the USA must cover you against damage to other people and property, though it is not compulsory for it to cover you against damage to your own vehicle. Collision damage waivers and theft waivers are expensive but it's worth checking to see if your credit card company offers special deals on car rentals and corresponding insurance, particularly to cover you if a car you are involved in an accident with is a stolen vehicle. American Express is one company to offer better prices for collision damage waiver insurance.

For a full resident's policy you must have a state driving licence, for which you must usually surrender any other driving licence you hold. You must also be resident in the state for a certain amount of time each year – this may range from six to 10 months. The average person pays $939 for insurance but this varies considerably depending on your age, sex, where you are resident and the corresponding rates of crime and traffic collisions, as well as the type of car you drive. In New Jersey, at the top end, residents pay an average figure of $1,365. Road tax is included in the price of the licence plate and cost of petrol, but there is an annual registration fee, which varies too, according to the state of residence. The cost of a routine service is about $100–$200, excluding replacement parts.

 A good place to start for information on car insurance is the Insurance Information Institute; 212 346 5500; www.iii.org.

The price of gas has rocketed recently, but this has not hampered the automobile market

Licences

You can drive legally in the USA on a UK full driver's licence or international licence for up to one year. After that you will need to get a licence issued by the state authorities. You can apply for this at the State Highway Department or DMV but you will probably have to take both a theory and practical driving test before you will be issued one.

Driving tests vary from state to state, but are generally very easy and can be arranged at short notice. They are usually taken in two sections, theory and practical, and most drivers need to purchase a driving permit (provisional licence) before they are allowed to take a test. Licences are valid for between two and five years, and are automatically renewable on payment of a fee of around $20.

In most states the legal age at which you are allowed to drive is 16, and there is a mandatory re-test at either 70 or 75. A small number of states have regulations which allow persons as young as 13 or 14 to learn to drive, providing they are operating farm machinery on their family's land. It is uncommon for them to be allowed to drive without supervision, however.

Car registration

Every car must have a Certificate of Title, or a Certificate of Ownership (the equivalent of a log book in the UK), which includes the driver's name and address and the vehicle licence plate number. A new Certificate is issued each time the vehicle changes hands. If you are buying a second-hand car, the seller will endorse the old certificate to say that they have sold the car, and it is then up to you to register it by sending the certificate to the Department of Transportation (www.dot.gov) or the Registry of Motor Vehicles (www.dmv.org) in your state. It will cost between $10 and $50 depending on the state. You will need proof of ownership, ID, proof of insurance and financial responsibility, and a current registration card.

Some owners like to keep their licence plates, especially if they are personalised. When you are issued the new registration certificate the plates will be transferred to your name, or you will be able to buy new ones. They cost between $8 and $52 per year and the price is often dependent on the weight or age of the car. An out-of-state car must be registered immediately, or within 10 to 60 days, depending on the state. If your children have just started in a state school or you have taken up employment, your car must be state registered.

In some states money for personalised ('vanity') plates is allotted to agencies involved in civic projects such as ecological reserves and wildlife parks: in California you will see plates displaying a variety of sentiments: IMMACHO, MAAHVLUS, SOLONG, or, typically, ALAPLAYA ('To the Beach!').

TIP

◼ It is sometimes possible to claim a refund on your licence plates if your car is scrapped or if you leave the state.

Car rental

You have to be at least 18 to hire a car, and some rental companies insist on a lower age limit of 25. Most of the larger companies require you to possess a major credit card as well, although they may waive that requirement if you can put down a large deposit (usually about 160% of the hire charge). Rental companies come in a variety of forms, from the outfits that hire out a couple of war-weary saloons (despite its ominous name, Rent A Wreck is an established company in this market), to the international and countrywide firms like Hertz, Budget, Enterprise or National Car Rental. If in doubt, go with the big firms: their cars will be newer and in better condition, and if they cost slightly more at least you have the peace of mind that the car is less likely to blow up. If it does, the agency has thousands of offices for you to get redress.

TIP

◼ It's normally cheaper to hire from an airport than from a city-centre office. Remember that most hire cars have automatic gearboxes – if you want manual (stick shift) you must ask for it.

The average price for a car ranges from $37 to $78 per day, including all insurance and unlimited mileage. Before you hire make quite sure that there is no drop-off fee if you want to take the car back to a different office, and ask the dealer if they will pick you up from home to collect the car. Sometimes in cross-continental journeys the drop-off fee may be as high as $1,000. Check too that the insurance comes with collision damage and theft waiver (see the 'Insurance' section above). You will normally be covered for up to $50,000, and can ask for extra cover if necessary. When hiring it's essential to check for hidden extras: a collision damage waiver is usually payable, even when a package contains 'free' car hire; additional charges include state tax and compulsory personal accident and

personal effects insurance as well as gasoline. If a car is not returned by the appointed time, high additional hourly charges are payable, plus an additional day CDW and insurance.

 The USA Travel Guide at www.usatourist.com provides a helpful comparative guide for car rental costs and tips on renting cars. For information on importing and buying a car, see the section 'Importing vs buying a car' in the *Before You Go* section.

◣ OTHER TRANSPORTATION

Air

Air travel in the USA is cheap and efficient. The alternatives of car, bus or train, usually take days rather than hours. A plane ticket doesn't usually cost much more than the cheapest train fare, although an increase in fuel prices is making this less common. In Alaska, air travel is the norm, even by light aircraft between smaller towns. Another advantage of air travel for non-residents is that there are several different discount packages, coupons and standby passes available only to foreigners.

Domestic airfares are determined by the popularity of the route and not by distance. It is cheaper to fly the 2,700 miles (4,345km) from Los Angeles to New York than it would be to fly many much shorter distances (though New York to LA is nearly twice as expensive). The most popular and therefore cheapest routes are along the eastern seaboard (Boston, New York, Washington, Miami), the west coast, and between the coasts.

Cheap deals available before you go

'Visit USA' fares (VUSA) are air passes offered by different American airlines allowing several stops within the country on one visit. You can opt to buy between three and 12 coupons, depending on the airline, for separate flights. But these deals are only available to residents of other countries so are not really applicable to readers of this guide except as an opportunity to scout out potential cities and towns before relocating to the USA. VUSA Air Pass Fares cannot, currently, be booked online. For American airline numbers in the UK see 'Getting There' in the *Before You Go* chapter of this book.

Cheap deals on the spot

To find cheap flights make sure you look through the weekend travel sections of the major newspapers, look up discount travel agencies in the *Yellow Pages*, try the websites listed in this book and check the websites of major airlines. In the big cities you will be able to find ticket consolidators for unbooked charter and commercial tickets. These are unofficial clubs with a membership fee of around $42. Consult www.airhitch.org for a detailed description of the process and local contacts. Southwest Airlines (www.southwest.com) is the best known low-cost airline in America and it serves 60 airports in 59 cities across the country. One-way tickets from LA to Las Vegas start at about $102 (£59) the best fares go to those willing to take less busy days (Tuesdays, Wednesdays, and Saturdays) and less-popular departure times (before 7am or after 7pm). JetBlue (www.JetBlue.com) is another no-frills airline with flights from New York to Florida (one way) from $180 (£104). A number of full-service airlines have launched low-cost subsidiaries, such as United's Ted (www.flyted.com). All the main cheaper American airlines are listed at www.etn.nl/lcostusa.htm with links to each carrier's website.

Courier travel

Another way to get discounted tickets is to fly as a courier. By allowing a shipping company to buy your checked luggage space, you are usually able to save around 50% of the ticket price, although you are obviously restricted to specific flights and hand baggage only. Once, such flights provided the cheapest tickets, but now their prices compare with other discounted fares. The advantage of couriering is that you get a scheduled flight so there are no obscure timings or roundabout routes to cope with. Your baggage is restricted to cabin baggage only, but some courier flights now allow more luggage. Most US courier flights start from New York.

Trains

Although there are high-speed commuter links in and around the big cities, and the Acela Express trains which run between Boston, New York and Washington are much used, most Americans don't choose trains for long-distance journeys due to the sheer length of time such a trip would take. But travelling by rail on Amtrak's stately and luxurious trains can be a delight. So keen is Amtrak, the National Railroad Passenger Corporation, to get people onto trains that they deny you no comforts. The trains are luxurious, with the best cabins equipped with sofas, armchairs and a private bathroom and shower. With such high-quality care offered to passengers, it is hardly surprising to learn that Amtrak has been forced to scale down its operations during the past decade yet again and axe several major routes while reducing frequency in others. Amtrak routes do still crisscross the country from Seattle to San Diego, Sacramento to Chicago, and New Orleans to Boston, however. Several of these routes are legendary rail journeys such as the Sunset Limited between Orlando and Los Angeles or the City of New Orleans, running from that city to Chicago. There is a wide variety of passes which allow unlimited travel valid for 15- or 30-day periods and prices vary depending on time of travel and where you are travelling. At the top end, a 30-day North American pass (which includes Canada) costs $999 during peak times and $709 during the off-peak season. Travel agents can supply these passes and advise you on the availability of special tours. More information is also available at www.amtrak.com. Frequent users of the service may qualify for the Amtrak Guest Rewards Program which awards points to be redeemed for travel, car rental and hotels.

The following two outlets supply details and tickets: *International Rail*: (08700 841 140; www.international-rail.com) and *Trailfinders* (0845 050 5900; www.trailfinders.com). In the USA, call 1 800 872 7245 for 24-hour recorded timetable information and reservations. The Amtrak website www.amtrak.com offers a comprehensive means of researching routes and prices and you will also find details of special deals and rail passes allowing unlimited travel within set periods and regions of the country. The site enables you to apply for brochures that are also stocked by most travel agents.

Bus travel

Buses are the cheapest form of travel in America. Cynics believe that only the terminally poor – those able to afford neither car nor air travel – or students go by long-distance bus. However, when you climb aboard a Greyhound you'll see exactly what they mean by their slogan 'leave the driving to us'. Taking a bus can be a romantic experience, and it is also the cheapest way of getting around. Greyhound is the largest operator, offering the best fares and a comprehensive network serving practically every city in the country (although it does not serve areas within national parks). You are allowed one piece of luggage in the cabin, and it must be able to fit under the seat or in the overhead compartment. You can check in two pieces weighing a total of 100lbs (45kg) for $5 and an individual item may not weigh more than 50lbs (22kg).

Greyhound's UK distributor, STA Travel (0871 230 0400; www.statravel. co.uk) sells the Ameripass, which can be used with another 54 participating bus lines for periods of 7, 10, 15, 21, 30, 40 or 60 days. A seven-day adult pass in high season is $219, 15 days is $319, and 30 days, $419. These passes are available from Greyhound distributors worldwide and are more expensive if bought within the USA. Call 1 888 454 7277 within the US, or if dialling from another country call 212 971 0492. Further details are available from Greyhound Lines (1 800 231 2222; ifsr@greyhound. com; www.greyhound.com). Information on the North America Discovery Pass, for travel on both sides of the US/Canada border, can be found at www.discoverypass.com.

TIP

■ For information on other bus companies, *Russell's Official National Motor Coach Guide* has countrywide timetables and route information for all companies other than Greyhound. It is available at bookstores, libraries and online at www. worldcat.org.

Two other companies run coach tours across the USA. Tauck Tours (1 800 788 7885; info@tauck.com; www.tauck.com) is a high-class operation doing 'all expenses' tours in the USA and Canada, including helicopter and boat trips to the less accessible parts of Alaska, and steamboat excursions in Louisiana.

For a more 'alternative' and leisurely way of seeing the country, Green Tortoise, based in California, operates reconditioned buses – 'hostels on wheels' – complete with sofa seats, stereos and dinettes. All meals are communal. The journey from San Francisco to Boston takes 10–14 days and costs around $709, with an extra $181 for food. They also do 'loop' tours, which include days on the beach and kayaking, going to national parks, Baja California, the Grand Canyon and Alaska. Book a good two months in advance, at a regional office (see the *Yellow Pages* at www.yellow.com) or at *Green Tortoise Adventure Travel* (www.greentortoise.com).

City transport

Transport within cities usually consists of buses, subways (underground railways), taxis, and streetcars (or trams) in a few cities such as San Francisco and New Orleans. In some cities (notoriously, Los Angeles), public transport is limited and unreliable so a private car is recommended. Some southern cities are so hot that taking any public transportation apart from air-conditioned subways is out of the question.

The big cities, of course, have sophisticated subways, and commuter rail networks. Taxis are always common and good value compared to Europe: a 1.8-mile (3km) taxi ride in New York should cost around $12. Except in New York and Chicago, taxi-sharing is common, although each passenger has to pay the full fare. Don't be surprised if your taxi driver does not speak very good English (especially in New York, Los Angeles, Washington and other big cities) and doesn't know their way about very well: have a map handy to help them out. New York cabbies often live up to their reputation for being rude, obstreperous and surly, but don't let it disappoint you if

TIP

■ Getting around cities in the States is no more easy or difficult than in any foreign country: make sure that you go to the tourist office on arrival, or get a decent map, and don't stray into areas that you are not sure of, especially at night. If in doubt, always take a taxi and don't travel alone.

they are helpful, polite and charming. Indeed, the new millennium has seen an unprecedented rise in politeness among New Yorkers in general. This phenomenon is laid at the door of the amazingly popular ex-Mayor Rudy Giuliani, who first introduced zero tolerance policing, and then set out to clean up the manners of the most ill-mannered city in America.

Getting around cities

American cities are often laid out in a grid pattern, with numbered streets and the spaces between streets called 'blocks'. This makes orientation slightly easier, but you must be sure that you understand the address. Americans do not usually bother with putting 'street' when writing an address, so '5th and 18th' in Manhattan means the junction of 5th Avenue and 18th Street. You will normally be able to pinpoint a block by this method. Pay attention to compass points in an address. In Washington, D.C., for example, street addresses are followed by NW, NE, SW, or SE, which are essential to get to the right district and the right end of

what might be a very long street. Brooklyn (NY) addresses use 'E' and 'W' in a similar fashion.

Except for a few of the older cities with condensed centres, like Boston and New York, walking within major urban areas is unusual and may even prompt suspicion. Remember too that in cities like LA and Houston, which are essentially designed to accommodate the car, distances can be great and walking a 'couple of blocks' may take you on a prolonged hike for a mile or more. This may be inadvisable in extreme temperatures or in the dark.

▉ HEALTH

Much of the disparity in American healthcare is attributable to the structure of American medicine, which is an extremely profitable industry. Pharmaceutical companies turn over millions of dollars in the search for new and lucrative drugs, doctors are highly motivated and even more highly paid, and hospitals are the best equipped in the world. But litigation is common and as a consequence all medical practitioners and institutions must take out punitive insurance policies, the costs of which are then passed on to the patients.

Unfortunately it is not the case that within this sophisticated health industry, every citizen is guaranteed similar standards of care. There are two state healthcare schemes, Medicare (for those over 65 and the

FACT

▉ The United States has some of the most expensive healthcare in the world and is the only developed nation that does not have a full government-supported healthcare system.

The importance of insurance   *i*

Although you will never be refused admission to hospital or left on the street by an ambulance because you cannot produce a credit card, it is crucial that you are insured for medical expenses. If there's only one piece of sound advice about visiting or living in the US, it's that medical insurance is mandatory before you set foot on American soil unless you happen to be very wealthy. An unforeseen medical emergency could literally bankrupt you within days. Admission for hospital treatment may require a deposit of between $5,000 and $15,000. The daily costs of a bed alone will seem extortionate: a private room alone can be around $1,000 a day and medical treatment will be added on top. Hospitals sometimes pass debts on to debt collectors who may follow you back to your own country and demand payment on behalf of their client. A half hour visit to a doctor in an ER may cost $300 alone without any tests, or it could cost $60 to see a GP.

disabled), and Medicaid (for those below a certain income level). Anyone falling outside the categories of the elderly or the very poor must pay. Personal medical insurance ensuring the best treatment is confined to those who can afford to buy it from personal income or those lucky enough to be employed by companies willing to offer corporate membership of a medical insurance scheme. Loss of employment can often mean an entire family will lose its coverage overnight.

If you have any illness that requires regular drugs make sure that you take sufficient supplies with you. American pharmacists will not honour foreign prescriptions.

If you are sent out to the USA with a company, it is more than likely that medical insurance will be part of the package – check this with your personnel department. Students will be able to benefit from cheaper premiums for the under 25s and most colleges have a clinic or health centre, which will offer free advice and basic treatment. They do not run emergency units or out-of-hours services so it is a good idea to check which hospitals and emergency units they recommend.

Restrictions on entry

No vaccinations are required to enter the USA as a visitor or non-immigrant from any country. If you are entering the country as a permanent resident for the first time, you will be required to show evidence of a history of vaccinations at the mandatory medical examination in your home country. If you cannot prove you've had all the required vaccinations you are under obligation to obtain them before your immigrant visa will be issued. Green cards will not be granted to applicants already in the USA as refugees or aliens on immigrant visas if they are found to have HIV antibodies or AIDS (or any other communicable disease) at the required medical examination. Irrationally, and unjustly, temporary visitors with HIV are also denied entry unless they have received a waiver, despite the fact that hundreds of thousands of Americans already carry the virus. Possession on entry of the drugs for treating HIV and AIDS may be sufficient to prevent entry, although recent legislation is working towards changing this rule. If you are HIV positive you must currently apply for a waiver to accompany your visa and indicate that you are not suffering from symptoms of infection, that you have sufficient insurance to cover any medical expenses and also that the visit will not exceed 30 days.

Finding a doctor

The treatment that you are offered in the USA will be very different from what you are used to in Europe or Australasia, though there are some marked similarities. Family medicine is still common and 'primary care physicians' are often consulted as the first point of reference, particularly by patients in HMO plans (see below) or if a patient is not sure whether they need a specialist or not. Sometimes a specialist in internal medicine – an 'internist' – functions as the equivalent of a European GP or general doctor who may then refer a patient to a particular specialist. It's quite common, particularly within cities, to use several separate specialists, such as a gynaecologist, dermatologist, or an osteopath. A mother will often use a women's clinic and her children will go to children's clinics and so on. Most doctors never make home visits, although in the larger cities there will be special 'house-call' units that will send a doctor to your house for a fee of $100–$200.

The patient as a consumer

For those who can pay, the quality of medical care in the US is extremely high and the country has some of the best hospitals and medical research facilities in the world. It's not uncommon for doctors to have their own testing laboratories within their offices so the process of testing is much quicker. In the highly litigious atmosphere of the USA, a doctor's greatest fear is a malpractice suit and, as a result, he is unlikely to advise a couple of days in bed when you complain of headaches and dizziness. They will take samples and carry out a series of tests for the simplest ailment in order to determine exactly what is wrong. You will be encouraged to have blood and cholesterol tests on a routine basis. Preventative medicine is therefore a major feature of American healthcare.

In the USA, the patient is the consumer, and you can take your custom elsewhere if you are not satisfied with the treatment. Hospitals are advertised on hoardings, on the radio, on TV, in magazines and on supermarket trolleys. 'We will help you realise your dream birthing experience', promotes a radio advertisement for a New York hospital. As the consumer, you have the choice, and as with all free market systems, this can overwhelm you to the point where you simply feel confused. Nevertheless the best hospitals in American cities, as in Europe, tend to be teaching institutions attached to local universities.

A great advantage of being the customer in the health market is that doctors will always tell you exactly what they are doing and what they propose to do. You will never be left in the dark, or patronised by a doctor who does not feel it is necessary to let you in on the complexities of the treatment. Appointments are comparatively easy to schedule and the doctor can give each patient ample time.

TIP

■ The best way to find a doctor is to discover which ones in your local area are affiliated with your health insurance plan. Your plan provider will have a list on their website of doctors who accept payment from them, so it's wise to choose one from the list before you become unwell.

TIP

■ The magazine *US News* and *World Report* publishes an annual survey of hospitals ranked according to specialties, which is available at www. usnews.com.

At the end of a course of treatment or a stay in hospital you will be presented with an itemised bill. Fees are quite steep: around $300 for a consultation, $100 for a lab test, and $50 for antibiotics. Refer all bills to your insurance company before you pay them if the hospital has not done so automatically, and if you are paying for your own treatment, double check the bill: it is common for hospitals to make mistakes and you may find yourself paying for treatment that you have not had.

Emergencies

In the USA, the emergency number is 911. Calling this number will alert the police as well as an ambulance. Most cities also have private ambulance services which will cost between $50–$200, but which will probably come more quickly than the public ambulance. They might also be covered on your insurance. Hospitals have emergency rooms, which are the equivalent of a casualty or accident and emergency department in the UK. Ambulances are obliged by law to pick you up for treatment; any scare stories about car accident victims being left in the road to bleed because they can't produce a credit card are almost certainly untrue.

Minor complaints

For minor complaints, tests and diagnoses there are 'walk-in centers' or 'urgent care centers', usually located in town centres or shopping malls.

Payment is on the spot, though some will defer payment until a patient's insurance comes through, and an average visit can cost between $30 and $100, depending on the diagnosis and treatment.

Dental treatment

Dentistry is a sophisticated science in the USA. It is unlikely that you will suffer any pain at all and it is more than likely that your dentist will exclaim over the gaps in your teeth (American teeth, as well as American dentists, are the best in the world) and refer you on for cosmetic treatment with an orthodontist.

If you plan to stay in the USA for more than a year, have your teeth checked before you go and take a copy of your dental records with you. This will save you time and money if you have to go for treatment. In the same manner as choosing a doctor, use your health insurance provider's website to find local dentists in your area which will accept your particular insurance.

TIP

◼ If you elect not to buy health insurance, use the recommendations of neighbours and colleagues to find a good dentist.

Optical care

Finding and being treated by an ophthalmologist in the USA is a simple procedure, and shouldn't be too expensive. The first time you visit one you may have all manner of tests conducted on your eyes, even if you've

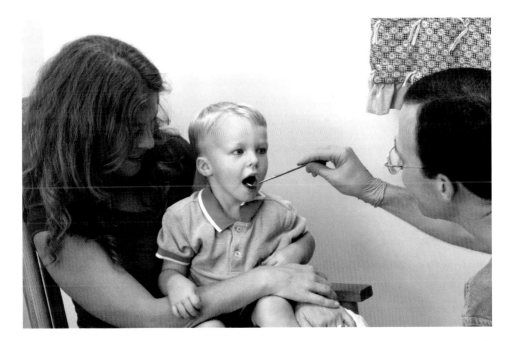

been wearing the same prescription, or none at all, for years. Opticians are likely to look at your eye pressure, examine you for colour blindness, test your long- and short-distance vision and may also dilate your pupils to check your retinas. If your prescription has changed or you just fancy new glasses or contact lenses, make sure your insurance policy will help to pay some of the costs. Contact lenses will usually be sent to you in bulk through the mail, and there are companies out there who will fill your lens prescription and send you a year's supply for a lot less money than your opthtalmologist. Once again, find an optician through your insurance company's website.

Group healthcare organisations

Health Maintenance Organisations (HMOs) are group benefit plans sponsored by a variety of different organisations ranging from the government to employers, hospitals and insurance companies. They can be independent or attached to a hospital, but they usually function quite separately, running their own clinics with independent doctors and nursing staff. They have grown over the last 15 years and now treat some 30 million patients a year. All medical costs are taken care of by a monthly subscription, generally much cheaper than conventional insurance premiums. While offering better value than individual insurance plans, HMOs generally offer more limited medical coverage. For example, you will have to choose a doctor from a more limited list of approved medical practitioners than an insurance company offers.

Preferred Provider Organisations (PPOs) are run on more or less the same lines, but are funded with greater collaboration between insurance companies and the medical profession to produce services at a better price. For contact information see the *'Useful Addresses' section*, below.

Insurance

Because of the costs of medical treatment in the USA, many European and Australasian insurance companies will not insure expatriates going out for a long period. Instead they advise you to get your insurance from a US company such as BlueCross or UK-based companies such as Expatriate Insurance Services Ltd or BUPA (whose addresses are also listed below) which specialise in expatriate insurance

It is not uncommon to find expatriates who decide to take the risk of having no insurance at all, weighing up the cost of treatment against the lifetime costs of an insurance policy. To reiterate, this is not a sensible course of action. American medical costs can be financially devastating. It is highly recommended you take out medical insurance during any stay in the USA. Planning for a medical emergency may seem unduly neurotic, but it only takes an accident while travelling or a case of severe food poisoning to send a 'healthy' person to hospital with all of the attendant costs.

> **Philip Jones stresses the importance
> of having healthcare insurance:**
>
> The one thing to be aware of is healthcare. We are fortunate enough
> to have health insurance and as a result our healthcare is excellent.
> However, many, many people don't have insurance. There is no
> universal coverage and should you not have insurance then you
> can be refused access to healthcare or be left with enormous bills. For
> anyone moving here, it is something to be aware of.

Costs

It's hard to outline a 'typical' policy because medical insurance is a complicated business. Costs vary according to a large range of factors, such as where you will be living, age, pre-existing conditions, number of children, and whether you are a smoker.

On a typical policy from a US insurance company, a couple aged between 25 and 34, with two children under 18, might pay $180 per month, with $34 extra for each child. The policy would have a $100 reserve, and costs of between $100 and $50,000 would be paid up to 80%. Costs of between $50,000 and $100,000 would be paid in full, and may in some circumstances stretch to a million dollars. Optional extras like maternity, dental or optical cover can be added too. There would be a $10,000 maximum evacuation payout (to get you back to your own country), which would kick in after five days in hospital.

There are companies who will insure students under the age of 26 for up to two years worldwide, fully comprehensive with upper limits in the millions. Adults travelling on non-student classification (not business) can also be insured. Endsleigh insurance (www.endsleigh.co.uk) offers very competitive quotes for worldwide travel, as does the Post Office in the UK (www.postoffice.co.uk) and www.travelinsuranceaustralia.com.au in Australia.

TIP

If you are going to be staying in the USA for six months or less it would be best to get a standard travel policy from an insurance company in your own country. They have the advantage of being cheaper, and have upper limits of around £2.5 million. However short your stay you should get a policy covering you for at least £15,000.

Things to look out for

When choosing an insurance policy you need to look out for certain conditions that apply to different policies. In particular you should look out for the following:

■ **Pre-existing conditions:** make sure that the policy defines this term. It can either mean the existence of a medical condition that has been treated, or simply a condition that has existed prior to taking out a policy. It becomes crucially important if you are unaware of such conditions as a heart murmur or ulcers. It is expensive to include pre-existing conditions in a policy, so look for policies with loose interpretations of the term.

- **Co-payment:** this is the reserve on a policy. Some policies pay out 70%–80% up to a certain amount and 100% thereafter. There may also be different co-payments for different medical conditions.
- **Specific limits:** some policies may specify dollar limits for certain conditions and ailments, and will only pay up to a certain amount.
- **Deductible:** Each year the policy holder might, for example, have to pay the initial $2,000 of costs before any reimbursement from the insurance company begins.
- **Exclusions:** Some policies exclude certain injuries, such as those incurred through dangerous sports.
- **Medical Evacuation:** J-1 exchange visas are required to have medical evacuation coverage. This will pay to have the insured transported home for treatment. It is rarely used and so is not an expensive addition to the policy.
- **Repatriation:** The policy pays to have the insured's remains transported home if they should die while in the USA. This is also a required benefit for J-1 visa holders.

Useful addresses

American Diabetes Association: 1701 North Beauregard Street, Alexandria, VA 22311; 1 800 342 2383; www.diabetes.org. Supplies ID cards with information on holder's condition and needs.

Centers for Medicare and Medicaid Services: *7500 Security Boulevard, Baltimore, MD 21244; 410-786 3000.*

International Association for Medical Assistance to Travelers (IAMAT): 1623 Military Road, Niagara Falls, NY 14304; 716 754 4883; info@iamat.org; www.iamat.org. Supplies free pamphlets, and a world directory of fixed-rate physicians. Membership is free, but donations are appreciated.

MedicAlert Foundation International: 2323 Colorado Avenue, Turlock, CA 95382; 209 668 3333; www.medicalert.org. For travellers with conditions such as weak hearts or diabetes, the MedicAlert Tag and membership costs $35 with $20 annual renewal fee, and gives information on the holder's condition in case of accidents.

Insurance companies

USA

BlueCross BlueShield Association: a countrywide network of health insurance organisations which are administered locally. Check www.bcbs.com for your local plan.

CNA: 1 800 437 8854; www.cna.com. Specialises in tailored insurance plans for students visiting the USA for studying purposes or for a cultural exchange.

International Medical Group (IMG): 317 655 4500 or 1 800 628 4664; insurance@imglobal.com; www.imglobal.com

UK

Atlas Insurance: 0870 811 1700; www.atlasdirect.net. An expert in travel insurance and works in partnership with American insurer CNA (see above).

Axa PPP Healthcare: 0870 608 0850; www.axappphealthcare.com

BUPA International: 01273 208181; www.bupa-intl.com

Columbus Travel Insurance: 0870 033 9988; @columbusdirect.com; www.columbusdirect.com

Endsleigh Insurance Services: 0800 028 3571; www.endsleigh.co.uk

Expacare: 01344 381650; info@expacare.com; www.expacare.net. Specialists in expatriate medical insurance.

Expatriate Insurance Services Ltd: 0700 340 1596 (UK), 1 800 341 8150 (US); info@expatriate-insurance.com; www.expatriate-insurance.com. Specialists in international health, travel and life insurance.

HMOs and PPOs

America's Health Insurance Plans: 202 778 3200; ahip@ahip.org; www.ahip.org. Represents companies providing health insurance coverage.

American Association of Preferred Provider Organizations: 502 403 1122; www.aappo.org

◼ SCHOOLS AND EDUCATION

The Structure of the education system

There is no federal government control over the education system in the United States, although legislature such as the No Child Left Behind Act do dictate certain regulations which must be abided by. Each state's department of education is controlled by an elected board and is divided into local areas. The public (state) schools system is funded by state and local governments, and receives only marginal funds from the federal government. The state board is responsible for setting educational policy and for deciding compulsory attendance ages, which in most states are between six and 16. Working within policies established at state level, school districts build schools, employ teachers, buy equipment, arrange dates of terms and holidays and generally oversee the daily operation of their schools.

Elementary and secondary education normally takes a child through school from the age of six to 18, moving up the system from Grade one to Grade 12. Most children, in fact, start their schooling at the age of five at kindergarten, where they learn basic numeracy and literacy. It is considered

TIP

◼ All elementary, junior high and high schools in America have a reputation in popular culture as being a place of cliques and divisions among the students. Children joining an American school from abroad may feel nervous about the experience if all they know of schooling in the USA is the geeks, jocks and cheerleader clichés. It is important to remember that the media portrays an exaggerated representation of the truth: schools in reality are far more likely to have children just like your own children's friends and they will probably find they fit in very quickly.

What should you expect from the school?

School lunches will probably be provided on-site, but lunchtimes will be very short, if the school has them at all. It is also becoming more popular to do away with any other form of break during the morning or afternoon, which you may need to warn your child about. In place of these breaktimes are after-school programmes, which range widely from sporting and musical activities to school productions and Knowledge Bowl leagues (an inter-school competition that is based on maths or general knowledge and is often associated with gifted students). In recent years funding for extracurricular activities has been dwindling, so schools will fundraise during the school year to pay for staff and resources to run these clubs. Don't be surprised, therefore, if a catalogue for frozen food arrives home with your child; proceeds from the sale of schemes such as this will keep their favourite activity alive for another year.

American schools don't generally have school uniforms, unless they are a private school, but there may be a dress code. Some schools, for example, have policies allowing only a single-coloured plain shirt and trousers, or they may not allow spaghetti straps on vests or tops which show a belly button. You may need to shop for clothes for school instead of reusing play clothes, but generally schools in the USA have a very informal dress code.

important for a child to attend kindergarten: entering Grade one without having done so can put a child at a disadvantage. Private nursery schools for four-year-olds have become very popular and day-care centres for pre-schoolers are also offering education-based learning for children as young as three months old.

Although it is legal to leave school at 16, in practice it is very uncommon. In most states those who have left school without completing Grade 12 would find it difficult to get a decently paid job. Proof of a high school diploma is often a requirement of employment, so adults do have the option of completing GED tests as an equivalent if they did not graduate from high school.

Grades K (kindergarten) to six are spent in elementary school, seven to nine in junior high or middle school, and the final grades, 10 to 12, in

senior high school. There are variations from state to state, but the system is more or less the same throughout the country.

Education in the state system is co-educational and comprehensive. Students are obliged to take a certain number of courses depending on their age and grade – courses are usually mathematics, English, health, physical education, general science and social science. Students specialise and choose extra subjects according to their individual interests and career choices, but unlike the UK system, for example, they do not specialise in those subjects only. Students in junior high and high school have to take compulsory subjects, but have the option of which type of topic within that subject they wish to study. In mathematics, for example, a student may choose calculus or applied mathematics; in science they might study biology or earth sciences. They will continue to meet subject requirements in this way until they finish high school. Some states also have graduation requirements where projects in certain classes must be completed: this ensures a wide range of subjects is taken. Minnesota is one such state, and students cannot finish high school if they have not completed and passed all the graduation requirement projects.

Students do not sit formal exams like GCSEs or A-levels, but are continually assessed throughout their 12 years of education. When they start in a school a folder is opened for them and they are given grades from A to F in each subject that they take, which depend on performance in tests that are set each term, homework, participation in class discussions, and so on. A new GPA (grade point average) is begun each year, and colleges will look at a high school senior's (12th grade) GPA as part of their selection process. GPAs are usually on a scale of 0.0–4.0, with 4.0 being a perfect score consisting of straight A grades. Naturally a GPA above 3.5 is very coveted, although anything above 2.0 is considered a good passing mark.

Upon graduation from high school, students are given a 'high school diploma'. Those who wish to go to university are assessed on a summary of their grades and also on the results of national college aptitude tests which are taken in the last two years of high school. These tests are designed to measure ability in verbal and mathematical skills and are not based on any specific course work. The most well-known of these are the Scholastic Aptitude Test (the SAT) and the Achievement Tests that are administered by the Educational Testing Service (609 921 9000; www.ets.org). It is possible to consult a database of tests on their website or, alternatively order them from there for student practice at home.

Foreign students

The procedure for foreign nationals to gain admission to the American public (that is, state) school system is fairly straightforward. If parents are studying, working, or on diplomatic service in the USA, then their children will be able to attend school on the basis of the parents' visas, without paying tuition fees.

A zoning system exists for public schools and children can usually only attend a school if it is in the area in which they live. Many parents, if they have the means, will make sure that they move to an area in which they like the schools. Children will be assigned to a school which will usually be the one nearest the home. Parents should enquire at the central office of the local school district for details of what documentation – such as records of immunisation and academic records – will be necessary. For many international students, a Hepatitis B inoculation will be mandatory, as well as a complete list of childhood vaccinations from your doctor.

The student's academic performance record is important and should be as detailed as possible as this will be used to place him or her in a suitable class. Worldwide Education Services provide grade translations for a fee at www.wes.org, although some countries are limited to only university-level transcripts on the website. As a general rule, UK grades A*-C at both GCSE and A-Level are equivalent to an American grade A at high school. It is important to find official documentation on this, however, as some high schools will only enter UK grades as they are listed without a transcript, meaning your child's GPA score will be much lower than it should be. If the student is planning to live with anyone other than his or her parents, an F-1 student visa is necessary. It is best to ask about visas in the US consulate in your home country, look online at www.internationalstudent.com, or apply through an international organisation such as The Rotary Club (www.rotary.org). Students whose ambition is to live and work in the USA can get a foretaste of life in the States through the Federation EIL programme, which offers homestays abroad with or without language courses, for individuals, couples and families (though not in the same home). There is also the US High School plus Homestay programme, which lasts for five months. Contact Experiment in International Living (details in the 'Useful Contacts' section below).

Parents should contact the school in question to see if it is eligible to meet visa requirements and admit foreign students. The school must be able to issue the form I-20 which must be used to apply for an F-1 visa.

Students attending a school on an F-1 visa can be charged for their tuition. This is up to the individual school and there is no central regulation (or any information available), so it is simply a matter of getting in touch with the school or education district in question and finding out what their policy is.

Foreign students and the private school system

American private schools are different from those in the UK, in that they have been established to fulfil a multitude of particular educational needs. There is no 'typical' private school: some will cater for a religious minority, some will be expressly for the purpose of pushing their pupils on to university, others will be for students with learning difficulties. There are schools devoted to pursuing creative or sporting talents as well as specialist academies for specific academic subjects; the list is endless.

Private school fees range from $20,000 to $27,000 per year for boarders and between $4,000 and $13,000 for day pupils, depending on whether the school is elementary, junior high or senior high, and whether it's religious or non-sectarian. The decision as to whether or not to send your child to private school is quite often based on the area you live in rather than personal (or political) choice. There are elite private schools – particularly in Connecticut and Massachusetts – but private education is not generally a question of elitism: some parents will meet the fees of a private day school because they consider that the public schools in their area are not safe. When considering a private school it is essential to examine the particular goals of the school to decide if they match with what you are after.

The application process for day and boarding private schools is much the same as for the public schools. You must first establish that the school is eligible to issue the form I-20, and then apply to the school itself for

TIP

■ Some students will arrive in the USA as foreign exchange visitors and may have to negotiate the school board's regulations by themselves. It is therefore imperative to equip your child with as much paperwork as you would take if you were accompanying them yourselves to live abroad. Take an official transcript of grade equivalences so they are ready to show the admissions counsellor – confusion over this has meant some students have been assigned lower grades than they should be.

The SSAT

Many private secondary schools require the SSAT, the Secondary Schools Admissions Test. This is administered by the Educational Testing Service and is held internationally in December and April. For more information and for application forms contact the Educational Advisory Service at the Fulbright Commission (020 7404 6880; programmes@fulbright.co.uk; www.fulbright.co.uk). It is advisable to begin the application process well in advance of the enrolment date in order to meet the school's application deadlines.

details of academic requirements. If your children are living with you as part of a parent's visa application an I-20 is probably not necessary. Check online at www.travel.state.gov if you are unsure.

The International Baccalaureate

If you are at secondary school in the USA but are planning to eventually return to Europe in order to go to university, it would be worth considering the International Baccalaureate (IB). This exam is designed to meet the university entrance requirements of most countries, and covers a broad range of subjects. It is taken in the final two years of secondary school, but you may have to study for it outside of normal lessons as it is not routinely offered in American schools.

For more information and a list of schools in the USA which offer the IB, contact the North America branch of the International Baccalaureate Organization (1 212 696 4494; ibna@ibo.org; www.ibo.org).

International schools

The European Council of International Schools (ECIS) is the oldest and largest of the associations that assess and grade international schools. The ECIS is responsible for school accreditation, teacher and executive recruitment, professional development, fellowships in international education, and entry into higher education. Most ECIS colleges in the USA prepare students for college or university on the basic US preparatory school programme, also teaching the standard UK GCSE, German Arbitur, French Baccalaureate, Swiss Maturité, and Spanish Bachillerato. More and more also do the International Baccalaureate.International. Schools are usually private, though ECIS members also include state schools. Instruction is given mainly in English, and the majority of students will be the children of US or British citizens.

The following schools are ECIS associate members. For further information, see the ECIS Directory of International Schools, or contact them direct (01730 268244(UK); 908 903 0552 (US); ecis@ecis.org; www.ecis.org).

Atlanta International School: 2890 North Fulton Drive, Atlanta, GA 30305; 404 841 3840; info@aischool.org; www.aischool.org. French, German and Spanish taught as second languages; 54 nationalities attend; co-educational (mixed sex).

Ecole Bilingue de Berkeley: 1009 Heinz Avenue, Berkeley, CA 94710; 510 549 3867; www.eb.org. French taught as a second language; 44 nationalities; co-ed.

The Masters School: 49 Clinton Avenue, Dobbs Ferry, NY 10522; 914 479 6400; info@themastersschool.com; www.themastersschool.com 14 nationalities; co-ed.

The Awty International School of Houston: 7455 Awty School Lane, Houston, TX 77055; 713 686 4850; www.awty.org. Arabic, English, French, German, Italian and Spanish taught as second languages; 35 nationalities (including 40% US, 30% French); co-ed.

Lycée Français de New York: 505 East 75th Street, New York, NY 10021; 212 369 1400; www.lfny.org

Lycée Français de Los Angeles: 3261 Overland Avenue, Los Angeles, CA 90034; 310 836 3464; www.lyceeonline.org

United Nations International School: 25-50 Franklin D Roosevelt Drive, New York, NY 10010; 212 684 7400; www.unis.org. Has a strong liberal arts tradition; 1450 students from 115 countries.

French-American International School: 150 Oak Street, San Francisco, CA 94102; 415 558 2000; www.frenchamericansf.org. 52 nationalities, mainly French; co-ed.

Washington International School: 3100 Macomb Street NW, Washington, DC 20008; 202 243 1815; admissions@wis.edu; www.wis.edu. French, Spanish and Dutch taught as a second language; other languages taken if necessary; co-ed; 80 nationalities.

Higher education

There are more than 3,000 universities and higher education colleges in the USA, many of them internationally renowned. The best-known are the Ivy League schools, which include the most famous names in American higher education: Brown, Columbia, Cornell, Dartmouth, Harvard, Pennsylvania, Princeton, and Yale. The term 'Ivy League' was first used by a sports writer to describe a sports league restricted to the eight oldest universities in the country plus the army and navy who formed their own sports league, and it simply alludes to the college buildings covered in ivy. These prestigious 'schools' have their own entrance requirements, but others – like the University of California at Los Angeles (UCLA) – and

TIP

 For details of 2,790 institutions in the USA that actively seek applicants from other countries see the *College and University Almanac* which is published by Peterson's in the US (www.petersons.com).

the Massachusetts Institute of Technology (MIT) also have excellent international reputations.

Each state administers its own university system, and each has an official state university and a number of private universities. Bachelor degrees are either four years (the standard BA, BSc), or two years (an Associate degree, after which it is possible to then move on to a four-year degree, described in the relevant section below). Masters degrees tend to be part-time for two years and PhDs can range anywhere from three to seven years, depending on whether you plan on obtaining a masters en-route.

American students tend to go to college near their hometown, or at least in their home state. Although this is of course not compulsory, the size of the USA and the difference in cultures across the country means that it is unusual to find students at university far from their home. In-state tuition is usually a third or a quarter of the cost of out-of-state, although some clusters of states offer in-state prices to students from any of its members. The five state area in the Midwest, for example, consist of North Dakota, South Dakota, Minnesota, Iowa and Wisconsin, and students can receive in-state tuition prices to any college in any of those states providing they

Knox College, Illinois

are a resident of at least one and not a visitor. It is certainly not uncommon to travel up to eight hours from home to attend college, but most students are from the same state.

An American degree is much more general than a UK degree. In the USA, a degree consists of a four-year programme of four courses taken simultaneously: a major, concentrated field of study, general education courses in a wide range of subjects, supporting courses for the subject majored in, and 'electives', which are chosen areas of particular interest to the student. Students tend to take compulsory courses in a similar manner to high school for the first two years, and declare a major before their third 'Junior' year. After this point, and for the next two years, they specialise in only that area.

Law and medicine cannot be studied at undergraduate level in the USA: these subjects must be taken at graduate school.

Foreigners at American universities

American colleges expect you to have qualifications that would admit you to higher education in your own country. Students from the UK should have at least two or three good A levels and between five and eight GCSEs in academic subjects. It is usually also necessary to sit the Scholastic Aptitude Test (SAT), which is held in Britain every year in October, November, December, January, April, May and June. American universities require SAT 1 and possibly up to 3 SAT II's. The SAT is administered by the College Board (www.collegeboard.com) and students can go to this site, register for the test, choose the date they want to sit it, and pay online. The official SAT test prep book (as well as more information on the test) is available from the Fulbright Commission's Educational Advisory Service, which offers advice and scholarships to UK students. For more detailed information you can read *Applying to Colleges and Universities in the United States* (2008) (www.petersons.com).

Financial costs and aid

State universities do not give financial aid to students though private colleges sometimes give partial scholarships. It is extremely common to take out a student loan to cover tuition, books and living expenses, although the repayment terms can be quite expensive for non-residents. A list of colleges giving substantial financial aid is contained in *Scholarships for Study in the USA and Canada* (Petersons 2007). The Fulbright Commission's Education Advisory Service can also supply *Study Abroad* (UNESCO 1999), or it can be purchased at www.portal.unesco.org

Tuition fees vary widely in the USA: generally, fees for state universities range from $6,000 to $15,000, and for private universities from $13,000 to $23,000, depending on whether the student is from inside or outside of the state. Remember you will need to provide for living expenses and course

TIP

■ A useful starting point is www.studyusa.com, which is aimed at foreign students and publishes a section called 'Financing Your Education'.

Forms of assessment

As in the secondary education system, assessment is continuous, and each course (or 'class') per term is awarded a number of credits that go towards making up the final degree. GPAs continue to be important at college level and, unlike in most foreign universities, grades are awarded for classes instead of a numerical mark. In terms of grade equivalencies, it is not until the third year of an American college that students study at the same level of difficulty as many of the international universities. Foreign students may, therefore, wish to choose the more difficult 300- or 400-level classes instead of the more popular level 100s which are routinely offered to new students. A UK 2:1 degree is equivalent to about an A- or a B in the States, or a GPA of about 3.6.

materials too. As a foreigner you will probably not be able to get financial aid from the state unless you have become a permanent resident.

Living costs also vary from state to state. They are highest in the big cities in the north-east and in California. You should expect to meet living expenses of between $8,000 and $15,000 per academic year, unless you live at home.

Which college?

It is advisable to start thinking about which colleges you would like to apply to at least 18 months before you want to enrol. It is also essential to meet the various deadlines for fees, financial aid and other parts of the application process. There is no clearing system in the USA and a missed deadline could mean having to wait another year to enrol.

When choosing a college, some of the things that you need to take into account are the location and size of the university – do you want to be in the centre of New York or in Mississippi; on a state university campus with thousands of new intakes each year, or in a small private liberal arts college? Of course, you also need to be sure that you can meet the costs, and that the university offers exactly the subjects that you want to study.

 A comprehensive list of all academic universities in the USA is available on the University of Texas' website at www.utexas.edu, and includes links to all their websites.

The SAT tests should be taken before you begin applying. You should first find out the application deadlines of the colleges of your choice, then contact the Fulbright Commission for information on taking the tests.

A timetable for applications would run roughly as follows: you should send off for application forms and prospectuses 12 months before enrolment – probably in August. By the autumn of the year before enrolment you should have submitted the completed application forms. Letters of rejection or acceptance will arrive in the following January. Finances can be sorted out in the months which follow, visas can be arranged, and final arrangements made to set off at the end of the summer.

It is impossible to give here all the information necessary for applying to an American college. The Fulbright Commission has an Educational Advisory Service which provides comprehensive information on all aspects of education in the USA and details can be found at www.fulbright.co.uk. The Commission have qualified advisors and a comprehensive reference library with information on all aspects of the American secondary and higher education system. They also organise lectures and information sessions which you could attend. A useful publication is the annual *College and University Almanac* (2009) (see www.petersons.com)

Athletic scholarships

Many colleges offer scholarships to students who are gifted in a particular sport. There is usually an upper age limit of 25, with other restrictions being that postgraduate students are not eligible and students must fulfil the normal entry requirements of the college. There is a UK placement service called College Prospects of America (www.cpoa.com) which will put together a résumé of your sporting achievements and send them to US colleges. The alternative is to contact colleges directly. A useful publication is *Sports Scholarships and Athletic Programs in the USA* (2004) (available from www.petersons.com) which not only lists thousands of scholarships worth millions of dollars, but also gives the names of individual coaches for specific sports at more than 1,000 US colleges. Expert advice on how to apply is also given.

Two-year colleges

Community, Technical and Junior Colleges – called two-year colleges because of the length of their courses – offer Associate Degrees in arts, science or applied science. These can be used as a basis for entering university in the third year of a four-year course, although this option is not always open to foreigners. There are about 1,500 two-year colleges and they are becoming more popular because of their reasonable fees; they are state and locally supported and tuition can be less than $3,000 per year. In order to enter, UK students should have completed their A-Levels and have passes in GCSE English and Maths; some colleges also require students to sit the SATS. American students normally live at home and commute when attending two-year colleges, and there are opportunities for foreign students to arrange home-stay with families on a term-by-term basis. Contact the Fulbright Commission for details.

Tuition Fees

Below is a list of 20 of the largest four-year colleges and their yearly undergraduate tuition fees for out-of-state residents (for state-run universities):

University of Austin, Texas	$14,254	www.utexas.edu
Ohio State University, Columbus	$21,285	www.osu.edu
Texas A&M University	$22,274	www.tamus.edu
Penn State University, Pennsylvania	$23,152	www.psu.edu
Arizona State University	$15,096	www.asu.edu
University of Florida	$17,150	www.ufl.edu
Michigan State University	$22,260	www.msu.edu
University of Illinois, Urbana	$22,526	www.uiuc.edu
University of Wisconsin, Madison	$21,438	www.wisc.edu
Purdue University, Indiana	$14,198	www.purdue.edu
University of Michigan	$16,655	www.umich.edu
University of California, Los Angeles	$27,066	www.universityofcalifornia.edu
University of Washington, Washington	$22,131	www.washington.edu
University of Minnesota, Twin Cities	$19,580	www.umn.edu
Indiana University, Bloomington	$22,316	www.indiana.edu
University of Arizona	$18,676	www.arzona.edu
San Diego State University, California	$10,578	www.sdsu.edu
New York University, New York	$35,230	www.nyu.edu
University of Maryland, College Park	$22,206	www.umd.edu
University of Kentucky, Kentucky	$15,094	www.uky.edu

Useful contacts

The Fulbright Commission: Educational Advisory Service, Fulbright House, 62 Doughty Street, London WC1N 2LS; 020 7404 6880; programmes@fulbright.co.uk; www.fulbright.co.uk

Experiment in International Living (EIL): 287 Worcester Road, Malvern, Worcestershire WR14 1AB; 0168 456 2577; info@eiluk.org; www.experiment.org

International Baccalaureate Organization North America: 475 Riverside Drive, 16th Floor, New York, NY 10115; 212 696 4464; ibna@ibo.org; www.ibo.org

ECIS: 21B Lavant Street, Petersfield, Hampshire GU32 3EL; 01730 268244; ecis@ecis.org; www.ecis.org

College Prospects of America Inc.: PO Box 269, Logan, OH 43138; 740 385 6624; homeoffice@cpoa.com; www.cpoa.com. This is an organisation dedicated to placing talented athletes in college and finding scholarships.

◼ CRIME AND THE POLICE

The bald statistics on crime in the USA are uncompromising. The most recent FBI report on crime comments that 20% of US citizens rate crime as the most serious problem in the country. The homicide rate is now seven times that of Canada and more than 20 times that of Germany; homicide is the third most common cause of death amongst elementary and middle school children and schools in many cities have airport-style X-ray screening to prevent pupils bringing weapons into class; 32 people per 1,000 households are likely to be the victims of violent crime in an average year.

The Clinton administration tried to pass a number of laws to deal with the problem between 1992 and 2000, but had to steer a complicated path between the Right, who were calling for more punishment and more executions, and the Left, who wanted rehabilitation and prevention. At the centre of the continuing debate is the gun lobby, which, in the form of the National Rifle Association (NRA) is a powerful political force with a large membership. The right to bear arms is a freedom enshrined in the constitution as a legacy of the Revolutionary militias created by local communities to resist British rule. It is a right cherished by many Americans but seen as baffling by many other nations where regulation of firearms is perceived as a logical attempt to protect the public. The debate over controlling weapons is frequently conducted in congress and during presidential elections.

FACT

◼ A child is 15 times more likely to die of gunfire in the USA today than in Northern Ireland at the height of the Troubles.

Gun crime

It is indisputable that President George Bush was far less inclined to propose or support gun control before Clinton's administration. Instead, he favoured stronger penalties against criminals. When he was governor of Texas he supported the state's highly controversial law that allows residents to carry concealed guns, ostensibly for protection. In other states, guns are licensed to be kept in the home for self-defence and must be locked up when not in use. To complicate matters, states each pass their own firearm laws in addition to federal regulation. Certainly the NRA favoured President George W. Bush in his 2000 presidential campaign, spending $10 million in advertising and political donations to defeat his opponent, Al Gore.

The crime bill passed in 1994 banned the manufacture and sale of guns classed as assault weapons – that is, semi-automatic rifles like AK47's. But observers say that as 83% of violent crime involves handguns, which are not touched by the law, it had limited effect. For all the power of the gun lobby, there are signs that Americans are getting sick of the ubiquity of firearms in their society. The terrible spate of playground and mass public shootings in recent years when schoolchildren brought weapons of war to the classroom (not by any means an exclusively American phenomenon), has woken many people up to the fact that guns mean less rather than more freedom.

Other new government measures to deal with gun crime include millions of dollars being spent on more police. However, as the most violent cities (Detroit and Washington) already have huge police forces, that does not seem to be the answer either. Some gun regulations in recent years have attempted to limit the availability of guns to felons and convicts, although in practice this has had little effect. There is also a 'cool-down' period during the sale of a gun, whereby a customer has to wait for a background check to be completed before they can leave the shop with gun in hand. The time delay varies from state to state, but for most it is at least 24 hours.

The most violent and crime-ridden cities are often not the ones that foreigners would go to: Odessa, Texas, is more dangerous than Miami or New York City, for example, and these cities actually often feel quite safe, owing to the fact that – almost unlike anywhere else in the world – the city is open for business around the clock. In Manhattan, you will frequently see people walking on the streets at four in the morning and you will pass shops and restaurants that have been open all night. But in other, newer cities that were largely planned with cars in mind, middle-class professionals have frequently left 'downtown' for the suburbs. A new trend too is for developers to build and maintain 'gated communities' whereby all visitors have to enter through a permanent security post.

FACT

▪ Recently, municipalities and crime victim groups have begun lawsuits to place responsibility for gun crime on the manufacturers. On their part, the gun makers have frequently counter-sued, arguing that their opponents are trying to interfere with free enterprise.

How afraid should you be?

For a great number of its citizens America is a dangerous place to live, more so than many other countries in the world. Many cities are still plagued by high rates of violent crime, often caused by turf wars among drug dealers or gangs. Having said that, it's important to keep this in perspective. Not all cities share the same crime rates, and urban neighbourhoods in the USA vary as much as they do in the rest of the world.

Some cities have gained from urban renewal and improved policing. Most notably, New York has famously experienced a dramatic decline in violent crime over the past decades. Some commentators have attributed this to higher police numbers and former Mayor Guiliani's policy of 'zero tolerance'. But this approach to urban policing remains controversial. New York police during this time have often been accused of brutality, particularly against minorities, and there have been several instances of individuals being inexplicably gunned down or seriously injured in custody.

Most murders happen within the family or within groups that know each other. They also happen in areas that it is not easy to stray into by mistake. There are parts of every city in which it is dangerous to walk, and it is a relatively simple matter to find out what those parts are. This does not mean that you have to be paranoid: the New York subway is marginally less populated at night but precisely because it operates a 24-hour service, you need never be alone on a station platform or in a carriage.

Listen to what people tell you about an area. A park might look charming and tranquil, but if the guidebook or a local tells you that it is unsafe, take their advice. It will take a long time to get to know an area well enough to make your own decisions. When driving, do not allow anyone except a policeman to flag you down. In cities, keep all car doors locked.

The most likely thing that will happen to you, if you do not take proper precautions, is that you will fall victim to a pick-pocket or bag-snatcher. The way to avoid this is to use your common sense: don't let your handbag swing ostentatiously on your shoulder, don't count your money in public and don't look too much like a tourist, ambling around appearing lost and wearing a camera around your neck! Those most likely to be robbed or mugged are those who appear vulnerable: don't stop on the street to peer at a map, or hurry along in a panic. Walk with purpose.

An increasingly popular movement across America is BAMM, which stands for Bay Area Model Mugging (www.bamm.org). Started in California,

TIP

■ You will always find the same advice on how to limit the dangers of mugging. In short: always carry $50–$100 'mugger money'; if threatened, don't try to resist or make sudden movements – your attacker will be extremely wound up and will not hesitate to use their weapon if panicked; direct their hand to your wallet or purse; stay absolutely still until you are sure they have gone; flag down a cab and go straight to a police station; collect the number of the police report to facilitate your insurance claim, and ask for a lift home.

it is an organisation which teaches women full-contact self defence against attacks, going against the prevalent myth that women are generally too weak to withstand a male attacker. You are taught not only how to fight back, but also how to observe your environment, prevent negative encounters, use your voice to attract attention, and gauge the weaknesses of your attacker. In short, you are taught how not to be – or seem to be – a victim.

The police

There are four main law enforcement agencies in the USA: city police, state police, the National Guard and the Federal Bureau of Investigation (the FBI, or 'Feds'). The state police (also known as state troopers) operate the highway patrol while the National Guard are civilian reservists who are called up to deal with civil disturbances (one-time Vice President Dan Quayle was, notoriously, a member of the National Guard during the Vietnam war, which some say was a form of draft dodging). The FBI deals with major crime and offences across state borders.

You are most likely to come into contact with the city police if you are mugged, or if you are caught jaywalking (crossing the road on a 'Don't Walk' signal). The state police are responsible if you break down, or are caught speeding. Needless to say, the police will not accept ignorance of the law in mitigation of a traffic violation or other misdemeanour. The law varies from state to state and from city to city, and it is important to be familiar with any peculiarities of the area you are living in. In some very popular tourist towns, special laws are reactivated every summer in order to cope with the artificially high population: you might find yourself up against summer drinking laws, or laws covering large gatherings, without realising it.

■ SOCIAL LIFE

There is nothing typical about America or Americans. The sheer size and diversity of the continent's 50 states make it difficult to draw any conclusions, and generalisations are always misleading.

Everything about America is unexpected, the more so to European or Australian eyes even though they have been brought up on a diet of Americana – films, TV, Marvel comics, fast food. They expect to understand and to recognise, so are all the more surprised when nothing is as they thought.

People from Britain, in particular, do not expect America to seem foreign, yet it is. Everybody speaks English, and the assumption is made that with the common tongue comes all the rest: people must think the same because they speak the same. One of the great delights of travelling in America is that you are always surprised when you expect not to be. You might think of San Francisco and immediately picture roller-coaster streets, clapboard houses and trams ... Dallas? No problem – oil wells and bootlace ties, steer horns on the fender and a gun rack in the cab, and as for New York, well that's easy – subways and cops, foul-mouthed cabbies and Huggy Bear on every corner...

The fact that all this actually exists delights the traveller, but what is really interesting is the fact that America is more more than that. If we think we know America we do not know the reality of it: the size of the country, the smells, the variety of the people. You realise you are in another country as soon as you step off the plane, but it is brought home to you with a jolt when you order a glass of water in a Pizza Hut in LA, and the waitress says 'What?' 'Er, water please' you repeat, at which she looks at you with scorn and incomprehension. Only after several repetitions do you understand that you must pronounce it 'wahder'. Without the hint of a smile she turns her back as you run a nervous finger under your collar and come face-to-face with the barriers of a common language.

Los Angeles, a vast conurbation of 9.9 million people, is spread out in a series of satellite communities, connected by 750 miles (1,207km) of freeway, in a 70-mile (112-km) wide basin between the Pacific and the mountains. The city basks in an almost constant temperature of 68°F (20°C). New York, by contrast, is more familiar. The climate is harsh in

America is more like a world than a country.
Martin Amis

winter and steamy in summer, but at least it changes. The city has a subway, and its people move around on foot. The country around New York, with its wooded hills and gorgeous autumn colours, is similar to a lot of Britain.

Between these two ends of the country lies a world. If you drive from the west coast to the east you pass through four time zones, and cover nearly 3,000 miles (4,828km). You may drive for hundreds of miles without seeing another car, and come across towns that are separated from their neighbours by a three-hour drive. Within this continent live people as diverse as the Texans, who still fly the confederate flag and call themselves the Lone Star State, liking to think that they are not quite a part of the union, and the Amish of Pennsylvania, who shun the 20th century in all its forms.

To attempt to describe the social life or customs of such a continent is difficult. Besides, there are several books on the subject already. There are, however, at least some generalisations which will at the very least give you a flavour of the country.

Manners, customs and social attitudes

America is a nation of immigrants. Vast numbers of Americans arrived – and are still arriving – as refugees, 'huddled masses yearning to be free'. Many, even those of the second, third and fourth generation, feel rootless. As a result, when they set foot in a new environment they make themselves at home as quickly as possible. In every town there is a civil society or social club of some sort: the Rotary, Kiwis, Elks, Lions, Jaycees, parent-teachers association, Junior League, Garden Club, Shriners.... the list is endless. These (especially the last one) are often an excuse for men to get together, throw bread at each other in restaurants, and play silly practical jokes. However, they are also ready-made societies that are instantly recognisable. In a new town you are unlikely to be lonely, with so many formal and informal organisations ready to welcome you.

There are two conflicting sides to the American character: on the one hand they are fiercely individualistic, but on the other they place great value on being a team player. To Americans the British are stuffy, tweedy, and too polite, but they themselves have rigid sets of rules. They mock the laid-back approach to life Australians and New Zealanders are famous for, but themselves like nothing better than a barbeque on the beach and drinking beer at a baseball game. One of the great myths about Americans is that they do not stand on ceremony, unlike the British, who are obsessed with protocol. Americans, however, can be very formal. You may go to a dinner party and find that your neighbour quietly stops you in mid-flow because the host is saying something and it is rude to talk at the same time. You may go to a party in California and find that although everybody is slowly getting drunk on watery beer, when you light a cigarette, it is regarded as the height of bad manners. Always expect the unexpected, and take your cue from what others are doing.

Americans have a reputation for spontaneity and openness. An English couple at a party in New York said that they were going to New England to see the fall, and were amazed when another couple whom they did not know offered them their house to stay in. They did stay there, and it transformed their holiday. To meet people as friendly as that is common, but it is equally common to meet the reverse side of that particular coin, and to assume that because everybody addresses you as an old friend they can be called upon to behave that way.

◼ FOOD AND DRINK

Apple pie, clam chowder, Louisiana gumbo, jambalaya, enchiladas, barbecued oysters, corn fritters, strawberry shortcake and pastrami, or beefburgers, Coca Cola and thick shakes. Every regional delicacy in the USA has its alter ego: for all the bland, mass-produced, cholesterol-rich quickie snacks there is also an abundance of delicious dishes that 200 years of immigration have contributed to the country.

The American palate is not very brave, and it is fair to say that everyday food tends to be tasteless and/or sweet. It is actually possible to be served M&Ms as an appetiser, and huge and sickly desserts are common. For all this there is a grand tradition of American food. In a country which

TIP

◼ When dealing with American manners, remember that the shared language might lead you to take things for granted that you would not do if you were in France or Germany.

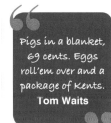

Pigs in a blanket, 69 cents. Eggs roll 'em over and a package of Kents.
Tom Waits

Local delicacies ℹ

In much of Europe, and especially in Britain, the tradition of sampling local delicacies has been lost. But this is truly one of the joys of a trip through America. The gumbo (okra soup) that you get in Louisiana really is the best, and the New England clam chowder is a reflection of the region's outstanding seafood. Cal-Mex and Tex-Mex are hybrids of American produce and traditional Mexican cooking which is much spicier than the usual American diet. It is possible to eat well in the restaurants of large cities as increasing affluence has prompted an interest in cookery from around the world, and hybrid foods from different cultures are popular menu choices. Other areas of the country specialise in local produce, such as Midwestern green-bean casserole or Southern baked-beans with brown sugar and bacon.

Tex-Mex food is popular in the USA, although it only vaguely resembles traditional Mexican cooking

is populated by Irish, Poles, Jews, Germans, Ukrainians, Chinese, French, Japanese, Thais, Vietnamese, Mexicans, English, Indians, Russians (and so on until you have named just about every nation on earth), diversity in dishes could be expected. Wherever you go in the USA you will find regional dishes.

Many scientists believe there is more obesity in America than in any other nation because of a genetic imbalance, but it could also be because of the amount they eat. In a restaurant, it is impossible to order a small portion. If, wishing to take the edge off your hunger, you order the small salad, you can be sure that it will come garnished with croutons the size of bread rolls, a large tub of fat-laden dressing, whole quarters of watermelon and an entire lettuce. French bread rolls are aptly called 'submarines'.

Typically, American meals are straightforward. Breakfast consists of either a doughnut or cereal and a cup of coffee, lunch of a sandwich, and supper of meat and two veg. Eateries and diners line every strip of highway from New York to San Francisco and it's nigh on impossible not to find something you like. There are 'family restaurants' which – predictably

– cater for whole families, and in every state the restaurants serve the local cuisine. In the Midwest and Texas beef features prominently, and fish and seafood can be found in towns along the coastlines of Florida, Louisiana, New England and California. In the south, soul food – grits, cornbread, beans – can be delicious. Mexican restaurants are ubiquitous, as are Chinese, Thai and Italian. In contrast to much of Europe, Indian food (that is, from the subcontinent) is quite hard to come by, although it's slowly becoming more commonplace.

Tipping

Rightly or wrongly, waiting staff depend on tips for much of their earnings. You should always tip at least 10%–15% in an American restaurant, and if the service is particularly good, then 20%. If you under-tip, it is possible that the waiter will ask, quite politely, if there was any problem with the meal, or you may run the risk of not receiving excellent service the next time you eat at the same restaurant. On the whole, however, service in restaurants far exceeds that of Europe. The USA

Unbeatable breakfasts

There is one culinary tradition that is done so well that to miss it is to miss one of the greatest pleasures that the country can offer. Ask an American expatriate what they miss most about living abroad, and they will talk about waffles, and maple syrup, and eggs roll'em over, and grits, and sourdough bread. Brunch is a great American tradition, a breakfast usually taken late in the morning on a weekend and so vast that lunch is unnecessary. Many restaurants and hotels will serve brunch, encompassing elaborate buffets of cereals, fruit, eggs, meats, and pancakes. Americans will try to make you understand, with the peculiar pride that people have in the seemingly trivial old traditions, that their breakfast cannot be beaten. It is true.

has cultivated a culture of service and a mantra stating 'the customer is king'. It's rare to meet a surly waiter or waitress who exudes resentment. In most diners, for example, you'll meet an effusively sunny Cheryl or Diane (names are often worn on badges) who greets you like a long-lost friend. They really work for their tip and they depend upon them. It's important to reward their efforts, particularly if you are going to be living in that community and plan to be a regular customer. In New York State, local sales tax (includes state and municipality levies) is 8.5% and diners simply double the tax (it is usually the last figure on a bill before the final sum).

Alcohol

Roadside bars are exciting: dark and forbidding, with one or two truckers sitting morosely at the end of a long bar, a pool table, and a person serving who is, at best, suspicious and at worst, hostile. If you go into one on a bright day you walk into darkness, and peer about for a while before you locate the bar. They are everything we expect from America but the beer (and don't share these feelings with the barman) is typically weak: Coors, Miller or Budweiser, and brewed locally. A new development is the microbrewery, or brewpub, where the beer is brewed on the premises and is often excellent.

If you are under 21, you cannot drink in bars in America. Bar staff work by the rule of thumb that you must *look* at least 25 if they are going to serve you without an ID, and some bars and restaurants have signs saying 'we card everyone $39\frac{1}{2}$ and under'. If you look young then you should

TIP

■ As a general rule, bars may open some time between 9am and noon, and will close between midnight and 3am. In many states you will find the sale of alcohol is forbidden on Sundays.

take identification with you whenever you go out, the best forms being your original passport or driving licence. A photocopy of your passport is often not sufficient, as bars are used to underage drinkers trying to pass off photocopies of their siblings' ID cards as their own.

Liquor laws vary from state to state, and affect such things as when and where you can drink or buy alcohol. In some states, mostly in the south and south-west, different counties have different policies: you may find that one county is dry or alcohol-free while the bars in the neighbouring county are raucous. Alcohol is completely banned on many Native American reserves.

The neighbourhood pub hardly exists in America, except in places like California and Florida where British or Australian expats live, and pubs with names like 'The Cock and Bull' cater for their nostalgic yearnings. Instead there is a multitude of bars that are either seedy or romantic, according to your state of mind. There will almost always be a pinball machine, and a pool table. They can be very lively places, with a good mix of different types of people (although the men usually outnumber the women by a large margin). There are also cocktail lounges, which are much more genteel affairs: your drink will be put on a little paper doily and the conversation, and music, is muted. You will be served by a waiter who you will pay when you leave, and a tip will be expected. Singles bars are a variation on the same theme: Americans tend to be more open about their relationships than Europeans, and consequently frequent such places in a much more phlegmatic frame of mind. There are plenty of bars and clubs in cities and college towns, and if you are a young person over the age of 21, the experience of going out on a Saturday night need be no different from in your home country.

In bars and restaurants beer is sold by either the glass, can or bottle in 12 fl. oz measures. It usually costs around $2.50, though this depends, naturally, on whether you're stopping in a roadside saloon or in a swanky Manhattan cocktail lounge. In most bars you can also buy a pitcher of draught beer, considerably cheaper than buying by the glass. Spirits are sold in measures which are approximately double the English optic measure, for around $2 or $3. The most popular whisky is Bourbon (Jack Daniels, Jim Beam or Wild Turkey), but scotch can be found in most places. The best scotch and malt whiskies (like Johnnie Walker Black Label, or Glenfiddich), can be twice as expensive as they are in Europe. Vodka and gin are also popular, as are rum and alcopops.

TIP

When you are drinking spirits, it is best to bear in mind that American spirits are generally much stronger than they are in the UK (80% or 90% proof rather than 70%).

◼ TAXATION

As a general rule, all non US citizens (foreign nationals) living, working or investing in the USA are subject to federal, state or local taxes. How much you are taxed as a foreign national depends on your status as a resident alien or non-resident alien: this is discussed further below.

The basic federal revenue law is the Internal Revenue Code, which deals with the collection of income taxes, estate and gift taxes, employment taxes and excise taxes. There is no VAT in the USA but states levy their own sales taxes at varying rates.

Federal taxes are administered by the Internal Revenue Service (the IRS), which is a government agency of the Department of Treasury. In addition to federal taxes, states and municipalities can also levy taxes, which can sometimes be fairly severe, although they are seldom above the level of federal taxes. Seven of the states do not require anyone to pay income tax and these are Alaska, Florida, Nevada, South Dakota, Texas, Washington and Wyoming. New Hampshire and Tennessee only levy a tax on dividends and interest income. Most charge up to 10% on income.

Income tax

As states and the federal government assess income taxes differently, if you are earning income you must file an income tax return on Form 1040, on or before 15 April: the tax year is 1 January to 31 December. Paying income tax, whether you are a permanent resident or not, is of crucial importance. US residents are taxed on their worldwide earnings, while non-residents are taxed on what they earn in the USA only. The income tax threshold (personal exemption) is $3,500, and taxes deducted from those earning less than that sum will be refunded. On top of that, couples or single persons can claim a standard deduction. In 2007 the standard deduction for a single person was $5,150. A portion of earnings is also subject to withholding taxes (which refers to the employer's responsibility in deducting the tax from your earnings) and you will be required to fill in a form W2 for federal withholding and a similar form for state and municipal withholding. State income tax is filed on a different form in each state and the forms will be available from the state tax office or the post office. Taxes can also be filed electronically for free if your gross income is below $54,000, or at a small cost if it is above this threshold.

> Filing electronically is now the most popular way to file your taxes in the USA, and details on how to do this can be obtained at www.irs.gov.

There are various tax treaties which have been set up with other countries (including the UK and Australia) which are designed to safeguard an individual or company against paying some taxes twice. A dual citizen of the UK or Australia and the US might be liable to tax on earnings in both countries. A Totalization Agreement assists with this and serves the same purpose in the case of social security payments, ensuring that people who

FACT

■ Student scholarships are liable for 14% federal taxation on living expenses but are tax exempt if used on tuition expenses. They are also subject to state tax. Non-resident aliens are taxed on all income derived from US sources. The statutory rate is 30% but this can be reduced by tax treaty.

earn an income in more than one country do not end up making social security or national insurance payments twice. Visit the Social Security Administration's website at www.ssa.gov for more information.

Green card holders, and those who have what is called a 'substantial presence' in the USA are taxed as US residents. 'Substantial presence' means (with various exceptions) those who are, at present, spending more than 183 days in the country at any one time over the course of that year and the previous two years. Be very careful of the 183 day rule: it is extremely complicated and you may or may not end up being a tax resident accordingly. For example, if you spent 120 days in the country during each year 2006, 2007 and 2008, you would count the whole 120 from 2008, 1/3 of the days from 2007 (40) and 1/6 of the days from 2006 (20), totalling only 180 days. Since this doesn't equal 183 you would not be considered a US resident for tax purposes. It is impossible, however, to go into the minutiae of federal tax law here: if you are not sure where you stand, get professional advice.

Generally speaking, if you are in the USA with no intention of abandoning your 'tax home' in another country, and if you have no application pending for permanent status, you are classed as a non-resident alien. Some individuals are exempt from resident's taxation - namely diplomats, employees of international organisations such as the United Nations, their families, teachers and trainees, students, and professional athletes - but tax exemptions are extremely complicated and cannot be covered in full detail here. Some types of employee with certain functions are exempt from specific taxes and aliens on temporary assignments in the USA - those working for multinationals for a set period, for instance - can deduct temporary living expenses (meals, lodging, transport, telephone and laundry expenses) from their gross earnings.

Earnings for personal services of holders of J-1 visas who are employees of foreign employers are specifically exempt from US taxes. The individual must not be in the country for more than 90 days, and must not be paid more than $3,000. Some tax treaties allow for a more liberal reading of this ruling, however, so again, it is important to get professional advice on this area.

As a rule, non-residents are taxed at a flat rate of 30% on earnings. Residents and citizens are taxed at the rates listed below.

Other taxes

Social security tax

Social Security tax consists of the Old Age Survivors and Disability Insurance (OASDI) which was introduced in 1935, and a programme of Health Insurance (HI), called Medicare, for people over 65. The programme insures for lost income due to retirement, disability or death and is administered by the Social Security Administration.

Almost all types of employment and self-employment are covered. Some non-resident aliens are exempt, depending on the type of visa they hold. Temporary workers on H visas are exempt, as are employees of foreign governments. Social Security payments are simply withheld by the employer.

In 2008, the social security tax rate was 6.2%, which applies to the first $87,900 of an employee's wages paid by the employer. The Medicare tax rate is 1.45%. The self-employed are also taxed at a rate of 15.3% on profits.

State and local contributions

State and local income taxes vary widely from state to state. In some areas, such as New York, they are fairly severe; elsewhere there are no state taxes, as in Nevada. Taxes paid to the state and locally can be counted as deductions from the gross wage for federal income tax purposes. Some states have different residency status and exemption rules; once again, the local tax office or post office will have more information. Alternatively, you can look online at www.irs.gov.

Gift tax

Gift tax applies to US residents and (with exceptions) to non-resident aliens on gifts of more than $12,000 annually.

Estate tax

There is no federal inheritance tax (although it is levied in some states). Estate tax applies to all deceased persons' estates.

Pension plan coverage

You may be eligible to participate in a US tax-qualified pension plan during your stay or assignment. For example, you may be able to join your company's 401(k) plan, which would permit you to contribute up to $15,500 of your salary during 2008 on a tax-deductible basis, enabling you to benefit from matching employer contributions. If you are aged 50 and over, an additional catch-up contribution is allowed. The additional contribution amount for 2008 is currently $5,000. You need to check with a professional adviser what the tax implications are in the USA and your home country. If you decide to withdraw the money from a fund on leaving the US, that sum will then be subject to US taxes.

Income Tax	
Married filing jointly	
Up to $15,650	10%
$15,650–$63,700	$1,565 plus 15%
$63,700–$128,500	$8,772 plus 25%
$128,500–$195,850	$24,972.50 plus 28%
$195,850–$349,700	$43,830.50 plus 33%
$349,700 or more	$94,601 plus 35%
Married filing separately	
Up to$7,825	10%
$7,825–$31,850	$782.50 plus 15%
$31,850–$64,250	$4,386.25 plus 25%
$64,250–$97,925	$12,486.25 plus 28%
$97,925–$174,850	$21,915.25 plus 33%
$174,850 or more	$47,300 plus 35%
Single	
Up to$7,825	10%
$7,825–$31,850	$782.50 plus 15%
$31,850–$77,100	$4,386.25 plus 25%
$77,100–$160,850	$15,698.75 plus 28%
$160,850–$349,700	$39,148.75 plus 33%
$349,700 or more	$101,469.25 plus 35%
Head of Household	
Up to £11,200	10%
$11,200–$42,650	$1,120 plus 15%
$42,650–$110,100	$5,837.50 plus 25%
$110,100–$178,350	$22,700 plus 28%
$178,350–$349,700	$41,810 plus 33%
$349,700 or more	$98,355.50 plus 35%

Further information

Further information on taxes can be obtained from:

Internal Revenue Services Department of the Treasury: 1 800 829 1040; www.irs.gov. Has local offices throughout the country.

Social Security Administration: 1 800 772 1213; www.ssa.gov. Has local offices also throughout the country.

TIME

FACT

■ The 24-hour clock is hardly ever used in timetables and public schedules.

Continental USA covers four main time zones: *Eastern Time* (the east coast as far as Michigan, Indiana, Georgia and Florida); *Central Time* (as far west as North Dakota and Texas), *Mountain Time* (south from Montana), and *Pacific Time* (the Pacific coast: Washington, Oregon, California and Nevada). Eastern time is five hours behind GMT, Central is six hours behind, Mountain seven hours and Pacific, eight hours. You will have to take account of time differences when calling within the States: remember that 9am in New York is 6am in California.

Working in the USA

■ THE EMPLOYMENT SCENE

The latest figures show that the employment market in the USA is struggling to stay afloat as a result of the national economic slowdown. In the first quarter of 2008 the economy lost 240,000 jobs, continuing the six-month long slowdown to a growth rate of just 0.3%. Currently, the unemployment rate stands at 5%, up from 4.5% in April 2007, or a jump from 6.8 million unemployed persons to 7.6 million in just over a year. Manufacturing and construction continue to be the worst affected areas, with mounting job losses each year, and the retail industry has recently joined ranks with them as it too sees recurring job losses and fewer big spenders. The rest of the non-manufacturing economy has managed to grow slightly, particularly in the professional and healthcare industries but sectors such as electronics, aviation, industrial machinery, and cars were badly hit by the economic downturn at the beginning of 2008 and US exports remain troubled.

According to the US Bureau of Economic Analysts, three sectors made notable contributions to faster US personal income growth in 2008 – professional services, finance, and healthcare. The area of the US with the lowest unemployment rate is the Great Plains region, which includes the Dakotas, Nebraska, Kansas, and Oklahoma. These states offer the greatest protection against the 'knock-on' effect whereby individual companies take down others in the same community in a chain reaction of bankruptcies. States most vulnerable to this effect are Hawaii, Alaska and Washington. The state worst hit by unemployment has most recently been Michigan, which in April 2008 reported unemployment figures of 6.9% – 1.9% higher than the national average. Contrary to popular belief, high-growth companies still exist in all sectors of the economy. Technology companies ranging from computing to bio-technology are not necessarily going to be the most successful companies, although they are likely to see the steadiest growth over time. A survey by the National Council on Entrepreneurship found that high-growth companies exist in all areas of the US and span the spectrum of economic activity. Finding the right job entails picking a well-managed company with good prospects for success and a contented workforce.

Opportunities for immigrants

The USA continues to be a favoured overseas posting for company employees. The London-based consultants Employment Conditions Abroad found in a survey that increasing numbers of foreign workers are now being posted to the USA. It is the largest area for expat movements both in terms of numbers and the size of the country, and they anticipate that the trend will continue. This does, however, apply only to those already employed by large companies with HQs, subsidiaries, branches or agencies in the USA, though this is hardly surprising.

> **FACT**
>
> ■ Currently, the unemployment rate stands at 5%, up from 4.5% in April 2007, or a jump from 6.8 million unemployed persons to 7.6 million in just over a year.

The view of the country sitting at the foot of the rainbow is nurtured by Hollywood, but its romantic appeal has such resonance that some people will literally risk their lives on fragile boats to get there. This continues a tradition first started by the *Mayflower* in 1620. The concept of the American Dream is irresistible to many people even if it is a schmaltzy simplification of the life lived by the majority of the population who must balance their salaried incomes against a stream of financial obligations, from running a car to paying taxes. Anyone who has spent time in one of America's downtown urban areas or passed through slums on a train can testify that entrenched poverty still exists within the US and that misfortune can literally take anyone off to Skid Row.

Nevertheless, it is important to acknowledge that the USA has historically seen immigration as representing a blood transfusion, a one-way flow of nutritious talent and drive. Certainly, emigrating to the USA for professional reasons continues to bear fruit for many individuals seeking the good life and a chance to improve their standard of living. These immigrants also make valuable contributions to their adoptive country.

Working in the US is often a boon to your professional credentials, especially if you return to your native country. But a sense of proportion is important. You will still encounter all of the problems of working life you experienced back home and you may well be working longer hours for that larger house and leisure activities.

TIP

■ Prospects for foreigners are best in high technology fields and niche markets. Highly-qualified engineers and managers in the computer industry, and in some areas of medicine such as physiotherapy and occupational therapy, are still in demand. Software designers and systems engineers with five to 10 years experience will find a ready market for their skills in the USA.

Although the outlook in some areas is not optimistic, foreign workers will always be popular. It is often cheaper to employ expatriates: recruitment costs may be higher, but there is less risk of the employee on a working visa being poached by rivals because of the bureaucracy and expense involved in giving sponsorship. Training costs may be minimal, and there is a better chance of loyalty from a foreign employee if she or he migrates from abroad expressly to work for a specific company. Foreign workers also tend to be highly motivated to succeed because they have invested their skills, education and resources in making the move.

Risks for immigrants

While employers may appreciate the value of hiring foreign employees, there are certain risks for those workers. The disadvantage of the working visa system is that someone can relocate to the USA to find that the job is unsuitable. They can even face redundancy without the opportunity to find new work. After navigating the legal and financial hurdles to obtain one job, are you likely to want to endure the application process for a second time within one year?

Another factor to consider is that some employers are reported to use the working visa system to pay lower wages. By law H1-B workers must be paid the median wage in their job category, but some foreign workers admit they ask for raises less frequently and are less likely to make complaints at work for fear of jeopardising the company's sponsorship. It might be easy in some cases to find work in the USA but you are also fairly expendable, particularly if you are a relatively new employee and cheap to fire. This is not to say individuals shouldn't try to find jobs in the USA, but they must understand the limitations of a working visa, which explains why a residency, with its freedom to move jobs, is worth its weight in gold.

Residence and work regulations

There is no work permit as such for the USA, instead the US Citizenship and Immigration Services (USCIS) issues a range of 'non-immigrant' visas (more than 70 in all), to cover every possible reason to enter and stay in the country for a time. Some visas allow you to work: the most common of these is the L visa, which allows the holder to work for the company which sent him or her to the USA, and for no other company. The B visa allows the holder to conduct temporary business in the US such as holding meetings, attending conferences and so on. A common application is for an H visa whereby an American company sponsors an individual for possessing specialised knowledge linked to a degree. Other visas are for different categories of work; for example J visas are for participants of an approved Exchange Visitor Program and O visas are issued to artists of 'extraordinary ability or achievement'. Another fairly common visa is the E

(Treaty Trader) visa, issued to nationals of countries with a treaty of trade and navigation with the USA, who are going to carry on trade with the USA and that country. There are about 50 treaty countries, including the UK and most of the EU. Because the USCIS rules are extremely complex, it is advisable to get professional advice from an immigration lawyer unless your company is taking care of the visa application for you.

Details and qualifications

The US State Department has given advance certification for work permits for people with advanced degrees in dietetics, nursing, pharmacy, physical therapy, medicine and surgery. The advanced degree requirement will sometimes be waived (with the exception of medicine and surgery) if you have a regular degree and specialised experience. This means that working visas in certain categories will be issued more readily.

The necessity for degrees and certificates varies from profession to profession. In some fields, such as computing, experience is everything and qualifications are almost worthless. The same applies in journalism, and many secretarial posts. To practise professional nursing or teaching it is, however, necessary to pass a state licensing exam, for which you need a qualification in your home country. Several professions require a qualification recognised by an American body. Librarians need a master's degree from a school accredited by the American Library Association, and entry to law, accountancy, banking and financial services is dependent upon a series of qualifications. If you are employed by a law or accountancy firm with operations in the USA, you will be able to get a posting without specific US qualifications. Although the US system is based on common law (as it is in England), as an individual it would be very difficult to find work in a US law firm without passing US law exams. Accountancy is regulated by state accountancy boards, 35 of which will consider applications from people with overseas qualifications.

TIP

■ *The Encyclopaedia of Associations* (updated quarterly on www. library-dialog.com) lists trade and professional associations in the USA that will be able to advise on the qualifications necessary to work in those particular professions.

■ SOURCES OF JOBS

The media

UK newspapers and magazines

Several newspapers published in the UK carry advertisements for jobs in the USA. Many papers can give excellent leads and useful information, even if they do not have formal 'Situations Vacant' advertisements. The *Guardian* carries international job adverts within its supplements between Monday and Thursday, and also on Saturday. The *Financial Times* carries adverts mainly for senior business and executive positions, and has regular supplements and special reports on countries and sectors. These will often

TIP

■ A UK paper specifically dedicated to job searching is *Jobsearch UK* (out weekly), which has one page of overseas jobs.

cover individual states in the USA. Contact the paper direct for details. *The Times* on a Thursday is particularly good for executive positions as is its 'Crème de la Crème' executive secretary section on Wednesdays; both it and the *The Independent* have overseas jobs listed, though not in dedicated sections. For academic positions, the *Times Higher Education Supplement* (published Fridays) is a fruitful source.

One of the best magazines to read is *The Economist*, which has an extensive section advertising senior positions in business, finance and industry. There are also a handful of dedicated magazines such as *Nexus* (which comes out monthly) and *Job Finder*.

New Scientist has advertisements for science and technology jobs, while *New Statesman and Society* and *The Spectator* have advertisements for jobs in particular areas, notably charities and politics. There will sometimes be US-based positions advertised there, or you could try *The Big Issue* for more charitable and non-profit jobs.

If you are looking within a particular sector, trade associations and their respective journals will be useful sources. The journals will be available in public libraries, and the associations themselves will often help you even if you are not a member. *The Directory of UK Associations* (Hollis Publishing 2005), has comprehensive listings and a copy may be obtained at www.hollis-publishing.com.

Other trade-orientated magazines can provide useful leads: *Campaign* (see www.brandrepublic.com/campaign) and *Marketing Week* (www.marketingweek.co.uk) may be helpful for those interested in advertising, the *Bookseller* for those working in publishing, and the *Administrator* for company administration and company secretarial leads. They are all available in newsagents and libraries. Accountants and lawyers should contact their associations for advice on job-hunting.

International and European newspapers and magazines

By their very nature the international journals are too broad in their outlook to carry many adverts for specific jobs. The exceptions are the aforementioned *Economist* and the *Financial Times* (which also has a US edition) – both are useful sources for senior managers. Otherwise, the *International Herald Tribune* (www.iht.com) and the *Wall Street Journal Europe* (www.online.wsj.com) are useful for general business information.

US newspapers and magazines

The best way to job hunt through the US papers is to look online for the domestic editions of the city or area that you want to work in: get a copy of the *Chicago Tribune*, the *New York Times*, the *Tennessean*, the *Cleveland Plain Dealer*, or the paper from whichever city in which you intend to work (see the 'Media and communications' section in the *Daily Life* chapter for addresses, or search online for a website). Otherwise, the only truly national newspapers are *USA Today* and the *Washington Post*. The *USA Today's* London office places adverts in the domestic edition and advises that it is worth buying the domestic editions for jobs vacant ('Help Wanted') advertisements, and the international edition for nationwide financial and industry news.

 For listings of US specialist journals see *Benn's Media Directory*, available from www.amazon.com.

Directories

The University of London Careers Group (020 7554 4500; careers@careers. lon.ac.uk; www.careers.lon.ac.uk) has a *Guide for UK and Overseas Students* with exhaustive information on companies offering employment in the EU or worldwide. This is aimed primarily at graduates. *Getting Computer Jobs Abroad*, published by the magazine *Computer Weekly* (www. computerweekly.com) has a detailed section on the USA. For directories it is best to go to main reference libraries as they can be extremely costly to purchase. In London, the Westminster Reference Library, (020 7641 1300; www.westminster.gov.uk/libraries) has many useful resources, or the Senate House Library at the University of London (020 7862 8500; enquiries@shl.lon.ac.uk; www.ull.ac.uk) is also excellent. Both have search capabilities on their websites.

Useful websites

There are literally hundreds of job hunt websites with lists of vacancies classified by professional categories or regions. Local newspaper websites are a quick way of finding vacancies whether you are abroad or within the USA when you look. Many allow you to post a CV (résumé), search for companies, view internship possibilities, and find advice about relocation to the US. Here is just a sample of some reliable job search sites:

CareerBuilder.com: www.careerbuilder.com. Leading recruitment resource which searches the classified ads of more than 130 local American newspapers.

Craig's List: www.craigslist.com. Site dedicated to classified advertisements and job opportunities.

JobBank USA: www.jobbankusa.com. Specialises in providing employment services to job seekers. Website includes a database of vacancies, news about job fairs, employer information and résumé posting options online.

Local Job Network: www.localjobnetwork.com. Site will automatically redirect you to a job search site local to you, such as www.milwaukeejobs.com or www.floridajobnetwork.com.

Monster: www.monster.com. A huge searchable database of jobs in the US and around the world, plus information on large employers.

TIP

◼ Crimson Publishing (www. crimsonpublishing. co.uk) publishes and distributes a number of annual directories covering short and long-term work. *The Directory of Jobs and Careers Abroad* is an excellent place to start, as it has guides to career opportunities divided by country and details of employers and agencies specialising in placements abroad. The *International Directory of Voluntary Work (2006)* lists a certain number of placements in the USA, as does *World Volunteers* and *Gap Years for Grown-Ups (2008)*.

Net-Temps: www.net-temps.com. Leading job board for temporary, temporary-to-permanent, and full-time employment.

Placing 'employment wanted' advertisements

There are some advantages to placing an 'employment wanted' advertisement in local newspapers or the *Craig's List* site of the state or city in which you want to work: you can write your own job description and you can be selective about where you work. As well as this, a foreign advertisement in a local newspaper will always get noticed (there is still some cachet in having an English administrator in certain types of firm, for example). Be cautious about respondents though. Ask how long they have been in business, if and where they are registered, how many other people they employ, and what the remuneration for the job is. If you are at all suspicious, get something in writing and contact the local city hall or chamber of commerce for advice on how to find out more about the company. You should not agree to meet anybody without being absolutely sure where you are going, and whom you are going to see. If in any doubt, make sure you let at least one person know your movements and how long you will be.

There is a list of major newspapers in the *Daily Life* chapter above. If the area in which you want to work is not listed, contact the local chamber of commerce for names of newspapers. Although each state has at least one daily that goes statewide, US papers are very local, so try to be fairly exact about the area you choose. You can also advertise for employment wanted on networking sites such as Facebook (www.facebook.com) or sites aimed specifically at classified ads like Craigs List.(www.craigslist.com).

The following is a sample advertisement. It is important to put it in the *weekend* edition, as well as the daily. Make sure you include your country code in the phone number and a registered email address.

> **SITUATION WANTED** *English secretary, computer literate (Word, Excel, Outlook), legal experience, some Spanish spoken. Seeks permanent position in Los Angeles or surrounding area. Resumé available. Contact Janet Ellis.*

Agencies and organisations

UK agencies

Engineering and construction

AndersElite: 02380 223511; contactus@anderselite.com; www.anderselite.com

Medical and nursing

O'Grady Peyton International: 0845 310 7310; europe@ogradypeyton.com; www.ogradypeyton.com

Computers and IT
Abraxas: 020 7255 5555; international@abraxas.com; www.abraxas.co.uk

Sales and marketing
Kelly Services: 001 248 362 4444; kfirst@kellyservices.com; www.kellyservices.com

Financial and banking
Robert Half Finance and Accounting: 020 7562 6500; londoncity@roberthalf.co.uk; www.roberthalf.co.uk

Other
VIP International: 020 7930 0541; vip@vipinternational.co.uk; www.vipinternational.co.uk. International hotel and hospitality recruitment company. Visa restrictions mean that there are very few opportunities in this area for executives, but the company also recruits for temporary positions onboard luxury cruise lines.

US agencies
Agencies specialise in particular disciplines, and the most prolific, as in the UK and Australia, are those offering temporary jobs in secretarial work. Fees are usually paid by the employer, but you should check whether you will be required to pay in advance. Look under 'Employment Agencies' in the *Yellow Pages* or search online at www.google.com.

 Guidance can also be sought from relocation and support agencies such as *International Consultants of Delaware* (001 215 222 8454; icd@icdeval.com; www.icdeval.com).

Chambers of commerce
There is a Chamber of Commerce in all major cities and in every state. They exist to promote business, and provide information on all aspects of living and working in the local area. State Chambers of Commerce supply information packs with business contacts, rates and taxes, commercial and residential property contacts and prices, business start-up materials and other relevant information. Addresses are commonly listed in the *Yellow Pages* or at www.uschamber.com.

BritishAmerican Business Inc (BABi) at www.babinc.org has more than 400 UK and US corporate members. Membership is by company only, with yearly fees of between £875 and £4,095. Membership gives access to various EU/UK/US committees, business information resources and databases, and an extensive events programme.

International Chambers of commerce
BritishAmerican Business Inc: 212 661 4060; www.babinc.org

US Chamber of Commerce: 202 659 6000; www.uschamber.org. (See the '*State-by-State Business Report*' section for addresses of City Chambers of Commerce).

Professional associations

Accountancy
National Society of Accountants: 1 800 966 6679; members@nsacct.org; www.nsacct.org
American Institute of Certified Public Accountants: 212 596 6200; www.aicpa.org
American Accounting Association: 941 921 7747; office@aaahq.org; www.aaahq.org

Agriculture
Agriculture Council of America: 913 491 1895; info@agday.org; www.agday.org
American Dairy Association: 315 472 9143; jtills@adadc.com; www.adadc.com.
American Forest and Paper Association: 800 878 8878; info@afandpa.org; www.afandpa.org

Banking/insurance/financial services
American Bankers Association: 1 800-BANKERS; www.aba.com
Financial Women International: 1 8660236 2007; email info@fwi.org; www.fwi.org
American Association of Insurance Services: 1 800 564 AAIS; info@AAISonline.com; www.aaisonline.com
Insurance Information Institute: 110 William Street, New York, NY 10038; 212 346 5500; www.iii.org

Chemical/pharmaceutical
American Institute of Chemists: 215 873 8224; email info@theaic.org; www.theaic.org
American Pharmacists Association: 202 628 4410; infocenter@aphanet.org; www.aphanet.org

Construction
American Institute of Constructors: admin@aicnet.org; www.aicnet.org

Electrical
American Electronics Association: 1 800 284 4232; email csc@aeanet.org; www.aeanet.org

Engineering
American Institute of Chemical Engineers: 1 800 242 4363; www.aiche.org
American Society for Agricultural and Biological Engineers: 49085; 269 429 0300; hq@asabe.org; www.asabe.org

American Society of Mechanical Engineers: 1 800 843 2763; infocentral@asme.org; www.asme.org
Institute of Electrical and Electronics Engineers: 212 419 7900; www.ieee.org
Institute of Industrial Engineers: 1 800 494 0460 or 770 449 0460; www.iienet.org

Legal
American Bar Association: 1 800 285 2221; www.abanet.org

Media/Performing Arts
Actors' Equity Association: 212-869 8530; www.actorsequity.org
American Federation of Television and Radio Artists: 212 532 0800; info@aftra.org; www.aftra.org
American Federation of Musicians: 212 869 1330; www.afm.org
National Writers Union: 212 254 0279; email nwu@nwu.org; www.nwu.org
Newspaper Association of America: 571 766 1000; www.naa.org

Medical
American Medical Association: 1 800 621 8335; www.ama-assn.org
American Nurses Association: 1 800 274 4ANA; www.nursingworld.org

Secretarial
International Association of Administrative Professionals: 816 891 6600; service@iaap-hq.org; www.iaap-hq.org

Miscellaneous
American Advertising Federation: 1 800 999 2231; aaf@aaf.org; www.aaf.org
National Retail Federation: 1 800 673 4692; www.nrf.com
American Association of Exporters and Importers: 202 857 8009; hq@aaei.org; www.aaei.org
Travel Industry Association of America: 202 408 8422; www.tia.org
American Institute of Mining, Metallurgical and Petroleum Engineers: 303 948 4255; aime@aimehq.org; www.aimeny.org

State employment agencies

Job Services, the state-operated employment service, operates a network of some 2,000 local offices in major cities around the country. These 'Employment Service Centers' provide free counselling, testing and job placements, and allow access to computerised listings of possible openings across the country. Each centre lists jobs for skilled and unskilled job seekers and their websites work in much the same way as privately-run recruitment sites do. They are listed in the *Yellow Pages* under 'Employment Service' or 'Job Service', and each state runs its own website.

TIP

■ Type 'Job Service' into any search engine for Employment Service Centers and select the state you wish to view from the list generated.

Company transfers

The 'special relationship' between the UK and the USA is now stronger than ever in industry and commerce. The American Chamber of Commerce in the UK lists 10,000 US companies that have subsidiaries, parents, distributors or agents in the UK, and 8,000 UK companies which have business links in the USA. Many of these companies will send staff overseas on secondment.

For more information see the *American Chamber of Commerce Directory* (you do not have to be a member of the Chamber to view this and it is available in most libraries). Alternatively, go to www.uschamber. com). You could also identify the major companies operating in both the UK and the USA in the following directories; for US companies and their subsidiaries see *Moody's Register*, *Ward's Business Directory* and *Thomas Register*, all of which list companies by industry sector; for UK companies and their subsidiaries consult *Kompass* (www.kompass.com), *Kelly's*, *Sell's Directories*, or *Who Owns Whom* (Dun & Bradstreet), which is a directory of companies and their subsidiaries throughout the world. In London, the Business Collections at the British Library (www.bl.uk) have extensive resources which give details of UK companies and their subsidiaries worldwide. Alternatively, the City Business Library (www.library.uncg. edu/news), run by the City of London, has a wealth of information on international business organisations.

 The UK Trade and Investment's excellent website at www.uktradeinvest. gov.uk gives detailed information on all aspects of exporting and building trade links.

■ APPLYING FOR A JOB

The best way to get a job, according to the US Bureau of Labor Statistics in the Department of Labor, is to apply to a company direct. At least 34% per cent of applicants are successful this way. The next best method is to network (including asking friends and relatives for help), which works for 26% of applicants. Contrary to popular opinion, therefore, buying the newspaper every day for the 'help wanted' columns or scouring the net is not necessarily as likely to end in success as sending your resumé on spec.

If there are many ways of finding a job, there are as many methods used by recruiters to find the perfect applicant. It is important to remember when applying for any job that the recruiter may be almost as apprehensive as you. Recruiting is a time-consuming and very expensive business, and it is essential to get it right first time. The consequences of bad recruiting – the person appointed turning out to be lazy or a disinterested employee who leaves after six months, for example – are serious and risky.

Companies use different systems to make recruitment less of a lottery. It is becoming more and more popular for large companies to hire a full-time recruiter, who will handle all the hiring and firing a corporation needs. Professional agencies will be used when a series of employees are required at once (for the opening of a new department, or a new plant), and head hunters will be brought in if a very senior post is vacant. Even if you do not apply for any jobs advertised on a recruitment website, it is worth keeping your CV posted and active so that employers can search for candidates in the same way that candidates search for jobs. Being headhunted in this way and asked to interview for a company you've never heard of is a popular way for employers to avoid paying expensive fees to websites *and* to find their perfect candidate. It can also be worthwhile to contact agencies that deal with recruitment in your field so as to cast your net as wide as possible.

Some companies use psychological tests to get to the 'real' character of the candidate. Opinion is divided as to the usefulness of the different tests that are in vogue at any one time. Psychometric testing is in favour at the moment (your personality is categorised according to a series of psychological tests), but handwriting analysis is still used by a surprising number of large and well-known companies. The theory behind all these tests is that you cannot get to the true nature of an individual through the formal setting of an interview, and that it is important to find out if the person will fit in with the group he or she will be joining. You will find that psychometric testing is used more at the senior end of the job market, and in certain professions such as banking and financial services. In the media and the creative, arts-based jobs, recruitment is often by the back door, but when a job is formally advertised the selection process will be conventional, as with the vast majority of jobs in the USA.

FACT

■ It is becoming more common for companies to set you an IQ-based test during an interview, the score of which will determine how well you will be able to handle the duties and responsibilities of the job you are applying for.

Letters of application

A letter of application – or cover letter as they are more commonly known – varies little in its US form from those in Europe or Australasia. It is important to follow the general rules of formal letter writing when attaching a cover letter to an application or résumé, so address it to Sir or Madam, include the date and your own address and close the document with "Yours sincerely" unless you've met them before. Be prepared to sell yourself: American employers are used to seeing flashy, professionally-written letters from people who truly believe they are the best in the market. As a foreigner you may feel that your own experience and qualifications do not stand up to American equivalents, which is why it is so important to sell your skills and knowledge as effectively as possible. If you worked for several companies as a temp during the past year, for example, list the skills you've acquired by constantly changing your role, such as flexibility, adaptability and an eagerness to learn. These skills transfer well to the American market, whereas lists of British companies who've hired you

TIP

■ When writing cover letters or résumés, make sure to use American-English spellings! You don't want your future employer to possibly dismiss you as a bad speller simply because you've used British-English terminology.

recently may not. The cover letter is an important opportunity to make the employer aware of those strengths not listed on your résumé, so highlight those skills you've acquired in your most recent jobs and word them in such a way that the hirer believes the fact you are foreign is a strength, not a weakness.

The résumé (curriculum vitae)

There are many different opinions about the writing and structuring of a résumé. Should it be short or long? Should you include a biographical paragraph in the third person (as in, 'Janie Jones is dedicated, careful, and likes to see a project through...')? Should you detail all your academic achievements, or none at all? Should you include referees, or say that they will be supplied on request? Certainly in America the norm is to have a single-sided sheet of A4 and only your most recent and relevant job experiences listed. Of course, if you have successfully used an existing CV to obtain employment in the past, it may be worth using it again.

There are certain facts about a résumé that are unalterable. It is a brief summary of your career; the 'hard' information about your qualifications and experience. It (and the covering letter) are either going to get you an interview, or get you nothing at all. It will sit in a pile of up to 500 other résumés, and will be allowed perhaps three minutes of somebody's time. Given these facts, certain decisions can be taken. The résumé should not be more than two sides of A4 (ideally just a single side), and it should be clear and well-laid out. Presentation is vital. The résumé is there to put across facts as efficiently as possible, and to show its subject in the best possible light. Try not to make it too shiny and overproduced. Avoid large blocks of text: it should be easy on the eye, with the important sections such as work experience easy to find and read.

Start with your name, address, telephone number and email address. List your work experience, starting with the most recent job, and say what the job was, the dates you were there, as well as some brief details of your responsibilities in bullet-point form. The more relevant this information is to the job you are applying for, the more details you should supply.

The parts of the résumé that are going to sell you should be on the first page. On the second page list your formal education (schools, dates attended, degrees and certificates – with US equivalents if possible – and major subject areas of specialisation). If you are a recent graduate, add extracurricular activities that relate to the job that you are applying for or awards you may have won.

After your academic history, list languages spoken, any volunteer activities you have done (if these are particularly relevant, put them on the first page, and draw attention to them in the covering letter), special skills (such as typing or shorthand), and any memberships of professional organisations.

TIP

The very fact your résumé will look different from all the other American candidates could work in your favour.

TIP

A photograph of yourself and the use of text boxes to section off areas of data can separate you from the crowd, but make sure you know how to use them properly. A good résumé can instantly look bad if the creator doesn't know how to use some software correctly.

Add a couple of lines outlining personal interests, what sports you play, or what you do for recreation. If the recruiter has reached this stage of the resumé, he or she will already be interested in finding out more about you, and a shared interest in an unusual sport or hobby could get you an interview. Never lie about or exaggerate your interests. If you say you have travelled extensively in Australia, be prepared for an interviewer who may have done the same. Admitting that you only spent a week in Sydney will not impress.

If you list referees, make absolutely certain they know they might be contacted, and why. It is usually sufficient to say 'Referees supplied on request' at the end of the résumé.

The interview

Interviews affect people in different ways. Remember that your interviewer may be as nervous as you are. Bad interviewers are a hazard: they will not know how to put you at ease, and they will not allow you to show yourself at your best. There is nothing you can do about it, except to be fully prepared for every eventuality.

You should find out everything you can about the company prior to your interview. Look up its website, or look in *Moody's Register of Companies*, *Hoover's Handbook*, *Forbes 500*, or any other directory that lists companies and their important characteristics. If you are able to show that you have taken the time to learn about the company, it will demonstrate that you are serious about the job.

Dress smartly. In the USA, dress codes are relatively casual, but men should never go to an interview without a jacket and tie, and women should always wear a suit, or very tailored trousers or skirt. Use your common sense; an interview in a bank will call for a smarter turnout than one in a newspaper office. If you find your interviewer in a T shirt, that is no problem: if you get the job you can moderate your dress accordingly. If you had turned up in jeans it would have looked as if you didn't care enough to make an effort.

FACT

Lighting up a cigarette in most American companies would get you thrown out before you got past the security guard.

Don't show that you are nervous. Any interviewer will expect you to be slightly apprehensive, and will make allowances. Remember, however, that the purpose of the interview is really to find out if you are the kind of person that will fit in: sweating and stammering too much will not bode well for future meetings.

An interview does not have to be an ordeal. One of the most important things to remember is that it is a tedious business for your interviewer, taking up time that could be better spent. If you can make the hour pass quickly and enjoyably, you will be remembered as good company. Try to turn the interview into a conversation, rather than a question and answer session. Most Americans like to deal straightforwardly with people, and are uncomfortable with ambiguity. Don't try to be clever, answer questions as honestly as you can, maintain eye contact, give a firm handshake, and look as if you are the sort of person it would be a treat to work with. Also remember to ask questions when prompted as this will make you look interested and prepared.

Useful publications for job applicants include *What Color is Your Parachute? A Practical Manual for Job-Hunters and Career Changers* (Richard Nelson Bolles, Ten Speed Press, 2008) and *Resumés That Get Jobs* (Jean Reed, Peterson's, 2002). As always www.amazon.com has the best database of business books.

■ ASPECTS OF EMPLOYMENT

FACT

■ Title VII of the Civil Rights Act 1964 enshrines in law the right of the individual not to be discriminated against on grounds of sex, age, race, colour, religion, pregnancy, disability or national origin.

The central piece of legislation applying to all areas of employment (hiring, promotion, performance appraisal, compensation and benefits, dismissal, redundancy and so on) is Title VII of the Civil Rights Act 1964. This enshrines in law the right of the individual not to be discriminated against on grounds of sex, age, race, colour, religion, pregnancy, disability or national origin. State and municipal governments often have their own regulations, causing some overlap with federal laws; some states have passed laws which restrict discrimination for other reasons also, for example. Claims against employers initially go to the Employment Equal Opportunities Commission (the EEOC), and if no settlement is reached they can then be taken to a federal court.

Wrongful dismissal is an area of law that is still developing. Some courts, for example, have interpreted possession of an employer's letter offering a job, or a company's personnel handbook, as an actual contract, making it much more difficult to dismiss the employee. Similarly, employees who have been sacked for refusing to carry out instructions that are dangerous or illegal have successfully sued their employers. It is also possible to sue an employer for causing emotional distress.

i For companies sending employees to the USA, *ECA International* (www.eca-international.com) is an employment consultancy providing information on all aspects of employment, including remuneration and benefits comparisons, taxation, cost of living indices, and so on. Membership is open to companies only.

Work practices

It would be impossible to attempt to describe here how American business functions as a whole. It is a huge subject, and one that has been covered by many experts. As always, there are a few generalisations that can be made, but they should be treated with caution: what is relevant in the east may be completely different in the west.

Americans have a strongly defined work ethic, and work is generally taken very seriously in the USA. They take fewer and shorter holidays than in Europe, and it is common for weekends and family life to be sacrificed if a job needs to be done. American businesses are often geared for quick results and present success: 'long-term' means looking ahead three years. Incidentally, this is thought to be one of the reasons why some industries are falling behind the Japanese and the Germans, who tend to look longer-term. You will be expected to work hard, with fewer breaks than you may be used to. You may find Americans are more aggressive and articulate in meetings than colleagues in Europe and that they are impressed by well-presented arguments backed up by hard-hitting data.

Confusingly, Americans are as renowned for their casual approach as they are for their punishing work ethic. First names are the norm (as indeed they are in most companies in Europe and Australasia these days), and networking on the golf course or squash court is common practice. The appearance of informality can be deceptive: business meetings are held at breakfast, lunch or dinner; business entertaining takes place at a ball game or other sporting event; and cocktail and dinner parties at colleagues' houses may well have a serious business purpose.

Another ritual that is gaining ground is dress-down Friday. Some major corporations have decided that if employees are allowed to wear casual clothes on a Friday it increases productivity. This of course comes with its own set of rules: if you are working for Chase Manhattan, dressing down is likely to require as much (or more) thought than putting on a suit and tie. Sports shirts, chinos and loafers are often the accepted casual uniform.

Observers of the American business ethic have identified three key ways in which companies work. The first is to have clear lines of management, and detailed instructions. 'Who do I report to?' is often the first question a new employee asks. Secondly, employees expect constant feedback on their work (continual assessment is also the basis of the schools grading system), and thirdly, close supervision is expected. If you are managing American employees, don't take it for granted that they will react in the same way as their British counterparts: if you have to correct someone for any reason, get the advice of an American colleague first.

A survey of *Fortune 500* company executives brought to light what they considered were the main elements to their success. The important thing was that they were all fully aware of the need to pursue their own careers, and the success of the company was seen as a means of achieving individual success, not as a means to an end. They also all embodied the great American values: they were pragmatic, assertive and, up to a point, egalitarian.

Teleworking

More than one sixth of America's working-age population – around 35 million people – do not owe allegiance to a single employer, and don't work in an

TIP

■ Good time keeping is important in America. Arriving five minutes late for a meeting calls for an apology; if you are going to be 15 minutes late you should telephone beforehand with a good excuse.

FACT

■ Achievement programmes in American companies are common and they often come complete with prize ceremonies.

FACT

■ The discussion of salaries is deeply taboo in the USA. Some companies will even write into their contracts that employees can be fired for initiating salary comparisons.

office; teleworkers – or 'techno-peasants' as they've been dubbed – are the growing army of workers who have taken advantage of the opportunities given by affordable home computers and who have set up home offices. There are two types of teleworker: the person who works from home for many different people – a freelance journalist or a plumber, for example – and the person who works for a single company, but does it from home instead of going into the office every day. Many companies are happy to have employees working from home – it means fewer overheads, and a happier employee is a more productive one. In the UK, teleworking is taking off at a slower rate. British Telecom (BT) has around 1,700 staff who work from home full time. It can seem very attractive – you don't need to put on a suit and subject yourself to the miseries of public transport. You can start and stop work when you like, and you can say goodbye to the backbiting and politics that colour office life. But be warned that many people find working at home lonely and depressing. While it can seem a luxury not to have to subject yourself to the 9am–5pm routine, when your computer is next door to the spare bedroom it can be impossible to stop thinking about work. One of the great advantages of going into the office is that you can keep it separate from the rest of your life; teleworkers sometimes find that far from casting off their shackles, they have simply brought them home.

> *i* For more information on teleworking and the 'soho' concept (small office/ home office) in the USA, WorkingSolo Inc (845 255 7171; wsoffice@ workingsolo.com; www.workingsolo.com) provides news, information, and encouragement to the self-employed and microbusinesses.

Political correctness and sexual harassment

TIP

■ The most important thing to remember is that America is a very litigious society, and issues are likely to go to law much sooner than in Europe.

Women in American companies have all the same problems and preoccupations as they do in other countries. The issues of sexual harassment and the glass ceiling preventing women from rising above a certain level in the hierarchy, are endlessly debated. Political correctness (being 'PC') is an area which should be given the same respect as an uncharted minefield.

Women should be aware of any male-female tensions that exist in a company, and take their cue from female colleagues. Men should be very careful of what they say and do. What might be light-hearted fun in London could be construed as the grossest politico-sexual incorrectness in Los Angeles.

Most company guidelines warn against behaviour that is likely to create 'a hostile and intimidating atmosphere', even though this may not be fully defined. Commentators have warned that to be accused of this sort of behaviour can carry the same sort of stigma as an accusation of indecent assault.

Salaries

Salaries in the USA are higher than in Europe and include more benefits and perks, although Americans have to spend considerably more time at work. As in Europe there are wide discrepancies between different occupations and between the public and private sectors. The notion of a national average is fairly meaningless without looking at different fields. The average salary for catering managers is $36,000 while the average salary for high school principals, for example, is $92,000 and a university dean can earn up to $230,000. An average salary for a data-processing manager is $98,000, but for an accountant it's $51,000. Starting salaries for graduates depend on a number of factors, including the profession they are joining and their qualifications. A recent graduate with a bachelor's degree in social work from California State University is earning, on average, $20,000 but if they are graduating from the computer science programme they are earning $45,000.

The federal minimum wage is set by the Fair Labor Standards Act of 1938. The act was last amended in 2007 to bring the minimum wage up to $6.55 an hour. This will increase to $7.25 per hour by July 2009. Additionally, the act stipulates that overtime be paid at time and a half after a statutory 40 hours a week, it places restrictions on child labour, and guarantees equal pay for all workers regardless of sex, age, religion or race. Some state laws will set a higher minimum wage, and companies working on government contracts come under the Public Contracts Act, which may also require a higher minimum wage.

FACT

■ The current minimum wage is $6.55 per hour, which will increase to $7.25 per hour by July 2009.

Benefits and perks

Benefits packages tend to be more generous than in the UK, with medical coverage, profit sharing and pension plans generally offered as standard. The situation as regards healthcare is undergoing major changes at the time of writing (see the 'Health' section in *Daily Life*) – as health insurance premiums increase, many employers are cutting back. At the same time, government health reforms may require employers to pay up to 80% of their workers' health insurance. Any contract should be studied carefully for healthcare provisions. Many employers offer life insurance as part of a benefits package. Pension plans are organised similarly to the UK system: there are government schemes to which the employer contributes and other schemes funded by employer and employee. Those on temporary and fixed-term contracts may not be eligible for company pension schemes.

TIP

■ Company cars are only provided to employees if it is absolutely necessary to the job. This is true even for senior executives.

Working hours, overtime and holidays

Americans are the most overworked people in the developed world and it is estimated that up to half of the workforce is suffering from symptoms of work-related stress. On average, Americans work 50 hours per week which is in stark contrast to the 35-hour working week in France.

Escape magazine calculated that Americans take only 9.6 days holiday per year and that a typical American couple are working 500 hours more per year than they were in 1980. As a consequence, there is growing pressure to readjust this balance so that Americans can have more time for their family life and relationships. The impact of overwork on health is also being hotly discussed in the media as a work/life balance. In the next five years this debate is likely to continue as a reaction takes place to a culture of excessive demands made by the workplace, with people desiring a better quality of life that is not simply measured in terms of income and promotion.

In factories working hours are normally from 8am to 4.30pm, and in offices 8am to 5pm. Overtime generally starts after a 40-hour week, although some unions have negotiated overtime after 35 or even 30 hours. You will frequently hear the phrases 'first shift', 'second shift' and 'third shift' to imply whether a worker is employed during the morning, afternoon or at night. Blue-collar workers are generally entitled to overtime pay or compensation but this depends on the individual industry.

You will find that working hours can vary because of the different time zones across the country. In banking and financial services and in the stock market, the necessity to keep pace with the opening of the New York stock exchange means that on the west coast the working day starts at least an hour earlier.

Trade unions

Union membership in manufacturing has fallen dramatically in the last 20 years, while there has been a corresponding rise in membership of federal and state government unions. In 1995, 14.9% of the workforce was unionised, against 12.5% today. Government workers are more unionised at 36.5%, compared to the private sector's rate of less than 8% or the finance, real-estate, and insurer sector at just 1.7%.

American trade unions are organised locally. Members of 'locals' all tend to work in the same industry or the same firm (which results in several different trades represented in one local). The locals are in turn members of a national union (such as United Auto Workers), and most of the national unions are in some way affiliated with the American Federation of Labor and Congress of Industrial Organisations (AFL-CIO). The balance of power is shifting away from the locals towards the big national unions.

Collective bargaining between the local union and the employer normally decides any dispute, rather than a strike. Collective bargaining agreements between employers and unions often have no-strike clauses, and clear and well-established guidelines for employees to air their grievances. With these sorts of safeguards, strikes are fairly rare.

In unionised industries the union is recognised as the spokesperson for any member with a complaint, and has a right to be present if the member wants to put the complaint to the management.

Employment contracts

Companies are not required by law to give their employees contracts, but in most cases there will be some sort of letter of agreement or contract offered. If you are being sent to the USA with your existing job, you should check your contract or agreement with the host company. In particular, you should be aware that the following areas are treated differently in the USA, and that there should be a provision for them in any contract of employment:

■ Sick pay

Employees are allowed to take a certain number of days off each year for illness (usually five), when they will be granted full pay. This is a statutory requirement, but the contract should detail any extra allowances the company gives.

■ Medical insurance

Check that the company provides this, and that it is sufficient to cover your needs (see the 'Health' section in *Daily Life*).

■ Housing allowance and Cost-of-Living Allowance (COLA)

US employees working outside their home states are often entitled to an allowance to cover extra costs. Sometimes this will include a certain number of days in a hotel. If you are coming out to the USA from the UK your company should make some sort of allowance for this, which will be detailed in the contract. A relocation package is often given to managerial employees and employees who are moving out-of-state, and this should cover removal and transport costs.

■ Termination period

Under federal law employers are required to give at least 60 days' advance written warning of any layoffs or plant closures. There are no other specific obligations covering termination periods, but your contract should specify a period of notice (usually from one to three months) that both employer and employee must work to.

Social security and unemployment benefit

Foreign nationals and their employers who are working in the USA may be subject to US social security taxes. These are imposed under three main pieces of legislation: the Federal Insurance Contributions Act (FICA), the Self-Employment Contributions Act (SECA), and the Federal Unemployment Tax Act.

TIP

■ Also check your contact for school fee allowances, overseas premiums, home leave allowances for family members, inclusion of a company car, moving expense reimbursement, 'settling-in' allowance, home maintenance expenses incurred in renting out your house in your home country, tax equalisation reimbursements, and other fringe benefits.

FACT

■ The UK has totalisation agreements with the USA, and international social security agreements that cover the payment of social security. This means that if you pay in one country you do not have to pay in the other. You can receive credit under the US system while paying in the UK, and vice versa.

Unemployment benefit is administered jointly by the federal and state governments. The state pays out benefits, which are financed by employer contributions, but in particularly difficult times, such as recession and major closures in one industry, the state and federal governments set up programmes to supplement the state funds. There may also be state-issued Stimulus Payments, which are paid to each taxpayer or family to stimulate spending in times of an economic slowdown. In early 2008, Stimulus Payment cheques were sent out to more than 130 million households for a value of up to $600.

Under FICA, social security and Medicare taxes are imposed on employees' income. Half of the taxes are withheld from the employee's wages, and half are paid by the employer. FICA taxes are imposed on all income earned in the USA, so even if you are exempt from income tax you may be liable for FICA taxes. Exemptions include holders of J, F, M and Q visas, and people covered under social security totalisation agreements.

Under the Federal Unemployment Tax Act, unemployment tax is levied on employers of one or more persons at 6.2% of the first $7,000 paid each year. Employers also pay into state unemployment insurance funds. Payments vary from state to state. Usually the amount of benefit paid, and the length of time that it continues, depends on the length of time you have worked for the company, and your salary. Allowances for dependants are also included in some states. Holders of J, F, M and Q visas, and employees of foreign governments are exempt.

The self-employed pay a SECA rate of 15.3% on profits and this applies to both US citizens and resident aliens. The Medicare portion is imposed at a rate of 1.45% on an unlimited amount of income, and matched by the employer to total 2.9% per employee (if the self-employed business owner has any). SECA tax is not imposed on non-resident aliens.

Reciprocal arrangements with the UK

The USA and the UK have various reciprocal arrangements whereby tax and National Insurance Contributions (NICs) do not have to be paid in both countries. Employees and the self-employed who are going to be in the USA for no more than five years, and who have been paying the required amount of Class 1 or Class 2 NICs, are covered by UK social security. If you are working under any other circumstances you may have to pay US social security. You should contact the local office of Social Security Administration and explain your status. If you are working for a UK-based employer, are ordinarily resident in the UK (i.e. intending to return within five years), or if you were a UK resident before you took up the job, you have to pay Class 1 NICs in the UK for the first 52 weeks you are abroad. Your UK employer should continue to do this automatically, and should write to the Overseas Benefits Directorate to avoid demands from the US Social Security Administration. If you or your company is in any doubt, contact the US Social Security Administration (www.ssa.gov) or HM Revenue and Customs in the UK (www.hmrc.gov.uk).

Pensions

Although there is no law in the USA requiring any employer to provide pensions for employees, most employers do provide some sort of retirement plan. It is an area heavily regulated by municipal, state and federal law and the most common forms are a 401k or IRA plan. The Pension Protection Act of 2006 allowed employers to automatically enrol employees into a 401k or IRA retirement plan in an effort to shore up schemes which stand to be under-funded when the employee reaches retirement age, so be aware that if you do not wish to set aside funds for a US retirement scheme through your employer, you must take measures yourself to opt-out. The Employee Retirement Income Security Act, administered by the Department of Labor, covers pensions, retirement plans and also employee benefit plans (health insurance, disability, accidents insurance and so on).

US retirement benefits are paid on a system of work credits, measured in three-month (quarter year) units called quarters of coverage. In order to draw benefits you need to have a certain number of years' work to your credit. Retirement benefit is paid to workers at the age of 65. A reduced amount can be claimed as early as age 62.

You should check whether you are entitled to join any US tax deductible pension plan while you are employed by a US company. You will be able to contribute up to about $10,000 on a tax-deductible basis, and to benefit from matching employer contributions. More information is provided in the *Retirement* csection of this chapter.

▉ UK state pension schemes

If you are entitled to a UK state retirement pension, and are living in the USA or spending most of your time there, you can draw your pension at the same rate as you would in the UK. National Insurance contributions and US insurance coverage can be combined to get you up to the required level. Widows' benefits are administered in the same way.

▉ Restrictions on UK-managed pension funds

If the company that is sending you to the USA has an occupational (as opposed to state) pension scheme in which you participate, you should check whether you will continue to accrue benefits while you are working in the USA. You should also check on the US income tax implications, because in many cases yours and your employer's contributions will be subject to US tax law.

▉ Entrance and exit interviews

Make sure that before leaving for the USA you let your accountant know exactly what you are doing, in order to get the best from your tax situation. When you arrive you should also have an entrance interview with a US accountant.

Useful addresses

UK

Pension Service: 0845 301 3011; www.dwp.gov.uk for details of the UK social security scheme.

US Embassy: 020 7894 0477; www.usembassy.org.uk

USA

Social Security Administration: 1 800 772 1213; www.ssa.gov/international

■ PERMANENT WORK

Executive employment prospects

The best prospects at the top end of the employment market for foreigners lie in the high technology areas: biotechnology, computer software and hardware, and networking technology. The medical and pharmaceutical professions are employing a lot of Europeans, the British in particular. One California-based executive search consultant said that at any one time in the pharmacy and biotechnology fields up to 15% of the top managers may be British. Hospital equipment manufacturers are fairly bullish about prospects, and hospital management is big business. One of the reasons for the strength of the healthcare sector is the ageing American population. This sector will not peak until the second decade of the 21st century: the majority of baby boomers, born in the 20-year period after the Second World War, are only just starting to reach retirement age. When they all do, the number of people over the age of 65 requiring care will reach unprecedented numbers.

The British are respected for their expertise in certain areas and are considered to be good at analysis and business development. In smaller companies European managers are sought after for their specialised knowledge of their home countries at a time when many American companies are seeking to forge links with Europe. From the foreigner's point of view this is good news on a number of counts: potential earnings are a good deal higher in the USA than in most of Europe, and there is also the chance of being at the top of a small firm, rather than further down the ladder in a larger one. It is important, therefore, for managers to stress their knowledge of European affairs. In general, American companies are meritocratic, and open to foreign nationals: they want the best person for the job no matter what his or her nationality.

When the economy booms consumers tend to buy luxury or 'greed' goods. Likewise, when the economy slows down, job opportunities in the retail and consumer markets tend to decline as consumers spend less. However, foreigners with experience of luxury goods such as high-class kitchen equipment, expensive domestic electrical equipment, and

TIP

■ The best areas for employment are on the east coast and in the states that are growing fast, including the Rocky Mountain states, Texas, Georgia and the Carolinas.

top-of-the-range prepared foods and bakery products should find openings in the big cities, as spending at the top end of the market has not yet slowed to the same extent as bargain goods.

Computers/IT

Prospects for work in the computer industry are still good but with one drawback: you can get the job easily enough, but you might have to wait four or five months for your H1-B visa. Clear that hurdle and you should be welcomed with open arms by UK recruitment companies working for clients in the USA. The skills most in demand since 2006 have been database export-orientated projects and knowledge of.Net and Java development. Maintenance of derivative and data feeds are crucial for the financial sector. Technical support for both IT and non-IT companies is likely to remain in high demand too, particularly for application development and help desk skills. Salaries are high for the most experienced: starting on around $65,000 a year, it can be possible to triple that on a five-year placement. For lists of recruitment consultancies see *Sources of Jobs* and the magazine *Computerworld* or go online at www.computerworld.com. Other helpful sites include www.itcareers.com, www.computerjobs.com or the federal job site www.usajobs.opm.gov which has a section dedicated to IT. Try also the established online IT hub www.zdnet.com for listings of tech jobs.

Medicine and nursing

The market for nurses in the USA is buoyant, especially for those with specialised knowledge such as paediatric intensive care nursing. America will need to recruit more than one million nurses by 2016 and has launched a recruitment drive in the UK and Australasia to help meet this goal. Perks include two months of rent-free accommodation, air fares, visas for family members, and the possibility of obtaining citizenship. By 2025 the shortfall of nurses may reach 500,000, making the nursing profession one of America's fastest-growing employment sectors. The current and projected shortfall, then, provides plenty of opportunity for nurses trained outside the US, but those thinking of taking up nursing in the USA should be warned that good experience is vital. With no state health service to support you through training, you are regarded very much as an independent practitioner. As a result, you will have a higher professional status than nurses in the UK. The average annual salary of a registered nurse (RN) in the US is $50,100.

British qualifications are highly respected, and the USA is currently a favoured destination for nurses and midwives, as it is for doctors looking for locum posts. To practise professional nursing in the USA you must pass a state licensing examination. The *Commission on Graduates of Foreign Nursing Schools* (info@cgfns.org; www.cgfns.org) holds an exam which it is necessary to pass in order to sit for the National Council of State

Boards of Nursing Licensure Examination (NCLEX). Passing the CGFNS is a requirement of the H1-A (Registered Nurses) visa, and you must have an offer of full-time work from a US employer.

The north-east has the highest doctor to patient ratio in the USA, and medical practitioners are in shorter supply in southern states. With the most expensive healthcare in the world, the best-equipped hospitals and R&D facilities, and with salaries a good deal higher than in Europe, working as a doctor or medical researcher in the USA is still an extremely attractive prospect. There are also opportunities on the non-clinical side. Working for a pharmaceutical company researching and testing drugs pays an average of $95,562 a year.

Useful contacts

O'Grady Peyton International: 0845 310 7310; europe@ogradypeyton.com; www.ogradypeyton.com

National Council of State Boards of Nursing: 312 525 3600; info@ncsbn.org; www.ncsbn.org. The NCSBN can provide addresses of state boards of nursing.

Teaching

One possibility for securing work as a teacher in the USA is to teach English as a foreign language to the thousands of immigrants who settle there every year. This kind of language teaching is known in the USA as TESL (Teaching English as a Second Language) or TESOL (Teaching English to Speakers of Other Languages). Countless programmes in English as a Second Language (ESL) are subsumed under several distinct programme types in America, in contrast to the heavy emphasis on 'academy' type EFL (English as a Foreign Language) or 'workplace' ESP (English for Special Purposes) in Europe. Just about every university and college in the major cities has an ESL programme, as do a range of government and charitable organisations. Commercial schools offer a wide variety of classes but tend to focus on survival ESL and EAP (English for Academic Purposes), with writing as a major component.

Although the demand for ESL teachers is enormous, it is very difficult for foreigners who do not have a green card to obtain the necessary working visa. The standard required qualification is an MA in TESOL, offered by universities and colleges in the USA, many of which are listed in the annually updated *EL Guide* (see 'Useful contacts' below). American organisations are beginning to recognise the Cambridge CELTA (Certificate in English Language Teaching to Adults) which can be obtained in four weeks at a large number of centres worldwide. *EL Prospects*, the monthly job supplement to the *EL Gazette*, carries some ads for openings in the USA, though most of those are academic posts in universities where it might be possible for the employer to overcome the visa problem in the case of highly-qualified candidates.

TIP

NMS and O'Grady Peyton (see below for contact information) are the two main UK organisations that sponsor nurses through NCLEX. They guarantee jobs at the end of the three- to four-month course and also sponsor applicants for a green card.

Bilingual/bicultural classes are run in thousands of high schools across the country. Many require staff who are not only state-certified teachers but also bilingual in either Spanish or exotic languages like Hmong or Gujarati. Most of the larger cities have at least one free or low-cost workplace literacy/vocational ESL programme which caters for immigrants needing assistance with basic English. Some of these programmes operate in outposts (such as churches and libraries) and many depend on local volunteers as tutors. Volunteer positions can conceivably lead to better things, and are particularly useful if you need references from American companies for your résumé.

Even for qualified American teachers, part-time seasonal work with full-time hours is the norm, often referred to as being hired as an 'adjunct'. Many contracts are not renewed each academic year, creating a transient English-teaching population. Pay is hourly and varies according to region, although an average wage of between $23 and $32 should be expected. Part-timers almost never get benefits, which means no health insurance, sick days or vacation pay. Even full-time teaching openings may be for just nine months, with pay as little as $25,000 in the Midwest.

TIP

■ One way of getting your foot in the door to teaching in America is to make yourself available as a substitute teacher. For this you will need a mobile phone and an email address at the very least.

i *TESOL* (Teachers of English to Speakers of Other Languages; info@tesol. org; www.tesol.org) is a non-profit, professional association which offers various services to members, numbering around 14,000 individuals and 45,000 organisations. The association offers an online job board, a job newsletter for TESOL members and an annual job fair, all of which may include English language teaching opportunities worldwide.

In most states you need to be a US citizen or resident in order to be employed in a public school. The same restrictions will seldom apply in private schools, where opportunities are better. Apply directly to the principal or through the school board's website. For addresses see the 'Schools and education' section in the 'Daily Life' chapter, above. Qualified UK teachers who want to arrange a temporary exchange with an American teacher should consult the section 'Short-term employment' below.

Applications for positions on the staff of a university are usually made direct. Several directories published by Petersons give details of schools and universities in the USA. Also see the *Directory of Postsecondary Institutions* (from www.amazon.com) for a complete list of American universities and institutes of higher education, or try the student website www.iamnext.com for links to each university's website. Lists of vacancies in modern language departments and English departments are supplied by the *Modern Language Association's* Job Information Service (www.mla. org). An online subscription to the jobs list costs $35 for a year for new members and $20 for graduate students.

Useful contacts

EL Gazette (monthly) and *EL Guide* (annual): 020 7481 6700; info@elgazette.com; ; www.elgazette.com. Relays news and developments in the industry; pitched at the professional end of the market.

Eflweb: editor@eflweb.com; www.eflweb.com. A leading provider of job and recruitment services to the EFL industry. The place for new and prospective EFL/ESL teachers.

Fulbright Commission: 020 7404 6994; education@fulbright.com; www.fulbright.co.uk/eas

Modern Language Association: 646 576 5000; www.mla.org

Teaching English Abroad (Susan Griffith, Crimson Publishing, 2008). Provides information on TEFL training and how to find work abroad and includes lists of language schools worldwide.

United Nations

The UN employs more than 16,000 people worldwide, and has a steady need for competent staff in various fields. Opportunities abound for clerical and administrative staff, as well as for professionally qualified lawyers, economists, scientists, IT specialists, translators and interpreters. The UN is particularly interested in candidates with international experience. Professional requirements usually include an advanced university degree and knowledge of both French and English, which are the two working languages of the UN. Each year the UN organises a National Competitive Recruitment Exam for entry-level positions. For more information have a look at the UN's website at www.un.org.

Most entry-level positions at the UN are for graduates under 39 who apply as 'junior professionals' for jobs in economics, finance, legal affairs or political affairs. These applicants must sit competitive exams and first need to contact the Office of Human Resources in New York (website below). Graduate students who are interested in doing an internship at the UN Headquarters in New York must submit an official UN Internship Application Form (P135), an up-to-date CV and a short essay. Applications are to be submitted between four and 12 months before the proposed start date and details of the scheme are available from the Internship Co-ordinator (OHRM_interns@un.org; www.un.org).

Other opportunities for work in the USA will be mainly in the UN's specialised agencies. With nearly 2,000 staff all based in Washington, the World Bank consists of the International Bank for Reconstruction and Development (IBRD), the International Development Association, and the International Finance Corporation. Qualified economists with experience in development issues are always needed.

The International Monetary Fund (IMF) employs economists, accountants, administrators, computer systems operators, language specialists and

TIP

■ More senior level positions at the UN are for experienced specialists and professionals. These applicants can contact the UN Information Office in their native country or the OHR in New York at the address given below.

lawyers. Jobs are open to graduates under 33 through the Fund's Economist Programme, or through direct appointment to the staff, for which a good deal of government, academic or financial experience is required.

The United Nations Development Programme coordinates and finances most UN development activities. It has a staff of 7,400, 80% of whom spend most of their careers in the field. Applicants, who should be postgraduates in the social sciences, should contact, in the first instance, the Information Centre at Millbank in London, or else the Office of Human Resources in New York. They will send the necessary information on to you regarding how to apply for a job. It is also worth checking out the websites of the various directorates; you will find them listed on www.un.org.

Useful addresses and websites

UN International Civil Service Commission: Two United Nations Plaza, 10th Floor, New York, NY 10017; 212 963 5465; icsc.un.org. Website lists all vacancies in the various UN divisions.

United Nations Information Centre: 1775 K Street NW, Suite 400, Washington, DC 20006; 202 331 8670; unicdc@unicwash.org; www.unicwash.org

Office of Human Resources Management: UN Headquarters, New York, NY 10017; 212 963 1234; www.un.org

■ SHORT-TERM EMPLOYMENT

Immigration officials at US entry points are notoriously efficient – if you do not have the appropriate work visa and they have the slightest suspicion that you are going to work they may search your luggage, confiscate your passport for two or three weeks and generally make you feel like a criminal. Despite this, many people have found it is possible to work illegally on a tourist visa by outwitting the immigration officials, although this is strongly advised against. It is helpful to have an address book full of US addresses of friends and relations with whom you might stay, and also enough money to support yourself, or bank letters confirming that funds are due to be wired over. On top of these, any documents that will convince the US Citizenship and Immigration Services (USCIS) that you are a legitimate tourist should be made available, including any that prove that you will be returning to your country by a certain deadline, say to take up a place in higher education or in a workplace.

Work Your Way Around the World by Susan Griffith (Crimson Publishing, 2007) is a popular and comprehensive source of temporary jobs for individuals who want to earn money while they travel. The book describes how to find employment on boats, at tourist resorts and national parks, in catering, agriculture, or by doing manual labour.

TIP

■ Further information on short-term employment is available at www.petersons.com, which has a broad range of summer opportunities to search online and is revised and updated frequently.

Work experience, internships and exchange schemes

For anyone looking for employment or work experience in the USA lasting up to 18 months, the schemes described here offer the simplest way of obtaining permission to work in the USA. A brief list of approved exchanges and internship programmes in the US is available on the *Fulbright Commission's* website at www.fulbright.co.uk.

Work and travel programmes

A handful of work and travel programmes are available in the USA through approved organisations. Application documents necessary for student-only programmes include a letter from your principal, registrar, or tutor showing that you are a full-time student in the year of travel. This should be done on college-headed paper. Gap-year students should submit evidence of an unconditional offer for the September/October after they have returned from the USA.

British Universities North America Club (BUNAC) administers a USA summer working programme in addition to its camp programmes whereby students are permitted to do any summer job they are able to find before or after arrival. In order to qualify for 'Work America' you have to be a full-time degree-level student returning to study at the end of the summer. The scheme provides a directory of jobs in the USA and organises loans for flights if necessary. There is a registration fee of around £260 (plus other associated costs, including mandatory insurance and visa application fees). To widen the scope of your job hunt, you might consult the section below entitled '*casual work*'.

The *Resort America* programme, administered by AIFS (American Institute for Foreign Study) and operated in the UK and Europe by Camp America, provides students with pre-arranged summer work across the USA. Positions available include working with food and beverages, guest relations, administration, housekeeping and general maintenance. Positions are in resorts, hotels, country inns and other establishments providing hospitality. The programme is from 12 to 16 weeks and pocket money starts at $1,375. The whole package is arranged for you and there is 24-hour support and advice available.

The other principal work and travel programmes are those of *Council Exchanges* (offered through *IST Plus* in the UK) and *Camp Counselors USA (CCUSA)*.

Camp Counselors USA's (CCUSA's) *Work Experience USA* (WEUSA) programme provides students aged 18 to 30 with the opportunity to live and work during the summer as an American citizen. You can choose from two different options, allowing you different levels of flexibility and independence – the Independent Option (costing £234) allows you to

TIP

You are usually required to have a minimum sum of money at your disposal: $400–$1000 in travellers cheques.

obtain temporary/summer work in many fields from forestry to finance, which may relate to future career plans, but requires that you find your own job – although CCUSA will offer you assistance. If you want CCUSA to do the work for you, you can choose the Placement Option (costing £460), which is geared towards working in seasonal summer jobs in the tourism industry, usually waiting tables, bar work, or working in country clubs or national parks. The CCUSA programme works with up to 250 employers in resort and vacation centres throughout the USA to find placements for participants. The programme guarantees a job to those who are accepted. Both packages include a Directory of Employers, assistance with return airfare from London to New York, four months' insurance, meeting on arrival and a two-day orientation in New York with accommodation. Most recruitment takes place before 1 April and the company has a network of interviewers around the UK who organise various open houses and recruitment fairs. Try visiting www.ccusa.com to find out more.

Useful contacts

AIFS Resort America (American Institute for Foreign Study):
020 7581 7373; enquiries@campamerica.co.uk;
www.resortamerica.,aifs.com or www.campamerica.co.uk
British Universities North America Club (BUNAC): 020 7251 3472;
enquiries@bunac.org.uk; www.bunac.org.uk
Camp Counselors USA (CCUSA): 020 7637 0779; info@ccusa.co.uk;
www.ccusa.com and 0131 665 5843; www.campcounselors.com
IST Plus: 020 8939 9057; info@istplus.com; www.istplus.com

Internships and work experience

'Internship' is the American term for traineeship. Placements are normally unpaid and provide a chance for undergraduates and recent graduates to get some experience in their career interest. The advantage of using an established exchange programme is that the organisers will handle complex and time-consuming administrative details so you don't have to worry about filling in forms incorrectly or applying for the wrong visa. You will be paying for these services but in exchange you should get a well-structured work-related placement and a J-1 visa, plus comprehensive insurance and accommodation if required.

For individuals who choose not to apply through an official exchange programme organiser in their home countries, it is possible to find a short-term training placement in the US through the *Association for International Practical Training* (AIPT) which sponsors most J-1 visas for on-the-job training. If you are not in a position to fix up your own internship independently, you can contact AIPT for help in finding a suitable placement.

If you want to try to go it alone, you can make use of the annually revised book *Internships* (Peterson's, 2005), which lists paid and unpaid intern positions lasting for a single summer, semester or an entire year. The

TIP

■ For a fee of £430 IST Plus' programme gives full-time university students the chance to work in the USA during the summer holidays. The price includes full insurance, US State Department fees, participant materials and 24-hour support and assistance while in the country. For more information go to www.istplus.com.

TIP

■ All applicants for J-1 visas will have to persuade the authorities that they will return home before the maximum period of 18 months expires.

book offers general advice (including a section called 'Foreign applicants for US internships') and specific listings organised according to field of interest – advertising, museums, radio, social services, law, etc.

Several exchange organisations in the UK arrange for students and graduates to undertake internships in the US. The most useful is IST Plus, which helps 1,400 students and graduates each year to arrange course-related placements in the US lasting from three to 18 months. The placement can take place at any time during your studies, during the summer, as a sandwich year, or up to 12 months after graduating. Although you are responsible for finding your own course-related position, often with the help of an academic adviser, IST Plus supplies practical advice on applying for work in their 'Internship USA' programme. Those who qualify receive a DS-2019, which allows them to apply for the required J-1 visa. The programme fees start from £430 for a two-month stint and go as high as £875 for 14 months. The programme works in association with the Council on International Education Exchange (CIEE) in Boston, which acts as a visa sponsor. Visa restrictions do not allow placements as nannies, au pairs or teachers.

Internship programmes are also overseen by *EIL UK, Cultural Homestay International* and a number of others listed under the *'Useful contacts'* section below. The *Central Bureau for International Education and Training* is a department of the British Council which supervises international exchanges and training programmes and is a point of reference for anyone hoping to navigate the rather complex subject of exchange programmes in the US.

Useful contacts

AIESEC: 020 7549 1800; national@uk.aisec.org; www.workabroad.org.uk; and 212 767 3774; www.aiesecus.org. Internships are offered to students studying economics, business, marketing, and computer science.

Alliance Abroad Group: 512 457 8062; www.allianceabroad.com. Offers work abroad, H2-B, Q, and J-1 visas, trainee and work/travel programmes.

Association for International Practical Training (AIPT): 410 997 2200; aipt@aipt.org; www.aipt.org

CDS International Inc: 212 497 3500; info@cdsintl.org; www.cdsintl.org. Practical training assignments lasting between three and18 months are open to British, European and certain other young professionals aged 18–35.

British Council Education and Training Group: 020 7930 8466; general. enquiries@britishcouncil.org; www.britishcouncil.org/learning

Challenge Educational Services: 01273 208648; www.challengeuk.com. The USA work placement scheme assigns unpaid interns aged 18–25 with UK nationality to a business for between one and four months. Previous internships have included marketing, banking, journalism, charity, computing and law.

Cultural Homestay International: 415 459 5397; www.chinet.org. Work and travel programme for full-time students aged 18–30 and two internship programmes for qualifying candidates; the short-term one (one, two, or three months) is for university students and recent graduates aged 20 to 30 and the intensive one (lasting six to 10 months) is for graduates and young professionals aged 22 to 35.

EIL:287; 0800 018 4015; info@eiluk.org; www.eiluk.org. Internships last three to 12 weeks year round. Interns aged 18–25 are assigned to a business in their area of interest and work in an unpaid capacity.

Global Vision International: 0870 608 8898; info@gvi.co.uk; www.gvi.co.uk; and 1 888 653 6028; info@gviusa.com; www.gviusa.com. Run conservation expeditions, volunteer projects and career development placements with partner organisations in 20 countries worldwide.

InterExchange: 212 924 0446; info@interexchange.org; www.interexchange.org. Offer work and travel, au pair, internship, career training, summer camp placements and H-2B programmes.

IST Plus: International experience programmes 020 8939 9057; info@istplus.com; www.istplus.com

Mountbatten Internship Programme: 020 7253 7759 (UK); 212 557 5380 (US); info-uk@mountbatten.org; www.mountbatten.org. Provides work experience in New York City for graduates and young professionals aged 21–28. Placements last one year and include free accommodation and medical insurance as well as a monthly wage of around $950. Interns pay a participation fee of £1,900.

Sister Cities International: 202 347 8630; info@sister-cities.org; www.sister-cities.org

Agricultural exchanges

Three British-based organisations offer work experience on farms in the USA:

International Farm Experience Programme (IFEP): 024 7685 7211; www.nfyfc.co.uk. Offers work experience in all land-based industries including agriculture, horticulture, rural tourism, landscaping and equestrianism. To qualify for a place you must hold a British or Irish passport, have a minimum of one year's relevant experience, and be between 18 and 28 years old. Placements last from three to 12 months and most can start at any time of year. The work is paid, but it is usually only enough to cover costs. You have the option of working on a farm or taking an exchange course at Ohio State University or Minnesota University.

Agriventure, International Agricultural Exchange Association (IAEA): 01945 450999; www.agriventure.com; and 1 800 263 1827; iaea@nucleus.com. Organises exchanges on farms mainly in Montana, North and South Dakota, and Minnesota. Individuals live and work with a host family. All-inclusive fees start from £2,245, which includes insurance,

visas, flights, orientation, and placement costs. Relevant experience is preferred but not essential. Placements are for between six and 12 months, with the return ticket valid for a year.

The International Rural Exchange Program UK: 01572 717381; ws@iepuk.com; www.iepuk.com. Places trainees with at least a year's hands-on practical experience in horse racing and equine work, agriculture, horticulture or oenology (wine making). The fee is £600, which excludes airfares.

US-based agricultural programmes

Ohio International Agricultural Intern Program: 614 292 7720; www.top.osu.edu

MAST International (Minnesota Agricultural Student Trainee): 612 624 3740; mast@umn.edu; www.mast.coafes.umn.edu

Teaching exchanges

Both the *British Council Education and Training* (www.britishcouncil. org) and the *Fulbright Commission* (www.fulbright.co.uk) run exchange schemes for teachers. The Fulbright Commission deals only with teachers at university level, and offers many grants for different categories of research and teaching. Teachers have to find their own exchange partner while the Commission helps with orientation and arranges the J-1 visa.

The Central Bureau (British Council) has a wider scheme, placing around 100 teachers a year in American schools at all levels, from nursery to 12th grade. In order to qualify you must be a qualified teacher with at least three years' experience, two of them in your current job, and you must have formal support from your head teacher. The Bureau will match you to a teacher in the USA as near to you professionally as possible, and will also take into account any preferences you have in terms of region. It arranges visas and organises orientation sessions for your US exchange partner: the same thing is done for you by the parallel organisation in the USA.

Business exchanges

Within the UK, the business association BritishAmerican Business Inc (BABi; www.babinc.org), runs a Professional Exchange Programme allowing employees of their member organisations to gain the experience of working in the USA on 18-month J-1 visas. BABI will process applications and organise insurance, income tax planning and relocation assistance. J-1 visas are handled through BABi's New York office.

Summer camps

Thousands of young people from around the world are needed each summer to be in charge of a cabin full of American youngsters and to instruct or supervise activities which can range from the ordinary (swimming and tennis) to the esoteric (puppet-making and ham radio). A number of agencies recruit and screen young people from abroad to work at US camps under the J-1 cultural exchange visa programme including those mentioned in the 'work and travel programmes' section above. The basic requirements are that you satisfy the age limits (usually 19–35) and that you have relevant recent experience working with children.

The minimum commitment, depending on the programme, is to work for the eight or nine weeks of camp, usually starting in May or June and finishing in either July or August. On completion, counsellors and other staff have six to 10 weeks' free time to travel and they normally return on organised flights between late August and the end of September. Participants in the summer camp programmes receive a free return flight between London and New York and guidance on applying for a J-1 visa. The camps provide free board and lodging plus pocket money. Interviews are compulsory and are held in university towns throughout Britain between October and May.

BUNAC is one of the two biggest summer camp placement organisations, sending up to 5,000 people aged between 18 and 35 to participate in the Summer Camp USA programme. The registration fee of £141 includes camp placement, return flight with land transport arrangements to camp and access to pocket money of $935–$1,075 (depending on age) for the whole nine-week period. In addition to the camp counsellor programme, BUNAC runs 'KAMP', the Kitchen and Maintenance Programme. KAMP is open only to full-time students, who are given ancillary jobs in the kitchen, laundry or maintenance departments at summer camps. They will be advanced

TIP

Placements are usually for one year from August to August, and you should apply as soon as possible in the autumn term for interviews in October/December.

TIP

There are fewer opportunities for Australian and New Zealand business exchanges than there are for the UK, although the American Australian Association (www.americanaustralian.org) may be able to point you in the right direction.

their airfare and paid more than the counsellors – at least \$1,350 for the nine-week period of work.

The other major camp recruitment organisation is *Camp America*, which arranges cultural exchange placements on summer camps across the USA for more than 10,000 people aged 18 or over, recruited from 30 countries. Two types of position are available through two different programmes: the Camp Counselor Program involves working directly with children aged six to 16, taking care of their welfare and teaching and guiding them; and the Campower Program, which is only available to students who are not in their final year, involves catering, kitchen work, ground work, and other activities necessary to keep the camp in good running order. The assignments are for nine weeks and pocket money varies according to age and experience. Positions are prearranged to suit your skills and interest and there is 24-hour support and advice.

Several other international camp placement organisations cooperate with camp directors to help recruit summer staff. For example, *Camp Counselors USA (CCUSA)* recruits young people aged 18–30 from more than 60 countries. Others are listed below.

Useful contacts

BUNAC: 020 7251 3472; enquiries@bunac.org.uk; www.bunac.org.uk
Camp America: 020 7581 7373; enquiries@campamerica.co.uk; www.campamerica.co.uk
Camp Counselors USA (CCUSA): 020 7637 0779; info@ccusa.co.uk; www.ccusa.co.uk; info@ccusa.com; www.campcounselors.com
Camp Leaders: 0845 430 1219; uk@campleaders.com; www.campleaders.com and 866 803 7643; usa@campleaders.com
International Counselor Exchange Program (ICEP): 212 787 7706; www.icep-usa.org
YMCA International Camp Counselor Program (ICCP): 212 727 8800; ips@ymcanyc.org; www.internationalymca.org

Soccer coaching

Soccer has gained huge popularity in North America over the past 15 years, especially among school children. Since British football is universally admired, demand is strong for young British coaches to work on summer coaching schemes. A number of companies recruit players and coaches to work all over the USA, including Hawaii:

Goal-Line Soccer Clinics Inc: 541 753 5833; trowney@goal-line.com; www.goal-line.com
Major League Soccer Camps: 1 800 536 9966 6272; www.mlscamps.com. The largest and best known.
Soccer Academy Inc: 703 3393 7961; esoccer@soccer-academy.com; www.soccer-academy.com

TIP

■ Organisations warn that camp counselling is not for people who are looking for a cheap way to see America. Those who have worked on a summer camp report that the work is hard and that you must have a genuine liking for children, including, but by no means limited to, the kind of indulged American child who can often seem spoiled and difficult to handle while on holiday.

Other companies advertise in the specialist press and BUNAC knows about these companies since they normally process the necessary J-1 visa. It is more important to be good at working with kids than to be a great football player, though of course it is easier to command the respect of the kids if you can show them good skills and a few tricks.

Working as an au pair

The only legitimate way for an au pair to work in the USA is on a J-1 visa, obtainable through US government-designated agencies. The official au pair programme allows young people with childcare experience to work for an American family for a minimum of one year, with numerous other conditions of participation.

A separate programme exists for qualified child carers or nannies called variously the 'Au Pair Extraordinaire' or 'Au Pair Elite' programme depending on the agency. Candidates with the appropriate nanny or childcare qualification (NNEB, BTEC, Diploma in Nursing, NVQ3) can earn more than an au pair ($220 a week as compared to $158) but are still limited to a one-year stay.

The basic requirements for au pairs in the USA are that participants are between 18 and 26, speak English to an acceptable standard, have a full, clean driving licence, and provide a criminal record check. They must also show that they have had at least 200 hours of recent childcare experience (which can consist of regular babysitting, helping at a summer playscheme or school). Anyone wanting to care for a child under two must have 200 hours of experience looking after children under two and should also expect the programme interviewers to delve more deeply than they would otherwise.

The fixed level of weekly pocket money paid on official au pair programmes to America has now been brought into line with the US minimum wage requirements. At the time of writing the weekly payment was $157.95 plus room and board in return for 45 hours of childcare (including babysitting) and domestic duties. Perks usually include a free

transatlantic flight plus one-way or return from New York to the family, a compulsory four-day orientation in New York, ongoing support from a community counsellor, up to $500 from the family to cover fees for a course of study, and two weeks' paid vacation.

Prospective au pairs around the world must apply through a small number of sponsoring organisations (currently six) which must follow US government guidelines. Applicants are required to pay an upfront fee of $500, $200 of which is returned to them at the end of 12 months if the programme is completed. *Au Pair in America* (part of the American Institute for Foreign Study) is the largest sender from the UK and worldwide.

Interviews are a necessary stage in the application process. In addition to the interviews, there will be a lot of form-filling, reference-gathering and letter-writing involved before you will be chosen. The most popular departure times are between January and March or between June and September, with the starting date of the majority of jobs coinciding with the beginning of the school year in September. The programme allows a 13th month of pure travel at your expense, providing you complete the initial 12 months as planned.

The *Educare America* programme is overseen by *AIFS* and uses a network of agencies to recruit candidates. Chief among them in the UK is *Childcare International Ltd* (office@childint.co.uk; www.childint.co.uk). Like the Au Pair Programme, Educare is a 12-month programme with departures in winter and summer, for which successful applicants must be interviewed and attend a four-day safety and childcare orientation on arrival. The families participating in the programme will have children at school and the work will involve supervising these children before and after school. The number of working hours is 30, the weekly pay is $118.46 and the programme fee is $850, which covers flights to the US. Participants study six hours a week at an accredited US post-secondary college or university during term-time for which they receive a contribution of up to $1,000 from their host families.

Useful contacts

American Institute for Foreign Study (AIFS): 020 7581 7300; info@aifs.co.uk; www.aifs.org. Runs the *Au Pair in America* Program. Has appointed interviewers located throughout UK and Europe.

AuPairCare Cultural Exchange: 415 434 8788; info@aupaircare.com; www.aupaircare.com. Also offers the Au Pair Elite Programme for qualified nannies.

Au Pair in America: 203 399 5000; aupair.info@aifs.com; www.aupairamerica.com

Cultural Care Au Pair: 1 800 448 5753; aupair.operations@culturalcare.com; www.culturalcare.com. Has overseas offices in Australia, Austria, Brazil, Colombia, Germany, Mexico, Poland, Russia, and Sweden, plus agents in countries such as South Africa, the Czech Republic, Peru, Panama, Croatia, and Hungary. Also operates through an agent in London.

EurAupair: 1 800 713 2002; info@euraupair.com; www.euraupair.com.
Experiment in International Learning (EIL) 802 257 7751;
info@worldlearning.org; www.experiment.org and 0168 456 2577;
info@eiluk.org; www.eiluk.org. Has offices in many countries worldwide.
Go Au Pair: 1 888 287 2471; inforequest@goaupair.com;
www.goaupair.com
InterExchange: 212 924 0446; info@interexchange.org;
www.interexchange.org

◼ CASUAL WORK

All US employers are obliged to examine the documents of anyone they employ to make sure that they are legitimate. The penalty for not doing so or for employing an illegal alien is a large fine, and, for the employee, deportation, with their chances of obtaining a visa in the future severely compromised. This has reduced the number of opportunities for casual work, but they do still exist, and there is apparently no shortage of people prepared to keep looking over their shoulder for immigration officials and to put up with long hours and low pay as the consequences of being outside the law.

Labour demands in summer resorts like Wildwood (New Jersey), Ocean City (Maryland), Virginia Beach (Virginia), Myrtle Beach (South Carolina) and Atlantic Beach (North Carolina) sometimes reach crisis proportions, especially along the eastern seaboard. Time can productively be spent looking for work in these areas by searching the internet. Dozens of sites may prove useful, though www.coolworks.com is especially recommended for seasonal jobs in the tourist industry and www.jobmonkey.com is also useful. Another job search website that lists summer jobs mainly in resorts and parks is www.seasonalemployment.com. Further contacts can be found in the annually revised book *Summer Jobs Worldwide* (Crimson Publishing 2008) and details in *Work Your Way Around the World* (Crimson Publishing 2007).

Ski resorts

Finding a winter job in a ski resort in Colorado, Montana, Utah, New Mexico, Nevada, Idaho and even California (the most difficult for illegal workers) is possible, although to turn up without anything arranged at all would be risky, given the price of accommodation and the competition for jobs, principally from American ski bums.

Recruitment fairs are held by resorts before the season starts and these are advertised in the local press and on billboards. Those without legal papers are obliged to ask for work in the restaurants, bars and hotels of the resorts that are not owned by a ski resort corporation. There are reports

TIP

◼ The most popular places for casual work are the obvious ones: in the cities, and the resorts of California, Florida, New England and the Gulf Coast, where it is still not difficult to pick up seasonal work in restaurants and bars.

FACT

◼ As most ski resorts are owned by corporations they will certainly not employ anyone without a social security number or valid visa.

If you want to work in a ski resort, plan ahead, as competition is fierce

of illegal workers in Colorado resorts such as Vail and Steamboat Springs. Cocktail waitresses, in particular, can earn a fortune thanks to the generous nature of American tipping. Further details of working in American ski resorts can be found in *Work Your Way Around the World*.

Useful addresses

Heavenly Mountain Resort: PO Box 2180, Stateline, NV 89449; 775 586 7000; www.skiheavenly.com

Mammoth Mountain Ski Area: Human Resources, PO Box 24, Mammoth Lakes, CA 93546; 760 934 0745; www.mammothmountain.com

Aspen Skiing Company: PO Box 1248, Aspen, CO 81612; 970 925 1220; www.aspensnowmass.com

Snowmass Village Resort Association: 16 Kearns Road, Suite 104, Snowmass Village, CO 81615; 970 923 2000; www.snowmassvillage.com

Breckenridge Ski Corporation: PO Box 1058, Breckenridge, CO 80424; 970 453 5000; www.breckenridge.com

Copper Mountain Resort Inc: PO Box 3001, Copper Mountain, CO 80443; 866 841 2481; www.ski-copper.com

Steamboat Springs Ski and Resort Corporation: 2305 Mt Werner Circle, Steamboat, CO 80487; 970 871 5132; personnel@steamboat.com; www.steamboat.com

Park City Mountain Resort: PO Box 39, Park City, UT 84060;
435 649 8111; info@pcski.com; www.pcski.com
Killington Ski Resort: 4763 Killington Road, Killington, VT 05751;
802 422 6100; humres@killington.com; www.killington.com
Jackson Hole Ski Corporation: PO Box 290, 3395 West Village Drive,
Teton Village, WY 83025; 307 733 2292; info@jacksonhole.com;
www.jacksonhole.com

Seasonal work

Seasonal harvest labour is another possibility for casual work, though quite a remote one, since many of the casual harvesting jobs are filled by Latin-American immigrants, legal or otherwise. Harvests include citrus fruit in Florida from October to May; wheat in the Great Plains (Kansas is known as 'the Wheat State') from May to August, soft fruits in the southern and eastern states in May and June; apples in the north-east in September – reputedly a good earner; and grapes in the wine-producing states of California, Oregon, Washington, Idaho, and New York.

If you have some experience, it might be worthwhile trying to get a job on an Alaskan shrimp, salmon or tuna boat – the pay can be good. Ask at Kodiak, Chignik, Petersburg, Ketchikan, Wragnell, or Newport and Astoria on the Oregon coast. Fishing ports along the Gulf of Mexico are also a possibility, although you will face fierce competition from Hispanic immigrants.

Although the national parks will normally only hire Americans there may be work opportunities during high season in May and June, and in September when the casual workers have gone back to school. You can also try theme and amusement parks, although again you will have to compete against local students for work.

■ VOLUNTARY WORK

If you are looking for a long-term commitment to volunteer work, your best bet is to look around your local community. If English is your first language, for example, you could try volunteering as a tutor to adult or child learners of English as a Second Language (ESL) through local libraries or schools. Full training is often given and the experiences are extremely rewarding, often resulting in long-term, fulfilling relationships with students and their families. Women's shelters usually need committed volunteers to help staff safe houses; after-schools clubs are often on the look out for experienced people to work with children; or you could look into schemes which help the elderly to run their errands. Whatever your interest and experience, volunteering is a wonderful way of giving something back to a community and adding some depth to an American résumé. Some useful websites which link volunteers to local and national schemes are www.volunteermatch.org and www.volunteer.gov. Alternatively, you could look at the *International Directory of Volunteer Work* (Crimson Publishing).

Short-term voluntary work for unskilled volunteers usually takes the form of workcamps. Working holidays on workcamps that last two or three weeks can consist of purely physical labour such as construction or environmental work, or they can have a more social emphasis, like playschemes for deprived or disabled children, hospital work, or community development. For example, volunteers clear trails in national parks and forests, assist with urban renovation and preservation of historic landmarks, and work with disabled children and adults at holiday centres.

The main workcamp organisations in the USA are *Volunteers for Peace (VFP)*, *Council Exchanges (International Volunteer Projects)* and *Service Civil International*. Prospective volunteers for these should register with the partner workcamp organisation in their own country. Other organisations accustomed to dealing with foreign applicants are included in the list below.

Useful contacts

American Hiking Society: 301 565 6704; www.americanhiking.org. Organises camps involving outdoor work, maintaining trails, fire watching, wildlife observation, and historical research. Minimum age is 16 and the minimum period of work is two weeks. Foreigners require work permit or J-1 visa.

Camphill Special School: 610 469 9236; www.beaverrun.org. Volunteers willing to stay more than six months help run programmes for children with disabilities. Volunteers are given a monthly stipend, health insurance and visa assistance.

Council Exchanges: 617 247 0350; info@councilexchanges.org; www.councilexchanges.org. Runs 600 International Volunteer Projects in 30 countries. Their directory of opportunities is available from April or can be viewed on their web page.

Quaker Information Center: 215 241 7024; www.quakerinfo.org. 'Smorgasbord' of listings of voluntary opportunities ranging from weekend workcamps through to two-year internships with aid agencies in USA and worldwide.

SCI International Voluntary Service: 206 350 6585; info@sci-ivs.org; www.sci-ivs.org. US branch of international workcamps organisation.

Société Bienfaisance Mutuelle: 415 477 3667. Helps British and French volunteers over 18 to work for eight weeks from early July for several San Francisco organisations including the California Pacific Medical Centre and the AIDS Service Foundation.

Student Conservation Association Inc: 603 543 1700; www.sca-inc.org. Organises conservation and environmental internships in national parks and forests nationwide, lasting from 12 weeks to 12 months. Travel expenses, housing, training and a weekly stipend are provided.

Tahoe Rim Trail Fund: 775 298 0012; info@tahoerimtrail.org; www.tahoerimtrail.org. Organisation that was formed in 1981 to help build and maintain a 165-mile (266-km) trail around the ridge tops of the Lake Tahoe Basin in California and Nevada. English-speaking volunteers are needed each year to help construct the trail during the summer and early fall months. Accommodation is not provided.

UVM Center for Career Development International Internships: 802 656 4200; living.learning@uvm.edu; www.uvm.edu. Has a database of thousands of internships in anything from teaching to conservation, many of which are based in America.

Volunteers for Peace (VFP): 802 259 2759; www.vfp.org. VFP places about 500 foreign volunteers on 40–50 workcamps in the USA. Details are included in its *International Workcamp Directory,* available to members from mid-April.

WinantClayton Volunteers Association: 020 8983 3834; wcva@dircon.co.uk; www.winantclayton.com Offers New York placements for approximately seven weeks from late-June to mid-August followed by two weeks independent travel time. Minimum age is 18 with no upper limit. Volunteers must hold full British or Irish passports.

■ BUSINESS AND INDUSTRY OVERVIEW

According to the Bureau of Labor Statistics, the US economy lost 240,000 jobs during the first quarter of 2008, continuing the economic slowdown of 2007. The main areas affected were manufacturing, construction and aviation, although the retail industry suffered major losses too, as consumers tightened their purse strings and began spending less. In contrast, positive contributions came from healthcare, IT and professional services, which all continue to grow at a healthy rate. The Federal Reserve's Beige Book, which covers economic activity, suggests that the economy has continued to weaken with decreased activity evident in all Federal Reserve districts.

The buoyancy of the 1990s illustrated the great inherent strengths of the American economy; its investment in research and development (particularly in new technologies), a lively venture capital market, and individuals and companies eager to innovate. At its best, the USA thrives on risk taking and hard work, though in the bad times it is the same industries which used to boom that are the most affected. Risk taking and hard work have historically produced great affluence, and some individuals have amassed vast fortunes. But brilliant ideas have also benefited large numbers of employees who have been fortunate to build their careers in dynamic companies. When times are good, the USA really lives up to its American Dream.

FACT

■ Oil prices have jumped above $130 a barrel at the time of writing; the price of gold is also on the rise and the weak dollar is putting pressure on import prices. All of these factors have contributed to a slowdown in the expansion of the US economy.

The improvement of the high US federal deficit in the early 1990s also built economic confidence, and the creation of the North American Free Trade Agreement helped to develop markets for US goods and services. The NAFTA is similar to the European Union, in that its policies affect a substantial number of people: almost 450 million, in fact. The EU has a similar population of around 490 million.

Franchising became more popular too, during the 1990s, as people sought to become self-employed – a trend which has continued into the millennium. Thousands of people every year are tempted to try running their own fast-food restaurant, dating service, home-cleaning operation or bagel shop. If you have a strong parent company with large advertising and marketing budgets (think along the lines of McDonalds), you have a massive advantage, although if your franchiser fails you will be carried down with it.

There are differences between north and south. It is generally considered that the north-east enjoys the highest standard of living while some of the southern states are among the poorest on the continent. However, over the past 20 years 'the South' has made great strides to modernise its economic base by improving standards of education and attracting investment and industrial plants with tax breaks. Atlanta is one of the fastest growing cities in the USA and widely regarded as a model for what is frequently called the 'new South': a region with better economic performances and improved race relations.

Despite advances in the southern states, the north-east of the country continues to have the highest disposable income, with the west close behind. In common with other highly industrialised nations the USA has shifted from being a producer of goods to a provider of services. Three-quarters of the workforce are now employed in service industries. The economy is also consumer oriented: two-thirds of all goods and services produced are bought by domestic users, while the remaining third is bought by business and government. It is for this reason that the economic slowdown has hit the USA so hard: when spending is reduced, services and associated industries suffer the consequences.

Automotive

The United States of America is the world's second largest car producer after Japan, accounting for one-fifth of the world's cars. The industry has faced its most intense competition in more than 50 years due to recession, the dramatic development of the Japanese car industry, global competition from growing economies like China, and the worldwide emergence of manufacturing overcapacity. The price of oil has pushed the cost of petrol to an all-time average high of $4.19 per gallon (£0.55/€0.69 per litre) at the time of writing, compared to $2 per gallon (£0.41/€0.52 per litre) in 2004. Despite the downturn in the US economy, sales of cars are holding

FACT

■ As far as standard of living is concerned, the south lags behind the north, with a disposable income at about 90% of the national average.

FACT

■ The motor industry is concentrated in Detroit (also known as Motown), which remains home to three of the largest car manufacturers in the world: Ford, Chrysler and General Motors.

up, largely due to financial incentives such as 0% interest on car loans being offered by the manufacturers, as well as big discounts. Some showrooms even offer a year's free gas for your car as an incentive to buy – in doing so, acknowledging the problems the industry is suffering.

Intense competition in the past has led to corporate restructuring, slimming of organisations and cost cutting, all of which will probably be necessary again. This will lead to many more job losses and plant closures, especially as factories become more automated.

There are two contradictory developments in consumer demand. While the market is increasingly concerned with 'green' issues – better efficiency, less fuel consumption and the development of hybrid vehicles – the average consumer is also clamouring for more comfort, more technology and more cup-holders. The demand for the controversial gas-guzzling four-wheel Sports Utility Vehicles is indicative of this trend, although sale prices for SUVs and pick-up trucks have seen a decline over the past year or so.

Fuel-efficient options

Hybrid cars are heralded as the next generation of automobile, paving the way for a reduction in petrol and oil and more energy-efficient options for the consumer. These new technology vehicles are becoming a more common sight on American roads and it is possible to pick up a brand-new, or even second-hand, model at most car showrooms. They are more expensive than the average car but you can drive away with a clearer environmental conscience and more money in your pocket at the end of the financial year. As a comparison, one of the smallest and most fuel-efficient regular cars in the current market, a Toyota Yaris, gets 31mpg (8mpl/13kpl) on average, whereas the hybrid Toyota Prius gets around 47mpg (12mpl/20kpl). It seems that with rising fuel costs showing no signs of declining, hybrid cars may be the future for American drivers.

Banking and finance

The pace of consolidation over the last decade has been more rapid in commercial banking than in any other industry. The House of Senate approved a bill in 1999 which allowed commercial banks, securities companies, and insurers to be affiliated under the same holding company, which in turn is regulated by the Federal Reserve. An interstate banking law also allows holding companies to acquire a bank in any state, and for banks from separate states to merge. Foreign banks now have the same right to open US branches as other banks, whether they operate directly in the USA or through a subsidiary.

The structure of the US banking system is more complex than that of the UK. There is no nationwide branch banking system and each state has its own banks which are regulated by the central bank, the United States Federal Reserve System (the 'Fed'). While most banks are local to a single state or group of states, some banks do have branches across the USA, such as US Bank, Wells Fargo and the Bank of America. There are also state-run banks, which are controlled by the state banking authorities.

National banks are required to be members of the Federal Reserve System, and must have 'National' or 'NA' (National Association) as part of their name. US commercial banks, chartered under the Federal Reserve System, offer the same kinds of business and individual banking facilities that can be found in the UK. These include collection services (debt collection and so on), cheque book and credit card services, and a variety of different current accounts.

The Federal Reserve also acts as a central clearing house for other banks, processing and clearing cheques, processing electronic transfers and federal securities and clearing customer payments. There are several local clearing houses which also have this function, the largest of which is the New York Clearing House. Banks also maintain accounts with other banks and can clear cheques through them. Other financial institutions include Credit Unions (similar to building societies), which provide interest-bearing deposits and loans to individual members.

Foreign banks in the USA

There are around 300 foreign banks which have banking operations in the USA. They account for a third of all commercial and industrial loans outstanding from all US

banking institutions. There are four types of operation that a non-US bank may set up in the USA. A representative office may not engage in actual banking activities, but is authorised to carry out various activities for the parent bank, such as arranging loans. Agencies – which are federally or state licensed – can conduct general banking business, their funds derived from the parent bank. Thirdly, branches can carry out all banking operations, again with capital derived from the parent bank. Lastly, subsidiaries can be set up, which are licensed and chartered in the USA. They have the same scope and are subject to the same restrictions as US domestic banks. Most foreign banks, whatever their status, provide most of the normal banking services: payments and settlements, obtaining foreign currencies, investment, and providing information on the state of the US markets and institutions.

The Stock Exchange

The USA has several stock exchanges in New York, Boston, Philadelphia, Chicago and San Francisco. The two largest – and most important – are the New York Stock Exchange and the American Stock Exchange (also in New York). For a company to be listed on the NYSE it must meet stringent

requirements. The company must submit past accounts to be audited, and the authorities must be satisfied that there is a wide enough market for the particular securities that it is listing. There must be at least 1.1 million shares, with a market value of at least $18 million, publicly held; the company must own net tangible assets of at least $18 million; and it must have earned, pre-tax, at least $2.5 million for the last tax year and at least $2 million in each of the two preceding years. Foreign companies must meet different, but no less stringent, requirements.

The US Stock Exchange is generally regarded as one of the most active in the world. There is excellent investor protection due to very strict disclosure laws, and, at the same time a prolific over-the-counter market for stocks not listed publicly. This is run by the National Association of Securities Dealers.

Chemicals and petrochemicals

The American chemical industry is the largest in the world and one the USA's most important manufacturing sectors. The industry produces more than 50,000 different chemicals in 12,000 plants and has an output of more than $400 billion a year. The chemicals industry covers products such as industrial gases and pigments, plastic resins and synthetic rubber, drugs and pharmaceuticals, soaps and detergents, cosmetics, paints, agrochemicals, and adhesives. Like many manufacturing areas, chemical companies have been merging and cutting back on costs as globalisation increases competition and the financial markets press for higher financial returns.

Problems facing the chemical industry are the same as those that face all major industries: competition, and domestic and international health and safety regulations. The industry is also suffering from the world's strictest environmental protection regulations – the 'Superfund' laws – although the industry remains a powerful lobby and is able, to a certain extent, to limit the passing of laws that would be too damaging to it.

Restructuring takes place frequently, with international companies from the UK, Germany, Japan, and France all acquiring US companies. Observers are saying that because the chemicals industry is at the forefront of the 'new materials renaissance' (advanced industrial ceramics, improved adhesives and other high-tech. substances), it will become an indicator for the health of the US economy as a whole. Another commentator has said that the long-term survival of the industry depends on how well it sells itself to the public, since it is, like the nuclear industry, producing essential materials by using processes that are potentially lethal to huge numbers of people. Moreover, these processes are extremely complex and difficult to explain and are thus liable to panic the average layman. The chemical industry's biggest problem may be a public relations one.

Food and agriculture

The USA is one of the most productive agricultural nations in the world, ranking near the top in global production of every major agricultural commodity except rice and coffee. The last agricultural census in 2002 found that agriculture contributed $197 billion to the US economy. But the figures confirmed the trend that farm numbers are declining as family farms become increasingly uneconomic and agriculture moves towards consolidation by large businesses.

Farms, especially in the great corn-producing states of the Midwest, cover many thousands of acres. Increasing automation of farm machinery is the trend of the future, as is the already established practice of growing corn for use as ethanol fuel instead of food. The genetic manipulation of crops is already commercial reality, and is a trend set to increase over the next few years despite resistance among some consumers, particularly in the European Union.

Other developments include increasing emphasis on healthy, organic, and low-fat foods, with a corresponding decrease in the production of processed and canned foods. As an indication of affluence, customers are aspiring to premium products such as more fresh meat and vegetables, reacting against the mass production of foodstuffs. As a consequence, there is growing interest in more 'European-style' foods such as speciality breads and exotic prepared meals that are made by small producers. There has been a wave of consolidations as manufacturers are forced to cope with lower margins and intense competition. Overall, the outlook for increased growth in the food industry is limited due to market saturation and rising prices.

As far as farming is concerned, the effect that increased efficiency will have on production will be immense. The downside to this is that employment in farming will fall off even further. American agriculture will continue to produce a wide diversity of products on a huge scale, but in a form that will not be recognisable as the traditional farming of the last hundred years.

The computer industry and IT services

Despite the onset of recession, the American computing industry remains a key component of its economy because the USA is the world leader in the production of both hardware and software. The world's top PC vendors are Compaq, IBM, Dell, Gateway, and Hewlett-Packard, all of which are American companies, though in the future they will be facing stiff competition from foreign rivals, particularly those located in Russia and China. While the industry continues to expand, its growth rate has slowed from 10.9% to just 4.7% in 10 years and, aside from economic conditions, many manufacturers are encountering problems of market saturation. The one exception to this rule is Apple, whose Macintosh computers and associated technologies

FACT

The world's top PC vendors are Compaq, IBM, Dell, Gateway, and Hewlett-Packard, all of which are American companies.

FACT

Security systems such as face recognition and intelligence, are emerging as essential areas for domestic defence in the war on international terrorism.

have seen a massive rise in sales in the past few years. Peripherals such as the much-coveted iPhone and iPod, plus the hugely successful iTunes application, have all shown that while there remains a market for home technology, the demand has changed from business and office-based software to creative technology used for visual and audio applications.

Silicon Valley remains the centre of innovation and enterprise in computing hardware and software. Start-ups exist alongside giant corporations, but the intellectual and financial environment enables the USA to remain at the forefront of Information Technology. This sector of the economy is a fertile source of employment and attracts migrants from all over the world.

Further north, in Seattle, Microsoft retains a virtual monopoly on the desktop operating system and, as such, is the industry Goliath. It finally resolved a long legal battle with the Justice department in 2004, which had alleged that the company was using anti-competitive practices. Having lost a series of legal judgments, Microsoft faced being split up into different companies but the threat receded as the two parties reached a compromise. In principle (though rarely or publicly announced in practice), it allowed software competitors access to Microsoft's five-year plans so that they could develop products for the Windows operating system which effectively still runs 95% of the world's desktop computers. At the beginning of 2002, the company was locked in a legal dispute with nine states who wished to see further penalties imposed on the company for conducting 'anti-competitive' practices, but the matter was resolved in 2004.

Now the internet bubble of massively inflated values has burst, online companies and services can concentrate on practical growth and product development that is governed by the normal market rules of profit and loss. Expectations were absurdly high for the internet, but it remains a key technical development and is revolutionising the way people communicate at home and at work. In the future, expansion of the convergence of media platforms – television with the internet and portable interactivity – is going to be a fertile area of activity for the IT sector.

The computer services industry supports the IT sector and is a substantial area of employment. Segments that are likely to grow here are outsourcing, systems integration, internet services and IT consultancy. Farming out computer services, for example, is an attractive way for businesses to cut costs. Internet support such as web and database management will continue to recruit significant numbers of skilled employees.

Transport and communications

The attacks on the USA on September 11, 2001 had a great economic impact on the airline industry. An estimated 100,000 people lost their jobs in the American airline industry practically overnight. The sector was arguably due for a round of cost cuts but the event exposed the airlines and plane manufacturers to a sudden catastrophic crisis which continues to affect the industry even now. The industry lost $3 billion in 2006, on top of the $30 billion that had already been lost since 2001. The immediate future, therefore, does not look bright for employment in aviation. But with improved security measures, higher prices and greater confidence, some airlines will naturally survive to service an essential aspect of American life: the need to travel huge distances by air for work or pleasure.

Deregulation of the air, road and rail industries during the 1990s led to many changes in the way the transportation network operated. Substantial deregulation of US airlines had already produced more competition and lower fares, but it also meant a loss of routes to the smaller cities. An 'open-skies' agreement between the USA and the European Union resulted in a number of cooperative ventures between US and European airlines, and new 'budget' airlines becoming more popular for inter-state journeys.

The railway played a historic role in opening up the USA to settlement in the 19th century though it now takes a backseat to air travel. Nevertheless, rail continues to be an important infrastructure, particularly for moving freight. Long-distance passenger rail travel has been almost eliminated by competition from airlines but several long-distance routes are still operated by Amtrak, with subsidies from the federal government. Amtrak plan to introduce high-speed services on the European and Japanese models to compete with airlines, and the lucrative east coast corridor – linking Boston, New York, Philadelphia, and Washington D.C. – will be the first high-speed route.

The road haulage industry is also benefiting from deregulation, and opening up more national routes. Although the railways are the major transporters of freight in the USA, the trucking industry is not far behind, though a rise in fuel costs may slow growth. Most goods are exported by sea, through the network of ports on the Atlantic seaboard and the Pacific coast, although there is an increasing amount of freight transported by air. As far as cars are concerned, travel between cities is still overwhelmingly by automobile on the network of highways built by President Eisenhower in the 1950s

■ STATE-BY-STATE BUSINESS REPORT

In the following state-by-state guide, major industries in each state are listed in descending order of significance. Each state runs its own website, and this is a good starting point for information about living and working there. Each website provides contact details for the departments of state government. Many of the chambers of commerce also produce relocation 'packets' containing information about local housing, health care, taxation, education and entertainment.

Alabama

www.alabama.gov

Major cities: Birmingham, Mobile, Montgomery (capital), Huntsville, Tuscaloosa

Population: 4,599,000

Chamber of Commerce: *Business Council of Alabama*: PO Box 76, Montgomery, AL 36101; 334 240 8714; www.bcatoday.org

Main industries (in order of size): manufacturing, wholesale/retail, services, mining, agriculture, forestry, fisheries, construction

Gross State Product: $161 billion

Income per capita: $32,404

Alabama, one of the poorest states, was, for a hundred years, the country's main producer of cotton. Nowadays the manufacturing industry, centred around Birmingham, and the space-related high-tech. industries, centred around Huntsville, dominate the state's economy. The state has always seemed to be the poor relation of neighbouring Georgia, whose capital, Atlanta, is one of the recognised hubs of the south. Professional and related industries (such as PR firms, marketing companies and training facilities) are expected to be the fastest growing industry group until 2012 and computer and mathematical science occupations are expected to provide the greatest opportunities. The state has a projected annual

average growth rate of 1.35% over the same period and the economy is expected to provide an estimated 299,000 jobs by 2014.

Alaska

www.state.ak.us
Major cities: Anchorage, Fairbanks, Juneau (capital)
Population: 670,000
Chamber of Commerce: *Alaska State Chamber of Commerce*: 217 2nd Street, Suite 201, Juneau, AK 99801; 907 586 2010; www.alaskachamber.com
Main industries: mining, construction, manufacturing
Gross State Product: $41 billion
Income per capita: $40,352

Alaska, the largest state in the USA in terms of land size, was purchased from Russia in 1867 for $7.2 million, but not officially incorporated into the Union until 1959. Gold was discovered there in the 19th century, but it was not until the late 1960s, when oil was discovered, that Alaska came into its own. Oil and related industries account for 90% of the state's revenue. Alaskans are so keen on development that they are considered to be the least 'green' of all Americans, but the state's natural beauty and pristine environment is the foundation of a growing tourist industry. While prospects for the fishing and timber industries are encouraging, the greatest opportunity for new jobs comes with the continued construction and maintenance of a gas pipeline, thought to be one of the state's most important economic developments.

Arizona

www.az.gov
Major cities: Phoenix (capital), Tucson, Mesa, Tempe, Glendale, Scottsdale
Population: 6,166,000
Chambers of Commerce: *Arizona Chamber of Commerce*;1850 N Central Ave, Suite 1433, Phoenix, AZ 85004; 602 248 9172; www.azchamber.com
Main industries: services, wholesale/retail construction, finance, manufacturing, construction
Gross State Product: $232 billion
Income per capita: $33,029

Admitted as the 48th state in 1912, Arizona's mainly desert climate meant that it remained sparsely populated until after the Second World War. Since air conditioning became widely available the state has been one of the fastest growing in terms of population. It is a light manufacturing centre, is popular with tourists and retirees, and has a high population of Native Americans (40% of all American tribal lands are in Arizona) and Hispanics. Arizona is economically healthy, with many credit card companies moving in, and the retail sector strong. Leisure and tourism are important sources of revenue and employment. Five million people visit the Grand Canyon every year.

Arkansas

www.state.ar.us
Major cities: Little Rock (capital), Fort Smith, North Little Rock, Pine Bluff, Fayetteville, Hot Springs
Population: 2,811,000
Chambers of Commerce: *Arkansas State Chamber of Commerce*: PO Box 3645, Little Rock, AR 72203; 501 372 2222; www.statechamber-aia.dina.org
Main industries: manufacturing, wholesale/retail, finance, agriculture/forestry/fishery construction, services, transport, public utilities
Gross State Product: $92 billion
Income per capita: $30,060

Arkansas, former president Bill Clinton's home state, is the South's smallest and least-populated state with an unfair reputation for being 'backward'. Cotton was the mainstay of its economy in the 19th century but although agriculture has remained an important part of the GSP (the state is a major lumber and poultry producer), it is now known as a strong manufacturing centre. There is no real attraction for investors in Arkansas and incomes are about a fifth below the national average. However, five of *Fortune 500's* companies are headquartered in Arkansas, mainly due to a long-standing relationship with the state: Alltel, Dillard's, Murphy Oil, Tyson Foods, and Wal-Mart. Manufacturers and service industries, particularly business and health services, continue to expand and create job opportunities.

California

www.ca.gov
Major cities: Los Angeles, San Francisco, San Diego, San Jose, Long Beach, Oakland, Sacramento (capital)
Population: 36,458,000
Chamber of Commerce: *California Chamber of Commerce*: 1215 K Street, Suite 1400, Sacramento, CA 95814; 916 444 6670; www.calchamber.com
Main industries: services, manufacturing, finance, wholesale/retail, construction
Gross State Product: $1,727 billion
Income per capita: $41,571

California, the 'Sunshine State', has the largest population and is one of the most affluent states in the USA. Despite major problems with inner-city poverty, it still has the eighth highest income per capita in the country. Financial services and manufacturing are the most profitable sectors. Although Bank America has its HQ here, as well as some of the country's largest aerospace and high-tech manufacturers, the wealth of the state rests on small businesses: one in five of the USA's fastest growing companies are in California. The state began to suffer at the end of the Cold War as many defence contractors are located in the state, but this loss was later balanced out in the mid to late 1990s by the boom in Silicon Valley where some of the world's most powerful computing and software businesses have their headquarters. Japan is California's biggest foreign investor and second largest trading partner after Mexico.

Colorado

www.colorado.gov
Major cities: Denver (capital), Colorado Springs, Aurora, Lakewood, Pueblo, Boulder, Arvada
Population: 4,753,000
Chamber of Commerce: *Colorado Association of Commerce and Industry*: 1600 Broadway Suite 1000, Denver, CO 80202; 303 831 7411; www.cochamber.com
Main industries: services, wholesale/retail, finance, manufacturing, construction, mining, agriculture/forestry/fisheries
Gross State Product: $230 billion
Income per capita: $41,042

One of the mountain states, Colorado has a history of economic success. In the 19th century lead and silver were mined, while the 20th century saw the seen the oil, coal and shale oil industries flourish and gradually recede in importance. The economy is sustained today by tourism (the state has some of the most beautiful scenery and first-class ski resorts in the USA) and manufacturing, as well as by its position as a centre for service industries and financial services. State unemployment is below the national average, and Colorado is host to telecoms company US West. Although the economy has slowed in recent years there were signs of improvement in 2007. Present high energy prices help keep the oil, gas, and coal industries alive but they in turn have had a minor negative effect on travel and tourism. Unemployment in Colorado is consistently less than the national average and is currently at 4.4%.

Connecticut

www.ct.gov
Major cities: Bridgeport, Hartford (capital), New Haven, Waterbury, Stamford, Norwalk, New Britain
Population: 3,505,000
Chamber of Commerce: *Connecticut Business & Industry Association, Inc.*: 350 Church Street, Hartford, CT 06103; 860 244 1900; www.cbia.com

Main industries: manufacturing, finance, wholesale/retail, services, construction
Gross State Product: $204 billion
Income per capita: $54,117

Connecticut is one of the oldest colonised states and used to be a centre for shipping, transatlantic trade and whaling. It is close to New York City, and many services and financial organisations have moved their offices to connecticut, attracted by cheaper rents. Connecticut is an important centre for the insurance and financial services industries, and is also known as a centre for weapons production. The rate of personal income is one of the highest in the country and recent increases in the defence budget have improved matters further: Connecticut is one of the Pentagon's biggest suppliers of equipment.

Delaware

www.delaware.gov
Major cities: Wilmington, Dover (capital), Newark
Population: 853,000
Chamber of Commerce: *Delaware State Chamber of Commerce*: PO Box 671, Wilmington, DE 19899; 302 655 7221; www.dscc.com
Main industries: manufacturing, finance, wholesale/retail, services, construction
Gross State Product: $60 billion
Income per capita: $40,608

The second smallest state by area, Delaware has one of the highest levels of income per capita, due largely to its small population and comparatively high GSP. Du Pont, the chemical manufacturing multinational, has its HQ here, and manufacturing in general dominates the economy. The state has liberal company incorporation laws and 80% of all American companies are registered here. Banking and insurance companies are major employers. Most businesses, and two-thirds of the population, are in the northern counties, while the southern counties are given over to orchards and some of America's most expensive real estate. A Delaware government initiative a few years ago included strengthening its largest employers, helping fledgling start-ups, and fostering small business, and this has sustained growth at a consistent rate.

District of Columbia

www.dc.gov
Major city: Washington, DC (US capital)
Population: 582,000
Chamber of Commerce: *DC Chamber of Commerce*: 1213 K Street NW, Washington, D.C. 20005; 202 347 7201; www.dcchamber.org

Main industries: federal government and the military, services, finance, construction, wholesale/retail
Gross Product: $88 billion
Income per capita: $61,092

District of Columbia, 68 sq miles (176 sq km), was designed as a capital under federal control. It has unique status in that it sends no representatives to Congress, and has no governor. The highest elected official is the mayor. It is the seat of the federal government, which is the major employer in the state. Beyond the impressive centre of town, where most of the government departments, museums and businesses are situated, lie some of the worst urban slums in the USA. It also maintains a high rate of crime.

Florida

www.myflorida.com
Major cities: Jacksonville, Miami, Tampa, St Petersburg, Hialeah, Fort Lauderdale, Orlando, Hollywood, Tallahassee (capital)
Population: 18,090,000
Chambers of Commerce: *Florida Chamber of Commerce*: PO Box 11309, Tallahassee, FL 32302; 850 521 1205; www.flchamber.com
Main industries: services, wholesale/retail, finance, manufacturing, construction
Gross State Product: $714 billion
Income per capita: $38,444

Together with California, Florida has been one of the fastest-growing states, in terms of population. At the beginning of this century Miami was a tiny village, but its high standard of living and warm climate have now made it a favourite with retirees from the USA, Canada and the UK. Tourism is an important industry, as well as financial services. Despite enormous growth in the past 30 years, Florida still retains impressive natural assets such as the Everglades and the Keys, long, sandy beaches, and a sub tropical climate. It has a vibrant economy despite being hit by frequent hurricanes, and this encourages high-quality jobs and a world-class business climate.

Georgia

www.georgia.gov
Main cities: Atlanta (capital), Columbus, Savannah, Macon
Population: 9,364,000
Chamber of Commerce: *Georgia Chamber of Commerce*: 235 Peachtree Street NE, Suite 900, Atlanta, GA 30303; 404 223 2264; www.gachamber.com

Main industries: manufacturing, wholesale/retail, services, finance, construction
Gross State Product: $380 billion
Income per capita: $33,457

Georgia is a major Deep South manufacturing state as well as a financial and services centre. Customer and business service centres, involving teleservice (inbound and/or outbound phone calling) and data centres, are a substantial component of the economy, contributing almost 100,000 jobs. Georgia is also home to the Lockheed Corporation, one of the largest aircraft manufacturers in the world, and Coca-Cola. Atlanta is regarded as the commercial capital of the South, and hosting the 1996 Olympic Games gave the region a great boost. Outside the prosperous cities, Georgia is still quite poor; low-wage industries such as paper and saw mills account for two fifths of jobs.

Hawaii

www.hawaii.gov
Major cities: Honolulu (capital), Pearl City, Kailua, Hilo, Aiea
Population: 1,285,000
Chamber of Commerce: *Chamber of Commerce of Hawaii*: 1132 Bishop Street, Suite 402, Honolulu, HI 96813; 808 545 4300; www.cochawaii.com
Main industries: services, finance, federal government and the military, wholesale/retail, construction, manufacturing, agriculture/forestry/fisheries
Gross State Product: $58 billion
Income per capita: $39,239

Hawaii was declared the 50th member of the Union in 1959. Tourism and agriculture dominate the economy though the federal government and military are also important sectors. Hawaii is committed to diversifying its economy, and industries encouraged are science and technology, film and IV production, sports, ocean research and development, health and education, diversified agriculture, and speciality food products.

Idaho

www.state.id.us
Major cities: Boise City (capital), Pocatello, Idaho Falls, Nampa, Twin Falls, Lewiston
Population: 1,466,000
Chamber of Commerce: *Boise Metro Chamber of Commerce*: 250 S 5th Street, Suite 800, Boise, ID 83702; 208 472 5220; www.boisechamber.org
Main industries: manufacturing, wholesale/retail, financial, services, transport and public utilities, agriculture/forestry/fisheries
Gross State Product: $50 billion
Income per capita: $31,197

Tourism (revolving around winter sports, hunting and fishing), mining, forestry and agriculture are the strongest sectors in idaho's economy. High costs in nearby California have meant that many high technology manufacturers have relocated to Idaho thus stimulating economic growth, especially around the capital, Boise City.

Illinois

www.illinois.gov
Major cities: Chicago, Rockford, Peoria, Springfield (capital)
Population: 12,832,000
Chamber of Commerce: *Illinois State Chamber of Commerce*: 311 South Wacker Drive, Suite 1500, Chicago, IL 60606; 312 983 7100; www.ilchamber.org
Main industries: manufacturing, wholesale/retail, services, finance, transport and public utilities, agriculture/forestry/fisheries
Gross State Product: $590 billion
Income per capita: $40,322

Chicago is one of the largest cities in the USA and it is a major financial and services centre. Agriculture is an important part of the economy (Illinois is the second largest producer of corn and soybeans in the USA), but the main strength of the state is In its reputation as a large and diversified manufacturing base dominated by heavy industry. Services account for a quarter of jobs in Illinois and 50 of the *Fortune 500* companies are located here. Tourism is a major growth industry, as is film-making.

Indiana

www.in.gov
Major cities: Indianapolis (capital), Fort Wayne, Evansville, Gary, South Bend
Population: 6,314,000
Chamber of Commerce: *Indiana Chamber of Commerce*: 115 W Washington Street, Suite 850, Indianapolis, IN 46244; 317 264 3110; www.indianachamber.com
Main industries: manufacturing, wholesale/retail, finance, services, transport and public utilities, agriculture/forestry/fisheries
Gross State Product: $249 billion
Income per capita: $33,616

'The Crossroads of America', as Indiana is known, is a particularly industrialised state with three in 10 workers employed in heavy industry. Auto-manufacturing (including components) and steel are the biggest industries in this sector. Farming is also an important sector. One of the major problems the state is having has to face is the closure of its military bases, which bring over $500 million a year to the economy.

Iowa

www.iowa.gov

Major cities: Des Moines (capital), Cedar Rapids, Davenport, Waterloo, Council Bluffs, Dubuque

Population: 2,982,000

Chamber of Commerce: *Greater Des Moines Partnership*: 700 Locust Street, Suite 100, Des Moines, IA 50309; 515 286 4963; www.desmoinesmetro.com

Main industries: manufacturing, finance, wholesale/retail, services, agriculture/forestry/fisheries

Gross State Product: $124 billion

Income per capita: $35,023

Iowa, the farming capital of the USA, grows 10% of America's food. It is the country's biggest producer of soybeans, and one of the leading producers of cattle and pigs. The state's manufacturing sector is largely geared around the farming sector and is mainly concerned with the processing of agricultural products. Three out of four workers in Iowa are employed in agriculture or related industries. There is also a fairly important service industry sector and Des Moines is a centre for insurance firms.

Kansas

www.kansas.gov

Major cities: Wichita, Kansas City, Topeka (capital) Overland Park

Population: 2,764,000

Chamber of Commerce: *Kansas Chamber of Commerce & Industry*: 835 SW Topeka Boulevard, Topeka, KS 66612; 785 357 6321; www.kansaschamber.com

Main industries: manufacturing, wholesale/retail, finance, services, agriculture/forestry/fisheries

Gross State Product: $112 billion

Income per capita: $36,768

Kansas, the epitome of middle America, has a diversified economy. Its agriculture (wheat and cattle) sector is one of the biggest in the country, while manufacturing industries, including an important aircraft sector, and extractive industries such as oil and gas both contribute significantly to the economy. Farming is in decline as an employer, if not as a producer.

Kentucky

www.kentucky.gov

Major cities: Louisville, Lexington-Fayette, Owensboro, Frankfort (capital), Covington, Bowling Green

Population: 4,206,000

Chamber of Commerce: *Kentucky Chamber of Commerce:* 464 Chenault Road, Frankfort, KY 40601; 502 695 4700; www.kychamber.com
Main industries: manufacturing, finance, wholesale/retail, services, transport and public utilities, mining, construction
Gross State Product: $146 billion
Income per capita: $31,111

The Kentucky Derby and bourbon are perhaps the best known things about this state, known as the 'Bluegrass State'. It is, however, one of the region's leading coal producers, responsible for about one fifth of the nation's output, and is also one of the important tobacco states, together with North Carolina and Virginia. Manufacturing is also a vital sector, accounting for almost a quarter of the GSP. Kentucky does contain some extremely poor areas, mainly in the desolate Appalachian region. Toyota gave a boost to the area about five years ago by building a $2 billion plant at Churchill, outside Lexington, and Kentucky remains keen on attracting more foreign investment.

Louisiana

www.louisiana.gov
Major cities: New Orleans, Baton Rouge (capital), Shreveport, Lafayette
Population: 4,288,000
Chamber of Commerce: *Louisiana Association of Business and Industry:* PO Box 80258, Baton Rouge, LA 70898; 225 928 5388; www.labi.org
Main industries: mining, finance, wholesale/retail, services, manufacturing, transport and public utilities
Gross State Product: $193 billion
Income per capita: $35,756

Louisiana still has a large population of Cajuns, descendants of French migrants to North America. French remains an official language in this state and the legal system is also unique in the USA because it is based on the Napoleonic code. The state is a major producer of oil and gas, petrochemicals and shipping and is also a popular tourist area, with visitors flocking to New Orleans for the festivals and the historic architecture, or to stare at the aftermath of Hurricane Katrina. One of the oddities of Louisiana is the mixed nature of its population: in the north is an Anglo-Saxon, conservative, protestant majority, while the south has a Latin and Creole catholic culture, with the vibrant New Orleans at its centre. State unemployment is constantly changing, and has gone from 11.4% to just 3.7% in under three years, one of the many fallouts of Hurricane Katrina.

Maine

www.maine.gov
Major cities: Portland, Lewiston, Bangor, Auburn, Augusta (capital)
Population: 1,322,000

Chamber of Commerce: *Maine State Chamber of Commerce*: 7 University Drive, Augusta, ME 04330; 207 623 4568; www.mainechamber.org
Main industries: manufacturing, wholesale/retail, finance, services
Gross State Product: $47 billion
Income per capita: $33,722

Maine is the largest New England state and is roughly the same size as the other five put together. Sparsely populated, the state draws on its abundant natural resources and farming, fishing, forestry and tourism are all major industries. In recent years, tourism has been growing as visitors come to enjoy the skiing in winter and the superb, granite coastline in summer. Fishing has been overtaken by tourism and light manufacturing as the main earner in this Atlantic state and more than half the state is owned by lumber- and paper-producing companies. Maine is one of America's largest blueberry growing states while potatoes rank third in acreage and fourth in production nationally.

Maryland

www.maryland.gov
Major cities: Baltimore, Rockville, Bowie, Frederick, Annapolis (capital)
Population: 5,616,000
Chamber of Commerce: *Maryland Chamber of Commerce*: 60 West Street, Suite 100, Annapolis, MD 21401; 410 269 0642; www.mdchamber.org
Main industries: services, wholesale/retail, finance, manufacturing, federal government and the military, construction
Gross State Product: $258 billion
Income per capita: $46,021

Maryland is a coastal state, well-known for its fisheries in Chesapeake Bay. Baltimore, the largest major city, is a regional services centre. Washington, D.C. abuts onto the state, and the federal government has several outposts in Maryland's suburbs, which make an important contribution to the economy of the state. The prosperity of the state has meant development: commuters now live as far away as the Pennsylvania border to the north and the hilly panhandle to the west and there is now very little open country left between Washington and Baltimore. Maryland's unemployment rate of 3.6% is well below the national rate. Growth sectors include the film industry, which provides roughly 2,000 full-time jobs. Over the past decade, filmmaking has had a total economic impact of more than $850 million.

Massachusetts

www.mass.gov
Major cities: Boston (capital), Worcester, Springfield, New Bedford, Brockton, Lowell, Cambridge, Fall River
Population: 6,437,000

Chamber of Commerce: *Massachusetts Chamber of Business and Industry, Inc*, 143 Shaker Road, PO Box 414, East Longmeadow, MA 01028; 413 426 3850; www.unitedchamber.org
Main industries: services, manufacturing, finance, wholesale/retail, transport and public utilities
Gross State Product: $338 billion
Income per capita: $49,082

Massachusetts is one of the original sites of European settlement in the USA, and was the first truly industrial state. The production of cotton and cloth made the fortunes of many families. The state is also home to many important educational institutions such as Harvard University and the Massachusetts Institute of Technology (MIT). It is a leader in high technology industries such as computers, photographic equipment, and defence electronics. Boston is the retailing, financial and service industry centre for the whole of New England although as Massachusetts imposes a tax burden on companies wishing to do business in the state, many are deterred from setting up there.

Michigan

www.michigan.gov
Major cities: Detroit, Grand Rapids, Warren, Flint, Lansing (capital), Sterling Height, Ann Arbor
Population: 10,096,000
Chamber of Commerce: *Michigan Chamber of Commerce*: 600 South Walnut Street, Lansing, MI 48933; 517 371 2100; www.michamber.com
Main industries: manufacturing, finance, wholesale/retail, services, transport and public utilities
Gross State Product: $381 billion
Income per capita: $35,086

Michigan, the eighth biggest state in terms of population, is one of the world's centres of car production. The 'Big Three' – Ford, Chrysler and General Motors – all have major plants here. Nearly all manufacturing is geared toward the production of cars, from processing raw materials to making components, and nearly a third of the state's workers are employed in this sector. Michigan also ranks in the top three states for industrial research and development spending. Situated on the shores of four Great Lakes, the state is also a prime destination for recreational boating and fishing. Michigan has, unfortunately, been the worst-hit state during the USA's recent economic slowdown, experiencing severe job losses, housing crises and a decline in development.

Minnesota

www.state.mn.us
Major cities: Minneapolis, St Paul (capital), Bloomington, Duluth, Rochester

Population: 5,167,000
Chamber of Commerce: *Greater Minnesota Chamber of Commerce:* 400 Robert Street N, Suite 1500, St Paul, MN 55101; 651 292 4655; www.mnchamber.com
Main industries: manufacturing, finance, wholesale/retail, services, agriculture, forestry, fisheries
Gross State Product: $245 billion
Income per capita: $41,034

Half of the population of Minnesota lives in the Minneapolis/St Paul metropolitan area, considered among the best US cities for quality of life, despite the long winters. Most of the state is made up of prairies and it is a major dairy producer. Minnesota is also a manufacturing centre, with companies such as General Mills and 3M boosting the economy. Other important sectors are mining, timber, and tourism. The Mississippi begins its 2,500-mile (4,023-km) journey in the north of the state and is a popular tourist destination each summer. Minnesota also has a tradition of political and cultural liberalism and is home to many large and successful companies.

Mississippi

www.mississippi.gov
Major cities: Jackson (capital), Biloxi, Gulfport, Meridian
Population: 2,911,000
Chamber of Commerce: *Mississippi Economic Council:* PO Box 23276, Jackson, MS 39225; 601 969 0022; www.msmec.com
Main industries: manufacturing, wholesale/retail, finance, services, agriculture/forestry/fisheries, construction
Gross State Product: $84 billion
Income per capita: $28,845

Mississippi has the lowest per capita income of all the states, and is considered to be the poorest state in the nation by a number of benchmarks. One fifth of the population now lives below the poverty line, it has had a weak education system, and it has no real manufacturing base – although in recent years it has made some headway in attracting light industry. The services and financial sectors are underdeveloped, but Mississippi's economy experienced a marginal upswing in employment and output in 2008, with most economic indicators showing improvement. Tourists are attracted to the state's image as the heart of the 'old South' and often visit the Mississippi River as a popular resort. Jackson, the state capital, is a fairly prosperous town of 180,000 with smart suburbs, and Clarksdale is a mecca for lovers of the blues: Muddy Waters and Howlin' Wolf both lived there.

Missouri

www.mo.gov

Major cities: Kansas City, St Louis, Springfield, Independence, Jefferson City (capital)

Population: 5,843,000

Chamber of Commerce: *Missouri Chamber of Commerce & Industry*: PO Box 149, Jefferson City, MO 65102; 573 634 3511; www.mochamber.org

Main industries: manufacturing, wholesale/retail, services, finance, construction

Gross State Product: $226 billion

Income per capita: $34,389

Missouri is a regional transport centre. The main industry is manufacturing, and several major companies are based here, including defence contractors like McDonnell Douglas and food-processing giants, Anheuser-Busch. The fastest-growing part of Missouri is the Ozarks area around Springfield where population has grown by nearly a fifth in the last decade, boosted by families and retirees. St Louis is one of the 20 biggest metropolitan areas in the country.

Montana

www.mt.gov

Major cities: Billings, Great Falls, Missoula, Butte-Silver Bow, Helena (capital)

Population: 945,000

Chamber of Commerce: *Montana Chamber of Commerce*: PO Box 1730, Helena, MT 59624; 406 442 2405; www.montanachamber.com

Main industries: finance, wholesale/retail, services, agriculture/forestry/fisheries, construction, mining

Gross State Product: $32 billion

Income per capita: $32,458

Known as 'Big Sky Country', Montana is one of the foremost ranching states. Its agricultural sector is sustained by the big ranch operations in the south and east of the state and the state is famous for its horses. The economy is otherwise dominated by mining, tourism and forestry. Hard metals mining is now in decline, but Montana still produces a large amount of coal.

Nebraska

www.nebraska.gov

Major cities: Omaha, Lincoln (capital), Grand Island, Bellevue

Population: 1,768,000

Chambers of Commerce: *Nebraska Chamber of Commerce & Industry*: PO Box 95128, Lincoln, NE 68509; 402 474 4422; www.nechamber.com
Main industries: services, finance, wholesale/retail, agriculture/forestry/fisheries, construction, manufacturing
Gross State Product: $76 billion
Income per capita: $36,471

'The Cornhusker State' produces a major percentage of the country's corn, wheat, and livestock. The east of the state is given over to corn production, while wheat is farmed in the west. Central areas of the state are dominated by vast cattle ranches. Nebraska was one of the dustbowl states, and abandoned farmhouses are still a reminder of the thousands of families that had to trek west in search of work during the Great Depression of the 1930s. Today, about half of the state's workforce is employed in agriculture or related activities, although it is still a precarious business, given the lack of rainfall. The small manufacturing sector is mainly concerned with food processing. More recently, Omaha has become a prime location for telephone call centres.

Nevada

www.nv.gov
Major cities: Las Vegas, Reno, Sparkes, North Las Vegas, Henderson, Carson City (capital)
Population: 2,496,000
Chamber of Commerce: *Las Vegas Chamber of Commerce*: 3720 Howard Hughes Parkway, Las Vegas, NV 89109; 702 735 1616; www.lvchamber.com
Main industries: services, finance, wholesale/retail, construction, manufacturing.
Gross State Product: $118 billion
Income per capita: $40,480

Nevada is the driest of the 50 states, but it also has a ski resort, Lake Tahoe, and two immense prehistoric inland seas, Pyramid Lake and Walker Lake. It is famous for Las Vegas (Nevada has legalised gambling), and for the Cornstock Lode, which was the largest silver mine in the world when it was first discovered. Tourism is the state's biggest earner; small-time gamblers and the merely inquisitive flocking to the casinos of Las Vegas – 'Armageddon in Neon'. Otherwise, mining is still an important industry. Nevada has one of the fastest-growing populations in the country, more than quadrupling since 1960. The state's lenient tax regulations make it a favourite of rich retirees wanting to make the most of their savings. Nevada's exports amounted to more than $5.7 billion in 2007, making it the state with the largest percentage increase in exports in the nation.

New Hampshire

www.nh.gov

Major cities: Manchester, Nashua, Concord (capital), Portsmouth, Dover

Population: 1,315,000

Chambers of Commerce: *Business and Industry Association of New Hampshire*; 122 N Main Street, Concord, NH 03301, 603 224 5388; www.nhbia.org

Main industries: manufacturing, finance, wholesale/retail, services, construction

Gross State Product: $56 billion

Income per capita: $41,512

New Hampshire is one of the smallest states in both population and area. It was one of the first industrialised states, and Manchester was the site of the world's largest cotton mill. The state is also, uniquely, the only one without a sales tax or state income tax, and as a result has attracted many high technology companies from neighbouring Massachusetts, where taxes are much higher. Tourism is also an important industry – the Granite State is famous for its lakes, and the beautiful White Mountains are a huge attraction. The New Hampshire primaries are the first to be held in any presidential election; unusually, both Bill Clinton and George W. Bush won the White House without coming first in their party's New Hampshire primary.

New Jersey

www.state.nj.us

Major cities: Newark, Jersey City, Paterson, Elizabeth, Trenton (capital), Camden

Population: 8,725,000

Chamber of Commerce: *New Jersey State Chamber of Commerce*: 216 West State Street, Trenton, NJ 08608; 609 989 7888; www.njchamber.com

Main industries: manufacturing, finance, services, wholesale/retail

Gross State Product: $453 billion

Income per capita: $49,194

Sandwiched between New York City and Philadelphia, New Jersey is an important services and financial centre and home to many commuters. It is the most urbanised and densely populated of the states (it is hard to believe that it used to be called The Garden State), and has one of the highest per capita incomes. Pharmaceuticals and chemicals are the dominant manufacturing sectors, and tourism on the Atlantic shore is also an important industry. Research and innovation has always been at the heart of the economy and for some years New Jersey has been laying the groundwork to move from a manufacturing to a high-tech.

economy. Today, it has one of the world's strongest pharmaceutical and biotechnology clusters with 75% of the world's top pharmaceutical companies headquartered in the state.

New Mexico

www.newmexico.gov

Major cities: Albuquerque, Santa Fe (capital) Las Cruces, Farmington, Roswell

Population: 1,955,000

Chamber of Commerce: *Association of Commerce and Industry of New Mexico* PO Box 9706, Albuquerque, NM 87119; 505 842 0644; www.aci-nm.org

Main industries: services, finance, mining, state and local government, manufacturing, construction, government and the military, agriculture/forestry/fisheries

Gross State Product: $76 billion

Income per capita: $31,474

New Mexico (whose 'greatness of beauty' D. H. Lawrence famously admired) is a vast state, sandwiched between Arizona, Texas and Mexico to the south. It has a higher proportion of resident Native Americans than all of the other states, and a large population of Hispanics. Mining of uranium, and production of oil and gas play a major part in the state's economy, and various government offices are situated here. The first atom bombs were produced at Los Alamos and the federal government chose Kirtland Air Base as one of four 'superlabs'. The New Mexico economy continues to expand at a moderate pace, although industries such as construction and manufacturing are experiencing the same downward shift as in the rest of the nation.

New York

www.state.ny.us

Major cities: New York City, Buffalo, Rochester, Yonkers, Syracuse, Albany (capital)

Population: 19,306,000

Chamber of Commerce: *Business Council of New York State:* 152 Washington Avenue, Albany, NY 12210; 800 358 1202; www.bcnys.org

Main industries: finance, services, manufacturing, wholesale/retail, construction

Gross State Product: $1,022 billion

Income per capita: $47,385

If New York were a country, it would have the ninth largest economy in the world. It has been overtaken by Texas in terms of population but still remains in third place and is an economic powerhouse. New York

City is the financial capital of both the country and the world, home to two of the main stock exchanges; the New York Stock Exchange and the American Stock Exchange, and two of the nation's three largest banks. Financial Services remain the city's leading sector for income while real estate and tourism are also strong. New York State has the head offices of many of the country's largest corporations and services and a very diverse manufacturing industry are also important sectors of the economy. Surprisingly, the state is also one of the nation's largest agricultural producers. New York City's fame draws huge numbers of tourists to the state. Although affected by the World Trade Center attacks, New York City is still one of the most dynamic urban centres in the world and its residents have a notorious resilience.

North Carolina

www.ncgov.com

Major cities: Charlotte, Raleigh (capital), Greensboro, Winston-Salem, Durham

Population: 8,857,000

Chamber of Commerce: *North Carolina Chamber of Commerce*: PO Box 2508, Raleigh, NC 27602; 919 836 1400; www.nccbi.org

Main industries: manufacturing, wholesale/retail, finance, service, construction, agriculture/forestry/fisheries

Gross State Product: $375 billion

Income per capita: $33,636

North Carolina has a varied economic base. Its income is derived from agriculture (tobacco), manufacturing (textiles, furniture and tobacco processing), banking and financial services, and high technology products (the state is home to the Research Triangle Park, a renowned centre for science and technology). North Carolina is also a regional centre for higher education. The economic success of the state could certainly be a model for the future of America as a whole.

North Dakota

www.nd.gov

Major cities: Fargo, Bismarck (capital), Grand Forks, Minot

Population: 636,000

Chamber of Commerce: *Greater North Dakota Chamber of Commerce*: PO Box 2639, Bismarck, ND 58502; 701 222 0929; www.ndchamber.com

Main industries: finance, wholesale/retail, agriculture/forestry/fisheries, services, mining, manufacturing, construction

Gross State Product: $26 billion

Income per capita: $34,846

North Dakota, situated in the heart of the vast expanse of the Great Plains, produces grain, corn ans livestock. It is also the country's main producer of wheat. It is first and foremost an agricultural state, and the manufacturing and services sectors are geared towards farms and farming products. There is also an important mining sector, producing coal and lignite. A variety of other industries are thriving in North Dakota: food processing, information management, engineering, and the service sector (including travel agencies, healthcare management companies, and computer technical support facilities). The state has the lowest crime rate in the country, the highest productivity rate, and the highest life expectancy.

Ohio

www.ohio.gov
Major cities: Columbus (capital), Cleveland, Cincinnati, Toledo, Akron, Dayton
Population: 11,478,000
Chambers of Commerce: *Ohio Chamber of Commerce,*: 230 East Town Street, Columbus, OH 43215; 614 228 4201; www.thechamberofcommerce.org
Main industries: manufacturing, wholesale/retail, finance, services
Gross State Product: $461 billion
Income per capita: $34,874

Ohio has many claims to fame: it has a large Native American population; flourishing iron, steel, and car industries; and it was in Ohio that the Wright brothers discovered flight. It is still a major industrial state, producing machine tools and consumer products as well as durable goods such as cars and agricultural machinery. In fact, Honda chose Ohio as the site for their first car factory in the USA. Ohio has managed to attract more than 300 foreign firms, including 100 Japanese ones. Retail, wholesale, and tourism are fast-growing service sectors in the state.

Oklahoma

www.ok.gov
Major Cities: Oklahoma City (capital) Tulsa, Lawton, Norman
Population: 3,579,000
Chamber of Commerce: *The State Chamber – Oklahoma's Association of Business and Industry*: 330 Northeast 10th Street, Oklahoma City, OK 73104; 405 235 3669; www.okstatechamber.com.
Main industries: wholesale/retail, manufacturing, finance, services, mining, government, agriculture/forestry/fisheries
Gross State Product: $135 billion
Income per capita: $34,153

Oklahoma was the centre of the drought of the 1930s, when thousands of farming families were forced off their land. The state was initially set aside for Indian reserves (implying that it was not regarded as prime land), and opened up for settlement in the late 19th century. It entered the Union as the 47th state in 1907. Oil and gas production is a mainstay of the economy, and the federal government is also a major employer. Tax and investment incentives have made Oklahoma a good location for small businesses. The regional economy is fairly robust, despite some inflationary pressures from higher energy prices. The state is currently experiencing a shortage of people in the labour market as the 'baby boomers' exit the market. There is also an increased demand for accountants, and opportunities in the retail, manufacturing, energy, and entry-level technology job markets.

Oregon

www.oregon.gov
Major cities: Portland, Eugene, Salem (capital), Medford
Population: 3,701,000
Chamber of Commerce: *Oregon State Chamber of Commerce*: 1401 Willamette Street, Eugene, OR 97401; 541 242 2350; www.aoi.org
Main industries: manufacturing, finance, wholesale/retail, services, agriculture/forestry/fisheries
Gross State Product: $151 billion
Income per capita: $34,784

Although the lumber industry has, for a long time, been the major employer in this very rural state (most of the towns have less than 20,000 inhabitants), the industry is in relative decline and there has been much activity in the high technology industries. Firms are regularly moving here from California, attracted by low rents. Oregon has been at the forefront of federal environmental regulation policies, which partly explains the decline of the logging industry.

Pennsylvania

www.state.pa.us
Major cities: Philadelphia, Pittsburgh, Erie, Allerton, Scranton, Harrisburg (capital)
Population: 12,441,000
Chamber of Commerce: *Greater Pennsylvania Chamber of Commerce & Industry*: 417 Walnut Street, Harrisburg, PA 17101; 717 720 5429; www.pachamber.org.
Main industries: manufacturing, finance, wholesale/retail, services, construction, mining

Gross State Product: $510 billion
Income per capita: $38,788

Pennsylvania is the birthplace of large-scale steel and iron production in the USA, but these industries are now in decline, and machinery production, metal working and coal mining are gaining in importance. After a century of heavy industry, it is now a prime target for environmental laws, and will need to be cleaned up in order to attract the high-tech businesses and tourists that are the key to prosperity in the future. The state is sometimes described as the birthplace of the Nation in honour of the central role that it played in the American Revolution – the Declaration of Independence was signed there. Pennsylvania is also well known for its Amish community, descendants of Dutch settlers who shun the 21st century in most of its forms.

Rhode Island

www.ri.gov
Major cities: Providence (capital), Warwick, Cranston, Pawtucket
Population: 1,068,000
Chamber of Commerce: *Greater Providence Chamber of Commerce*: 30 Exchange Terrace, Providence, RI 02303; 401 521 5000; www.provchamber.com
Main industries: services, wholesale/retail, manufacturing, finance
Gross State Product: $46 billion
Income per capita: $39,463

The principal economic activities of Rhode Island are manufacturing and services, with contributions made by construction, agriculture and forestry. For such a small state (the smallest in the union), fishing has an important part to play in the country's economy. It was an early area to industrialise, and the manufacturing industry in the state has been dominated for many years by silver, jewellery, and textiles. A quarter of the state's million inhabitants claim Irish descent. Service producing industries (primarily tourism, health services, and financial services) are Rhode Island's chief sources of income. Tourism generates more than $3.2 billion annually. Retail and manufacturing are the second and third largest segments of the economy. Other important sources of income are agriculture (dairy and poultry products), fisheries (especially shellfish), and biotechnology/pharmaceuticals.

South Carolina

www.sc.gov
Major cities: Columbia (capital), Charleston, North Charleston, Greenville
Population: 4,321,000

Chamber of Commerce: *South Carolina Chamber of Commerce*: 1201 Main Street, Suite 1700, Columbia, SC 29201; 803 799 4601; www.scchamber.net

Main industries: manufacturing, finance, services, state and local government, federal government and the military

Gross State Product: $149 billion

Income per capita: $31,013

Up until the end of the Second World War, South Carolina's economy was dependent on textile manufacturing and agriculture. Today it is more diversified, with other industries (and real estate) playing an important part in the economy. Agricultural land takes up 25% of the state's land area. (Cotton was the major crop in the 19th century and formed the basis of South Carolina's textile wealth.) South Carolina is also now a major tourist destination, the government is an important employer, and BMW opened its first-ever North American plant in South Carolina.

South Dakota

www.sd.gov

Major cities: Sioux Falls, Rapid City, Aberdeen, Pierre (capital)

Population: 782,000

Chambers of Commerce: *South Dakota Chamber of Commerce & Industry*: PO Box 190, Pierre, SD 57501; 605 335 6060; www.sdchamber.biz

Main industries: finance, wholesale/retail, agriculture/forestry/fisheries, services, manufacturing, construction

Gross State Product: $32 billion

Income per capita: $33,905

With farmland covering 90% of South Dakota, it is naturally one of the country's main agricultural producers, with large grain crops and livestock herds. The most important manufacturing products are farm-related, but the state is also a large producer of gold. The population, though increasing slightly, is minute for the size of the state, as is the GSP. Tourism is a thriving industry: South Dakota is home to the Badlands National Park, and the equally famous sculpture of four presidents carved into Mount Rushmore. One of the state's initiatives is to promote the creation and development of new businesses that will contribute $6 billion to its GSP.

Tennessee

www.tennessee.gov

Major cities: Memphis, Nashville (capital), Knoxville, Chattanooga

Population: 6,039,000

Chambers of Commerce: *Tennessee Chamber of Commerce & Industry:* 611 Commerce Street #3030, Nashville, TN 37203; 615 256 5141; www.tnchamber.org

Main industries: manufacturing, wholesale/retail, services, finance, construction

Gross State Product: $238 billion

Income per capita: $33,280

Agriculture used to be Tennessee's biggest economic sector, but with the advent of the Tennessee Valley Authority in the 1930s, which rejuvenated the area by ambitious federal government projects, the economic base changed to manufacturing as the state rapidly industrialised. Now, although agriculture still plays an important part, the manufacturing of textiles, food processing and chemicals constitutes the major sector, and there is also a uranium enrichment facility, the Oak Ridge National Laboratory. Tourists make a significant contribution to the state's economy, largely visiting Elvis' Graceland mansion in Memphis, or Nashville, the home of country music.

Texas

www.state.tx.us

Major cities: Houston, Dallas, San Antonio, El Paso, Austin (capital)

Population: 23,508,000

Chamber of Commerce: *Texas Association of Business:* 1209 Nueces Street, Austin, TX 78701; 512 477 6721; www.txbiz.org.

Main industries: wholesale/retail, manufacturing, services, finance, mining, construction

Gross State Product: $1,066 billion

Income per capita: $37,187

In 1901, oil was discovered at Spindletop on the Gulf coast, and since the 1970s the economy of Texas has relied extensively on its oil and gas wealth. Much of the industry in the state is related to petroleum refining and the production of petrochemicals. Other important manufacturing sectors are aerospace and high technology products such as semiconductors and microprocessors. Cropland and pasture make up more than 80% of the land area of Texas, and beef is a major product of the state. In the nineties Texas began diversifying away from oil: financial services are now an important sector, and four fifths of non-farm jobs are in the service sector. In recent years, venture capitalists have continued to invest primarily in the Texas software, telecommunications, semi-conductor, industrial/energy, networking and equipment, medical devices, and equipment industries.

Utah

www.utah.gov

Main cities: Salt Lake City (capital), Provo, Ogden, Sandy City, Orem

Population: 2,550,000

Chamber of Commerce: *Salt Lake City Chamber*: 175 E 400 Street, Salt Lake City, UT 84111; 801 364 3631; www.saltlakechamber.org
Main industries: manufacturing, wholesale/retail, services, finance, state and local government, federal government and the military
Gross State Product: $98 billion
Income per capita: $31,189

Manufacturing, services, and the wholesale and retail trade are the most important parts of Utah's GSP. Famous as the home of the Mormon Church, the economy is dominated by metals mining, smelting, and iron and steel production. In recent years companies involved with light industry have been attracted to the state, and tourism (there are some bizarre and arresting natural sights in Utah, such as the great Salt Lake itself, and the Bonneville Salt Flats) is a major earner. The federal government is also an important employer.

Vermont

www.vermont.gov
Major cities: Burlington, Rutland, South Burlington, Barre, Montpelier (capital)
Population: 624,000
Chamber of Commerce: *Vermont Chamber of Commerce*: PO Box 37, Montpelier, VT 05602; 802 223 3443; www.vtchamber.com
Main industries: manufacturing, finance, services, wholesale/retail, construction, agriculture/forestry/fisheries
Gross State Product: $24 billion
Income per capita: $36,670.

Vermont was the first state to be admitted to the union after the founding 13 states. Its principal economic activities are manufacturing, wholesale and retail trade, services, finance and real estate, tourism, and agriculture. Tourism is a major part of the economy due to the excellent skiing in the state and the thickly wooded mountains that turn a thousand shades of red and gold in autumn. Major manufactured products include machine tools and electronic equipment.

Virginia

www.virginia.gov
Major cities: Virginia Beach, Norfolk, Richmond (capital), Newport News, Chesapeake.
Population: 7,643,000
Chamber of Commerce: *Virginia Chamber of Commerce*: 9 South 5th Street, Richmond, VA 23219; 804 644 1607; www.vachamber.com
Main industries: manufacturing, services, finance, government and military, construction

Gross State Product: $369 billion
Income per capita: $41,347

Eight of America's presidents have been Virginians. Government is the largest employer in the state – partly due to the number of military bases, and partly because Washington, D.C.'s southern suburbs are located in Virginia, and many residents work for federal offices there. One of the largest naval bases in the world is in south-eastern Virginia at Norfolk. Important manufacturing sectors include food products, tobacco and chemicals.

Washington

www.access.wa.gov
Major cities: Seattle, Spokane, Tacoma, Bellevue, Everett, Olympia (capital)
Population: 6,396,000
Chamber of Commerce: *Washington Association of Business*: PO Box 658, Olympia, WA 98507; 360 943 1600; www.awb.org
Main industries: wholesale/retail, finance, manufacturing, construction, agriculture/forestry/fisheries
Gross State Product: $294 billion
Income per capita: $40,414

The Seattle region, where Boeing manufactures planes (the head office moved to Chicago) and where Microsoft is based, is the services and manufacturing centre of the state. Washington is also a leading lumber state, producing the most timber of any state apart from Oregon and California. Farming (mainly dairy products, fruit and wheat) is also an important sector. There is some tension between industrialists and environmentalists over conservation. For example, moves to protect the habitat of the spotted owl may cost thousands of logging jobs.

West Virginia

www.wv.gov
Major cities: Huntington, Charleston (capital), Wheeling, Parkersburg, Morgantown
Population: 1,818,000
Chamber of Commerce: *West Virginia Chamber of Commerce*: PO Box 2789, Charleston, WV 25330; 304 342 1115; www.wvchamber.com
Main industries: manufacturing, mining, construction, services, finance, wholesale/retail
Gross State Product: $56 billion
Income per capita: $29,537

West Virginia's economy is heavily dependent on coal mining and other extractive and heavy manufacturing industries. As is the case with other Appalachian states, West Virginia is relatively poor, and unemployment is higher here than the national average. Steel and chemicals production are the leading manufacturing industries. Only the state's eastern panhandle is in a strong economic condition, mainly through tourism, though West Virginia is home to some of the world's best-known companies, such as Toyota and Amazon.com.

Wisconsin

www.wisconsin.gov
Major cities: Milwaukee, Madison (capital), Green Bay, Racine, Kenosha
Population: 5,557,000
Chamber of Commerce: *Metropolitan Milwaukee Association of Commerce*: 756 N Milwaukee Street, 4th Floor, Milwaukee, WI 53202; 414 287 4100; www.mmac.org
Main industries: manufacturing, finance, wholesale/retail, services, agriculture/forestry/fisheries
Gross State Product: $227 billion
Income per capita: $36,047

Wisconsin's biggest economic activities are manufacturing and agriculture, particularly dairy farming. Important manufacturing centres are located in Milwaukee, the state's largest city, and Madison. Wisconsin also has a thriving tourist industry owing to shorelines on two of the Great Lakes; Superior and Michigan. The Mississippi flows down its western border. Manufacturing accounts for more than a quarter of the GSP: among its most important products are food products, machinery, transportation equipment, and paper and wood products. There are several large shipment centres on The Great Lakes.

Wyoming

www.wyoming.gov
Major cities: Cheyenne (capital), Casper, Laramie, Gillette, Rock Springs
Population: 515,000
Chamber of Commerce: *Greater Cheyenne Chamber of Commerce*: 1 Depot Square, 121 W 15th Street, Cheyenne, WY 82001; 307 638 3388; www.cheyennechamber.org
Main industries: mining, finance, construction
Gross State Product: $30 billion
Income per capita: $43,226

The population of Wyoming has climbed back from a decline after a boom in the 1970s and it no longer has one of the lowest per capita incomes in the country. There are three times as many cattle here as people. Mining of sulphur coal has become the major contributor to the state's economy, as well as other forms of mining such as uranium mining. Ranching is an important employer (there are about 70,000 farms) Tourism too is an important sector, since Wyoming has spectacular Rocky Mountain scenery and contains one of the USA's most popular national parks, Yellowstone.

■ RETIREMENT

The USA has the most diverse landscape in the world, along with the most varied climate. Several states have the perfect weather for those who like their sunshine gentle, and many retired people love the year-round blue skies of Florida or California, with their constant temperatures and warm seas.

As well as the climate and the landscape, America offers a great variety of leisure activities. From the natural and dramatic beauty of the Grand Canyon, Monument Valley, or the redwood forests of northern California, to the grand *kitsch* of Disneyland, everything for the tourist is done in style and (usually) with taste. Above all, Americans know how to build museums. They are expensive, but informative and interesting and often very big. It is very difficult to be bored in the USA.

For the British retiree, another inestimable advantage to America is the common language. This is important for anybody moving to a new country, but doubly so if you are retiring, as you will probably be at an age when learning a new language would be an effort you could do without. For other Europeans, the fact that at some stage in her history America has taken in representatives of almost every race on earth means that it is always possible to find a community from your own country if you know where to look.

There is one major disadvantage in looking to America as a place to retire to: immigration laws. The zeal of the Immigration and Naturalization Service is discussed elsewhere, but it is important to mention here that America, unusually, has no special retirement category in its immigration laws. If you want to retire, you have to do so on one of the visas available to everyone: there are no special dispensations for the over 65s. This is all covered in greater detail throughout this chapter but the important fact to remember from the outset is that unless you have a green card or are a US citizen, you will probably only be able to stay in the country for six months at a time.

Staying in the country for only six months at a time may be no great disadvantage. A lot of people will regard it as the perfect way to spend their retirement: six months in the sun and six months at home seeing the grandchildren. This need not be too expensive: because many people are in the same boat, the rental sector in popular retirement areas like Florida is geared towards six-month lets.

The decision to leave your home country

Unless you are marrying a US citizen, already have citizenship or are a green card holder, the decision to leave your home country permanently need not be taken. For the reasons given above and in the following sections, the vast majority of retired foreigners in the USA spend only part of the year there. This makes life much easier. You need make no irreversible decisions about selling the house and moving wholesale to the other side of the Atlantic. It also gives you the opportunity to get to know the country and decide which state suits you best. If (or when) you are certain that you want to settle in the USA, you can take the necessary steps towards getting more permanent status. This is not easy, but it is a good deal easier if you know the country. The following sections give details on the various immigration options open to retirees.

TIP

■ Visa categories change constantly, and there may well be a new retirement visa introduced in the future, or one which allows an eight-month stay, for example. Meanwhile, think of the advantages in spending six months a year in the country and enjoy your retirement.

Residence and entry

There is no provision in federal immigration law for retired people. Unlike many other countries, anybody wishing to retire to the USA, even those with enough funds to support themselves, cannot do so on a special retirement visa. The regulations stand for anybody of any age who wishes to spend time in the USA.

However, retirees with $500,000 or more to invest can take advantage of Treaty Trader legislation, which created a retirement visa in all but name. The USCIS has redefined the EB-5 visa where applicants may invest in a USCIS-designated Regional Center and apply for a green card, issued to the applicant, spouse, and all children under the age of 21. Regional Centers offer 'immigrant programs' which require virtually passive investments, enabling you to genuinely retire, or for that matter, do anything you choose. They are usually organisations or agencies which deal with specific geographical locations and their aim is to improve the economic viability of that area. Visa processing takes about a year, and 21 months after entering the USA you have three months to apply for removal of conditions, after which the investment may be sold.

Another option is to use a B1 or B2 visa for temporary visitors on business or pleasure, which is valid for six months at a time. These visas used to be valid indefinitely, but are now only valid for ten-year periods with strict rules on which activities you are allowed to participate in while you are visiting the USA. They do allow multiple entry though, so the holder can spend six months in the country, leave, and return for another six months, subject to the discretion of immigration at the port of entry. Opinion is divided as to whether it is a good idea simply to cross the border into Canada, Mexico or the Bahamas, and return after 24 hours: the immigration authorities are increasingly denying entry if they suspect that you are using your visa to reside permanently in the USA. As a B visa holder you must retain a home outside the USA.

Some retirees decide that six months of the year is enough for them – they can spend the winter in America and return home for the spring and summer. Those who are semi-retired may set up a company or buy an existing business (on an E-1 visa), or try for an intra-company transfer visa (an L-1). Both have advantages. The E visa is potentially renewable every five years, as long as the business is maintained and you fulfil your obligation to employ a few US citizens. To qualify for an E visa you need to have made an investment in your company in the USA (usually a sum of around $100,000, though you may have an application approved for less than that), to employ people (usually one or two), and to show that the business is profitable.

The L visa allows you to apply for a green card after two or three years and exempts you from a major step in the application process: that of

FACT

■ Without a green card or the funds for an EB-5 visa, it is impossible to legally spend more than six months of the year in the USA.

labour certification (proving that your job cannot be done by an American). The disadvantage for those on the way to retirement is the work involved in starting or working with a new business, and the additional risk of doing so in an unfamiliar environment. This, of course, applies to both E and L visa applicants.

There are two ways to qualify for an L visa. The first is to be transferred by your company to a branch, affiliate, subsidiary or joint venture in the USA. You must have been employed outside the USA for at least one of the past three years as either a manager, executive or person with specialised knowledge. Another way of qualifying is to set up a branch, or sister company to a company that you already run in your own country: you will then have L visa status as an employee of the American side of the company. The two operations can be run in tandem until you are eligible to apply for a green card, and then the home country branch can be wound down, and you can retire on your resident's status. This sounds simple, but there are major pitfalls. It is essential to get professional advice to ensure that you are applying for the right visa for your status (see the section entitled 'Visas, work permits and citizenship' in the *Before you go* chapter of this book).

Where to live

It is unlikely that you will be thinking of spending most of your retirement in America without having some knowledge of the country and the advantages and disadvantages of the various states. The most important criteria are probably affordability (the daily cost of living in that state as well as the cost of property purchase or rental), climate, and the ease of getting there from your home country. Another consideration should be the numbers of fellow expatriates that you are likely to meet – some people would prefer to be somewhere with a sizable community from their own country while others would prefer to be somewhere where there are few other expats.

There are few statistics available on the number of foreigners actually retiring to the USA. According to a survey from the American Association of Retired Persons, more than 50% of the country's older population – around 16.8 million people – live in just nine states. California, New York, Florida, Pennsylvania, Texas, Illinois, Ohio, Michigan and New Jersey all have more than one million people aged over 65.

One of the problems of retirement in the USA is that, without a specific 'retirement visa' there is no real community or club for retired foreigners. There are a few associations, such as the Florida Brits Club (see below), which have been set up to bring general expatriates together, but there is little that is aimed specifically at retired expatriates. The last section in this chapter has some addresses of clubs and organisations for expatriates

Popular retirement destinations

The most popular states for expatriates of all nationalities – and for American retirees – are Florida and California. Both have agreeable climates and affordable property, and Florida has the added advantage for foreigners of being readily accessible from Europe. Another advantage is that, owing to its popularity as a holiday destination, flights are frequent and comparatively cheap. California's popularity is waning slightly, mainly because it is 3,000 miles further away from Europe. New York State and Massachusetts have always been popular, but the soaring price of property in these states has dissuaded a lot of people from buying there. Arizona and Colorado are attracting more foreigners for as they are both in the early stages of rapid development, property prices are low while the economy and facilities are getting better. A recent US survey found that they are the two most popular states for Americans to own a home, and observers say that many foreign buyers are following suit.

while this section outlines selected states that are popular with foreigners. The descriptions cannot begin to be exhaustive and for more information on the individual areas, you should refer back to the regional guide above. You should also contact state chambers of commerce for real estate guides.

Florida

There are vast areas of Florida that are in the process of development and, as a result, the state is being heavily advertised as the most desirable place to buy a home. Retirement developments are being sold at the moment, some with several golf courses and gyms attached. Florida is the main expatriate and retirement state, popular with Europeans, Australians and New Zealanders, as well as Canadians and Americans. It has the biggest concentration of over-65s (16.8%) in the country, and the smallest population of under-18s.

Being on the east coast, Florida is easily accessible from Europe and has a far warmer climate than the rest of the east coast states. One of the reasons for Florida's popularity is the number and variety of diversions it is home to: Disney World, the Everglades National Park, Universal Studios, the Kennedy Space Center, and hundreds of beaches. The areas south of Orlando, Palm Coast, and Amelia Island in the north-east of the state, are spots that attract the most British property buyers. Other popular areas are Naples (southwest), Newport (south) and Sarasota (on the central west

FACT

■ Between 4,000 and 8,000 British people own second homes in Florida, a figure which does not take into account the large number of people who rent their holiday home year after year.

coast). At the bottom of the range it is possible to find a three-bedroom freehold house with two bathrooms for $160,000 though prices can then go sky high depending on what you are looking for. Probably as a result of foreign investment, Florida seems to be riding out the housing crunch a little better than most other states and house prices haven't changed a great deal in the last couple of years. The larger and denser cities and the particularly attractive areas along the coastline can still command extremely high house prices however.

If you're a Brit who is looking for advice and information about becoming an expatriate in the USA, the Florida Brits Group (www.FloridaBritsGroup. com) is a good place to start. Established in 1990, the group has a membership of around 1,200 couples, all of whom own holiday homes in the sunshine state of Florida. The group gives advice on buying and running holiday property in Florida and also organises regular events in the UK for British homeowners. Membership is a one-time joining fee of £20 per couple. The group also sells a Florida Homeowners Information Pack which provides advice on wills, taxes, legal issues and rentals (price £16.50, includes P&P) and has good associations with business brokers in Florida and visa consultants in the UK who can help assist would-be immigrants source visa-qualifying businesses for E2 visas.

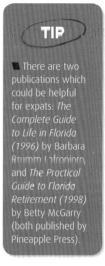

TIP

■ There are two publications which could be helpful for expats: *The Complete Guide to Life in Florida (1996)* by Barbara Brumm Lafronioni, and *The Practical Guide to Florida Retirement (1998)* by Betty McGarry (both published by Pineapple Press).

Two retirees relaxing on Bonita Springs beach, Florida

Property Contacts

Florida Home Realty: 10200 State Road 84, Suite 107, Davie, FL 33324; 954 475 4860; info@floridahomerealty.com; www.floridahomerealty.com
Florida Property & Business Services LLC: PO Box 41, Chichester, West Sussex, PO20 1UZ; 01243 536026; admin@floridapbs.com; www.floridapbs. com. Accountants providing a service to property owners in Florida.
World of Florida: St Ethelbert House, Ryelands Street, Hereford HR4 0LA; 01432 845645; homes@worldofflorida.co.uk; www.worldofflorida.co.uk. Specialists in villas to buy and rent in Florida.

Colorado

Colorado is one of the most beautiful states, with 35% of it given over to national parkland in some form. Colorado is in the process of development, and its economy is considered healthy. Along with Florida and Arizona it is one of the most popular states for expatriates. Fort Collins, situated in northern Colorado, is an attractive part of the state, and is reported to be one of the fastest-growing communities in the USA. It has over 300 days of sunshine a year, and is close to the Rocky Mountain National Park, Estes Park and the Poudre Valley, all of which have wonderful views. There are a number of developments springing up there, and houses are reasonably priced – a single mid-range three-bedroom family home will cost around $230,000–$270,000. (Of course, it's possible to find a cheaper home or one that costs far more). Developments around Fort Collins have facilities for golf, horse-riding and boating.

Arizona

Arizona has recently been at the top of the tables for activity in the homes market: there has been almost 30% more new sales and increases in employment. It is one of the boom states, with land being reclaimed from the desert and turned into new business parks at an unprecedented rate. Real estate prices are still reasonable, although they are climbing steadily: the price of an average new home in Scottsdale costs around $310,000. The cost of living is one of the lowest in the country: Phoenix, the largest city in the state, is an affordable place to live. Winter temperatures in the high 60s make Arizona a favourite with retirees, as does the famous scenery. During the summer, however, the desert setting is merciless as temperatures climb above 100°F (37°C), making it unwise to spend any length of time outside an air-conditioned environment.

Arizona is the Grand Canyon State, and is also home to Monument Valley and some wonderful desert scenery. It is a prime tourist state: the Grand Canyon is one of the seven natural wonders of the world and often one of many people's 'must see' sites. A lot of property developers are concentrating on the Scottsdale/Phoenix area, where 'gated' communities

TIP

■ One of the great advantages of Colorado is the varied landscape and climate: although it has the highest average altitude of any of the states, and more famous-name ski resorts (among them Aspen and Vail), it also attracts walkers and hikers in the summer.

TIP

■ The one benefit to Arizona's heat is the lack of humidity; the dry desert heat can often be suffered longer than the humid, sticky heat of states further north and east.

are being built with secure entry, pools and sports facilities. These communities also have golf clubs, restaurants and shopping nearby.

California

The state that for many people sums up America has long been a mecca for sun-worshippers and those in search of a better quality of life. The climate hardly changes in California; apart from a few days of light rain in the spring, the sun smiles down on the reclaimed desert that makes up most of the south of the state – the most populated part. It is a popular retirement state, though less so with Europeans than with Americans. One of the best things about California is the variety of the landscape, as there is everything from the high Sierra mountains to the desert: Death Valley is the lowest point in the country, 656 ft (200m) below sea level. There are also the Redwood forests in the north, the vineyards of the Napa Valley, and the Pacific coastline which stretches the length of the state. The weather changes gear the further north you go: the climate of San Francisco is markedly cooler and wetter than Los Angeles.

FACT

◼ California's economy has been continuously growing since 2000 at a rate of about 2.8%, ranking it fifth in the USA. Residential construction has also increased again.

View of a vineyard in Napa Valley

A popular area is Santa Monica, 15 miles (25km) west of downtown LA. It is near the sea, with all amenities close by, but with practically no public transport. The Santa Clarita Valley is a community development appreciated by families while another planned community is Westlake Village – Agoura Hills. The official real estate brochure for the area says the 'quality of life is enhanced by the relative serenity of ocean breezes'. In the San Francisco area, Palo Alto is an old-fashioned community with trains to the centre; Los Altos is a dormitory town popular with foreigners because of its European appearance.

Texas

Another popular retirement state with Americans, Texas has a high standard of living, a healthy economy (ranked fourth in the USA), and an excellent climate in the south. It is the second biggest state after Alaska, with relatively cheap real estate – although it is extremely difficult to find rental property. Because of its many advantages, the state is attracting international companies, and the main expatriate population is a shifting one of workers and executives on temporary contracts and secondment. Galleria, west of Houston, is a mixed residential and business area with good access to shopping and recreational facilities. There are international schools in Houston and Memorial (a quiet, wealthy, tree-lined neighbourhood) and high quality public (state) schools throughout the entire state. Another popular area is Plano, to the north of Dallas. It has lakes and reservoirs nearby for boating and fishing, and public transport is excellent.

Pensions

If you are living in the USA (or visiting regularly), and you are entitled to a UK (or EU) state retirement pension, you will get the same rate as if you were at home, including all state pension increases. You should let your local Social Security office know your date of departure and your overseas address. When you return to your own country it is essential that you tell the relevant office that you are back. You can receive a retirement pension from both the USA and your own country if you have enough insurance under each country's scheme to qualify you for a pension. The social security reciprocal agreement between the USA and most European countries or Australia (although not New Zealand or South Africa) will help you to receive a US pension if you do not have enough UK, European or Australian insurance. The normal system that operates is that if you have at least six quarters of insurance coverage (the equivalent of one and a half years full employment) in the USA, but you do not have enough to qualify for a US pension, the insurance that you have paid at home can be combined with your US insurance to help you qualify for a US pension. The amount of money that you are entitled to will be calculated in your country of origin, based on the amount you would have earned if you had been paying insurance there all along.

i For a clearer picture on reciprocal agreements, visit the Social Security Administration's website at www.ssa.gov/international/agreements.

Reciprocal agreements usually apply only to a basic retirement pension, not to state earnings related pensions and any occupational pensions. If you have a personal pension scheme in your own country, then this can be transferred to a US personal pension scheme by the insurance company that provides the scheme. The company has to make an application to the Inland Revenue Pension Schemes Office (or the appropriate office in your country) in order for the transfer to be approved, and then arrange for the scheme to be transferred across to a US insurance company. If you have been sent abroad by your company you should have been continuously covered by the company's occupational pension arrangements, which will enable you to build up rights towards your pension. Your employer will have made one of three arrangements for you: you may have remained in the home company pension scheme, transferred to your host company's scheme, or you may have been transferred to an international offshore pension scheme. Depending on length of service, you should be entitled to draw your pension in the USA (for more details on this see the 'Taxation' section in 'Daily Life').

Widow and widower benefits can be paid in the same way as retirement pensions. If your husband or wife was insured under both US and European or Australian schemes, then the same rules apply as for retirement pensions. If you are entitled to US Retirement or Disability Benefit, it may be reduced if you are drawing a retirement pension at home under rules called the Windfall Elimination Provisions. However, these rules do not apply if you are drawing UK widow's benefits, so it may be worthwhile to continue drawing UK widow's benefits until you are 65, rather than claiming UK retirement pension at 60.

TIP

■ Regulations governing pensions are complicated, and you should get professional advice before deciding on any course of action

Useful addresses

Centrelink (Australian Pensions) Retirement Services 13 2300; www.centrelink.gov.au. For information on the Australian social security scheme.

HM Revenue & Customs (previously Inland Revenue): 0845 600 2622; www.hmrc.gov.uk

Overseas Pension Service – Department for Works and Pensions: 0845 60 60 265; www.thepensionservice.gov.uk. For information on the UK social security scheme.

United States Embassy: 020 7499 9000; www.usembassy.org.uk. For information on the US social security scheme in relation to the UK.

US Social Security Administration: 800 772 1213 (US); www.ssa.gov

Taxation

Taxation is covered in more detail in the *Daily Life* chapter. If your pension is being paid from your home country into a US bank account and if you are non-resident in the USA and are resident abroad (for taxation purposes), your pension will be taxed at source by the local tax office at home, and paid to your US bank account net of tax (i.e. with the tax already deducted). For UK residents, if you are claiming exemption from UK taxes on the basis of non-residence in the UK, then your pension will be paid gross to your US bank account, and taxes will be deducted in the USA. Under present laws, 85% of your UK government social security income may be taxed, if it reaches levels of $30,000–$40,000. It is important to understand also the tax treaties and totalisation agreements in force between the USA and other countries. Generally, if you are a non-resident of the USA and a resident in one of the countries it has a Totalization Agreement with, even if you are spending six months of the year in the USA, these agreements ensure that you do not have to pay income tax or social security in both countries.

Useful addresses

Ferrell Wealth Management Inc: 407 629 7008; info@ferrellwm.com; www.ferrellwm.com
Expatriate Advisory Services: 01509 670 918

US pensions

US retirement benefits are paid on a system of work credits, measured in three-month (quarter-year) units called quarters of coverage. In order to draw benefits you need to have a certain number of years' work to your credit. Retirement benefit is paid to workers at the age of 65. A reduced amount can be claimed as early as age 62. Your eligibility for state retirement benefits from your country of origin and from the USA will vary – see above fpor details. Under reciprocal arrangements you may combine national insurance payments to make you eligible for a pension in either country.

Occupational (company) and personal pension plans are similar to those available in much of Europe. Company tax deferred retirement plans are usually called 401(k) plans: you are allowed to invest a certain percentage (adjusted annually) of your income and your company may match 50% to 100% of the money you put in, depending on the scheme. Personal retirement plans, either an Individual Retirement Account (IRA), or a Keogh Retirement Plan for the self-employed, are also available, although they are not as widespread in the USA as they are in Europe. They are sold by most financial institutions, including banks, insurance companies and savings associations.

Occupational pension schemes are extremely complex. They generally fall into two broad categories; those that are financed entirely by the employer, and those to which both employer and employee contribute. Within these categories are defined contribution plans and defined benefit plans (fixed contributions and fixed benefits respectively). There are many other types of pension scheme, including profit share schemes, employee stock ownership plans (ESOPs), money purchase schemes and simplified employee pension plans. Employers will supply all their employees with information on the pension scheme that they operate.

 For further information, contact The Pension Rights Center (202 296 3776; www.pensionrights.org).

Health insurance

You are not eligible for Medicare until you have been resident in the USA for at least five years. Medicare is the federal programme of health insurance (HI) included in the social security provisions. It is available to all US citizens who are over 65, who have paid social security taxes. Those over 65 are automatically covered, unless they have not been in the USA for five years. It is essential that you are covered by an insurance policy from your own country if you are thinking of going to the USA for any length of time. Even if you have secured a green card and you are going to live in the USA, if you are over 65 and have not been in the country for five years, you will not be eligible for Medicare. It will also be almost impossible to buy insurance at this age. Any American over the age of 65 who is buying insurance is doing so only to top up Medicare (which typically pays hospital bills less deductibles – such as drugs and dental costs – for the first 60 days of treatment), and no insurance company would cover you for the sort of sums necessary for full insurance.

Wills – taxation and legal considerations

The making of wills is also covered in the 'insurance and wills' section of *Setting Up Home*. This section will deal with the various legal and taxation considerations that have to be taken into account should you die while living in the USA.

You should get the advice of an attorney when making your will. There are two types of inheritance law for those who die intestate. Most states have common law: the estate is divided among all surviving relatives, including the spouse and children. Nine states (Alaska, Arizona, California, Idaho, Louisiana, Nevada, New Mexico, Texas, Washington and Wisconsin) have community property law, in which property acquired by a husband and wife after their marriage is regarded as owned by them in community, and is divided up as such after death.

You should make a will regardless of the size of your assets. If you get married, the marriage automatically revokes previous wills, and if you separate or divorce, you should change your will. Remember that it will be to your advantage to establish your domicile outside the USA in order to avoid US death taxes. If you have a green card or have become domiciled (see below), this option is not open to you. If you are domiciled, you can make a will that establishes a 'credit shelter trust', which ensures that both you and your spouse can use the $2 million estate tax exemption amounts separately.

The US equivalents of inheritance tax or death duties are Estate and Gift Taxes. A federal estate tax is imposed on the market value of assets that an individual owns at death. In addition, all the states impose death taxes at much lower rates than the federal rates.

The important criterion with estate taxes is not whether you are resident or non-resident, but whether you are domiciled or non-domiciled in the USA. This matter is very subjective, but as a basic rule of thumb, if you have a green card or have been permanently in the country more than five years (normally this will be holders of L, E and G visas), you will be considered domiciled. If you have been in the country for fewer than five years, or if you stay for a few months at a time, and have a home in another country, you will be considered non-domiciled.

Tax rates have been cut following the budget bill introduced by President Bush in 2001. Estates of domiciled people are now taxed at a maximum of 45%, and will stay at this rate through 2009. An exemption is allowed on the first $2 million, which will rise to $3.5 million in 2009. Non-domiciled people are taxed at the same rate but only on US assets, with an exemption limited to the first $60,000.

Gift tax is only imposed for non-domiciled people if the gift is tangible (real estate). A gift of property, therefore, is liable to gift tax, but US stocks or bonds, which are considered intangible, are not. Stocks and bonds will, however, be subject to estate tax on your death. You should also make your spouse the owner of any life insurance policies.

One method of distributing assets after death is to set up a revocable living trust, which effectively puts all your property into a trust. The advantage here is that you remain in control of decisions affecting the property but on death all assets are not put into probate. In many states, if land or homes exceed a valuation of $20,000, the estate is automatically entered into probate, the process whereby each will is ratified by the courts and involves unnecessary expenses which may cost up to 10% of the entire assets. Consult the Estate Plan Center (www.estateplancenter.com) or the American Association of Retired People (www.aarp.org) for further detailed advice. The International Law Partnership also has an excellent website, full of useful international tax laws information and advice at www.lawoverseas.com.

FACT

■ There is a gift tax in the USA which is designed to prevent people giving away all their assets before death.

TIP

■ It is important to remember that if you buy a US home, no matter what your nationality or visa status, it will be subject to estate tax when you die. In addition to the Federal Estate Tax, there may be levies imposed by state governments, so this needs to be considered in estate planning too.

Death

There are various things to be taken into account when arranging a funeral in the USA. The most important decision is whether you would like the body to be shipped home or not. After registering the death with local authorities in the USA, you will need a death certificate from the funeral director before you can attempt to send a body home. The cost will vary depending on the state: in New York it costs around $1,500, plus the standard airfare, although companies such as Inman Nationwide Shipping can arrange everything for as little as $750. Pricing is fixed by weight. In the *Yellow Pages* (www.yellow.com) under 'Funerals' you will find several funeral directors who specialise in shipping. Cremation costs start at around $500, but will normally cost much more. For funerals being held in the country, The American Association of Retired People says that the average total cost of a traditional funeral is $4,600, although flowers and other costs can add another $1,300. Burial can cost a further $2,600 and cremation can amount to about $1,800. In certain states this will be higher or lower, depending on the density of the population and the availability of space.

TIP

■ All deaths must be reported to the local town hall; the death of a foreigner should also be reported to the relevant embassy or consulate in order that it can be registered in the deceased's country of birth.

Hobbies and interests

The over 65s are a powerful and vocal lobby. They are also numerous, and wherever you go you will find an array of societies and a range of recreational activities all designed expressly for the retired.

There are sports and social clubs with expatriate members in all areas of the USA, particularly in metropolitan areas, states such as Texas or Florida, and the east and west coasts where expats congregate. Membership of a sports club can be expensive, but fees vary so widely depending on the state, city, and type of club that it is difficult to give an average. In general, the YMCA (www.ymca.net) is one of the most reasonably-priced organisations, with annual subscriptions of between $400 and $1,000 (seniors enjoy better rates than other users). For more information, contact the local chamber of commerce, visit a library's notice board, go online or look in the local *Yellow Pages* under 'Clubs'.

The USA has a tradition of religious tolerance and freedom of religion is enshrined in the First Amendment of the Constitution. The Roman Catholic Church has around fifty million members, and the nearest equivalent to the Church of England, the Episcopal Church, has some three million. You will find that church attendance is higher in America than it is in Britain and many parts of Europe. Because of the history of immigration to America, you will also find that no matter what your nationality or denomination, there will be a church to cater for your needs. In many communities the church is the social as well as religious centre, organising discussion groups, outings, sports events, dinners and musical evenings. If you are not a churchgoer but are at a loss as to how to start meeting people and making a social life in a new area, you will find that the local church will often still make you feel extremely welcome. Americans are very friendly towards new arrivals, and never more so than in a church group.

Whatever your hobby or interest, it is unlikely that you will struggle to make friends.

Clubs and association contacts

The Florida Brits Group 01904 471800; FlaBritsCl@aol.com; www.floridabritsgroup.com. Has a membership of 1,200 Florida-property-owning couples.

Union Jack: 1 800 262 7305; ujnews@ujnews.com; www.ujnews.com. A very useful source of contact information for British expats; it is a monthly newspaper that can be obtained on subscription for $35 per year. Lists expat clubs and organisations and holds classified advertisements for immigration attorneys and shippers.

American Association of Retired Persons: 1 800 687 2277; www.aarp.org. Offers advice on relocation, retirement housing, taxation and financial planning. Also has a bibliography of retirement directories.

What's on?

As an example of the variety of clubs, meetings and events available in the USA, here is a selection from the *What's On* column of a local paper in New York State. In a packed week, there was a meeting of CHANGES (Citizens Helping A New Generation to Evolve Sustainably), an archaeology lecture on 'New perspectives on prehistoric cultural change', the twice-monthly meeting of the New Horizon Senior Citizens Club of Yorktown ('New members welcome!'), a meeting of Suburban Singles ('tonight's discussion topic: How do you feel about the risks/joys of 'falling in love'?'), several harvest suppers, a keep-fit evening run by the American Heart Association, a traditional clam chowder lunch, a slide lecture on 'The history of England thru embroideries', craft fairs, roast beef dinners, turkey dinners...the list goes on. This sort of thing is replicated in tens of thousands of small towns throughout America, and the hospitality of the average American will ensure that you are made welcome.

Administration on Aging: 202 619 0724; www.aoa.gov. Provides lists of local services for seniors. Of limited help to individuals but may be able to provide some useful contacts.

SeniorNet: 408 615 0699; www.seniornet.org. An online community and resource for retirees, with chat rooms, news, and advice.

Firstgov for Seniors: www.usa.gov/topics/seniors. The federal government's online information hub for retirees.

Starting a Business

■ HOW TO GET STARTED

The USA and the UK have always been enthusiastic business partners, and the EU is following suit. Each year the UK and the USA conduct trade with each other worth $85 billion, on top of a two-way investment worth $290 billion. With the formation of the North American Free Trade Area (NAFTA), consisting of Canada, Mexico and the USA itself, there is an area of free trade equal in size to Western Europe containing an estimated 400 million consumers. The US economy is a cornerstone of international commerce.

For those thinking of exporting to the USA from the UK, UK Trade and Investment (www.uktradeinvest.gov.uk) is actively supporting the UK's share of North American imports. This includes a series of initiatives and programmes aimed at encouraging UK businesses to consider America as an option. Export USA is designed to assist small companies to introduce innovative products or services to the American market. Another source of help is available from BritishAmerican Business Inc (BABi), which has offices in New York and London (www.babinc.org). BABi is an affiliate of the British American Business Council (BABC), serving a membership base of more than 700 and aiming to promote transatlantic business development. The organisation produces publications, organises networking events and maintains a database of contacts. BritishAmerican Business Inc is the incorporation of the British American Chamber of Commerce and the American Chamber of Commerce in London. The BABC has offices throughout the UK and USA.

Chambers of Commerce are reporting an increased interest in the USA from companies of all sizes, despite the recent economic slowdown. There is an awareness on both sides of the Atlantic of the need to create partnerships with American business organisations and, as a result, it is common to be met with extreme courtesy and helpfulness by organisations who are determined to attract companies and individuals.

The US market is highly sophisticated. It consists of a population of 304 million with an average standard of living higher than most other western countries. It has traditionally had a very inward-looking business culture – a market of that size means it was less necessary to look beyond the USA borders. This has all changed in the last few decades with the advent of globalisation and rapid international communications. It is now as easy for a Texas company to supply Montreal as it is for them to supply Houston. This means that the business climate is more open than ever before. Importing from around the world is now common practice, and exports have become the bread and butter of thousands of companies.

Another advantage to running a company in the USA is in auditing procedures: it is not necessary, as it is in the UK and other parts of Europe, to submit annual audited accounts. There are also few rules on disclosure

The perks of setting up a business in the USA

Setting up a business in the USA is, in many ways, easier than in Europe. There is little federal government restriction and generally there is less regulation, less union activity, and altogether a more laissez-faire attitude. Different states have different laws, but as a rule of thumb it is recognised that the southern and southwestern states are freer in this respect. In the north you will find that the state will take more interest in your business and you will be subject to more regulations than in Texas, for example. For the specific details of each state's commercial regulation it's best to contact local chambers of commerce or state governments (see the state guide in the 'Working in the USA' chapter for contact details).

and you will not have to file lists of directors and principal shareholders of a private company. A company is not required to carry on its business in the state in which it is incorporated (incorporation is the equivalent of forming a limited company), which means that you can take advantage of the liberal tax and incorporation laws of certain states to register a company that is located somewhere else. A factory can be placed where the right sort of labour is available, it can be equipped with technologically advanced machinery and production techniques, and it can then supply markets throughout the country.

Incorporation itself is straightforward, and can be done in a matter of hours. It is usually a simple matter of registering with the State Corporation Department, and can cost as little as $100.

Starting a business is as easy for a foreigner as for a native entrepreneur. State departments and chambers of commerce are geared to encourage new businesses, and you will find that they will go out of their way to help. In one instance, a woman who happened to be a single mother went on a fact-finding visit to Georgia, and found that the local chamber had made sure that her escort was another single mother, in order to point out all the relevant facilities that she would be able to take advantage of.

Choosing a location will be one of the most difficult early decisions. Unless you already have a clear idea of where you want to be, there are many different factors, such as local regulations, local tax regimes, labour pools, real estate values and so on, that should be taken into account. Relocation agents and local chambers of commerce can advise on this. See also the 'Choosing an area' section, below.

TIP

■ It is wise to hire an attorney to take care of your incorporation; this will cost upwards of $750.

As with any business venture, it is essential to have the right advice, and a detailed business plan. The USA is a tempting place to start a business for its very culture is based on individual entrepreneurship. It is also daunting because of its size and the sheer wealth of opportunity, so it is important to be focused. This chapter can give some useful pointers, but there is no substitute for contacting the relevant organisations in the individual states that you have identified and building up your knowledge of the business environment from there.

Procedures involved in starting a new business

Preparation from scratch

Within the scope of this book it is not possible to detail all the preparation that is necessary before contemplating a business start-up. Because of the size of the country, when considering business opportunities, it is necessary to regard the USA as a collection of small countries rather than as single entity. Each state has different laws, and, more importantly, different ways of doing business. The north-east has an industrial history, and factory labour will be more plentiful than in southern states where small, high-tech. industries are more common. Southern states often have the advantage of migration workers, who will work seasonally, whereas northern states usually have more fixed labour pools. For details on the advantages and disadvantages of different states see the 'Choosing an area' section below. Also contact chambers of commerce in your area, as they will have lists of contacts in the USA.

Assuming that you have decided on an area, one way to start is to source all your information from your own country. It is better to build up a client relationship with a firm that can then introduce you to associates in the USA than to contact US firms direct. See the 'Accountants' section below, for a list of accountancy firms in the UK.

If you are in the UK, regional chambers of commerce are a possible starting point. Bear in mind that they exist to promote trade between the UK and other countries, not to help people work and invest abroad, but they can give limited advice to people wanting to set up business abroad. Regional chambers in the USA are likely to be more fruitful sources of information. UK chambers that have links with the USA are Bedfordshire and Luton, Birmingham, Edinburgh, Manchester, the North East, North Hampshire, Nottinghamshire, Renfrewshire, Coventry and Warwickshire, Dorset, Isle of Wight, Northamptonshire, and Sheffield. If you are from outside of the UK, try visiting www.uschamber.com for a guide to international chamber relations. See also the end of *Working in the USA* for a 'State-by-State Business Report with addresses of US chambers of commerce.

Two organisations that offer specialised advice to British exporters are the *British Chambers of Commerce* (www.britishchambers.org.uk) and Link 2 Exports (www.link2exports.co.uk) which provide both export advice and country profiles.

Other starting points for information are the state development agencies. These are agencies of state governments, and are set up to give advice on all areas of business in the state, from location information to financial incentives offered by the state. They are fiercely competitive organisations, and are keen to attract foreign investment. The quality of free advice you will get and the help with financing in the form of introductions to banks and so on, will be excellent. Many state development agencies have well-established offices in Europe. They may also be called Departments of Commerce, or Economic Development Agencies.

Accountancy firms and lawyers who deal with the USA work on the principle that no one organisation can know everything that there is to know, and they will advise up to a certain point and then hand you over to their counterparts in the USA. Similarly, US chambers of commerce in the UK are concerned with attracting US businesses to the UK, and not vice versa. If you are dealing directly with US government and state departments it is always best to use sources actually in the USA. *Bierce & Kenerson* (www.biercekenerson.com) is a law firm specialising in support for business investment in the US. Their website publishes a legal guide to investment issues and procedures. They also assist both US and foreign businesses in structuring international new and joint ventures that involve trade in goods, services and/or technology.

Preparing to go...

Preparation should include extensive visits to the area. Relocation agents and real estate agents can do all the ground work necessary, advising on suitable premises and organising meetings with businesses for sale, but although it is theoretically possible to set up a branch or an export outlet solely through the medium of advisers, this would be courting disaster. You should spend as long as possible getting to know the area and its business climate, and also meeting your advisors. The more familiar they are with your particular circumstances, the more efficiently they will be able to cater for your needs.

It is important to be fully aware of the local and federal laws operating in the state in which you wish to set up. Federal law will regulate matters which affect interaction between states (such as interstate trade), and state laws will cover such things as company compliance. The formalities of incorporation will be different in New York and Louisiana, and this should be taken into account when deciding where to go. You must also make sure that there are no state regulations covering the particular business you are setting up: this information will be available from professional associations and from the city hall of the area in question.

The *Service Corps of Retired Executives* (www.score.org) is a nationwide group of business counsellors which gives advice on local laws, raising finance and other aspects of starting a small business. There are 389 chapters spread across the country with 10,500 volunteers as staff.

Accountants

The biggest accountancy firms have branches in major cities across the USA, and will advise individuals setting up businesses, as well as large corporations. In addition, they publish a variety of free books and materials on a wide range of business topics, from setting up a business to importing and exporting, and immigration regulations. (See also the 'Accountancy advice' section below.)

The head offices of the biggest accountancy practices in the UK are as follows:

PricewaterhouseCoopers: 1 Embankment Place, London WC2N 6RH; 020 7583 5000; www.pwc.com

KPMG: 8 Salisbury Square, London EC4Y 8BB; 020 7311 1000; www.kpmg.com

Ernst and Young: 1 More London Place, London SE1 2AF; 020 7951 2000; www.ey.com

Deloitte, Touche and Tohmatsu: Stonecutter Court, 1, Stonecutter Street, London EC4A 4TR; 020 7936 3000; www.deloitte.com

Grant Thornton: Grant Thornton House, Melton Street, Euston Square, London NW1 2EP; 020 7383 5100; www.grant-thornton.co.uk

Horwath Clark Whitehill: St Bride's House, 10 Salisbury Square, London EC4Y 8EH; 020 7842 7100; email enquiry@horwathcw.com; www.horwathcw.com

Robson Taylor Chartered Accountants: Charter House, The Square, Lower Bristol Road, Bath BA2 3BH; 01225 428114; info@robsontaylor.co.uk; www.robsontaylor.co.uk

Institute of Chartered Accountants in England and Wales (ICAEW): PO Box 433, Chartered Accountants Hall, Moorgate Place, London EC2P 2BJ; 020 7920 8100; www.icaew.co.uk

Association of Chartered Certified Accountants (ACCA): 29 Lincoln's Inn Fields, London WC2A 3EE; 020 7059 5000; www.acca.co.uk

Choosing an area

The USA should be looked at as a group of individual economic areas, each with its own strengths and weaknesses. Thus New England and New York State are regarded as concentrations of 'intellectual capital' and are the most expensive states to run a business from; the Rocky Mountain states have poor infrastructure, yet are among the fastest growing in the country in terms of employment figures, and so on.

The problem of deciding where to move to is compounded by the states' individuality. You will be able to get a wealth of information from their development agencies and chambers of commerce, but it is difficult to find an overall picture. *The Economist* publishes *Pocket USA*, a guide to manufacturing and industry in all the states, and the regional guide in the previous chapter will give some background on industry.

All these questions will influence your decision. For example, if you are setting up a small high-tech. electronics business, there is no need to tap into a heavy industrial labour pool. You would be far better off in a southern state such as Texas which has a burgeoning high-tech industry. If you are setting up a telephone sales business, one of your main criteria may be the regional accent, and if you are starting a financial services operation you will need to be in New York or the north-east, the US centre for that industry. In some cases it may be better to locate yourself in one of the poorer states which are keen to attract inward investment. If you do not need a sophisticated transport infrastructure, a southern state like South Carolina has a poor road and rail network but gives excellent grant funding if you are going to provide jobs in the state. Similarly, you might need to be in California because your product will sell best there, but it would be better to move across to Arizona, which has a more lenient tax regime and is desperate for investment.

Relocation questions

When deciding where to locate, a number of factors have to be taken into account, such as the following:

- What type of business are you setting up?
- What markets are you aiming at?
- What type of labour force do you need?
- What are the relative costs of wages, real estate, utilities and cost of living?
- What is the transport and infrastructure base like?
- What government and state incentives are available?

It is yet more difficult to identify states that will still be prosperous in ten years' time. Utah benefited from the investment of the Winter Olympics in 2002, and Michigan has been hit hardest by a slowdown in both the automobile and national economies. California's recession has already been mentioned, but many advisors hold that if you go anywhere in the USA it should be west in order to cash in on the long-term potential based on trade with the Pacific Rim countries. Florida is a favourite location for expatriates, largely due to its superb sub-tropical climate and access to the ocean, but there is a danger of saturation. On the other hand, the state is also a gateway to trade with Latin America and the Caribbean.

One of the trends that have been identified in the USA is the growing need of businesses for 'knowledge workers'. As work becomes more high-tech. and computerised, workforces get smaller and all levels become more skilled. This means that businesses will have to locate in areas that an educated workforce is going to be attracted to: that is, areas with good schools and good leisure facilities. Some of these are in what is being called the 'second tier' cities: ones that have been modernising themselves for the past 10 years or so and are now pleasant and stimulating places to live. Examples include Albany, New York; Birmingham, Alabama; Austin, Texas; Salt Lake City, Utah; and Oklahoma City, Oklahoma. The biggest cities will still remain centres of activity: New York for financial services, trade and media; Boston for computer services, medicine and teaching; Chicago for heavy industry and teaching; San Francisco and Silicon Valley for information technology; Los Angeles for entertainment; and Houston for oil and gas, and high-technology.

It is also important to take into account the incorporation regulations of the different states. Generally, the southern and south-western ones

Fast growers

The fastest-growing states in terms of job creation are the four mountain states: Montana, Wyoming, Utah and Colorado, together with the neighbouring desert states, Nevada and Arizona. The fastest growing city in the country is Las Vegas. During the past 40 years there has been extensive migration from the industrial heartland of the north-east and mid-west, often known as the 'rust-belt', towards better economic opportunity in what is known as the 'sun-belt': the states of the far south and south-west, like Georgia and Arizona. Both Atlanta and Phoenix are rapidly growing metropolitan areas that are attracting investment and skilled workers who appreciate a higher quality of life than in older, larger cities.

are the most relaxed about regulations. In Texas, they will let you set up your company and then will ask questions; in the north, they are far more likely to make you comply with state bureaucracy before you start up. California, for all its laid-back image, has some of the most crippling company regulations in the USA – so much so that many companies are moving east to the mountain states, to avoid them. The southern states are also cheaper: the cost of living and of property still reflects the states' relative obscurity in the business world. Naturally, this will change, but at present the south is one of the most attractive areas in which to invest or start a business.

Raising finance

If you are intending to live abroad on a permanent basis it is improbable, but not impossible, that you will be able to borrow start up capital from a bank in your home country. This of course is dependent on a series of factors: your credit history, your standing with the bank, your business history, and the collateral that you can provide. If you are able to mortgage or sell your house at home, or provide it as collateral against a loan, that would be seen as sufficient by many UK and European banks. You would not be able to get a loan simply on the basis of a start-up in the USA. On the other hand, if you are opening a branch or a distribution operation in the USA and using the parent company at home as a base, the best way to raise finance would be from your home bank. It is unlikely that an American bank would lend money to an unknown quantity with no trade record. Bank references from your home country would not count for much in this situation as the bottom line is that the bank does not know you.

If you are trying to set up in the USA with no umbilical cord to your own country, then the first port of call should be a state development agency. You will be advised on all aspects of business in the state and will be put in touch with small local banks, which will be a better prospect than a large bank in another state.

You should be aware that all banks advise of the difficulty of getting a loan for a business start-up. There are, however, numerous state and federal incentives (described below) and government loan guarantees that banks are using to increase their loans in this sector. Some banks, such as First Interstate and Union Bank, have programmes specifically developed for small businesses. There are other sources of credit, although these will come with hefty repayment packages. Commercial finance companies will base their credit on accounts receivable: you can pay back the money depending on your cash flow. Insurance companies will also offer seven- to 15-year loans, and there are also venture capital firms that provide loans to smaller businesses as well as corporations. For more information, contact the relevant state development agency.

TIP

■ Further advice should be sought from relocation consultants (see the 'Relocators' section in 'Setting Up Home'), accountants, and professional associations in the USA.

FACT

■ It should be possible to borrow up to $350,000 from a small bank for a small operation, although the collateral that you would have to provide on that sort of sum would be upwards of 50%.

The investment climate within the USA is generally favourable for foreign investors and there should not be any unusual problems in obtaining finance. There are no legal restrictions on foreign investors' access to financing in the USA. The *National Association of Small Business Investment Companies* (www.nasbic.org) has a membership made up of investment companies that provide small businesses with venture capital and management guidance.

Investment incentives

The federal government has a policy of neutrality towards encouragement of foreign investment. The system treats US and foreign investors as equals, which is believed to lead to healthy investment. The state governments, however, see foreign investment as very positive; something that improves the local economic environment by enlarging the tax base, creating new jobs and reducing unemployment costs. The states are fiercely competitive, and each will try to tempt foreign investors and foreign businesses. The US Department of Commerce provides information on markets, financing, and other related areas to foreigners intending to invest in the USA. It will also put investors in touch with US firms which are interested in opening up a joint venture, and will provide lists of state development agencies.

All foreign investors are eligible for available investment incentives at state, federal and local levels. These include tax breaks (such as provisions for the allowance of accelerated depreciation of assets), property tax exemptions for new industry, exemption of business purchases, and income tax write-offs for certain types of investment. Other incentives include more than 100 Foreign Trade Zones, known as free ports or free zones. These are overseen by the federal government, and are operated by private and public corporations under government grants. Operating in almost all the states, they are areas where imported and exported goods can move freely without paying duty: goods can be manufactured, stored and transported, and duty is only paid when the goods enter the US market, and then at preferential rates. This is very attractive to foreign importers: when goods enter the USA, the assessment for duty does not include the cost of processing and profit realised. For more information contact the Foreign Trade Zones Board (www.ia.ita.doc.gov).

State development credit corporations can make credit available to businesses that are finding it difficult to get financing. They lend for property, land, equipment, working capital and other uses. They also provide recruiting and training services for industrial employees. For more information contact the relevant state development agency.

Small and medium enterprises

There is no standard definition of a small and medium enterprise in the USA. Generally, a small business will employ between two and 50 people, and is 'independently owned and not dominant in its field of operation'

■ The Small Business Administration (www.sba. gov), under the Small Business International Trade and Competitiveness Act of 1988, helps small businesses in a number of ways, such as by providing capital for the purchase of plant and equipment. It also helps with export competitiveness through various local support programmes.

TIP

(Small Business Act, 1988). The importance of small businesses to the US economy is widely recognised: small firms make up 99% of all US businesses and provide around 40% of the GNP. In 1991, there were an estimated 1.3 million small business start-ups. When the recession began in the early 1990s, millions of highly-qualified people were made redundant as companies shed staff in an effort to contain costs. This created a pool of motivated and experienced individuals who turned entrepreneur and started up on their own. In the past few decades, according to Dun and Bradstreet surveys, businesses with fewer than 50 employees have accounted for more than two-thirds of new jobs.

The umbrella group which provides help to small businesses is the Small Business Administration, which has regional offices throughout the USA (many are located in the chambers of commerce). There is also an organisation for the self-employed: the National Association for the Self-Employed (www.nase.org). State development agencies can also provide useful advice and contacts to anybody setting up a small business. Local chambers of commerce are valuable sources of business intelligence.

FACT

■ Half of all new enterprises in the USA start with less than $10,000 in capital; two-thirds of those start with less than $5,000.

Useful publications

All these books are available in bookshops and through www.amazon.com. In addition, information packs, including advice and standard forms, are available from all chambers of commerce and state development agencies.

Exporting to the USA: (Edward Hinkelman, World Trade 1995)

Commerce Business Daily: Overseas Subscriptions, US Department of Commerce

Small Business Kit For Dummies: (Richard D. Harroch Wiley Publishing, 2004)

Business Plans for Dummies (Serial): (Steven Peterson Wiley Publishing, 2005)

Accounting for Dummies (Serial): (John A. Tracy Wiley Publishing, 2008)

121 Internet Businesses You Can Start from Home: Plus a Beginners Guide to Starting a Business: (Ron E. Gielgun, Actium Publishing, 1997)

Operating a Really Small Business: (Betty M. Bivins; ed. Beverly Manber Crisp Publications, 1993)

What No One Ever Tells You About Starting Your Own Business: (Jan Norman, Dearborn Trade, 2005)

The Small Business Handbook: A Comprehensive Guide to Starting and Running Your Own Business: (Irving Burstiner, Fireside, 1997)

Succeeding in Small Business: The 101 Toughest Problems and How to Solve Them: (Jane Applegate, Plume Books, 1994)

Entrepreneur Press, affiliated with *Entrepreneur Magazine*, publishes books for small businesses and start-ups. To see the list go to www.entrepreneur.com. Titles include *Start an Import/Export Business* (2008) and *Creating a Successful Business Plan* (2008). The website also publishes information on franchises, start-ups, marketing and e-commerce.

Periodicals and websites

Journal of Small Business Management: www.icsb.org. (International Council for Small Business).

Entrepreneur Magazine: www.entrepreneur.com. (Entrepreneur Group).

Fortune Small Business: www.fsb.com. A supplement published by *Fortune Magazine*.

Inc Magazine: www.inc.com. Offers advice on starting and developing a small business.

Small Business Network: www.snbpub.com. Offers assistance with growing a business.

Regional investment offices

Every state and major city has an economic development office which gives advice on all aspects of setting up a business, including investment advice. Regional chambers of commerce will supply contact details (see 'State-by-State Business Report').

Relocation agencies and business services

Relocation agencies provide a variety of different services from advising and helping employees who are being relocated (either within the USA or overseas), to advising companies and individuals who want to set up an office or business in a new area. The former services are covered in the 'Relocators' section in 'Setting Up Home'. Commercial relocation specialists offer services that are designed to meet the needs of companies that are relocating, and will also advise individuals needing to find office space. Site selection used to be a relatively simple process that included an assessment of real estate prices and the pros and cons of various locations based on transport systems, local wage rates, and so on. Now that there is such fierce competition between states to attract firms, however, it has become big business. As always, the best source of information will be the state development office (see above for selected addresses or contact the regional chamber of commerce). Companies that are relocating, or opening large plants in the USA, usually prefer to enlist the services of outside consultants who will not be biased towards any particular state or area. This should not be an issue for a small business.

Real estate agents are useful sources of information on relocation. The large international accountancy firms – in particular Deloitte, Touche Tohmatsu, PricewaterhouseCoopers and Ernst & Young – also now advise on site selection and relocation. They have the advantage of being able to use their huge client bases and expertise in taxation, management consulting and real estate to give an all-round service. When dealing with firms of this size, it is worth remembering that they would be charging around $400 per hour, and would farm out minor consultancy work to a smaller consultant. It is best to go to the small consultant first, who would charge an hourly rate of $100–$120).

As well as site selection and relocation, there are a number of companies that offer advice on formation. Jordans, based in Bristol, gives information on existing companies worldwide and advises on the company formations. They can incorporate a British company in the US for around £450.

Most of these services can be found in the *Yellow Pages* (look also under 'Relocators', 'Movers', and 'Moving Services' on www.yell.com or www.yellow.com), or from regional chambers of commerce.

Useful contacts

Association of Relocation Professionals: 0870 073 7475; www.arp-relocation.com
Avalon Overseas Movers: 020 8756 4040; www.avalon-overseas.com
Employee Relocation Council: 703 842 3400; www.erc.org
Fluor Daniel Consulting: 469 398 7000; www.fluordaniel.com.
(Fluor Daniel also have offices in Georgia and the Netherlands.)
Jordans: 0117 923 0600; customerservices@jordans.co.uk; www.jordans.co.uk
Schuyler, Roche Law: 312 565 2400; www.srzlaw.com. Legal services for international business.
Mayer Brown: 312 782 0600; www.mayerbrown.com
Weichert Relocation Resources (WRRI): 020 7802 2500; info@wrriworld.com; www.wrri.com

Business structures and registration

An important consideration for any company setting up in the USA is the choice of business entity. There are several types of business entities in the USA: sole proprietorship, three types of partnership, corporation, and joint venture. Each is subject to a particular tax regime, and affects the owner's legal liability in a different way.

Sole proprietorship

A sole proprietorship is a business owned and operated by one person. It is the easiest type of business to run because it is subject to the minimum of setting up and disclosure requirements, although all profits and losses are filed on an annual tax return. Your personal assets are not protected, and as owner you are fully responsible for any debts.

The procedures for registering a new business this way vary from state to state, as do the costs involved. Although it is relatively simple (depending on the state), it is best to get an attorney to take care of the formalities, if only to save time and trouble. If you want to register your company yourself, the state development agency or the chamber of commerce will provide you with information and a business start-up

TIP

■ Law firms provide advice on areas such as structuring business organisations, employment and labour matters, tax and real estate, and litigation and arbitration.

kit. Generally, a business is registered with the county clerk of the area in which you intend to incorporate. Registration necessitates the filing of a fictitious name (the name of the company), which costs between $50 and $90, paying a sales tax deposit ($500+) and an initial business tax, and compliance with zoning regulations (ensuring that you are entitled to carry out your business in a particular area) which costs between $50 and $75. In addition, you must have a business licence for each city in which you intend to do business. A sole proprietor or partner is not required to pay employee taxes, but if you are intending to employ staff there are further taxes to be paid. Depending on your business, there are also different laws and regulations to be complied with; for example, if you are handling food or controlled waste.

FACT

■ Family members can be considered employees in the USA.

Partnership

In the legal and financial world, a partnership is the most common form of business set-up. A partnership is an association of two or more people running a business for profit, and it can be either 'general' or 'limited', depending on the responsibilities and liabilities of each partner. In a general partnership all the partners take responsibility for the running of the business, and all have liability for any debts. In a limited partnership, there is at least one general partner who is liable for debts, as well as one or more limited partners, who have limited authority and limited liability. Rules for limited partnerships vary from state to state and if the partnership is not set up strictly within a state's particular requirements, limited partners may find that they are fully liable as if they were general partners. The regulations for registering a general partnership are more or less the same as for a sole proprietorship (see above). Many states have also set up a recent entity called a Limited Liability Partnership (LLP). Many professional service organisations have adopted this structure, which is similar to a general partnership but allows partners to benefit from partial limited liability.

Corporation

A corporation is a separate legal entity with the right to sue or be sued, the right to own property, borrow money, buy its own shares, and enter into legally binding contracts. A corporation consists of its owners (shareholders), a board of directors, and company officers. The main advantages of running a corporation are that shareholders have limited liability and banks and other lenders are usually more willing to lend to it than to other types of business.

FACT

■ A corporation does not have to register (incorporate) in the state in which it operates.

Setting up a corporation is a lengthier and more complicated business than for either of the two entities above. A corporation is formed by completing a certificate of incorporation and filing it with the Secretary of State of the state in which you will be incorporated (not necessarily the state in which you intend to do business). The certificate should include the name of the corporation, the purpose and length of time for which it is being formed, the names and addresses of the incorporators, the location of the principal office, the maximum amount and type of capital stock, the capital required at the time of incorporation, the names of stockholders, the number of shares they hold, and the names and addresses of directors. Very few state incorporation laws specify a minimum amount of paid-in capital and it is up to the owners where they incorporate. Most lawyers will recommend Delaware, as it has ideal incorporation laws, and the vast majority of foreign (and US) companies are incorporated there. One of the attractions of Delaware is that there is no need for any of the incorporators to be a US citizen, neither is there any need for the directors to meet formally. There is also great freedom over the payment of dividends, and firms are allowed to keep the minute book, stock transfer ledger and other books outside the state. It normally takes between two and 14 days to form a corporation. Visit www.chamberofcommerce.com for more information.

Limited liability company

In a fairly recent development, some states have adopted laws allowing for the formation of Limited liability companies. This is a new kind of entity that is, in effect, a cross between a corporation and a partnership. It is taxed as a partnership (i.e. taxes are paid directly by the shareholders on their share of the company's income) but shareholders are granted limited liability as if under a corporation. It is too soon to tell if LLCs will expand any further, but the idea has gained acceptance very quickly.

Joint ventures

These can be any combination of two or more enterprises associated with a single business objective. For legal and tax purposes a joint venture is normally considered a partnership, and is limited in scope and duration.

Importing and Exporting

Imports

Most goods may be imported free of any import restrictions, although many consumer products will have to satisfy federal and state health and safety requirements. Certain categories of goods may not be imported, such as certain drugs and materials which are deemed to have been produced by forced labour. Within 10 days of importation a number of documents must be filed with customs. These include entry documents, entry summary documents, bills of lading, customs bonds to cover payment of duty, and powers of attorney documents. For detailed information consult the US customs website at www.customs.gov.

FACT

■ Imports from Cuba, Iran, Iraq, Libya, and North Korea are generally forbidden.

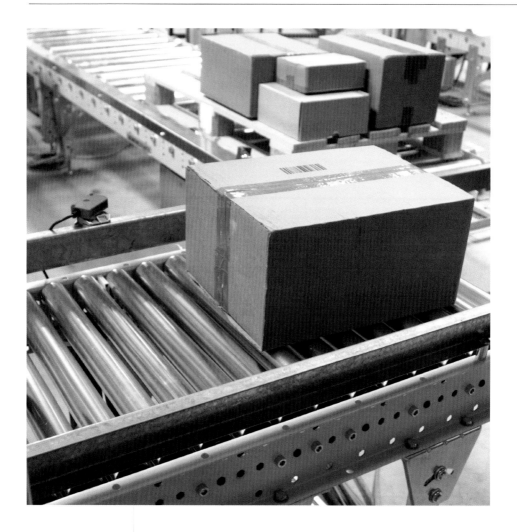

Exports

Most exports are free of restrictions. However, to protect US security interests there are restrictions on the export of goods, technology (including hardware) and technical data. Exports to certain countries are strictly prohibited, and the specific export of oil and arms to certain African countries is also prohibited.

◼ IDEAS FOR NEW BUSINESSES

European and Australasian businesses have a particular advantage over American firms: their nationality. American consumers have a weakness for anything European in particular, especially when they are thinking in terms of quality and lasting value, and snob appeal. Among Europeans, the British have the additional advantage that when it comes to buying branded luxury goods, Americans perceive 'Britishness' as an appealing quality. This goes for many different market sectors, and brand name is often more important than price. Burberry, Wedgwood, Royal Doulton, all signify quality and taste. In general, playing on the European origins of the product is an effective way of signalling old-fashioned craftsmanship and quality as these are all attributes that will strike a chord with an American audience. For UK and Australasian businesses common language is, of course, another advantage.

If you are thinking of setting up a business in the USA, the importance of thorough market research cannot be overstressed. The following factors need to be examined in detail: the size of the target market; the size of the niche that makes up the core of the market; the trends that are affecting the market at any one time; who exactly the customer market is, and what makes those customers tick – why should they buy your product? Who are the distributors, and what will it cost you to use them? What sort of price should your product be fixed at? What is the competition, and what are its strengths and weaknesses? You must also decide if it would be better to manufacture your product in your own country, and simply distribute it in the USA. Again, market research will help with this decision. What are the costs associated with manufacturing the goods on site, rather than shipping them over? In some cases it may even be cost-effective to manufacture in the USA and to export the goods back into Europe before selling them.

There are other options open to those who are keen to do business in the USA but who do not have the resources to set up a new company from scratch. One of the ways that those who want to stay in the USA get around visa restrictions is to buy a business in order to qualify for the E-2 'treaty trader' visa. This allows the investor unlimited time to live and work in the USA, providing the business remains viable. Unlike some other visas, this one must be approved by the American Embassy in your country of residence and they will certify that you are buying a genuine business. A minimum of $100,000 is required but that is qualified by the fact that the business cannot simply support a family. Instead, it must be generating a profit of around $70,000. This means that you should really be looking at a minimal investment of around $120,000–$140,000 in order to generate that level of profit. It is expensive, but does remain a very useful way of gaining a working visa and a means of earning a living once in the US.

There are consultants who advise on buying businesses, and state development agencies will also offer information and counselling as well as a range of small business incentives and grants. Local newspapers have 'business opportunities' columns which advertise everything from garages, nurseries and antique shops, to pizzerias, sandwich shops ('a great little

TIP

■ A UK firm setting up in the USA would do well to capitalise as much as possible on its nationality. This of course depends on what is being sold: it is more important in the marketing of marmalade than semiconductors.

TIP

■ The US market is vast, and competition is intense. Unless you can identify a particular niche that is not already exploited by a domestic manufacturer, you will have little hope of competing against companies that know the country and its peculiarities.

TIP

■ Be aware that in recent years the American Embassy has been getting stricter about approving business-purchased linked visas. It is possible to top up your purchase fund with a loan but generally the embassy will only approve a maximum of 25% of the purchase price.

business with some real old-fashioned heritage started in 1948, $345,000'), hotels, beauty salons and dry cleaners ('discount dry cleaning super store and laundry, 60% cash business, state of art new equipment. High traffic mall location, $150,000'). Prices and conditions vary from state to state, as do state and local regulations. In Florida, for example, to run a hair and beauty salon you will need qualifications and a licence.

The web is a good place to look for businesses to buy across the USA. Businesstown.com provides information on valuing a business, raising venture capital, hiring and firing, and managing a business. It also lists other contacts. Listings of businesses to buy are available on the Business Resale Network (www.businessresale.net) where you can search by category of business, city or state. You might also want to try www.franchising.com for franchise opportunities, or the publications *Businesses You Can Start Almanac* (Adams) or *Streetwise Small Business Start-Up* (Adams).

For more information contact the relevant state development agency. *Going USA* (Outbound Publishing) is a subscription title published in the UK which focuses on emigration to the USA for people who want to live and work there. Opportunities to buy businesses, such as hotels, are often advertised in its pages. The publishers also hold two annual fairs – the 'Emigrate' fair, held in March; and the 'Opportunities Abroad' fair, held in October, both at Sandown Exhibition Centre in Surrey. Here, exhibitors offer advice on starting and buying businesses in the USA as well as giving information on more general services for emigration.

Clothing, fashion and textiles

As consumer confidence grows there is considerable opportunity to capitalise on the British reputation for quality, particularly in the area of high-quality fashion fabrics. American consumers are also very fond of traditional European fabrics such as tweed and textured fabrics from UK businesses. The bulk of the population is now aged 50 or older, and there is demand for career and casual clothing: knitwear separates, fashion accessories, cheap designer and casual sportswear. There is competition from the Pacific Rim countries, where labour and materials are cheap, but

European businesses have the advantage of being able to play the 'quality' and 'tradition' cards.

Reproduction furniture

This is another area where European manufacturers have a potential edge over domestic and Pacific Rim or Far Eastern countries. The worldwide furniture market is expanding, with forecasts putting the increase at 5%–10% over the next decade, and the American market seems to be fairly stable. Consumers prefer traditional designs, which are sure to retain their value, over experimental, modern furniture. The UK and other European countries have a reputation for quality furniture, and British reproductions are regarded as the best in the world.

Gardening products

Around 78 million US households participate in at least one form of indoor or outdoor gardening activity. It is a sector that is growing fast, and anybody from the UK setting up would be able to exploit the British reputation for gardening. Opportunities in this area include seeds, tools, merchandise, garden statues (including gnomes), wild bird and pet products, planters and books. The garden machinery sector is not an opening – tools such as lawnmowers, strimmers, and mini tractors are dominated by US and Japanese suppliers.

FACT

■ You will need to have a good idea of what sectors you are thinking of buying in: it is no good approaching a consultant and hoping to be spoon-fed a business plan.

TIP

■ A small furniture or cabinet-making business would be well-placed to capitalise on the strong reputation of British and European furniture makers.

Environmental products

The Environmental Protection Agency is currently using a multi-billion dollar superfund authorised by Congress to clean up 1,700 dirty sites contaminated by hazardous waste which were created in the time before the introduction of environmental standards. Observers reckon that the market for environmental products, technology and services is recession-proof due to government regulations, public concern, social responsibility and health issues. Recent ideas for business have included environmental cleaning products, home recycling equipment and paperless companies. Because of the highly specialised nature of their instruments, manufacturers of environmental products are extremely diversified, ranging from individual, small companies to larger corporations. One particular type of water filter, for example, will only be available from a German company and indeed most equipment has its specialist manufacturer.

FACT

■ US firms lead the world in their knowledge of hazardous waste treatment.

Water pollution is considered the most significant issue in the environmental sector and new technologies are constantly being sought for the treatment of water and the removal of a growing list of pollutants. Any company setting up in this area would have to find a niche product that was not being manufactured by a US firm. This should not be an impossible search, given the size of the sector and the vast range of equipment and services that are needed.

Food and drink

A highly sophisticated market, the food and drink sector is the largest in the USA, with sales of around $395 billion and an expected growth of nearly 18% until 2011. UK and European products have an excellent reputation with the 34–55 age group, which has a high disposable income. This is a very competitive market and anybody thinking of setting up a business should research it thoroughly. The fact that it is concentrated on the east coast implies that it would be worthwhile looking into the possibility of manufacturing in Europe and importing to the USA. Again, European goods have a reputation for quality and tradition which give a competitive edge over domestic products. However, many of the major players (companies like Sainsbury's, Tesco and Diageo) have a stake in the USA and supply lines set up: it would be very difficult to get contracts to supply the big supermarkets. On a much smaller scale there will be local markets for niche products: confectionery, bakery items (cakes, pies and breads), dairy products and preserves (jams, marmalades and jellies). If these are marketed with the emphasis on their traditional, European origins they should be well received.

Restaurants

Americans love eating out, and restaurant prices are noticeably cheaper than in Europe. It's possible to have a hearty, filling breakfast in a diner for around $6. Changes in family dynamics and the increase in working mothers have increased the pool of those likely to eat out, and higher incomes have boosted the amount of money they have to spend. Add to this Americans' appetite for the perceived quality inherent in European goods – whether we're talking about Scottish woollens or English marmalade – and opening up a restaurant becomes an interesting business proposition, especially in an area popular with tourists. If you're catering for the locals it might be an idea to look at the possibility of opening a place with a British or European theme – a tea room, for example, or a bar specialising in English breakfasts. Remember also that Florida, California, Arizona, Colorado and other states with sizeable expat communities would be good places to open a genuine pub with decent beer that would help to drown any homesickness. Chambers of commerce can advise on likely pitfalls, current trends and so forth.

FACT

■ Food eaten away from home accounts for between 25% of the household food budget (for low-income families) and 50% (for the highest earners).

Sports goods

Americans have an appetite for gadgets and convenience products, and a business that could discover a niche in a particular area would do well. The most popular American 'sports', by the numbers participating, are walking, swimming, cycling, fishing, camping, bowling and working out. Golf comes 14th on the list; hunting (shooting) and tennis, 18th. Schools still concentrate on the traditional American sports and soccer (football) has been slow to take off, but with the interest in the USA World Cup team, this is poised to become as big there as it is in almost every other country in the world.

In other areas, there is a market for garden games that families can play together, for licensed sports goods (clothes and other products with the logo of a particular team), and for fitness products. Cycling is big business. Until recently Americans were only interested in off-road biking, but new government initiatives are encouraging people to bicycle to work. Under Clean Air legislation, every state must present a plan to encourage bicycle use. Massachusetts is investing in adapting roads for bicycle use, and other states have similar projects in the pipeline. This means that there is a fledgling market for bicycle lights and other safety gear. Bicycle

FACT

■ Women's soccer is a far bigger deal in the USA than in most other countries, so a girl's or women's coaching club is not a bad investment.

Following government initiatives, cycling has become more popular, and with gas prices rising, now could be the perfect time to open a bike shop

fashion accessories sell well but again, it is essential to identify a niche that has not been penetrated. As one of the country's biggest and most profitable areas, there is intense competition for a market share in sporting goods.

High-technology and computers

Despite a recent recession, the IT economy continues to offer good prospects. Even though internet stocks were vastly overvalued before the combustion of the 1990s, the excitement that generated such speculation stems from the knowledge that IT is becoming integrated into every aspect of the developed world.

Dell Computers sees bright prospects for servers and the storage market. If this analysis is correct, there is likely to be a corresponding high demand for the skills that support servers and networks. Naturally, this requires a high degree of training but offers ample opportunity for contractors. General internet support, from web design to programing, will continue to be in demand, but perhaps not rewarded with quite the same degree of generosity as before the stock slump.

Technology and gadgets will continue to be big business in the USA

One valuable starting point is www.techies.com, which is a professional resource. The site conducts surveys on the field and publishes advice for the self-employed in the IT sector.

Many foreigners identify niches in this sector and start up small businesses. The sector has the advantage that it is not labour intensive, and manufactured goods tend to be easier to transport. A firm can set up in one state and supply to states several hours away so that it is possible to operate in Texas, for example, where transport is cheap, and compete with firms in New York.

Despite the internet bubble breaking, Venture Capital companies remain interested in internet and communication start-ups, though they are applying more rigorous criteria before lending money. Provided that individuals have innovative ideas and robust business plans, potential investors can still be persuaded to lend capital. After all, opportunity continues to arise from technological progress, though the process of assessing the true value of products and services has since returned to earth. The 'war on terrorism' has prompted investors to be particularly interested in the forthcoming prospects of specialised security technologies.

FACT

■ Many IT professionals in the USA begin their careers as employees and moved toward self-employment, often setting up their own businesses as consultants.

Licensing arrangements

A good way to make the best of the US consumer market is to license your technology in the USA. To license technology a company does not need to make a capital investment in the USA, or maintain a full-time staff. The US system of patenting and trademark licensing is comprehensive and you will have full legal protection for a statutory number of years. For more information contact the *US Patent and Trademark Office* (www.uspto.gov).

Accountancy

Following the collapse of the USA's seventh largest corporation, Enron (the biggest bankruptcy in US history), the accounting profession was thrown on the defensive. Andersen, the auditor and one of the five accounting firms involved, faced congressional investigations over its role in the energy giant's demise, and this eventually led to its own voluntary closure in 2002.

The trend for many large accounting firms to provide parallel business strategy services is already being questioned as being in direct conflict with the traditionally impartial role of the auditor in ensuring strict compliance with financial law and honest reporting to shareholders.

In order to do audit work (potentially the most profitable area of accountancy) in the USA you will need to be qualified as a Certified Public Accountant. Most state accountancy boards will insist on at least a degree before you can take the exam: it is not sufficient to be qualified with an ACCA or ICAEW, or any other foreign accountancy qualification. If you wish to practise without the CPA, and you cannot do audit work, there are possible openings in acting as a conduit for European companies wishing to set up in the USA. You would be able to offer incorporation and registration services, help with business plans, payroll and tax administration, tax preparation, tax audits, and a number of other services that would be invaluable to a new company that wanted somebody speaking a familiar language. Smaller operations will not be able to afford the services of the big firms, and the right sort of advertising (in chambers of commerce in your own country, for example) should bring you to the attention of people thinking of setting up in the USA. UK accountants operating in New York have said that they have not yet seen evidence of a surge in foreign investment, whether this is companies setting up or investors simply putting money into US companies. New York is a heavy tax state, however, and it is important to look at the states where foreign companies are likely to set up.

When deciding how to set up, you can choose between incorporation, sole proprietorship, or partnership. Many accountants are now going for the Limited Liability Company Partnership (LLCP) option (see the '*business*

structures and registration' section above) which would shield the other partners should one of their partners' work involve malpractice.

Real estate agency

There are a number of opportunities for estate agents to set up, particularly in the states where there is a heavy expatriate population. For all practical purposes this will be Florida, although observers say that desert states such as Arizona and New Mexico, which are rapidly developing, are becoming popular. In order to practice as an estate agent you will need to collaborate with a licensed agent, or get a realtor's licence. This requires a one-year course, at the end of which you will be able to practice as a realtor but not as a broker. In Florida and in many other states, only brokers are allowed to take a commission on property sold, and the broker's licence is only issued after the agent has practiced for a certain amount of time (usually three years) as a realtor. The normal route therefore is to work with a broker until you become eligible for a broker's licence.

Women and minority-owned businesses

Banks are increasingly lending their support, in the form of loans and guidance, to women- or minority-owned business enterprises. Most state development agencies have women's business development centers which cater entirely for women. In some states these centers will be set up for women and minorities. Men are not absolutely excluded: in most states the business must be 51% owned by the minority, or by women, in order to qualify for assistance and set-aside perks. Professional women's organisations and further reading includes:

American Business Women's Association: 1 800 228 0007; abwa@abwa.org; www.abwahq.org. Publishes *Women in Business* magazine.

American Society of Women Entrepreneurs: 1 888 669 2793

Small Business Administration's: Office of Women's Business Ownership, 202 205 6673; www.sba.gov

National Association for Female Executives: 800 927 6233; www.nafe.om. Publishes *Executive Female* magazine.

Careerpreneurs: *Lessons from Leading Women Entrepreneurs on Building a Career Without Boundaries* (Dorothy Perrin Moore, Davies-Black Publishing)

Mompreneurs: *A Mother's Practical Step-By-Step Guide to Work-At-Home* (Ellen H. Parlapiano, Patricia Cobe)

National Association of Black Women Entrepreneurs: 248 737 7124; info@nabwe.org; www.nabwe.org

Sister Ceo: *The Black Woman's Guide to Starting Your Own Business* (Cheryl D. Broussard, Penguin USA)

TIP

■ While real estate agency is well-regulated in the USA, property management is not, and it is possible to set up as a property manager with no qualifications or licence. See the section in *Setting Up Home* for useful addresses and telephone numbers.

Law

Expertise in the law is one of the least exportable of skills as the national legal systems differ enough from country to country to make it impossible to practise abroad without retraining. The law of the USA is based on the English common law system, which means that an English or Welsh lawyer would have less difficulty than some other nationalities. Because of the federal government's interest in promoting trade between the USA and the UK there is a good deal of activity that requires professional legal input, and in some states it is possible to practise as a foreign legal consultant. The globalisation in trade and the corresponding growth of multi-national corporate activity is pushing up the demand for experts in foreign jurisdictions. Nineteen US states and the District of Columbia allow foreign lawyers to act as foreign legal consultants.

In order to practice as a US attorney, a foreign lawyer has limited choices: they can attend an accredited law school and pass the state bar exam; in some states an individual may qualify to take the state bar exam by completing an M.C.L. or L.L.M. degree or through spending an equivalent number of hours at an accredited law school. New York allows lawyers who practised in a country using common law to take the bar without further education; alternatively, you can certify as a foreign legal consultant.

 Each state has an admitting authority responsible for bar admissions and will have its own rules for admitting foreign-qualified lawyers. Contact the *National Conference of Bar Examiners* (www.ncbex.org) or any state association of bar examiners for further information.

Buying a franchise

One valuable opportunity for starting a business in the USA is to buy a franchise. This option has several advantages, namely that you are likely to be investing in a proven product or service which is manufactured or distributed by a company which has national brand recognition, customer loyalty, a large national marketing budget, and quality control. You will also receive help with training staff and promoting the business locally.

TIP

■ Buying a franchise is one method of changing career but with ample support.

The advantage in immigration terms is that it is a means of obtaining an E-2 work visa because franchises are recognised as legitimate businesses. Each year The International Franchise Expo is held where franchise businesses exhibit their products. Contacts include:
International Franchise Expo: 201 226 1130; www.franchiseexpo.com
Franchise Times: 612 767 3200; info@franchisetimes.com;
www.franchisetimes.com
International Franchise Association: 202 628 8000;
ifa@franchise.org; www.franchise.org

Useful business websites

Yahoo small business: smallbusiness.yahoo.com. Information, articles and features for small businesses.

Working Solo: www.workingsolo.com. Lists of hundreds of related websites on subjects including associations, organisations, education, business planning and management, shipping goods, and taxes.

SOHO America: www.soho.org. Offers online help for the small office/ home office.

Small Business Administration: www.sba.gov. Government site.

SCORE (Service Corps Of Retired Executives): www.score.org. Caters, for small American businesses.

Asset Financial Management: www.afm-business.co.uk. Offers online help and advice on how to build and grow your own business.

NBIA (National Business Incubation Association): www.nbia.org. The NBIA provides management assistance, access to financing, and technical support services. (Incubation is the maturing of young firms under the wing of more established companies.)

◤ RUNNING A BUSINESS

Employing staff

What is an employee? It is important to be certain of the status of those working for you. It might seem that there is nothing ambiguous about an employee; that someone either works for you or they do not. However, there are some people who you may not consider employees because you do not pay them: your partner (husband or wife), for example, or other family members. Usually, these are considered employees and should be classed as such for tax purposes. There may also be some ambivalence about part-timers: how many hours does someone have to work before she or he is considered an employee?

Employee taxation is subject to federal law and the IRS is diligent. You must be absolutely certain of the status of those that are working for you, as a mistake could be costly and dangerous. If an independent contractor does not meet all the required criteria, for example, you could find yourself liable for all the employee's taxes, which can amount to tens of thousands of dollars for one wrongly classified worker.

The IRS classifies people working for a business in one of four ways: as independent contractors, statutory non-employees (direct sellers who sell your product door-to-door), statutory employees (drivers), or employees. The first two are not employees for tax purposes, and the second two are, meaning you must file certain forms for them to deduct taxes. You yourself are not an employee of your own firm. In a book of this scope it

◤ Some employers may hire subcontractors as a way of avoiding payroll taxes: this is a loophole that the Internal Revenue Service is looking at closely.

is not possible to go into all the criteria that make up the classifications so you must look at this yourself closely. The tests for an independent contractor are that they must use all their own tools, offer their services to the general public, and be in full control of the methods they use to do the work. If part of the contract allows you to tell a contractor when to work, then he is an employee. The law is extremely complicated and it is essential to get the advice of an attorney or accountant when deciding the status of an employee.

Labour laws

US labour law is based on the doctrine of 'employment at will'. This gives employers the right to terminate any job without justification. This right is seldom abused, but it means that the contract becomes very important, usually including clauses guaranteeing at least two years' employment. Contracts tend to be drawn up by collective bargaining and are renegotiated every two or three years, although in areas where there are no unions an individual is responsible for their own salary and contract negotiations. Despite the basic freedom of 'employment at will', most legislation is designed to protect the worker, and in any dispute it is usually the employer who is required to prove innocence. Neither courts nor auditors will show any leniency because of a firm's ignorance or its small size.

Equal opportunities is an area that is also being looked at closely by the courts. This is covered in more detail in the employment sections in the 'Working in the USA' chapter. The federal law covering employment discrimination is Title VII of the Civil Rights Act of 1964, which applies to all employers with 15 or more employees. Over the past 30 years civil rights movements have made great progress in protecting the rights of these groups, and in many companies equal opportunities are mainly protected by executive orders from the president of the company and incorporated into the contract.

Within states the courts have been capricious in their judgments, and almost identical cases from different states that have gone to the Supreme Court have been dealt with differently. The whole area (like that of sexual harassment and political correctness at work) is fraught with contradictions and emotion, and you should get professional advice before dealing with any case that seems to touch on it.

Employers are required to verify the identity and eligibility to work of all employees hired after 1986. This entails filling in form I-9 from the US Citizenship and Immigration Service, and non-compliance means a heavy fine. If you are employing friends and relatives without papers, you should be very careful how you fill in the I-9.

Most states have passed additional employment laws with which it is necessary to comply. Chambers of commerce will supply details of state and federal laws. You will also be able to get free advice in the form of booklets and other publications from major law and accountancy firms which deal with the USA.

Taxation

A corporation (a company, however large, which is incorporated under the laws of any state) is liable for federal, state and local taxes. Depending on the size of your operation, if you decide not to incorporate, you will be liable simply for individual income tax. You may also choose to register as an S corporation. This means that you are classed as a corporation, but taxed as an individual. There are certain restrictions, such as your corporation can have no more than 35 shareholders. Obviously, if you are an individual of some wealth, it will not be to your advantage to have your personal income taxed in this way.

Any company with a permanent presence in the USA has to pay federal, state and local corporation taxes and other taxes on its income. Having a 'permanent presence' refers to the setting up of a branch, office, warehouse or distribution centre in the USA.

There are various tax treaties which operate between the USA and other countries (including most European countries and Australia). These exempt companies which are paying taxes in their own country from paying them again. This should not apply to anyone living and working in the USA, especially with their own company, but if you are not sure of your status, get the advice of an accountant.

A corporation formed in the USA is subject to US federal tax on its worldwide income using a sliding scale according to revenue. There is a federal alternative minimum tax (AMT) which is intended to prevent corporations with large incomes from using various deductions and so on to limit their tax liability. This is imposed at a rate of 20%. Companies are also subject to capital gains tax (maximum 34% rate) and withholding tax on dividends, royalties, and interest paid to foreign recipients (generally 30%). Companies have to assess their own income and estimate how much tax they should pay. A form 1120 must be filed with the IRS within two months from the end of the fiscal or calendar year.

Most states also impose their own corporate tax. This ranges from a 2% single business tax in Michigan, to 12% in Iowa (at the top end of a sliding scale within the state). Nevada, Washington and Wyoming have no state corporation tax. Taxation varies widely from state to state. In all states apart from Alaska, companies are taxed on their US ('water's edge') profits, as opposed to worldwide profits. In California, Idaho, Montana and North Dakota, worldwide taxation is the norm but companies can opt for water's edge. Many states are now taxing services in an attempt to expand their tax base.

Local taxes are complicated by the mass of incentives in the form of tax 'holidays', tax breaks and so on that states, municipalities, and counties are granting in order to attract new business. Chambers of commerce can give details of incentives; see also the 'Investment incentives' section above.

Tax on branches of foreign corporations in the USA are heavy. The source of the income and deciding whether it is 'effectively connected' with a US business is the most important consideration affecting the rate of tax. It is better to set up a corporation in the USA than to set up a branch of a European business, since the federal government imposes a branch profits tax (BPT), usually 30%, on repatriated earnings of a branch of a foreign company. For more information on taxation see the 'Daily Life' chapter. The larger firms of accountants publish free guides on taxation abroad: PriceWaterhouseCooper's *Doing Business Guide: United States* is particularly comprehensive, although written by accountants for accountants, and therefore in need of occasional translation. The guide can be ordered online at www.pwc.com.

Accountancy advice

Most medium-sized accountancy firms in the USA and in Europe are very keen on gaining international business and will be very willing to help the prospective entrepreneur and small company looking for start-up advice. Accountants are always best placed to offer the widest range of advice, and most firms with international aspirations will be able to introduce you to US firms with which they have made contact. Small companies and individuals will always be better off contacting the smaller firms, not only because the hourly rate will be less, but because you will get a more personal service. Typically, a medium-sized accountancy firm with American contacts will advise you from scratch. What is the best vehicle for your business: should you set up a partnership, a corporation, a branch? They will take into account the size of the business that you wish to set up, and the nature of the product. They will then advise on the best location, from the point of view of taxation regimes in different states, infrastructure, and all the available regional and state grant funding and investment incentives.

There is no one firm of accountants that can advise on all aspects of US tax, and at some stage you will be given contact numbers of affiliates in the US who will be able to advise you further.

Depending on your level of knowledge of the USA, there is no doubt that it is best to start with a firm in your own country. However, if you do wish to deal straightaway with a US firm of accountants, one of the associations below will be able to recommend its members across the country.

Useful contacts

For local chambers of commerce refer back to listings in the 'State-by-State Business Report'.

Council of Better Business Bureaus: 703 276 0100; www.bbb.org
Small Business Service Bureau Inc.: 800 343 0939;
membership@sbsb.com; www.sbsb.com
Small Business Legislative Council: 202 639 8500; www.sblc.org
US Chamber of Commerce: 202 659 6000; www.uschamber.org
US Department of Commerce (Office of Economic Development):
202 482 2000; www.commerce.gov. View website for regional contact
numbers.
National Association of State Development Agencies: 703 490 6777;
www.nasda.com
British Standards Institution: 020 8996 9001; cservices@bsigroup.com;
www.bsi-global.com
Colliers Erdman Lewis Ltd: 020 7629 8191
National Society of Accountants: 1 800 966 6679; www.nsacct.org
American Institute of Certified Public Accountants: 212 596 6200;
www.aicpa.org
American Accounting Association: 941 921 7747; office@aaahq.org;
www.aaahq.org
Small Business Administration: 1 800 827 5722; www.sba.gov. Lists all
local offices of the SBA across the US, offering a full range of advice and
services.

Time Off

F or a country so utterly devoted to work and the workplace, America is a nation obsessed with the pursuit of leisure. It is the country which brought the world baseball, basketball, convenience food and drive-thru liquor stores, lawnmowers built like small tractors, and cable television. The USA's performances at international sporting events such as the Olympics usually puts other countries to shame, and it's the interest and financial support from spectators that make Olympic dreams possible for American children throughout the USA. Sport is taken very seriously in this country, and the nation divides itself every spring and fall for the baseball and American football seasons.

The USA has more fast food restaurants than any other country in the world. Most don't even require their customers to leave their cars, and it can often prove cheaper to buy junk food at a drive-thru than prepare a fresh meal at home. You don't even have to leave your car to see a movie; just visit one of the famous drive-in movie theatres on a clear evening and tune in the radio for sound.

FACT

■ With all the competitiveness and money available, it's no wonder an American team always wins the World Series of baseball.

Cultural classics

America has some of the most wonderful and bizarre traditions ever heard of, most of which the average tourist never gets to experience. For example, the township of Brasstown in North Carolina copies the New Years Eve traditions of New York in their own style every year by slowly dropping a caged possum from the top of a flag pole at the stroke of midnight instead of a giant Swarovski crystal ball. In the town of Danville, Vermont, dowsers from all over the country come together during the third week of September every year to show off their uncanny ability to find water or gold buried underground by waving a Y-shaped stick around. There are also some highly unusual sights seen on every road trip taken across the USA, the least of which are the roads themselves. Take Route 46 in North Dakota for example, which has the longest and straightest strip of road in the country. They say you can set your steering wheel in one position and not have to change a thing for nearly two hours flat. Of course, any good road trip would not be complete without a visit to either the World's Largest Ball of Twine (Minnesota), the World's Largest Peanut (Oklahoma), the Poultry Hall of Fame (Maryland) or the Cartoon Hall of Fame (Florida). It's probably fair to say that America creates its own definition of 'cultural classics'.

On every street corner there is an opportunity to be active or lazy, depending on your preference, as baseball quadrangles, swimming pools and tanning salons beckon you. The humble barbeque has grown into a propane monster, complete with grill, hob and condiment tray to be used every spare minute of a Sunday afternoon in July. Entire stores have been built to accommodate America's interest in leisure pursuits: those selling sporting goods, hunting and camping supply stores, children's toyshops, giant warehouses full of hot tubs, swimming pools and whirlpools, huge bookshops complete with cafes, armchairs and CD listening stations, and shopping malls that are so large their walkways are used by 'mall walkers' for exercise.

It's fair to say that while America may not have much free time, it sure uses it wisely.

◾ PUBLIC HOLIDAYS AND EVENTS

The following is a list of public and federal holidays. Some holidays, such as New Year's Day or Independence Day, will always fall on the same date every year. Others, such as Memorial Day or Thanksgiving, will follow a set pattern from year to year – they may be on a certain weekend in a certain month, for example. If a holiday date (such as Independence Day – 4 July) falls on a weekend or mid-week, a federal holiday is usually given on the closest Monday or Friday.

New Years Day	1 January
Birthday of Martin Luther King, Jr.	Third Monday in January
Washington's birthday	Third Monday in February
Memorial Day	Last Monday in May
Independence Day	4 July
Labor Day	First Monday in September
Columbus Day	Second Monday in October
Veterans Day	11 November
Thanksgiving Day	Last Thursday in November
Christmas Day	25 December

Festivals

There are events and festivals happening all the time in the USA, from Mardi Gras in the two weeks before Shrove Tuesday in New Orleans, to small state fairs throughout the country in the summer.

The following is a brief list of some of the main festivals around the USA. Nothing is more galling than to arrive in a place only to discover that the most exciting festival of the year has just ended: it is thus well worth checking with the state tourist offices before you go travelling so that you can plan your route accordingly.

February
Daytona 500: Daytona Beach, FL. The most famous stock car race in the world. Book accommodation at least six months in advance and visit www.daytona500.com.

May
Indianapolis 500: Indianapolis, IN. A month-long festival of events leading up to the famous car race. See www.indy500.com.

June
A Taste of Chicago: Chicago, IL. A gigantic food festival that takes place in June and July, serving food from the city's restaurants to some four million people. Go to www.tasteofchicago.us for more information.

July
Boston Pops Fourth of July Concert: Boston, MA. One of the thousands of Independence Day events: can be particularly moving. Try visiting www.july4th.org.

Kutztown Folk Festival: Kutztown, PA. A celebration of the culture of the Pennsylvania Dutch. See www.kutztownfestival.com.

Cheyenne Frontier Days: Cheyenne, WY. The biggest rodeo event in the world takes place the last full week in July. Visit www.cdfrodeo.com for more information.

August
State agricultural fairs: take place in almost every state, usually in August. The biggest are in Wisconsin (Milwaukee, early August; www.wistatefair.com), Illinois (Springfield, early August; www.illinoisstatefair.info), and Minnesota (St Paul, last week in August and first week in September; www.mnstatefair.org).

Burning Man: Black Rock Desert, NV; www.burningman.com. A festival dedicated to alternative performance and art which transforms the desert into a temporary city of 25,000.

September
Pioneer Days: Fort Worth, TX. Good 'ole boys in western-style celebrations in the stockyards. Three days in late September. Go to www.city-data.com for more information.

Misissippi Delta Blues Festival: Greenville, MS. One of the biggest blues events in the country, with details at www.deltablues.org.

October

The State Fair of Dallas: The Dallas State Fair Park is a national monument, and this three-week extravaganza is held in and around it. For details on prize cattle, livestock and more good 'ole boys in the Lone Star State, see www.bigtex.com.

November

Macy's Thanksgiving Day Parade: New York City. Held annually on Thanksgiving Day, a parade of carnival animals, balloons and floats takes all day to pass through the 'canyons of Manhattan' from 86th Street and Central Park West to Macy's department store at 34th Street and 7th Avenue. See www.macysparade.com.

December

The National Christmas Tree Lighting/Pageant of Peace Washington, D.C. Annual festival that begins with the lighting of the presidential tree on the White House lawn on the second Thursday in November, and is followed by nightly choral performances at the Ellipse. Visit www.whitehouse.gov for more information.

These are thousands of festivals and events that take place across the USA every year. These include local village fairs, corporate-sponsored festivals

The South by South West annual music festival, Austin, Texas

(try Burlington's *Chocolate Fest* in Wisconsin, sponsored by the local Nestlé factory) and large events drawing hundreds of thousands of people from across the country. Visit www.festivalfinder.com for information about the 2,500 music festivals that occur across North America. The guide at www.festivals.com has many global festivals but also provides extensive details on events in each of the US states. There is also a list of every state tourism website.

■ SOCIALISING

Making Friends

The shifting American population is romanticised in literature and films (think of Kerouac's *On The Road*, as well as the hundreds of road movies made). There's an enduring appeal in the USA in the idea that moving on holds the promise of a better life, something that is encapsulated in the American Dream philosophy. The average American moves once every four or five years, and companies often relocate their employees every two years. Professionals accept the fact that in order to progress in a country the size of a continent they may need to relocate frequently and across great distances. Many employers, especially the large ones with

offices across the nation, make every effort to make relocation attractive. There will be company social clubs and special events within firms so that new arrivals can meet their co-workers. Local communities are also active in helping new arrivals meet 'the neighbours' and will often invite them into their homes. Culturally, Americans invite participation. This might involve joining the Parent Teacher Associations (PTAs) or attending events organised by local churches or women's groups, or it might involve joining a local golf, tennis or country club.

Students, in particular, may move far from their home towns and states to study at good colleges. Having made a circle of college friends they might, upon graduation, then need to move thousands of miles away again. So many Americans expect to relocate and are used to making new friends with frequency. Frankly, this social fluidity is often a welcome relief from the formalities and strictures of European or Australasian social interaction. If you attend a party in the USA, particularly if you're new to your area, people will show a genuine interest. They will ask about you and your family with a genuine interest and your accent will certainly more than likely draw a crowd. At times their approach may seem pushy to the more reserved European, but it does usually demonstrate a spontaneous hospitality.

> **Anthony Goodman found Americans to be incredibly welcoming to new neighbours:**
>
> When we arrived we were showered with homemade cookies and invitations to visit. Having previously lived in London in apartments where you didn't really even know the people living below you, this was very supportive.

To outsiders, Americans have a reputation for forming superficial friendships, something that is probably reflective of an eagerness to expand social circles and contacts with greater ease than many European people. Despite this, as an expat, you should expect to spend a year or more finding compatible people with whom you can form close friendships, although attending and hosting gatherings will speed the process up dramatically. See the *Daily Life* chapter for more tips on making friends and settling in.

> Americans are amazingly friendly and generous. They traditionally love the Brits and are very welcoming. There are also an enormous number of English people in the States. That has always been the case but it is even truer now. It is hard to go anywhere in New York now and not hear English accents.
> **Philip Jones**

The novel foreigner

The average American is always incredibly interested to learn about other cultures, even if they have the reputation of never wanting to experience them for themselves. For this reason, try starting conversations with strangers on local topics such as the weather or price of gas – you'll soon find the conversation will quickly turn to your foreign accent and you'll be asked questions about your home country. As a generalisation, Americans love to hear foreign idioms and expressions, and, given enough time, will sometimes attempt to use them in their own speech, so don't be afraid to stand out a little: your differences will often even help you to assimilate.

For British people in the USA, to communicate with and find other expats, you might want to take out a subscription to *Union Jack* (www.ujnews.com), a national newspaper published for Brits in the USA. The paper lists adverts for clubs, immigration lawyers, shippers, and also publishes news about the UK.

Dating

TIP

■ The expression 'dating' in America usually refers to a single person going out on several evenings with different people. It is unusual to only date one other person at any one time: it is more common to be dating several people at once. The slightly worn phrases 'going steady' or 'being exclusive' usually refer to having only one other person in your love life.

If you are planning on moving to the USA as a single person, America is a fantastic place to find a date. The dating culture in America is quite unlike any other country, and whole industries have sprung up around the idea of finding a soulmate for everybody. If you are new to an area, try going out to the local bars or nightclubs, or even keeping an eye out at the library, coffee shop or gym. It's also important to not be afraid to speak up: American men and women are more than happy to ask each other for a drink and are equally unafraid of subsequent rejection. However, if you are a little more reserved, a good place to start is an online dating service. For both gay and straight online dating, try www.match.com or www.eharmony.com, two of the largest and most successful dating services on the internet. List your interests, qualities and quirks and search a database of millions to find someone who sounds fun and interesting. Alternatively, try joining a local book club, volunteer service or even a theatre company. The important thing is to get out there, even in the smallest of American communities. After all, you are more likely to find someone with similar interests to you if you join a group of like-minded people.

◼ ENTERTAINMENT AND CULTURE

There has been so much talent and creativity to have emerged from the American entertainment industry that it seems an almost impossible task to narrow down what the most influential or impressive aspects are. Certainly the theatre industry has produced an impressive array of plays, musicals, actors, directors and playwrights, but it seems to be more than the sum of its parts. Going to see a theatrical production or concert in New York or Chicago is truly a unique experience. In a similar fashion, visiting the movie theatre in your local town seems to have a different feel to it in the USA. Perhaps it's the buttery popcorn or the large, comfortable seating, but the idea of settling down to watch your favourite actors onscreen in the dark remains an ever-tempting notion to millions of Americans every single weekend. Even the music and gaming industries are big business in the USA, expanding the entertainment industry at an ever-growing pace.

FACT

◼ The smaller and often more experimental theatres are known as 'off-Broadway' where you will find more company-based and ensemble theatres. The smallest theatres on the fringe, often fifty-seat studios, are known collectively as 'off-off Broadway.'

Theatre

New York is the heart of American theatre and its centre, known across the world as 'Broadway,' invented the modern musical as we know it today. Broadway roughly corresponds with London's West End and it is here where you will find all the most successful shows, many of which are the popular musicals which originated in Londonover the past 25 years.

Take a credit card for booking. The most comprehensive listings are in the Sunday edition of the *New York Times* (www.nytimes.com), the *New York Magazine* (www.nymag.com), the *Village Voice* (www.villagevoice.com), the *New Yorker* (www.newyorker.com) and *Time Out New York* (www.timeout.com/newyork). There is also a telephone listings service; New York City on Stage (212 768 1818).

There are free summer shows at Shakespeare in the Park in the Delacorte Theater in Central Park. In the big cities you will find the best Broadway shows in the larger theatres and smaller theatres putting on a selection of fringe shows. Some cities like Chicago, Boston and San Francisco have particularly active and critically successful theatres. Contact the local tourist office or chamber of commerce for details.

Prices on Broadway can be high, often as much as $100 for the best seats, and going to see a show is still an event worth dressing up for. Elsewhere, tickets are more affordable, and you can buy unsold (standby) tickets half-price on the day of the performance. This must usually be paid for in cash only. The best place to buy cut-price tickets for both Broadway and off-Broadway shows is the TKTS booth on Times Square or Bowling Green Park near Wall Street. Each day at 11am unsold theatre tickets go on sale for 25%–50% less than the normal price. You may need to queue but it's the best way of seeing a show for far less. Bear in mind too that the booths only take cash or traveller's cheques.

> *i* For updated daily information on performances, callTKTS on 212 221 0013.

Classical music, opera and ballet

TIP

■ In the summer the New York Philharmonic gives free performances in Central Park. Outdoor classical concerts are also held in many venues across the country, including the Hollywood Bowl in Los Angeles.

Some of the most famous companies in the world are based in the USA, where corporate sponsorship of classical music, opera and ballet is as common as it is in Europe and Australasia. In New York, the Lincoln Center is home to some of the world's leading performing arts organisations: the New York Philharmonic, the Metropolitan Opera, The New York City Opera, the New York City Ballet, and the American Ballet. The Center has several auditoria: the Metropolitan Opera House (the Met), Avery Fisher Hall, and the Alice Tully Hall. The great American orchestras are in Boston (the Boston Symphony's classical season, The Boston Pops, takes place from mid-May to mid-July), Chicago, Cleveland, New York and Philadelphia, while the leading opera companies include Boston, Chicago, New York, San Francisco, Santa Fe and Seattle. The San Francisco Opera is the oldest major company in the west though the San Francisco Ballet (which is more than 60 years old) and the San Francisco Symphony are equally distinguished companies. The country's most famous ballet companies are the New York City Ballet, the American Ballet, the Joffrey Ballet (New York, Chicago and San Francisco), the National Ballet in Washington, and the Pittsburgh and Philadelphia Ballet Companies.

Prices are as high as you would expect for major establishment performing arts: a ticket to the opera or ballet in the big cities costs between $50 and $200. However, although standard prices are high, tickets are often subsidised, and some performances can be seen for as little as $30. Standing tickets at around $10 are sold at some of the big venues like the Met in New York. Concerts and performances are of course not limited to the major halls: in every large city there are hundreds of smaller and more intimate venues with correspondingly cheaper seats.

Syracuse offers an extremely rich cultural life, with opera, a symphony orchestra, and world-class chamber music. It also has a good theatre and New York City is not too far away (only a five-hour drive!).
John Philip Jones

Popular and mainstream music

The USA has given the world Jazz, Blues, Motown, R&B (Rhythm and Blues), Rap and Country music, and it is even possible to isolate individual cities where each genre began. Music historians will point out that Detroit,

Michigan was the hometown of Motown, New Orleans is famous for its Jazz, and Nashville, Tennessee, is the capital of country music. If your interests lie in the history of popular or mainstream music, it's always worthwhile taking a trip down to a musical city to tour Berry Gordy's Motown studios, or going to see the place where Elvis recorded 'Hound Dog'. If you're not sure where you'd like to go first, try visiting www.motownmuseum.com or www.musiccitytours.com for an introduction to some of the sights musical cities can offer.

Rap and pop music, alongside country and western music, continue to generate the most commercial sales of music in the USA today. The Billboard Music Chart (www.billboard.com) records the progress of all singles and albums released in the USA and their progress in terms of volume of sales. As a historical marker it's interesting to look at their catalogue of Charts, reaching as far back as 1956, to see how difficult it has been for artists not born in America to gain chart positions. America continues to dominate music and commercial singers worldwide, and the influence of the USA cannot really be underestimated. It is interesting to see, however, that the biggest-selling singles and albums in US sales do show a healthy mix of US and foreign-born musicians, even those placed as high as the top five.

Biggest-selling records in US sales		
Biggest singles:		**Copies sold**
Candle in the Wind (Princess Diana tribute)	Elton John	37 million
White Christmas	Bing Crosby	30 million
Rock Around the Clock	Bill Haley and his Comets	17 million
I Want to Hold Your Hand	The Beatles	12 million
Louie Louie	The Kingsmen	12 million
Biggest albums:		
Their Greatest Hits	The Eagles	28 million
Thriller	Michael Jackson	27 million
The Wall	Pink Floyd	23 million
Led Zepplin IV	Led Zepplin	22 million
Back in Black	AC/DC	21 million

Cinema

Hollywood dominates in America just as it does in the rest of the world. Tickets cost $5–$12 and are usually bookable by credit card. In New York there is a special cinema hotline (777 FILM), with details of screenings around the state.

Cinemas are usually classed as 'first-run', or 'revival and art-house'. The former are everywhere and the latter can be found in most big cities. One of the great symbols of America – the drive-in movie – has sadly lost out to the DVD, though some people are nostalgic for their youth and are renovating drive-ins. They are still few and far between, but if you ask around you may find one not too far away. Enthusiasts should check out some of the devotees' websites. A particularly good one is the Drive-In Theater Guide at www.driveintheatre.com.

Small towns have multi-screen complexes which show all the latest releases: it is difficult to find anything remotely art-house or avant-garde outside the big cities. Some small cities with large student populations, however, will have independent movie theatres, so it's useful to check an online listings guide such as www.yahoo.com/movies to see all the cinemas in your local area.

Gambling

Americans have a strangely ambivalent attitude towards gambling. It is illegal in most of the country, yet they spend $637 billion a year on legal

FACT

■ Films are classified G (general audience), PG (parental guidance), PG-13 (parents strongly cautioned, some scenes may be unsuitable for children under 13), R (no children under 17 unaccompanied by an adult), and NC-17 (no children under 17). You will probably not need any form of ID to get into a movie at the cinema, but it's always worth bringing one when renting a DVD.

gambling with a further $375 billion wagered illegally on sporting contests – more than on cinemas and sport combined. Although gambling is, as referenced above, banned in most states, gambling cities such as Las Vegas in Nevada and Atlantic City in New Jersey (as well as some Native American reserves, which are exempt from state laws), make up for the lack of opportunity elsewhere. Nevada's state revenue depends on gambling, as did the revenue of the Mafia, although recently the Mob – or what remains of it – is turning elsewhere for funds, and legitimate companies are buying up and building casinos.

In a place like Las Vegas ('Armageddon in neon', as it's been dubbed) it is difficult to resist at least a flutter, then just as hard to stop. In contrast to the popular portrayal of casinos in the movie industry, the main clientele of the big casinos is as far from sophisticated as it is possible to be: housewives, with shopping baskets full of quarters feeding the slot machines, their husbands at the roulette tables, or elderly gamblers taking advantage of the free drinks offered to lure punters through the door. Casino owners recognise that it is essential that gambling is not perceived as seedy or in any way disreputable, or else the ordinary punters – those who would otherwise be sunning themselves in Florida, and on whose endless supply of small change the business relies – would stay away. Although in many casinos the drinks are free and the layout is designed for maximum disorientation to make it as difficult as possible to leave, children are allowed and a family atmosphere is encouraged.

As well as casino gambling, there are state lotteries and, of course, the horses and greyhound dogs. Horse racing is mostly limited to flat racing, and off-track betting is illegal in all but three states: Connecticut, New York and Nevada. All betting is based on the totalisator (tote) system, where the total amount placed is divided among the winners. Bets are placed to win, place (come second), or show (third). An each way bet is the same as in the UK: first, second or third. For listings and a guide to form, buy *Daily Racing Form* which can also be viewed at www.drf.com.

TIP

■ Gambling is not seen as a problem, generally, and Americans tend to only sit up and take notice if a family member or friend becomes addicted. With the ever-expanding online gaming industry becoming more commonplace, however, the USA has seen a rise in gambling addictions and a surge in those seeking help.

Museums

America has some of the best museums in the world, usually very well-presented, informative and interesting. Museums like the Metropolitan in New York, the National Gallery in Washington, and the Getty in Los Angeles all have outstanding collections on a level with the great collections of Europe. However, in the USA these collections were built up and then donated by families which grew enormously wealthy in the 19th century on commodities and services like oil, steel, or banking. Most large cities like Boston, Chicago, Philadelpia, Houston, and San Francisco also have superb collections of art and antiquities that can take days to view in their entirety, reflecting the wealth of the country and its diverse immigrant heritage. The Smithsonian Institution in Washington, D.C. houses a range of separate museums dedicated to space, natural history, ancient civilisations and American history. Prices for normal museums are $10–$20. In the cities, get hold of a local newspaper for listings.

Art museums and galleries are one of America's specialities, and the giant collections and exhibitions of the Guggenheim Museum in New York and the National Gallery of Art in Washington, D.C. are testament to this. In the same way opera stars desire to perform in the Sydney Opera House in Australia, and classical musicians want to play at the Royal Albert Hall in England, so artists relish the thought of their work being displayed in one of America's prolific galleries. Artists as diverse as Michelangelo and Andy Warhol, the architect Frank Lloyd Wright and even Kandinsky, as well as thousands of other international artists from every era, have all been on proud display in at least one of America's galleries. The USA remains at the forefront of artistic development, with a strong tradition of modern and contemporary art continuing to grow.

Living museums are one of the things that Americans do particularly well. Every state has its particular piece of history which it wants to preserve, and often this is done (in typically grandiose style) in the form of a living museum. All over the country historical towns, battlefields, houses of the famous and landmarks are preserved and in some cases rebuilt. Some of the best known are Colonial Williamsburg in Virginia, an entire 17th-century town that has been preserved and recreated, Dearborn in Michigan, Sturbridge Massachusetts, Mystic Connecticut, and the seaports of New York and Baltimore. Presidential libraries such as the Kennedy Library in Boston and the Reagan Library outside Los Angeles are popular tourist sites as they commemorate both the achievements of individual presidents and also particular eras of American history.

All of these are well worth a visi, but are unfortunately very expensive, as tickets can be as much as $22 for one person: to take a family, and pay for all the souvenirs that your children will demand, can be a chastening experience.

TIP

■ Admission to art galleries is usually quite reasonable: the Guggenheim Museum is currently $18 for adults most days, with a 'pay what you wish' honour system on a Friday.

■ SPORTS

As mentioned previously, America is a nation in love with sport. Millions of dollars are pumped into the industry to produce the fastest, fittest and strongest athletes, and – with a few notable exceptions – the USA continues to largely dominate the international sporting world. Of course, those sports which hold little interest to Americans are naturally those which they do the least well in, such as football (soccer) and rugby. Even so, interest in these sports is growing.

So enthusiastic are Americans about their sports and games that much of their leisure time is taken up with them. Whether they're working out at the gym, encouraging their children in Little League baseball or watching a basketball game on television, most Americans would agree that sport is a major part of their lives.

Baseball

Baseball is the great American unifier. More than (American) football, baseball is the sport that most regard as quintessentially American. Every major city has a nationally competing team, and every county has a league. Fathers tutor their children early on in the mysteries of the game and often

Major League baseball Teams	
American League	**National League**
Baltimore Orioles	Arizona Diamondbacks
Boston Red Sox	Atlanta Braves
Chicago White Sox	Chicago Cubs
Cleveland Indians	Cincinnati Reds
Detroit Tigers	Colorado Rockies
Kansas City Royals	Florida Marlins
Los Angeles Angels of Anaheim	Houston Astros
Minnesota Twins	Los Angeles Dodgers
New York Yankees	Milwaukee Brewers
Oakland Athletics	New York Mets
Seattle Mariners	Philadelphia Phillies
Tampa Bay Rays	Pittsburgh Pirates
Texas Rangers	San Diego Padres
Toronto Blue Jays	San Francisco Giants
	St Louis Cardinals
	Washington Nationals

like to see it as more than a game, but rather as preparation for life, learning to be a team player. Just as the British have any number of cricketing metaphors, Americans talk about 'ballpark figures', meaning a very rough estimate. An outing to a baseball game is a highly recommended way to immerse yourself in authentic American culture. You'll eat popcorn and hot dogs while watching a game among an enthusiastic crowd of families with little of the aggression sometimes found in European football stadiums. There's even an organ which is played to build up the excitement. One advantage to baseball is that it is quicker than cricket and does not last longer than a few hours.

The rules of baseball are very similar to rounders: teams win by scoring a number of runs around a circular pitch. 'Hitters' are given three attempts ('strikes') at balls thrown by a pitcher (who pitches from the 'mound'), and they run as far as they can round the pitch – though at least to first base – without being struck out. A home run is when the hitter runs all the way round without stopping.

There are two main leagues: the National and the American. Each team plays 162 games a year – five times a week – in the spring and summer, leading up to the World Series in the fall, which is played between the winner of each league. Although it is called the World Series, Canadian teams are usually the only ones from outside the USA to participate.

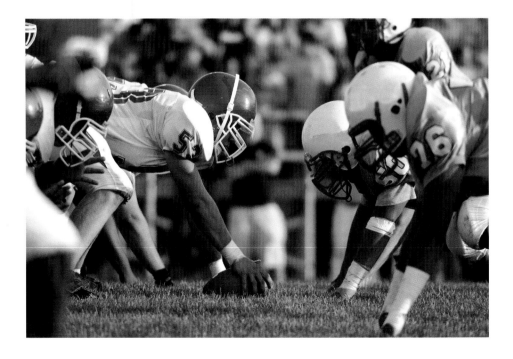

There are more than 6,000 baseball-themed books in print. As a starting point try *Total Baseball: The Official Encyclopaedia of Major League Baseball* (ed. John Thorn, 2001) or *The Great American Novel* (2006) by Philip Roth.

Football

In fall and winter, football is played. Americans call European football 'soccer', and the football that they play more closely resembles rugby.

To most Europeans, American football is as incomprehensible as cricket is to Americans. It has the same amazingly well-informed following and draws the same eccentric fans (Richard Nixon said that if he hadn't gone into politics he would have been a pro-football commentator, and was by all accounts an expert in the game). There are stupendous amounts of money to be made in the sport, and one of the major breeding grounds is the college football league played in the summer – many colleges will recruit promising players at this time in the hope that they will nurture a future star.

In football, an egg-shaped ball (similar but smaller than a rugby ball) has to be thrown and caught over a line to score a goal. That is the general point, but, like all games, it becomes more complicated the more the game is studied. What baffles foreigners is the endless parlaying on the pitch, and the set moves that seem to take away all spontaneity. One of the most important (and highest paid) players is the quarterback, on whom most of the set moves depend. It is their job to throw the ball an

FACT

One drawback of this sport is the fact that the player's faces are hidden by visored helmets, obscuring the human drama of their emotions from the spectators.

National Football League teams	
AFC-North	**NFC-North**
Baltimore Ravens	Chicago Bears
Cincinnati Bengals	Detroit Lions
Cleveland Browns	Green Bay Packers
Pittsburg Steelers	Minnesota Vikings
AFC-South	**NFC-South**
Houston Texans	Atlanta Falcons
Indianapolis Colts	Carolina Panthers
Jacksonville Jaguars	New Orleans Saints
Tennessee Titans	Tampa Bay Buccaneers
AFC-East	**NFC-East**
Buffalo Bills	Dallas Cowboys
Miami Dolphins	New York Giants
New England Patriots	Philadelphia Eagles
New York Jets	Washington Redskins
AFC-West	**NFC-West**
Denver Broncos	Arizona Cardinals
Kansas City Chiefs	San Francisco 49ers
Oakland Raiders	Seattle Seahawks
San Diego Chargers	St Louis Rams

immensely long distance, after it has been passed to them in a series of preordained moves. The other members of the team take out their opposite number, again in a predetermined fashion. Teams spend days watching and re-watching their own and their opponents' moves on video to try to spot weak points.

Teams play 16 games throughout the fall and winter on Sunday and Monday evenings, and this culminates in the Superbowl in January, an event watched by millions of men and women at home, who spend time eating snacks, drinking beer, and throwing popcorn at the screen.

Other Sports

Other important American sports are basketball and ice hockey, played in indoor arenas throughout the USA. Like some football and baseball players, basketball and hockey stars can achieve fabulous wealth and superstar status.

Soccer (football) is becoming increasingly popular in America, especially among schoolchildren. The resounding success of America's hosting of the 1994 World Cup and their team's passionate performance in Korea and Japan in 2002 has boosted the game's ratings. It also didn't hurt when England's David Beckham joined the LA Galaxy team in July 2007. Although it is unlikely to ever gain recognition as a national sport, more than 11 million Americans now play soccer regularly, and there are plans to begin a new national league. It is particularly popular amongst schoolchildren and women, and women's soccer is so full of talent in the USA that they are

frequent winners and finalists in the Women's World Cup.

Cricket, sadly, has less chance of finding a place in America's heart. For those Brits and Aussies who cannot bear to do without the thwack of leather on willow and who get dewy-eyed at the thought of the shadows lengthening on the village green, the West Indian community in New York plays every weekend for 12 weeks during the summer in Van Cortland Park. On Staten Island there are also frequent games between the British and the West Indians. The United States of America Cricket Association also has timetables of games across the country at www.usaca.org.

Amateur sports

Americans take their sport very seriously and never more so than when it is amateur.

National parks

The website www.gorp.away.com has a wonderful selection of Top 10 lists of national parks. The following are a selection of parks which have made it to the number one slot on at least one list:

Readers' Choice	Glacier, MT
Parks for spring	Yellowstone, WY, MT, ID
Parks for winter	Yosemite, CA
Rock climbing	Joshua Tree, CA
Endangered parks	Fire Island National Seashore, NY
Biking parks	Acadia, ME

Hunting, shooting, fishing, tennis and golf are all extremely popular. By 'hunting', the Americans mean taking a rifle and shooting birds and/or other animals. They do not mean foxhunting, which is regarded as an English aberration, and is practised only in Virginia, Maryland and other parts of New England. In America, riding to hounds is certainly an elitist occupation, but other forms of hunting are followed by all income groups, particularly in the Midwest.

Tennis and golf, in a country where land is plentiful and relatively cheap, can also be played by those without huge incomes. There are public courses and clubs, which will allow anyone to play cheaply, and mini-golf is a common pastime at family fun centres.

Camping and hiking

Camping and hiking are very popular pastimes. Contact the National Parks Service in Washington, D.C. (www.nps.gov) for details of parks and the best times of year to go. You can also look for campsites in each state and make reservations at www.reserveamerica.com.

◼ THE USA FOR CHILDREN

It's interesting to compare the upbringing of American children to those of say, Germany or New Zealand, because the USA seems torn over its expectations of what children should be. On the one hand, it keeps its children at home and as child-like as possible until the age of six or seven, and doesn't expect them to be able to read or write until they reach school. On the other hand, it seems to be in a rush to tell children to behave like adults, with children's toys involving very adult situations and practices

Spending a weekend in the great outdoors is a great way to explore the USA. Log Ranch House, Montana.

involving makeup and cell phones, for example. America also seems confused over whether it wants its children to be split down their gender, racial or class divides, or if every child is to be treated equally. Toy shops firmly distinguish between toys for girls and toys for boys, with entire sections of the store coloured either a garish flamingo pink or bold, vibrant blue, and yet on a Little League baseball team, the two sexes compete as one team. Rather brilliantly, though, America has managed to create entire industries devoted to keeping the eternal child inside every human being regardless of age, with companies such as Disney and Microsoft's XBox firmly leading the way.

Activities

Most American children will, at some point, be enrolled in some kind of after-school or weekend activity, whether it be sporting, musical, theatrical or artistic. American schools really seem to excel at encouraging children to try their hand at a thousand different projects until they find one they like. Unfortunately a lot of after-school programmes are experiencing funding cuts, so if your child has a firm interest in an activity no longer offered at the school, you should try looking for other programmes in the area with a similar theme.

There are many clubs and groups in existence: try The Boys and Girls Clubs of America (www.bgca.org) for after-school sports, arts and crafts and outdoor pursuits or The YMCA (www.ymca.net) for sporting activities. For more specific activities, try baseball's Little League group (www.littleleague.org), farming's 4-H Club (www.4-hafterschool.org) or use the internet to search for theatre and dance schools in your local area. For a really useful, general guide to after-school programmes, try using www.afterschool.gov, a government-run website which helps you make the most of the activities that are available in your local area.

About the USA

◼ POLITICS

The USA has one of the best-known written constitutions in the world. It was drawn up in 1787, ratified by the 13 original states by June 1788, and has been continuously in operation ever since. In a country which is made up of representatives of just about every nation on earth, the constitution is the glue that holds everyone together. All nations and populations have something which they consider gives them 'nationhood' – this might be language, race, history or a past struggle for independence. For Americans, the most powerful thing that they have in common is the belief in individual freedom, enshrined in the constitution. The constitution's aims were to create a 'more perfect union' through justice, domestic tranquillity, common defence, general welfare and liberty. Today, anybody wishing to become a citizen of the USA must swear to uphold the constitution, and must also be able to answer a series of questions about its meaning and purpose.

There is a historic distrust of regulation by the federal government which goes back to the roots of the Revolution, and this suspicion of authority is reflected in well-organised resistance to the regulation of firearms and any new forms of taxation. Competition for power between the federal government and the states has a long history and reflects the constitution's concern for the balance of power between local communities and the centre. These disputes are often resolved by the Supreme Court. Contempt for Washington was most horrifyingly demonstrated in 1995 when a federal government building in Oklahoma was blown up with a 4,000lb bomb. In an outrage that was at first pinned on radical Islamic terrorists, though was later linked to a home-grown bomb; 162 people lost their lives. Speaking after this disaster, President Clinton felt compelled to remind the

Roots of freedom

The structure of American government and politics has always been rooted in individual freedom. The Bill of Rights is designed to protect the average citizen from governmental abuse of power: the rights of women, ethnic minorities and all other groups are taken for granted by all Americans. This has led to a highly litigious society (Americans are quick to use the law to assert their rights), and there are more lawyers per head in the USA than in any other country. One of the most notorious of these rights, the right to bear arms, is jealously guarded by many Americans.

The iconic White House building, where the US president officially resides

nation that government officials and institutions are both honourable and respectable.

The key to understanding American politics lies in the pioneering history of the country. Among the first settlers were English puritans who were escaping religious persecution. They landed at Plymouth Rock in 1620, and over the next few decades were joined by successive waves of their countrymen, as well as numbers of Dutch (who bought Manhattan from the native Indians in 1624), Scots, Irish and Germans. Gradually the frontiers of the new colonies were pushed westwards over the Appalachians and beyond, until by 1763 the whole of the continent east of the Mississippi had been colonised. Over the next century, millions of new settlers from Europe fought and traded with the Native Americans for land, and as they became more powerful, they herded them into reserves. This was the frontier spirit that opened up the west.

Americans by and large order their lives in the belief that they have built the greatest and most powerful country on earth. The cowboy with pistols and a rugged sense of justice might be a Hollywood invention, but myths are rooted in reality. There are more handguns than TV sets in the USA – 223 million at the last count – and that amounts to almost one for every man, woman and child in the country.

Independence was fought for. The Native Americans were displaced from their territories, a precarious living was wrested from the soil, and the British colonial government was defeated. In the popular imagination, hostile inhabitants and unfamiliar lands were subdued and civilised by a pioneering spirit. In 1789 America was a tiny nation of 13 states hugging the Atlantic seaboard; today it is a federation of 50 states and 303 million people. The early Americans knew as much about California as they did about the moon: today it has a population of 36.5 million.

All this was built from nothing. When we say glibly that America has no history, we are speaking in terms of time. The quality of its history is a distillation of the dreams of millions. To Americans it is a vast history packed into 200 years, the history of the greatest nation on earth. Each individual, arriving with a handful of precious belongings, carved out a detail of it. This is echoed again and again in the lives of Americans: they love their country powerfully and emotionally because they believe they created it, and are thus responsible for its welfare. Never was an anthem sung with as much feeling as 'God Bless America'. Perhaps more than any other nation in the world, Americans believe their country has a unique destiny which is often attributed to the religious nature of the Plymouth colony that was founded by the Pilgrim Fathers – religious refugees looking for a safe harbour and a pure expression of their faith.

Americans believe that they have intrinsic human rights which are articulated in the Constitution as the inalienable right to 'life, liberty, and the pursuit of happiness.' When this phrase was written, these were radical ideas, and these beliefs continue to inspire people around the world. Historically, then, Americans have valued individual effort and merit. But the country can be introspective despite its enormous power, wealth and influence in the world. In the early years of the 21st century it stands as one of the world's indisputable superpowers. The population, however, particularly beyond the two coasts, leans towards isolationism – the feeling that the USA should not be active in international affairs unless there is a distinct threat to American security. Often in the past 60 years, American presidents have cajoled their countrymen to sanction a greater role for the country overseas in order to maintain the international order.

■ There are more handguns than TV sets in the USA – 223 million at the last count – and that amounts to almost one for every man, woman and child in the country.

The architects of the constitution believed that they were creating the formula for the perfect balance of power between the people and the government. Democracy in America is as good and as bad as democracy everywhere, but with all its problems, at its best it can still be a beacon for liberal democratic values. However, as the infamous events of September 11 illustrated, the USA is seen by some groups around the world as an enemy to be confronted and even aggressively attacked. The long-term historical significance of the destruction of the World Trade Center remains uncertain but what is clear is that while the USA continues to be an inspirational force for its economic and cultural vigour following the end of the Cold War, such a status unfortunately also attracts a degree of fanatical hostility and anger.

Government

The United States of America is a federal republic with a government composed of three separate branches: the Executive, headed by the president; the Legislature (Congress, which includes the House of Representatives and the Senate); and the Judiciary, headed by the US Supreme Court.

The president is both head of the Executive and Head of State (in contrast to various European systems, for example, where the two are separated). The president must be at least 35 years old, a US citizen by birth, and have been resident in the USA for at least 14 years. Presidential elections are held every leap year on the day after the first Monday in November. Each president is limited to two terms of four years each and he (or she) is elected along with a vice president who takes over if a

FACT

■ The revolution was built on the notion of freedom instilled by the original pilgrims in resistance to 'taxation without representation.'

TIP

■ Not since the outbreak of World War Two have Americans been so pressed to examine their place in the world.

State government

Each of the 50 member states has a measure of self-government. The federal government is responsible for defence, foreign affairs, justice at the higher levels, internal security, the coinage, and the mail. In many ways the USA is a collection of independent states and it is sometimes easy to see how – after the War of Independence – the architects of the Union were not at all sure that it would work. When Pennsylvania was created, for example, it was considered imperative that it had a corridor leading up to the Great Lakes so as to avoid having to go through New York State. To this day, too, many Texans will not accept that their state is part of the Union.

president dies, is removed from office, or is unable to continue. The last time that this happened was when Gerald Ford took over from Richard Nixon when the latter resigned.

The Legislature is made up of the House of Representatives (the House) and the Senate. The House of Representatives consists of 435 representatives, or congressmen and congresswomen, elected every two years by universal suffrage. The number from each state is determined by the population of the state: Florida sends 25 representatives to the House, Idaho only two. The Senate has 100 senators, two from each state, who are elected every six years.

The Judiciary, which is made up of the US Supreme Court and various lower federal courts, interprets, reviews, and applies federal laws. Federal courts can also apply state laws in certain cases. Supreme Court judges are nominated by the president and approved by the Senate. Although the Supreme Court is not the final authority on state law (that function is fulfilled by a supreme (state) court in each state) they can declare void any state law that conflicts with federal law and also have the final ruling in test cases which cannot be settled by the state courts and may have a profound impact on the country. In 1954 it was the Supreme Court that ruled segregated education as a violation of the US Constitution during Brown v. Board of Education. In 2000, the presidential election was locked in conflict over disputed ballots in Florida. Eventually, the decision about how to proceed fell to the US Supreme Court which ruled that the relevant Florida election officials could declare a final result in George Bush's favour. It remains a highly controversial decision even now but illustrates the power of the court to influence American life as the final arbiter of the Federal Constitution.

Each state has its own constitution and a government modelled on the federal one, with a state legislature, a governor, and a court system. Within each state, power is devolved even further, to city and county authorities.

In the USA television has long played a vital part in the voting process, with election campaigns focusing heavily on the visual and instantly recognisable qualities of the leader and of the party's policies. Because the population identifies a national president when it is voting (although in a presidential election an entire administration is voted in), a presidential campaign usually articulates simple and powerful themes of patriotism, defence, crime and the family. One of the reasons for Ronald Reagan's popularity was his ability to articulate the most traditional of American ideals, namely, individual success and freedom. He preached the message that American power should be revived after the humiliations caused by the Iranian revolution and subsequent hostage taking of more than 400 US citizens. He then wrapped the whole thing in layers of easily-digested policy: fight crime, fight drugs, and defend the country against Communism. Bill Clinton too – despite the Monica Lewinsky scandal – was immensely popular, in part because of his telegenic charisma and talent for connecting with ordinary Americans.

Unlike European parliamentary democracies, the US cabinet members are not members of the Legislature, but political appointees of the president. There are 14 executive departments which they head, of which the most important are the State Department, responsible for foreign policy, the Treasury, and the Defense department. Other departments deal with agriculture, transportation and so on.

The two houses of Congress sit at either end of the Capitol Building in Washington, D.C. Both houses are extremely powerful, possessing the legislative power both for proposing bills and passing them into law. The party system is less rigid than the British model in which executive authority depends upon strict party discipline in Parliament. Both congressmen and senators are, by nature, more independent figures who tend to build coalitions of interest across the two parties according to factors like regional influence and personal ideology. As a result the president can be frequently thwarted in his or her wishes.

When George W. Bush became President in January 2001, he enjoyed narrow Republican majorities in both the Senate and House of Representatives, but in an illustration of the power of American legislators, particularly in the senate, Senator Jim Jeffords of Vermont 'crossed the

The 2008 elections

The heavily publicised struggle for dominance in the run-up to the November 2008 elections between Republican candidate John McCain and Democratic candidates Hillary Clinton and Barack Obama led many voters to switch political allegiance and focus on issues that were previously marginalised. The role of women and minorities in politics came under close scrutiny and it was the first time in American politics that gender and race played such a huge part in the Presidential campaign. With President Obama's clear victory on 4 November, Americans are now expecting the 'change' that he promised.

aisle', leaving the Republicans to become an independent. The Democrats controlled the Senate by one vote, but this gave them the power to derail the president's legislative agenda. The tables turned and a Republican president compromised with Congress as his Democratic predecessor learnt before him. Clinton lost, for example, his radical proposal to reform the American healthcare system. Each scenario illustrates well the system of divided power which the Founding Fathers conceived in the effort to prevent any re-emergence of the 'tyrannical' government they experienced under British rule.

Written into the constitution, therefore, are checks and controls to prevent the state from becoming too strong. All laws have to be ratified by Congress: they have to run the gauntlet of both houses, and are often heavily revised in the process.

Political parties

At both federal and state level, the American political system is a two-party system. The Democrats and the Republicans are among the oldest political parties in the world: the Democrats were formed at the beginning of the 19th century, the Republicans (known as the GOP, the Grand Old Party) in 1854 by opponents of slavery, with Abraham Lincoln as their first President. Both parties are not really parties in a strictly whipped sense, but more broad coalitions encompassing wide ideological spectrums and regional interests. During the first stages of any presidential campaign (known as the primaries), candidates from the same party will run against each other, often with devastating results. In 2008, the race between Hillary Clinton and Barack Obama stirred new interest in the primaries and the stance each candidate took on the minutest of political issues became of the utmost importance to the American people.

There are many different factions within the parties. One of the best known is the Jesse Jackson's Rainbow Coalition, another is the Christian Coalition – a powerful lobby made up of various groupings of the evangelical right. There are fewer differences between the parties than we expect though. A right-wing democrat could be mistaken for a left-wing Republican and it is not uncommon for politicians to change parties. Occasionally an independent candidate will make an impression on the voting public, especially in times of great disaffection with the government. In 1992, the Texan Ross Perot won 19% of the vote as an independent. In 1912, Theodore Roosevelt got 27% of the vote: this is the nearest an independent has ever come to the White House.

This may be changing, however. In the USA, party allegiance is less important than it is elsewhere. The public prefers to see things in terms of individual personalities and single issues: a politician's stance on abortion or homosexuality is more important than which party he or she belongs to, for example. Congressmen and women rely far more on the ability of the media to put their personalities across than on standing on a particular party platform. In the past, voters were loyal Republicans or Democrats, but many more are now registering as independent, and voting for the individual rather than the party.

■ THE ECONOMY

The United States is the world's largest economy and continues to be highly productive and successful, despite its recently feared recession. In fact, while America may only contain 4% of the world's population, it produces 25% of the world's economic output. This fact alone explains the nation's enormous importance to the world economy and its influence on it. It is self-sufficient in every major product except for petroleum, chemicals and some manufactured items and has a strong, resilient, and diversified economy. Balancing the budget remains an annual battle between the Executive, led by the President, and the Legislature on Capitol Hill. Taxation remains highly contentious and politically perilous.

Following the national deficits of the early 1990s, President Bill Clinton pressed for a deficit reduction package which also included new taxation. After a mighty struggle, the proposed budget was passed by the narrowest of margins in both houses of Congress, and many observers attribute the booming economy of the 1990s to this measure. Furthermore, when George W Bush assumed office in 2001, he cut taxes to add an approximate 1% growth and by the end of 2006 had cut the budget deficit by nearly a half. However, the sub-prime mortgage crisis and subsequent housing market downturn of 2007, combined with a major increase in the price of oil and gold and a global weakening of the US dollar, led to a slight recession in early 2008. Experts have predicted that by the time a new president takes office in January 2009, the growth of the American economy may have

The richest country in the world

Current GDP is around $19000,000,000,000. The country consumes a massive percentage of what it produces and exports only account for 11.3% of the GDP, as compared to a European average of 25%. The USA uses a quarter of the world's energy resources even though it has only 4% of the world's population. It imports 33% of its oil, and 18.8% of the country's energy is produced by nuclear power.

slowed down to just 2.2%. While this is frightening for most Americans, the good news for prospective immigrants is that housing prices remain cheaper than most other comparative countries and your home country's currency will buy you a lot more when you first arrive.

Economic pressures remain on the 'middle class'; the vast majority of working Americans. Whereas in the 1950s only one breadwinner was necessary to keep the average middle-class family in comfort, now normally both parents have to work. At the same time, there is still a substantial underclass (especially in the inner cities) that remain trapped in poverty. Caught in vicious circles of poverty, inner city decay and a reluctance by the middle class to finance remedies, 12.3% (or 35 million) Americans, a disproportionate number of them black or Hispanic, live below the poverty line. In some regions, such as in the South, 13.8% of the population is extremely poor. Despite this, the USA remains a phenomenal economic power.

■ The strongest industries overall are those dealing in steel, motor vehicles, aerospace, telecommunications, chemicals, electronics and computers, and a broad range of consumer goods. Other leading sectors are pharmaceuticals, entertainment and the media, and financial services.

Industry and military spending

The economy is now overwhelmingly based on service industries. Agriculture accounts for 1% of the GDP, the manufacturing industry 18.2% and services 67.8%. The principal components of the manufacturing industry are machinery and transport, which also make up the major percentage of US exports.

After 1992 the US economy expanded at a gallop for eight years. The takeover mania that took hold as the recession came to an end in the early 1990s continued well into 1998. During the Clinton presidency enormous corporate mergers took place in an economic climate of growth. The government also encouraged the process of globalisation, whereby trade tariffs were lowered and multi-national companies supported. Clinton saw the creation of NAFTA, the North American trading area consisting of the USA, Canada, and Mexico as one of his greatest achievements. It faced substantial opposition from the unions and American nationalists who predicted that American companies would be free to move production lines to Mexico where they could employ labour at a fraction of the usual cost.

Following the end of the Cold War, politicians in both parties supported the notion of a 'peace dividend' which would arise from reduced military spending. Funds could now be channelled towards national infrastructure or social programmes, or returned to the citizens through tax cuts. This had a profound impact on military manufacturers and many areas of the country, like southern California, suffered high unemployment; $12 billion was spent on programmes to retrain workers and help companies to adapt and develop lines for civilian use. Fortunately too, the economy continued to expand, enabling the government to keep unemployment low.

After a decade of lower military spending, President Bush proposed a massive increase in the military budget for 2003 of $45 billion – an increase of 15% – to equip the country for the 'war on terrorism'. The 2008 budget proposal included a controversial $481.4 billion allocation for the Department of Defence's base budget, which was a 62% increase over their starting budget funding in 2001. The ability to spend this sum is actually a direct reaction to the recent recession. A weakened dollar has paved the way for increased rates of international US exports and a reduction of the deficit, providing more stable funding patterns in the budget.

Farming

Farmland makes up 46% of US land surface. In 1900, half the US workforce were farmers. Continuing the 20th century trend, numbers employed in farming have fallen further in the new millennium. Now just 0.6% of the population work in either farming, fishing or forestry. The traditional family farm is under severe pressure because economic pressures favour agribusiness – agriculture on an industrial scale. Increased mechanisation and biotechnological advances have made agriculture an exact and efficient science. At the same time, the farming world is coming under serious public pressure to reduce the use of chemical pesticides and factory farming and switch to more earth-friendly or organic methods.

Outlook

The US economy grew by 4.4% over the whole of 2004, the fastest pace since 1999, creating 2.23 million jobs. By the first quarter of 2008 it had slowed, however, to just 1.1%, due to a crisis in the housing market, a weakened dollar and an increase in oil prices. When the economy first began to lose its momentum at the end of 2000, the picture was complicated by the terrorist assaults on the country in September 2001 and the ensuing 'war against terrorism,' which certainly affected consumer confidence, particularly in the travel and tourism sectors. The simultaneous hijacking of four planes had a devastating impact on the airline industry

FACT

■ The chief crops produced in the USA are cereals, cotton and tobacco. Cattle ranching for beef is another important sector.

– 100,000 Americans in the aviation industry and 80,000 travel agents lost their jobs. At the time of writing, the national rate of unemployment was up to 5.1%, and average annual earnings per capita rose only 1.5% between 2004 and 2005 (the most recent figures available), setting a trend for future years. However, although inflation was picking up, wages and salaries had risen 1.2% more than inflation, thereby increasing disposable incomes. The Federal Reserve (the US's central bank) made 10 cuts in the interest rate during 2001 in an attempt to prevent recession but at the end of 2004, 11 of the 12 Federal Reserve districts were not experiencing expanding economic activity. This was compounded in late 2007 and 2008 when further economic disappointment did lead to a brief American recession.

Regional trends

Since the 1970s there has been a migration of industry from the north of the country to the Sunbelt regions of the west and south which have a heavy concentration of light and high-tech. industries.

The economies of the individual states vary widely. California is known for the San Francisco high-tech. industries and the Los Angeles entertainment industries, but manufacturing and farming are also found throughout the state. It is one of the largest and most prosperous states and tops the league in terms of gross state product (GSP), although it is now declining as businesses move east to Arizona and north to Oregon, where the tax burden is less. In the fourth quarter of 2004 personal income grew by 2.6%, the fastest pace since the beginning of 2000. Despite the economic slowdown, the most recent figures available for 2008 show that California's GSP continues to grow at a rate of 4.2%.

Other states with a high GSP are Texas, New York, Florida, Illinois, and Pennsylvania. The least productive states are Vermont, North Dakota, Wyoming, Montana, and South Dakota. Measuring the prosperity of states by the rate at which they are developing gives a different picture. Recent figures for job creation show that the fastest-growing states are Idaho, Utah, Arizona, Oklahoma and New Mexico, all of which are in the Rocky Mountain or Southwest districts. California used to be the Golden State, the favoured destination for entrepreneurs and businesses, but years of recession caused many organisations to think again and to locate themselves in cheaper areas that are seeing faster growth, particularly those in close proximity.

The decline in the heavy industrial base of the north-east, (the Rustbelt, ranging from Pennsylvania to Iowa) has been largely offset in New England by an expansion in the service industries, and now Boston, for example, is a centre for computer services. American concerns have recently been directed towards Michigan, in the Great Lakes district, which has been hit hard by a decline in its industries, particularly construction. Its GSP growth was the only one in recent years to decline and latest statistics put its growth at -0.5%. However, despite its recent slowdown, Michigan still places in the middle of the GSP leader's table.

■ GEOGRAPHY

The United States of America is the fourth largest country in the world. The North American continent, consisting of Canada and the Arctic archipelago as well as the USA, covers 8.3 million sq miles (21.5 million sq km), of which the USA takes up 3.6 million sq miles (9.3 million sq km). It is bounded in the north by Canada, in the south by Mexico and the Gulf of Mexico, in the east by the Atlantic Ocean and in the west by the Pacific Ocean. From east to west, New York to San Francisco, it is 3,000 miles (4,800 km). From the town of Brownsville, the southernmost point of Texas, to the 49th parallel (the boundary between the USA and Canada), it is 1,600 miles (2,560 km). This vast landmass covers a huge spectrum of different landscapes, environments and climates. The eastern coast (New England, where the first white settlers landed) is rocky and richly wooded. South and west of New England are the Appalachian Mountains, which rise up out of the Atlantic coastal plain. Further west are the Great Lakes and the central

■ Another state which is regarded as up-and-coming is Texas, which has diversified away from oil into high-technology and computers. It has benefited from its proximity to Mexico, as the North American Free Trade Agreement increased cross-border activity. Florida is also benefiting from increased Latin-American trade.

The sheer magnitude of the USA means the terrain varies from deserts to mountain ranges, such as the Alaskan Mountains

Supersized country

To a European, the size of the USA is difficult to imagine. We tend to think of it as one country (as indeed it is) but forget to take the size of the continent into account. New York is almost as far from San Francisco as it is from London; Texas is bigger than France while Alaska is twice the size of Texas. You can drive west from Houston all day and still not have left Texas. To drive from New York to California is the equivalent of driving from London to Cairo.

lowlands, undulating plains cut through by the mighty Mississippi, which begins its journey near the Canadian border and finally flows into the Gulf of Mexico, 2,348 miles (3,779 km) later. It is, by then, a huge and sluggish river, broad and deceptively slow. Going west from the Mississippi the landscape changes to the Great Plains, often referred to as the breadbasket of America. It then rises to the Rocky Mountains, a massive range that runs north to south. The highest point in the Rockies is Mount Whitney in California, standing at 14,495 ft (4,418m). Further west still is the great Californian valley, half of it desert, half fertile land, and the Pacific Ocean. Mt McKinley in Alaska is the highest point at 20,321 ft (6,194m) while Death Valley in California is the lowest at −282 ft (−86m).

Regional divisions and main cities

The USA is a federal republic of 50 states. The capital is Washington, the District of Columbia. The first states of the Union were Maine, New Hampshire, Vermont, Massachusetts, Connecticut, Rhode Island, New York, New Jersey, Pennsylvania, Delaware and Maryland. As the 19th century progressed, further states were added to the union: Louisiana in 1812, Alabama in 1819 and Arkansas in 1836. California became a state in 1850, Alaska and Hawaii, the newest additions to the union, in 1959. The states vary greatly in size (Rhode Island is tiny at just 1,200 sq miles or 3,107 sq km, while Alaska covers 600,000 sq miles – equating to 1,553,994 sq km), geography and population. Each state organises its affairs independently, with a government that is designed to mirror the federal government. States set their own taxes and pass their own laws, and they also have their own police forces and jurisdictions.

Each state has its own capital, which may not be the largest or best-known city. The capital of New York state, for example, is Albany, while the capital of California is Sacramento. The largest cities (by population) in the USA are New York (8.2 million), Los Angeles (3.8 million) and Chicago

(2.8 million). Dallas, Houston, Philadelphia, Phoenix and San Diego all have populations of more than a million.

The fastest-growing cities, in terms of population growth in the last decade, are Las Vegas, NV (83.3%), Naples, FL (65.3%), Yuma, AZ (49.7%) and McAllen-Edinburg-Mission, TX (48.5%). Other towns that are growing fast are Austin-San Marcos, TX (47.7%), Fayetteville-Springdale-Rogers, AK (47.5%) and Boise City, ID (46.1%). All the top ten fastest growing cities are based in the South except one, reflecting the South's new taste for technology and industry. The states with the highest standard of living are New Jersey, Maryland, Hawaii, Connecticut and New Hampshire, all having an average income per head of more than $60,000 and growing steadily. Mississippi, Arkansas, Louisiana, West Virginia, and Alabama have the lowest standard of living in the country with household incomes below $38,000 and falling.

The most rural states are Vermont and West Virginia, where less than 40% of the population live in urban areas. In California, New Jersey, and Hawaii more than 89% live in an urban area.

The 'State-by-state business report' section of the 'Working in the USA' chapter lists all the states and their important statistics. A list of state abbreviations is given in 'Daily Life' and more information on living in the different regions of the USA is given in 'Setting Up Home'.

FACT

■ American cities tend to sprawl and merge, and huge metropolitan areas are continuously forming. New York City spills over into suburbs in New York, New Jersey, and Connecticut, forming an almost continuous conurbation with a population of 18.8 million. The same has happened on the west coast, with Los Angeles, Long Beach and Santa Ana in California forming a metropolitan area of 12 million people.

Yellowstone Park is know for its geothermal features – geysers, mud pots and hot springs

Average temperature (°F/°C)		
	January	July
Atlanta, GA	42.7/5.9	80.0/26.6
Boston, MA	29.3/−1.5	73.9/23.2
Chicago, IL	22.0/−5.5	73.3/22.9
Denver, CO	29.2/−1.5	73.4/23.0
Honolulu, HI	73.0/22.7	80.8/27.1
Los Angeles, CA	57.1/13.9	69.3/20.7
Miami, FL	68.1/20.1	83.7/28.7
New Orleans, LA	52.6/11.4	82.7/28.2
New York, NY	32.1/0.1	76.5/24.7
Phoenix, AZ	54.2/12.3	92.8/23.7
St Louis, MO	29.6/−1.3	80.2/26.7
San Francisco, CA	49.4/9.6	62.8/17.1
Seattle, WA	40.9/4.9	65.3/18.5
Sioux Falls, SD	14.0/−10.0	73.0/22.7
Washington, D.C.	34.9/1.6	79.2/26.2

Climate

FACT

■ Some of the greatest seasonal differences can be seen in the Midwest region, where hot and humid summers are followed by blizzards and ice showers in the winter.

Climatic variation within the USA is enormous, ranging from the Arctic conditions in Alaska to the deserts of the south-west. Winter temperatures in Alaska plummet to -19°F (−28°C), whereas in Florida they are a steady 66°F (19°C) for most of the year. In California the weather hardly varies: it is constantly mild with a range of only 16°F (9°C). On the east coast the climate is similar to much of Europe, with more severe winters and hot summers. New York City has particularly cold and wet winters, and hot and muggy summers. The centre of the continent is dry, but both the north-west Pacific (Oregon and Washington) and the New England Atlantic coast are humid, with a heavy rainfall.

Much of the USA is prone to the most powerful of nature's forces: the north-eastern coast is vulnerable to blizzards, the southern lowlands are susceptible to thaw flooding in the spring (the Mississippi recently flooded vast tracts of land), and in the desert areas of the south, tornadoes are a hazard. Sometimes the most devastating events can be the result of a single unpredictable act of nature. The tragic loss of life and livelihood caused by Hurricane Katrina, which hit New Orleans in the summer of 2005, was one such catastrophe.

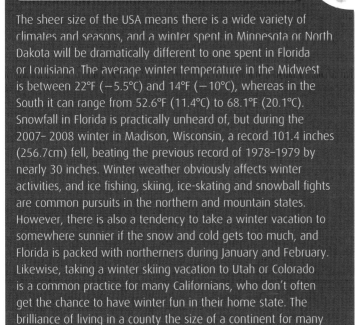

Global warming and US pollution

The USA is one of the world's worst polluters when it comes to greenhouse gas emissions. President Clinton agreed to back the 1997 Kyoto conference treaty to reduce emissions from cars, factories, homes and other energy users, but his successor 'President Bush' decided, in 2001, to revoke that support, provoking a storm of criticism around the world. His administration argued that the treaty unfairly penalised the USA for its dynamic rate of growth and productivity. Bush instead proposed that the USA offer incentives to its domestic consumers for reducing greenhouse gas emissions. He also argued that the burden for reducing them should be more evenly distributed across the globe. Much, though, could be achieved by improving conservation within the USA and by supporting renewable sources of energy. The Kyoto Protocol has now come into effect (February 2005) committing the 34 countries that signed the agreement to cut emissions by 2012. President Bush expressed a desire to 'work together' on environmental issues and introduced his own 10-year programme to

FACT

■ The USA is one of the world's worst polluters when it comes to greenhouse gas emissions.

reduce carbon intensity of the US economy by 18%. It remains to be seen if his successor will implement more change in US foreign and domestic policy to effect enough change in emissions and climate control.

Population

The population of the USA is 303 million, having grown 0.9% between July 2006 and July 2007. The latest national survey found a birth rate of 14.3 per thousand and a death rate of 8.2 per thousand, 20% of the population is under 15, 12.6% over 65. There are 79.6 people per sq mile. Of the total population, 73.9% identified themselves as white, 12.2% as black, 4.4% as Asian and 14.8% as Hispanic within all ethnic groups. Continuing a historically high rate of immigration, 9.5% of the US population was born in another country.

◼ RELIGION

Total freedom of religion is written into the American Constitution. Church and State are separate. More than 90% of Americans claim to be members of one of the hundreds of Christian denominations and of these, 40%–50% are regular churchgoers. The main Protestant denominations are Baptists (36.6 million), Methodists (13.5 million), Lutherans (8.4 million)

and Episcopalians (2.5 million). There are some 60 million Roman Catholics and 5.9 million Jews. Since the 1980s there has been a steady increase in the power of the Evangelical movement and 42% of all Americans describe themselves as 'born-again' Christians. 'Televangelism' is an established part of the American scene. There is no animosity between Protestants and Catholics (the latter tacitly accept divorce and contraception) and shared services are commonplace. Many of the ethnic minorities practise their own religions and there are many other sects, such as The Church of Jesus Christ of the Latter Day Saints (Mormons) of Salt Lake City in Utah, who account for 1.7% of the total population as well as small sects or new age spiritual groups with members from different ethnic groups. There are estimated to be around four million Muslims.

Fundamental Christianity

The USA has seen a massive growth in the number of Fundamental Christians over the past 50 years, possibly as a result of a 1963 Supreme Court ruling banning state-sanctioned prayer in state schools. Also known as The Christian Right, this group of Southern Baptists, Independent Baptists and Assembly of God worshippers (amongst others), are very likely to be active in the political sphere. This has led to many political activists, particularly presidential campaigners, attempting to appease The Christian Right during their campaigns. The 2008 presidential race between John McCain and Barack Obama was one example, with each candidate either distancing themselves from religion (left-wing Democrat Obama), or encouraging links with major fundamental leaders (right-wing Republican McCain). The Christian Right is so influential that entire policies have grown up around it: abstinence-only sex education in schools was a George W. Bush policy directly influenced by his own religious beliefs, and an attempt to maintain a stronghold with the religious right. The main beliefs of Fundamental Christians often include the rejection of popular secular music, dancing and cinema; abstinence from pre-marital relations, alcohol and drugs; a traditional style of dress and extremely divided, 'traditional' gender roles for men and women.

Appendices

Editors of *Time. Time America: An Illustrated History.* (Time, 2007). A pictorial guide to the history of the USA from *Time* magazine.

■ USEFUL WEBSITES

The following is a list of some useful websites, divided by subject matter. Many of these websites can be found listed throughout the book and this list is by no means exhaustive. More specific details and other websites can be found in each chapter correlating to the subject matter.

Cars and automotive

American Automobile Association: www.aaa.com
AAA Foundation for Traffic Safety: www.aaafoundation.org
BP Motor Club: www.bpmotorclub.com
Department of Motor Vehicles: www.dmv.org
Department of Transportation: www.dot.gov

Educational resources

AfterSchool: www.afterschool.gov
College Board: www.collegeboard.com
College Prospects of America: www.cpoa.com
Educational Testing Service: www.ets.org
European Council of International Schools: www.ecis.org
Experiment in International Living: www.experiment.org
Fulbright Commission: www.fulbright.co.uk
International Baccalaureate Organization: www.ibo.org
International Student: www.internationalstudent.com
List of USA Colleges: www.utexas.edu
Peterson's: www.petersons.com
The Rotary Club: www.rotary.org
United Nations International School: www.unis.org
Worldwide Education Services: www.wes.org

Embassies and consulates

Australian Embassy in USA: www.austemb.org
British Embassy in USA: www.britainusa.com/embassy
Irish Embassy in USA: www.embassyofireland.org
New Zealand Embassy in USA: www.nzembassy.com
USA Consulate Northern Ireland: www.usembassy.org.uk/nireland
USA Embassy Edinburgh: www.usembassy.org.uk/scotland
USA Embassy London: www.usembassy.org.uk

Appendices

◼ USEFUL BOOKS

Chapter One: Why Live and Work in the USA?

Franklin, Paul , *Basic and Tourist Information: USA* (DK Travel: 2004). An Eyewitness Travel Guide that is useful for tourist, travel and accommodation information, particularly for short breaks.

Chapter Two: Before You Go

United States Department of Labor, *Dictionary of Occupational Titles* (Fourth Edition: Revised, 1991). A complete guide to every single occupational title in the USA.

Kelley Blue Book, *Kelley Blue Book Used Car Guide* (Kelley Blue Book Co., Inc., 2008). An extremely helpful guide to buying and selling used cars throughout the USA.

Chapter Three: Setting Up Home

Blake, Fanny, *A Place in the Sun* (Channel 4 Books, 2002). Outlines ways to live and buy property in many foreign resorts, including the sunniest parts of America.

Chapter Four: Daily Life

Russell's Official National Motor Coach Guide (Russell's, 2008) A helpful guide to travelling across America by coach and bus.

Peterson's College and University Almanac (ed. F.Oram, Peterson's, 2009) Complete list of all universities, colleges and community colleges in the USA.

Applying to Colleges and Universities in the United States (Peterson's, 2005) Handy how-to guide for applying to university, or consult Peterson's website.

Scholarships, Grants and Prizes 2008 (Peterson's, 2008) Top tips and a list of scholarships available to US and foreign residents.

Studying Abroad (UNESCO Publishing, 1999) A guide on how to study abroad, for any prospective student from any country considering study in any other country.

Sports Scholarships and Athletic Programs (Peterson's, 2004) Top tips and a list of sports scholarships and programmes available to US and foreign residents.

Chapter Five: Working in the USA

Griffith, Susan, *Work Your Way Around the World* (Crimson Publishing, 2007). Offers tips and frank advice on how to seek employment while travelling abroad.

Nelson Bolles, Richard, *What Color is Your Parachute? A Practical Manual for Job-hunters and Career Changers* (Ten Speed Press, 2008). An excellent guide for all job-seekers.

Reed, Jean, *Résumés That Get Jobs* (Peterson's, 2002). How to write a résumé from an American perspective.

Chapter Six: Starting a Business

Applegate, Jane, *Succeeding in Small Business: The 101 Toughest Problems and How to Solve Them* (Plume Books, 1994). Problem solving advice from a professional.

Bivins, Betty, *Operating a Really Small Business* (Crisp Publications, 1993). An oldie but a goodie: really good advice for owning a small business.

Burstiner, Irving, *The Small Business Handbook: A Comprehensive Guide to Starting and Running Your Own Business* (Fireside, 1997). Another useful guide for small business operators.

Gielgun, Ron, *121 Internet Businesses You Can Start from Home: Plus a Beginners Guide to Starting a Business* (Actium Publishing, 1997). Offers advice for all budding internet entrepreneurs.

Harroch, Richard D., *Small Business Kit For Dummies* (For Dummies, 2004)

Hinkelman, Edward, *Exporting to the USA* (World Trade, 1995). A guide to exporting goods from any other country into the USA.

Norman, Jan, *What No One Ever Tells You About Starting Your Own Business* (Dearborn Trade, 2005). Little known facts for the uninitiated business owner.

Peterson, Steven, *Business Plans for Dummies* (For Dummies, 2004).

Tracy, John A., *Accounting for Dummies* (For Dummies, 2008).

Various, *Businesses You Can Start Almanac* (Adams Media, 2006).

Various, *Streetwise Small Business Start-Up* (Adams Media, 2006).

General books

Bryson, Bill, *The Lost Continent: Travels in Small-Town America* (Harper Perennial, 1990). A hilarious introduction to local America from one of the kings of travel guides.

Zinn, Howard, *People's History of the United States: 1942 to Present* (Harper Perennial Modern Classics, 2005). A weighty, academic walk through America's history, but nevertheless brilliant.

Editors of *Time. Time America: An Illustrated History*. (Time, 2007). A pictorial guide to the history of the USA from *Time* magazine.

◼ USEFUL WEBSITES

The following is a list of some useful websites, divided by subject matter. Many of these websites can be found listed throughout the book and this list is by no means exhaustive. More specific details and other websites can be found in each chapter correlating to the subject matter.

Cars and automotive

American Automobile Association: www.aaa.com
AAA Foundation for Traffic Safety: www.aaafoundation.org
BP Motor Club: www.bpmotorclub.com
Department of Motor Vehicles: www.dmv.org
Department of Transportation: www.dot.gov

Educational resources

AfterSchool: www.afterschool.gov
College Board: www.collegeboard.com
College Prospects of America: www.cpoa.com
Educational Testing Service: www.ets.org
European Council of International Schools: www.ecis.org
Experiment in International Living: www.experiment.org
Fulbright Commission: www.fulbright.co.uk
International Baccalaureate Organization: www.ibo.org
International Student: www.internationalstudent.com
List of USA Colleges: www.utexas.edu
Peterson's: www.petersons.com
The Rotary Club: www.rotary.org
United Nations International School: www.unis.org
Worldwide Education Services: www.wes.org

Embassies and consulates

Australian Embassy in USA: www.austemb.org
British Embassy in USA: www.britainusa.com/embassy
Irish Embassy in USA: www.embassyofireland.org
New Zealand Embassy in USA: www.nzembassy.com
USA Consulate Northern Ireland: www.usembassy.org.uk/nireland
USA Embassy Edinburgh: www.usembassy.org.uk/scotland
USA Embassy London: www.usembassy.org.uk

Employment and investment resources

Ambler Collins Visa Specialists: www.amblercollins.com
American Australian Association: www.americanaustralian.org
British American Business Inc: www.babinc.org
British Universities North America Club (BUNAC): www.bunac.org.uk
Career Builder: www.careerbuilder.com
Dictionary of Occupational Titles: www.oalj.dol.gov
Do Something Volunteer Opportunities: www.dosomething.org
ECA International: www.eca-international.com
Investments: www.americanlaw.com/investor
IST Plus: www.istplus.com
Job Bank USA: www.jobbankusa.com
Local Job Network: www.localjobnetwork.com
Monster: www.monster.com
National Association of Small Business Investment Companies: www.nasbic.org
Net-Temps: www.net-temps.com
Robinson O'Connell: www.robinsonoconnell.com
RWH International Inc.: www.usjoboffer.com
Small Business Association: www.sba.gov
UK Trade and Investment: www.uktradeinvest.gov.uk
Union Facts: www.unionsfacts.com
US Chambers of Commerce: www.uschamber.org
Volunteer Match: www.volunteermatch.org
Working Solo Inc: www.workingsolo.com

Finances, imports and tax advice

American Accounting Association: www.aaahq.org
Bank Rate: www.bankrate.com
Centrelink: www.centrelink.gov.au
Conti Financial Services: www.mortageoverseas.com
E-Loan: www.eloan.com
Fannie Mae: www.fanniemae.com
HM Revenue & Customs: www.hmrc.gov.uk
Home Shark: www.homeshark.com
Internal Revenue Service: www.irs.gov
Mortgages Expo: www.mortages-expo.com
Quicken Loans: www.quickenloans.com
Social Security Administration: www.ssa.gov
Tax Net USA: www.taxnetusa.com
The Pension Rights Center: www.pensionrights.org
US Customs: www.customs.gov
US Patent and Trademark Office: www.ustpo.gov

General immigration advice

American Association of Retired People: www.aarp.org
American Immigration Center: www.us-immigration.com
Diversity Visa Lottery: www.dvlottery.state.gov
General Travel and Tourist Information: www.travel.state.gov
House of Representatives: www.house.gov
US Citizenship and Immigration Services (USCIS): www.uscis.gov
Visa Now Immigration Advice: www.visanow.com

Healthcare (USA only)

America's Health Insurance Plans: www.ahip.org
American Association of Preferred Provider Organizations:
www.aappo.org
American Diabetes Association: www.diabetes.org
BlueCross BlueShield Association: www.bcbs.com
CNA: www.cna.com
International Medical Group: www.imglobal.com
Medic Alert Foundation: www.medicalert.org

Immigration advice specific to home countries

Australian Dual Citizenship: www.immi.gov.au
European Union Dual Citizenship: www.europa.eu
UK Dual Citizenship: www.ukba.homeoffice.gov.uk

Immigration and real estate lawyers

American Bar Association: www.abanet.org
Brownstein, Brownstein and Associates: www.brownsteinlaw.com
Chang and Boos: www.americanlaw.com/investor
Ferman Law: www.fermanlaw.com
Find Law: www.findlaw.com
Four Corners Emigration: www.fourcorners.net
Global Visas: www.globalvisas.com
Richard Goldstein: www.goldsteinvisa.com
Laura Devine Solicitors: www.lauradevine.com
LaVigne, Coton and Associates: www.lavignelaw.us
Law Society of England and Wales: www.lawsociety.org.uk
Richard Madison: www.lawcom.com/immigration
Margaret M. Wong and Associates: www.imwong.com
New Horizons Group: www.newhorizonsgroup.com

Travel Document Systems: www.traveldocs.com
USA Immigration Law Center: www.usailc.com
Workpermit: www.workpermit.com

Insurance

Association of British Insurers: www.abi.org.uk
Atlas Insurance: www.atlasdirect.net
Axa PPP Healthcare: www.axappphealthcare.com
BUPA International: www.bupa-intl.com
Columbus Travel Insurance: www.columbusdirect.com
Endsleigh Insurance: www.endsleigh.co.uk
Expacare: www.expacare.net
Expatriate Insurance Services Ltd: www.expatriate-insurance.com
Insurance Information Institute: www.iii.org

Pets

American Society for the Prevention of Cruelty to Animals:
www.aspca.org
Animal Health Divisional Offices: www.defra.gov.uk
Centers for Disease Control and Prevention: www.cdc.gov
US Public Health Service: www.usphs.gov

Property

American Society of Home Inspectors: www.ashi.com
Homebuyer Events Ltd: www.homebuyer.co.uk
Home Buyer Show, AU: www.bcec.com.au
Homestore: www.homestore.com
Moves International Relocations: www.moves.co.uk
Multiple Listing Services: www.mls.com
National Association of Estate Agents (UK): www.naea.co.uk
National Association of Home Inspectors: www.nahi.org
National Association of Realtors: www.realtor.com
National Association of State Utility Consumer Advocates:
www.nasuca.org
Pricoa Relocations UK: www.pricoarelocation.com
Property Abroad: www.property-abroad.com
Prudential Florida WCI Realty: www.prudentialfloridawcirealty.com
Rental Law: www.rentlaw.com
Right Move: www.rightmove.co.uk
Runzheimer International: www.runzheimer.com
US Department of Housing and Urban Development: www.hud.gov
USA Home Exchange: www.ushx.com

US Treasure House Auctions: www.ustreas.gov
Weichert Relocation Resources Inc: www.wrri.com
The World of Florida: www.worldofflorida.co.uk
The World of Property Show: www.worldofproperty.co.uk

Relocation and removal firms

Anglo-Domus: www.anglodomus.com
Association of Relocation Agents: www.arp-relocation.com
Avalon Overseas Movers: www.avalon-overseas.com
Bishop's Move Group: www.bishopsmove.com
Britannia Movers International: www.britannia-movers.co.uk
The British Association of Removers: www.removers.org.uk
Community Connections: www.communityconn.com
Davies Turner Worldwide Movers: www.daviesturner.co.uk
Direct Moving: www.directmoving.com
Doree Bonner International: www.doreebonner.co.uk
International Federation of International Movers: www.fidi.com
John Mason International: www.johnmason.com
Oceanair: www.oceanairinternational.com
PSS International Removals: www.pss.uk.com
Worldwide ERC: www.erc.org

Retail

AT&T: www.att.com
Bloomingdales: www.bloomingdales.com
MCI/Verizon: www.consumer.mci.com
Outlet Bound: www.www.outletbound.com
Sears: www.sears.com
Sprint: www.sprint.com
Time Warner Cable: www.timewarnercable.com
US Cellular: www.uscellular.com
Verizon Wireless: www.verizonwireless.com
Wal-Mart: www.walmart.com

Other interesting and useful sites

Amazon: www.amazon.com
Bay Area Model Mugging: www.bamm.org
BBC World Service: www.bbc.co.uk
Billboard: www.billboard.com
British Expats: www.britishexpats.com
City Search: www.citysearch.com

Craig's List: www.craigslist.org
Digital City: www.digitalcity.com
E-Harmony: www.eharmony.com
Expats Voice: www.expatsvoice.org
Facebook: www.facebook.com
Festival Finder: www.festivalfinder.com
Life in the USA: www.lifeintheusa.com
Mates Up Over: www.matesupover.com
Myspace: www.myspace.com
National Parks Service: www.nps.gov
Newslink: www.newslink.org
Wikipedia: www.en.wikipedia.org
Yellow Pages USA: www.yellow.com
YMCA: www.ymca.net

Travel and flights

Air Canada: www.aircanada.com
Air New Zealand: www.airnewzealand.com
American Airlines: www.americanairlines.co.uk
Amtrak: www.amtrak.com
British Airways: www.britishairways.com
Continental: www.continental.com
Courier Travel: www.couriertravel.org
Delta: www.delta.com
Expedia: www.expedia.com
Flightclub: www.flightclub.co.uk
First American Travel: www.1111trip.com
Greyhound Buses: www.greyhound.com
International Association of Air Travel Couriers: www.courier.org
International Rail: www.international-rail.com
Lastminute.com: www.lastminute.com
Northwest/KLM: www.nwa.com or www.klm.com
Opodo: www.opodo.com
Qantas: www.qantas.com
STA Travel: www.statravel.com
Trailfinders: www.trailfinders.com
Travelocity: www.travelocity.com
Travel Supermarket: www.travelsupermarket.co.uk
Unijet: www.unijet.aero
United Airlines: www.unitedairlines.co.uk
US Airways: www.usairways.com
USA Tourist: www.usatourist.com
Virgin Atlantic: www.virgin-atlantic.com

US banks

Bank of America: www.bankofamerica.com
Chase Bank: www.chase.com
Citi Bank: www.citi.com
Key Bank: www.key.com
US Bank: www.usbank.com
Wells Fargo: www.wellsfargo.com

US SYSTEM OF MEASUREMENT

The USA uses the imperial system, but it is known as the USA system of measurement. Temperature is always measured in fahrenheit.

Length (NB 12inches = 1 foot, 10 mm = 1 cm, 100 cm = 1 metre)									
inches	1	2	3	4	5	6	9	12	
cm	2.5	5	7.5	10	12.5	15.2	23	30	
cm	1	2	3	5	10	20	25	50	75	100
inches	0.4	0.8	1.2	2	4	8	10	20	30	39

Weight (NB 14lb = 1 stone, 2240 lb = 1 ton, 1,000 kg = 1 metric tonne)									
lb	1	2	3	5	10	14	44	100	2246
kg	0.45	0.9	1.4	2.3	4.5	6.4	20	45	1016
kg	1	2	3	5	10	25	50	100	1000
lb	2.2	4.4	6.6	11	22	55	110	220	2204

Distance									
mile	1	5	10	20	30	40	50	75	100	150
km	1.6	8	16	32	48	64	80	120	161	241
km	1	5	10	20	30	40	50	100	150	200
mile	0.6	3.1	6.2	12	19	25	31	62	93	124

Clothes							
USA	6	8	10	12	14	18	
UK	8	10	12	14	16	18	20
Europe	36	38	40	42	44	46	48

Shoes								
USA	2.5	3.3	4.5	5.5	6.5	7.5	8.5	9.5	10.5
UK	3	4	5	6	7	8	9	10	11
Europe	36	37	38	39	40	41/42	43	44	45

Temperature						
Fahrenheit	50	70	80	90	100	200
Celsius	10	21	26	32	38	93

Volume (1 US gallon = 3.8 litres 1 litre = 0.26 US gallons 1 US gallon = 0.83 UK gallons 1 UK gallon = 1.2 US gallons)

■ INDEX

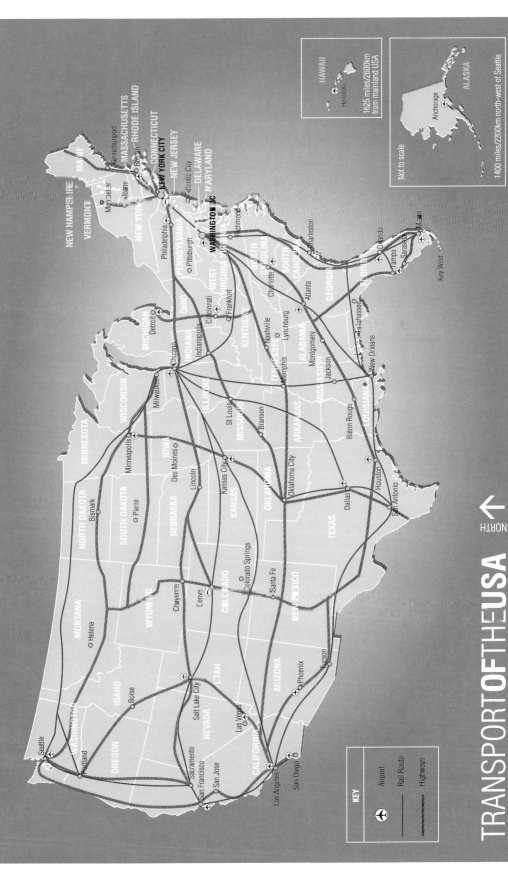

TRANSPORT**OF**THE**USA**

← NORTH

KEY
- ✈ Airport
- Rail Route
- Highways

HAWAII
Honolulu

1625 miles/2600km from mainland USA

ALASKA
Anchorage

Not to scale

1400 miles/2300km north-west of Seattle

Seattle · Portland · Boise · Helena · Bismark · Pierre · Minneapolis · Des Moines · Lincoln · Cheyenne · Denver · Colorado Springs · Santa Fe · Salt Lake City · Las Vegas · Sacramento · San Francisco · San Jose · Los Angeles · San Diego · Phoenix · Tucson · San Antonio · Dallas · Houston · Oklahoma City · Kansas City · St Louis · Branson · Baton Rouge · New Orleans · Jackson · Memphis · Nashville · Montgomery · Lynchburg · Atlanta · Tallahassee · New Orleans

WASHINGTON · OREGON · IDAHO · MONTANA · WYOMING · NEVADA · UTAH · CALIFORNIA · ARIZONA · NEW MEXICO · COLORADO · NORTH DAKOTA · SOUTH DAKOTA · NEBRASKA · KANSAS · OKLAHOMA · TEXAS · MINNESOTA · IOWA · MISSOURI · ARKANSAS · LOUISIANA · WISCONSIN · ILLINOIS · MISSISSIPPI · ALABAMA · TENNESSEE · KENTUCKY · INDIANA · MICHIGAN · OHIO · GEORGIA · SOUTH CAROLINA · NORTH CAROLINA · WEST VIRGINIA · VIRGINIA · PENNSYLVANIA · NEW YORK · VERMONT · NEW HAMPSHIRE · MAINE · MASSACHUSETTS · RHODE ISLAND · CONNECTICUT · NEW JERSEY · DELAWARE · MARYLAND

Chicago · Milwaukee · Detroit · Indianapolis · Cincinnati · Frankfort · Charlotte · Charleston · Orlando · Tampa · Sarasota · Miami · Key West · Richmond · WASHINGTON DC · Philadelphia · Pittsburgh · NEW YORK CITY · Albany · Montpelier · Atlantic City · Boston · Kennebunkport

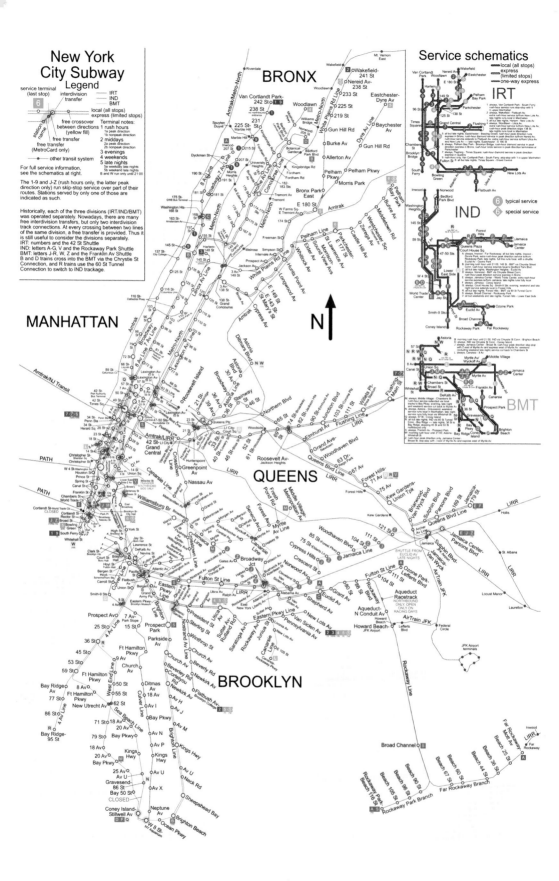